Ulrike Joras
Companies in Peace Processes

Ulrike Joras (Dr. rer. nat.) works in the area of »Business & Peace« for swisspeace in Bern, Switzerland. Before joining swisspeace, she worked for the United Nations in New York and the Center for Development Research in Bonn.

ULRIKE JORAS
COMPANIES IN PEACE PROCESSES
A Guatemalan Case Study

[transcript]

Bibliographic information published by Die Deutsche Bibliothek
Die Deutsche Bibliothek lists this publication in the Deutsche Nationalbibliografie;
detailed bibliographic data are available in the Internet at http://dnb.ddb.de

© 2007 transcript Verlag, Bielefeld

All rights reserved. No part of this book may be reprinted or reproduced or utilized in
any form or by any electronic, mechanical, or other means, now known or hereafter
invented, inlcuding photocopying and recording, or in any information storage or
retrieval system, without permission in writing from the publisher.

Cover layout by: Kordula Röckenhaus, Bielefeld
Typeset by: Ulrike Joras
Printed by: Majuskel Medienproduktion GmbH, Wetzlar
ISBN 978-3-89942-690-8

Distributed in North America by:

Transaction Publishers
New Brunswick (U.S.A.) and London (U.K.)

Transaction Publishers Tel.: (732) 445-2280
Rutgers University   Fax: (732) 445-3138
35 Berrue Circle   for orders (U.S. only):
Piscataway, NJ 08854   toll free 888-999-6778

Table of Contents

List of Boxes	7
List of Graphs	7
List of Tables	8
List of Maps	8
List of Acronyms	9
Acknowledgment	13
1 Introduction	**15**

I Conceptual Framework

2	**The Business Sector in Conflict Prevention, Conflict Settlement and Peacebuilding: Potentials and Limits of a New Type of Partnership**	**23**
2.1	Corporate engagement in conflict management: Background of a new concept	23
2.2	Businessmen, business associations and economic elite: A closer look	28
2.3	Potential roles for business in conflict management: From conflict prevention to post-conflict peacebuilding	33
2.4	Who, how, where and why: A brief analysis of the demand for corporate engagement in conflict management	45
3	**Corporate Costs of War and Peace**	**51**
3.1	Costs of war	52
3.2	Costs of peace	68
3.3	Is there a role for business participation in conflict management? Some conclusions	79

II Case Study

4   The Economic and Social Structure of Guatemala   85
4.1 The Guatemalan economy and the dominance of coffee   85
4.2 Economic impacts of the war   96
4.3 Excursion: The indigenous population in Guatemala   103

5   Structure and Role of the Private Business Sector in Guatemala   107
5.1 The private sector in Guatemala –
     its characteristics and historic political role   108
5.2 Business organizations in Guatemala   113

6   The Private Business Sector during the Civil War   125
6.1 The war begins: The period between 1960 and 1970   126
6.2 A violent interlude: Low-intensity warfare as a business climate   131
6.3 The second war peak: The business sector between fleeing
     the country and developing new conflict management strategies   137

7   The Costs of Peace: Entering the Peace Process   151
7.1 Negotiating interests: The business sector during the
     commencement of the peace process   152
7.2 Progress and setback during the government of Serrano   164
7.3 The business sector gets more involved:
     The peace process during the De León- administration   177
7.4 The private sectors concurrence:
     The peace process comes to an end   201

8   Complying with the Peace Accords: The Private Business Sector's Role during Peace Building   213
8.1 No war but no success: A brief overview of the implementation
     of the peace accords   214
8.2 Is there a role for the business sector in the post-settlement phase?
     Some general thoughts   217
8.3 Difficult dialogues: Still no climate for peaceful conflict settlement?   219
8.4 The constitutional referendum of May 1999   222
8.5 Economic dimensions of peace   226

9	**Conclusion and Policy Implications on Business Engagement in Conflict Management**	247
9.1	The business sector in the Guatemalan peace processes: Findings from the case study	247
9.2	Comparison of the Guatemalan case with other peace process	260
9.3	Policy implications	269

Appendices   271
Appendix 1: Maps   271
Appendix 2: Destruction and damage of fincas (1978-1994)   274
Appendix 3: Destroyed infrastructure (1981-1995)   276

Bibliography   279

List of Boxes

Box 1:	Violent conflict and peace: Some definitions	24
Box 2:	Definition of conflict management and related expressions	34
Box 3:	Policy Implications	269

List of Graphs

Graph 1:	Area planted with coffee and production between 1961 and 2002	88
Graph 2:	Area planted with sugar cane and production between 1961 and 2002	89
Graph 3:	Area planted in with bananas and production between 1961 and 2002	90
Graph 4:	GDP growth rates in Guatemala between 1971 and 2003	93
Graph 5:	Gross Domestic Product to constant market prices from 1995 in million USD between 1950 and 2001	93
Graph 6:	Percent of killings and disappearances occurring in rural areas by year, 1960-1995	99
Graph 7:	Number of visitors for the years 1973-2000	101
Graph 8:	Foreign exchange from tourism in million USD from 1973-2000	101
Graph 9:	Export value of main traditional product between 1995 and 2002	102

List of Tables

Table 1:	Examples of business activities in different stages of a violent conflict	41
Table 2:	Direct and indirect economic effects of violent conflict	55
Table 3:	Growth rates of the industrial production	90
Table 4:	Share of the industry in GDP	90
Table 5:	Income from principal exports, tourism and remittances (in USD millions)	92
Table 6:	Estimated killings and disappearances between 1960 and 1996	96
Table 7:	Central-American war affected countries, where over 0.5% of the population died, 1970s and 1980s	97
Table 8:	Estimates of cumulative GDP loss for Nicaragua, El Salvador and Guatemala	97
Table 9:	Ranking of human rights violations and acts of violence in percent according to department	100
Table 10:	Gross internal investment in percent between 1995 and 2002	103
Table 11:	Mayan language groups	104
Table 12:	Timetable of the different statements regarding the peace process between May and June 1992	168
Table 13:	Overview of the content of the accord on socioeconomic aspects and the agrarian situation	203
Table 14:	Kidnappings between 1997-1999	216
Table 15:	Case studies, supporting and contradicting the results from Guatemala	267

List of Maps

Map 1:	Main geographic zones of Guatemala	271
Map 2:	Areas of main human rights violations during the civil war and major coffee zones in Guatemala	272
Map 3:	Major fighting zones during the first and second phase of the civil war	273

List of Acronyms

ACECOGUA	Asociación General de Comerciantes Guatemaltecos (General Association of Traders in Guatemala)
ACOGUA	Asociación de Caficultores del Oriente de Guatemala (Association of Coffee Cultivators of Eastern Guatemala)
ACU	Asociación de Caficultores Unidos (Association of the United Coffee Cultivators).
AGA	Asociación General de Agricultores (General Association of Growers)
AGEXPRONT	Asociación Gremial de Exportadores de Productos No Tradicionales (Non-Traditional Products Exporters Association) (formerly GEXPRONT)
AMCHAM	American Chamber of Commerce
ANACAFÉ	Asociación Nacional del Café (National Coffee Association)
ARENA	National Republican Alliance (political party in El Salvador)
ASAZGUA	Asociación de Azucareros de Guatemala (Association of Sugar Producers in Guatemala)
ASC	Asamblea de la Sociedad Civil (Civil Society Assembly)
ASIES	Asociación de Investigación y Estudios Sociales (Research and Social Science Association)
AUSA	Association of the United States Army
BANDEGUA	Guatemalan Banana Company
CACIF	Comité Coordinador de Asociaciones Agrícolas, Comerciales, Industriales y Financieras (Coordinating Committee of Agricultural, Commercial Industrial and Financial Associations)
CACM	Central-American-Common Market
CAEM	Cámara Empresarial de Guatemala (Business Chamber of Guatemala)
CAG	Cámara del Agro (Chamber of Agriculture)
CAN	Central Auténtica Nacionalista (National Authentic Centre Party)
CARCOR	Coordinadora de Asociaciones Regionales de Caficultores Organizados de la República (Coordinator of Regional Associations of Organized Coffee Cultivators of the Republic)
CBI	Confederation of Business and Industry
CBM	Consultative Business Movement (South Africa)
CEG	Conferencia Episcopal de Guatemalteca (Guatemalan Episcopal Conference)
CEH	Comisión para el Esclarecimiento Histórico (Historical Clarification Commission)
CEPAL	Comisió Ecónomica para América Latina (UN Economic Commission for Latin America)
CEPAZ	Comisión Empresarial para la Paz of CACIF (Business Commission for Peace)
CERIGUA	Centro de Reportes Informativos sobre Guatemala (Information Centre about Guatemala)
CGTG	Central General del Trabajadores de Guatemala (Head Office of Guatemalan Workers)
CIIDH	International Center for Human Rights Research in Guatemala

CNOC	Coordinadora Nacional de Organizaciones Campesinas (National Co-ordinating Office of Peasant Organizations)
CNR	Comisión Nacional de Reconciliación (National Reconciliation Commission)
CNUS	Comité Nacional de Unidad Sindical (National Committee of Trade Unions)
COCIPAZ	Coordinadora Civil por la Paz (Civil Coordinator for Peace)
CONAGRO	Coordinadora Nacional Agropecuaria (National Agricultural Coordinating Office)
CONAVIGUA	Coordinadora Nacional de Viudas de Guatemala (National Coordinating Committee of Guatemalan Widows)
CONIC	Coordinadora Nacional Indígena Campesina (National Coordinating Committee of Indigenous Peasants)
CONTIERRA	Comisión Nacional para la Resolución de Conflictos de Tierra (National Commission on the Resolution of Conflicts over Land)
COPAZ	Comisión de la Paz (Peace Commission of the Guatemalan Government)
COPMAGUA	Coordinadora de Organizaciones del Pueblo Maya de Guatemala (Coalition of Mayan Peoples Organizations)
COS	Colectivo de Organizaciones Sociales (Collective of Social Organizations)
COVERCO	Comisión para la Verificación de Codigos de Conducta, Verification of Codes of Conduct
CPN-M	Communist Party of Nepal Maoist
CPPF	Comisión Preparatoria del Pacto Fiscal (Preparatory Commission of the Fiscal Pact)
CSIS	Center for Strategic and International Studies
CSR	corporate social responsibility
CUC	Comité de Unidad Campesina (Peasant Unity Committee)
DC	Democracia Cristiana (Christian Democratic Party)
DDR	disarmament, demobilization and reintegration
EGP	Ejército Guerrillero de los Pobres (Guerrilla Army of the Poor)
ESTNA	Centro de Estudios Estratégicos para la Estabilidad Nacional (Centre of Strategic Studies for National Stability)
FAR	Fuerzas Armadas Rebeldes (Rebel Armed Forces)
FARC	Fuerzas Armadas Revolutionaire Colombia
FDI	foreign direct investment
FEPYME	Federación de la Pequeña y Mediana Empresa (Federation of the Small and Medium Enterprise)
FLACSO	Facultad Latinoamericana de Ciencias Sociales (Latin American Faculty of Social Sciences)
FMLN	Farabundo Martí Front for National Liberation
FOCIDEP	Foro Cívico Democrático por la Paz (Civil Democratic Forum for Peace)
FUNDAPAZ	Fundación para el Desarrollo en Justicia y Paz
FONTIERRAS	Fondo de Tierras (The Land Fund)
FRG	Frente Republicano Guatemalteco (Guatemalan Republican Front)
FUNDAZUCAR	Fundación del Azúcar

FUNDESA	Fundación para el Desarrollo de Guatemala (Foundation for the Development of Guatemala)
FUNRURAL	the foundation of Anacafé
GAM	Grupo de Apoyo Mutuo (Mutual Support Group)
GDP	gross domestic product
GUATEL	Empresa telefónica guatemalteca (Guatemalan phone company)
IEMA	commercial and agricultural enterprise tax
IGSS	Instituto Guatemalteco de Seguridad Social (Guatemalan Social Security Institute)
INCEP	Instituto Centroamericano de Estudios Políticos
INCORE	International Conflict Research
INDUPAZ	Industrias para la Paz (Industries for Peace)
IPM	Instituto de Previsión Militar (Institute of Military Planning)
IPP	Inversiones para la Paz (Investments for Peace)
IUSI	Impuesto Único Sobre Inmuebles (single property tax)
IVA	Impuesto Sobre Valor Agregado (value added tax)
LAC	Latin American and Caribbean
LDC	least developed countries
MANO Blanca	Movimiento Anticomunista Nacional Organizado (Nacional organizad Anticommunist Movement), also known as the White Hand
MAS	Movimiento de Acción Solidaria (Movement of Solidarity Action)
MINUGUA	Misión de Verificación de las Naciones Unidas en Guatemala (UN Verification Mission in Guatemala)
MLN	Movimiento de Liberación Nacional (National Liberation Movement)
MNC	multinational company
MR-13	Movimiento Revolucionario 13 de Noviembre (November 13 Revolutionary Movement)
NGO	nongovernmental organization
OAS	Organization of the American States
ODHAG	Oficina de Derechos Humanos del Arzobispado de Guatemala (Archbishop's Human Rights Office in Guatemala)
OPIC	Overseas Private Investment Corporation
ORPA	Organización del Pueblo en Armas (Organization of People in Arms)
PAC	Patrulla de Autodefensa Civil (Civil Self-Defence Patrols)
PAN	Partido de Avanzada National (Party of National Advancement)
PELC	Political & Economic Link Consulting
PGT	Partido Guatemalteco de Trabajo (Guatemalan Labour Party, Communist Party)
PMA	Policía Militar Ambulante (Mobile National Police)
PMC	Private Military Company
PPP	public-private partnership
PRA	Political Risk Analysis
PREN	Plan de Reorganización Nacional (Plan for National Reorganization)
PRIO	International Peace Research Institute, Oslo

PROTIERRA	Comisión Interinstitucional para el Desarrollo y Fortalecimiento de la Propiedad sobre la Tierra (Interinstiutional Commission for development and Strengthening of Landownership)
PSC	Private Security Company
REMHI	Recuperación de la Memoria Histórica (Recovery of the Historical Memory)
SAT	Superintendencia de Administración Tributaria (Superintendancy of Tax Administration)
SEGEPLAN	Secretaría de Planificación y Programación (Secretariat for Planning and Programming)
SEPAZ	Secretaría de la Paz (Peace Secretariat of the Guatemalan Government)
SITRABI	Sindicato de Trabajadores de las Bananeras de Izabal (Labour Union of Banana Workers in Izabal)
TNC	trans-national company
UASP	Unidad de Acción Sindical y Popular (Labour and Popular Action Unity)
UCN	Unión del Centro Nacional (National Centrist Union)
UGT	Unión Guatemalteca de Trabajadores (Guatemalan Workers Union)
UNAGRO	Unión Nacional Agropecuaria de Guatemala (National Agricultural Union of Guatemala)
UNSITRAGUA	Unión Sindical de Trabajadores de Guatemala (Trade Union Unity of Guatemalan Workers)
URNG	Unidad Revolucionaria Nacional Guatemalteca (Guatemalan National Revolutionary Unity)
USAC	Universidad de San Carlos (National University of San Carlos)
USAID	US Agency for International Development
UTJ	Unidad Técnico Jurídica
VAT	value-added tax
VESTEX	Guatemala Apparel and Textile Industry Commission

Acknowledgment

The author wishes to acknowledge the following people, without whom this thesis would not have been possible: Prof. Dr. Wolfgang Schoop from the RWTH Aachen, for supervision, guidance, advice and a lot of patience and understanding when things were again not moving forward as anticipated. Prof. Andreas Wimmer, Department of Sociology, UCLA, and former Director of the Center for Development Research in Bonn, for providing the initial opportunity to undertake this PhD-thesis and for guidance and advice. Dr. Conrad Schetter from the Center for Development Research in Bonn for advice during the very first steps into this field, for maintaining interest, for constructive suggestions throughout the process of writing and for all the things he and Maaren helped out with (such as a place to sleep when I did not have an apartment). Dr. Tobias Debiel, INEF, for helpful comments to earlier version to some of the chapters. I also want to thank my sister, Elisabeth Joras, for helping with the maps and Philippe Rudaz for his assistance, patience and humour when formatting the document for printing.

For the period of field research in Guatemala, I am particularly grateful for help, guidance, support and advice from Dr. Andrea Althoff and Andreas, Magalí and Joschua Bouke. A very warm thank you also to Rocio Aroujo for making my time in Guatemala pleasant and interesting. The work would not have been possible without all the people who sacrificed time for interviews. I am particularly grateful to Peter Lamport, Max Quirin, Luis Reyes Mayen, and Víctor Suárez for their repeated willingness to give interviews.

Going through the years of writing the thesis was made much easier through the encouragement and backing from three people: My parents, Werner and Marion Joras, and my husband, Charlie Palmer. I would like to dedicate this work to two people: To my father, Werner Joras, who died shortly before the book went to print and to Charlie, for providing moral support, for his incomparable patience and repeated willingness to read chapters as well as for his flattering ways when correcting my English. I hope the times of lap-top in bed on a Sunday morning will be over now.

1 Introduction

Background of the Study

In April 2004, the Security Council of the United Nations discussed the role of business in conflict prevention, peacekeeping, and post-conflict peacebuilding. Secretary-General Kofi Annan argued that "'business itself has an enormous stake in the search for solutions', adding that companies require a stable environment in order to conduct their operations and minimize their risks". All relevant United Nations bodies, the Bretton Woods institutions and civil society were asked to "cooperate closely with the private sector to support the climate of peace in conflict-prone regions, help mitigate crisis solution, and contribute to reconciliation processes" (UN Security Council Press Release 2004).

Kofi Annan's statement for the UN is exemplary for an increasing number of governmental as well as non-governmental organizations, which argue that the private business sector has a role to play in preserving peace and ending conflict. Companies are assumed to have the potential as well as the interest to contribute to the maintenance or reestablishment of a peaceful and stable environment.

The idea that private firms are deemed partners in conflict management is a relatively new phenomenon. Until recently, these activities were considered the responsibilities of governments and state institutions alone. The end of the Cold War, however, changing patterns in conflict emergence and settlement as well as the steadily expanding movement of corporate social responsibility and public-private partnerships, have resulted in the business sector being increasingly identified as a potential player in preventing and resolving armed strife.

Paradoxically, the discussion about the possibly conducive role of private business actors in conflict management in part originated from a debate mostly ignited by NGOs, showcasing how companies generated or prolonged armed hostilities. Primarily transnational firms in the resource-extracting sector including Shell, DeBeers or Talisman have been accused of doing business in conflict-ridden countries, contributing to the maintenance of violence.

Since private companies are involved in the emergence and maintenance of violent conflict they were now also considered necessary partners in strategies aiming to resolve armed strife. In addition, NGOs and governmental institutions increasingly asserted that while some companies thrive during warfare, the majority of private firms prefer a peaceful business environment without the insecurities of conflict. Since private companies are believed to have self-interest in peace, the implication seemed to follow that they are willing to contribute to activities supporting peace. However, whereas the active participation of NGOs became a common feature in many contemporary peace processes, there is still little knowledge of and practical experience in business participation in conflict management.

Goals and Relevance of the Study

The aim of the study is to provide some insights into corporate perceptions of violent conflict, peace and peacebuilding in order to better assess the potential as well as the obstacles for corporate engagement in conflict prevention, conflict settlement and post-conflict peacebuilding. The study seeks to explore the conditions under which peace and conflict are considered economically detrimental by companies in order to shed some light on whether or not business is self-interested in peace. Moreover, this study aims to better understand if certain economic branches or groups are more inclined to support peace-related activities than others.

It is assumed that private companies are only self-interested in peace and more willing to support and participate in conflict management if the corporate costs for war exceed the corporate costs for peace. The study argues that although peace, in the sense of an absence of violence, may be considered beneficial by the majority of private companies, conflict transformation that addresses the root causes of violence may not be regarded as being economically profitable. The majority of those who argue that private companies have a self-interest in peace seem to disregard the fact that not only violent conflicts but also peace may result in costs and disadvantages for firms. While entrepreneurs may have a preference for a stable and peaceful business environment, they may reject structural changes, such as reforms in the economic rules of the game that potentially accompany conflict transformation. Peacebuilding may force the private sector to compromise over its economic interests, and businesses may consequently reject more comprehensive conflict management strategies.

The scope of the inquiry is limited to four selected foci:

i. Internal conflicts: Since the end of the Cold War, internal conflicts have been the predominant form of war compared with inter-state conflicts. Therefore, intra-state conflict will be the focus of this study.

ii. Domestic businesses sector: Most studies published so far on the role of companies in conflict and peace highlight international enterprises. However, it

has been acknowledged that the domestic private sector assumes a crucial role when it comes to corporate engagement in peace and conflict.
iii. Business associations: Particular attention will be paid to the organized business sector and not so much to individual businessmen.
iv. Legal business: The study will not address the role of illicit business activities such as smuggling, kidnapping, drug trafficking. Furthermore, companies, such as those that produce weapons may have an interest in the maintenance of armed hostility and hence, will not be considered in this study. Instead, it will focus on those economic branches that do not directly profit from violence.

Selection of the Case Study and Major Findings

This study explores the questions and assumptions outlined above for the case of Guatemala. It looks at the strategies of the Guatemalan business sector in the context of the emergence and settlement of the Guatemalan civil war (1960-1996), as well as during the peace negotiations (1986-1996) and the first five years after the formal ending of the conflict (1997-2002).

Guatemala was chosen as the case study for this work for a number of reasons. First, the civil war formally ended about five years prior to the field research in 2001. This provided the opportunity to explore all the major phases of a violent conflict and a peace process (pre-conflict phase, conflict phase, conflict settlement and post-conflict phase). Second, Guatemala provided a relatively diversified economic structure. Although coffee dominates the economy, commerce, industry and the service industry (in particular tourism) are of some economic significance for Guatemala. Therefore, the role and perception of various branches could be explored, and not only a single, dominant economic sector. Third, Guatemala has a very well-organized and vocal business sector. The business community did not remain a passive observer of the Guatemalan peace process, but instead assumed an important role. This happened despite the fact that at the time of the civil war and peace negotiations, the idea of corporate engagement in conflict management was hardly of any relevance in the international debate conflict management.

For the Guatemalan case, it is shown that the organized private business sector held in large parts a recalcitrant position vis-à-vis the peace process, even though they were in favour of an end to violence. There were certainly variations in this position among the different groups and over time, but overall, "nobody in the Guatemalan private sector applauded the peace process", as one Guatemalan executive put it. Businesses in Guatemala preferred peace to war, but they opposed peace negotiations over political, social and economic issues since they expected results that would be detrimental to their interests. The Guatemalan private sector experienced relatively low corporate costs during the violent strife, in comparison to the potentially high costs accruing from an ample process of conflict transformation. In this sense, the case of Guatemala supports the assumption that the business sector had a self-interest in peace. However, it also shows that conflict transformation may result in risks for companies, which may therefore cause resistance rather than support for peace processes. The study thereby alluded to the importance of differentiating between the private sector welcoming a cease fire or a comprehensive peacebuilding process.

With regard to differences in perception among branches or groups it is shown that contrary to prior assumptions, major variations in the perception of and strategy towards the armed rebellion and the peace process ran along ideological lines, and not according to branch. Rifts emerged primarily between the hard-liners and the moderate factions within the different branches rather than between branches.

To the best of my knowledge there are only very view comprehensive case studies that have examined the way business entrepreneurs approach peace processes and violent conflicts in their political lobbying strategy as well as operational decisions. The study at hand seeks to contribute to this body of literature, trying to contribute to a better understanding of firms in violent conflicts and peace processes in general.

Methodology and Information Sources

A qualitative approach has been chosen as the methodology for this inquiry. Primary and secondary sources have both been used. With respect to primary sources, over 80 semi-structured interviews were conducted between January and October 2002. These included interviews with Guatemalan entrepreneurs from different branches, governmental officials involved in the peace process, members of non-governmental organizations, executives of internationals organizations, and researchers and experts. The interviews generally lasted from 30 minutes to two hours. Some interviewees were interviewed once, and others several times, depending on their availability, reliability and involvement in and knowledge about the peace process. Interviews were largely conducted in Spanish in Guatemala City but trips were also made to Quetzaltenango, the second biggest town in Guatemala, and to a number of fincas.

The interview partners were chosen according to their knowledge on different matters and their involvement in different periods and historical stages of Guatemala's conflict and peace process. Throughout the field research, emphasis was put on corroborating the information gathered by interviewing at least two sources. Interviews were recorded, transcribed and than analysed. It was agreed with the interviewees not to disclose the sources of information.

The interviews provided insights into how the private business sector perceived the civil war and the peace process as well as information about the different events in this period. Given the fact that some of these events occurred more than 40 years ago, the quality of the information was sometimes weak. In addition, some of the questions asked touched upon highly sensitive issues and some of those interviewed refused to provide information or provided false information, as was found out through other sources.

With regard to secondary sources, a thorough literature review on the Guatemalan armed conflict as well as related theoretical fields was carried out. In addition, data were collected through a comprehensive review of Guatemalan newspapers, particularly for the time during and after the civil war. The following Guatemalan newspapers and weekly newsmagazines were used: *Crónica, El Gráfico, La República, Prensa Libre,* and *Siglo XXI*. The weekly news service CERIGUA was also used as a source.

The newspapers provided important information on some of the key events during the period under scrutiny. However, allowance must be given to the fact that national newspapers were censured or could not report freely during the civil war. Throughout the study, information was verified either through interviews or through other written sources. The following archives were used: The newspaper archives of the *Biblioteca Nacional* in Guatemala City as well as the *Universidad de San Carlos* in Guatemala City and to a limited extend the *Archivo General de Centro América*.

In addition, some of the *campos pagados* (public announcements) and documents were provided directly by various organizations such as CACIF, Anacafé or MINUGUA. Statistical data were taken from various sources, in particular from on-line databanks belonging to international organizations such as the United Nations.

Structure of the study

The work at hand is structured into two major parts. First, a theoretical part is presented (chapter 2 to 3.3), followed by a second part comprising the Guatemalan case study (chapter 4 to 8). In a smaller concluding section (chapter 9), the principal findings of the study are summarized, with the results analysed in relation to other armed conflicts. The major policy implications are also presented in the concluding section.

The case study is largely structured chronologically, starting with the civil war, and followed by the period encompassing the peace negotiations and the post-conflict peacebuilding phase. Additional chapters in the second part describe the structure of the Guatemalan private business sector as well as the indigenous population and discuss the economic losses inflicted by the civil war on the national economy and the private sector. Throughout the second part, the major corporate costs of war are analysed along with the predominant conflict management strategies used. Part two also links the findings of the empirical chapter to the theoretical (first) part of the study.

I Conceptual Framework

2 The Business Sector in Conflict Prevention, Conflict Settlement and Peacebuilding: Potentials and Limits of a New Type of Partnership

2.1 Corporate engagement in conflict management: Background of a new concept

How violent conflict[1] and economy are interrelated has been discussed from various angles for quite a long time. There has been research on the impact of trade on war and peace; debates on poverty and its interrelation with violent conflicts, or works discussing links between the World Bank's and IMF's Structural Adjustment Programs and war (Brock 1997; Anderton 2003).

Although not a new theme, **economic aspects of violent conflicts** have arrested more and more attention since the demise of communism. The discourse around "Greed or Grievance", for example, that emerged after the end of the Cold War strongly influenced the current debate on violent conflicts. It raised awareness about economic factors in contemporary civil wars and how they may shape their emergence, course and ending (Collier/Hoeffler 1998; Keen 1998; Berdal/Malone 2000; Collier 2000b; Ballentine/Sherman 2003; Humphreys 2003).

One aspect of the debate is the **role of private companies in conflict zones**. In particular NGOs, such as CorpWatch, Fafo, Global Witness, Human Rights Watch or Project Underground scrutinized in recent years how corporations are involved in violent strife. They mostly unveiled the negative impacts of private entrepreneurs in war ridden societies. Primarily transnational companies in resource extraction have been put in the spotlight. Shell in Nigeria, Unocal in Burma and Afghanistan, diamond traders like DeBeers and oil companies such as BP-Amoco, Elf, Total and Exxon in Angola (Global Witness 1998; Global Wit-

---

1 See Box 1 for definition.

ness 1999), Freeport in West Irian, Talisman in the Sudan (Harker 2000)[2], or H.C. Starck in the Democratic Republic of Congo (Evangelischer Entwicklungsdienst 2002) were accused of prolonging armed conflict, being involved in human rights violations or supporting illegitimate regimes.

Box 1: Violent conflict and peace: Some definitions

> The notion **"violent conflict"** is not defined consistently. It is instead a vague term that is often used interchangeably with other notions, such as "civil war" or "rebellion".
> Depending on the context, the terms are based on different concepts and ideas, using different criteria for differentiation (see for example Miall et al. 1999). In a statistical context, for example, a "civil war" may be defined numerically to separate it from "rebellion" and related terms. Collier for example defines civil wars as follows: "An internal war occurs when an identifiable rebel organization challenges the government militarily and the resulting violence results in more than 1,000 combat-related death, with at least 5 percent on each side" (Collier et al. 2003: 11).
> In the study at hand, the term "violent conflict" describes disputes over incompatible interests in which at least one side of the conflicting parties resort over a longer-term period to the use of direct, physical violence.
> No differentiation will be made between "civil war" and "violent conflict". The notions "armed conflicts", "deadly conflict", "belligerent violence" and so on are used interchangeably.
> The notion **"peace"** is even vaguer than the term "war". In the study at hand, peace exists when the use of violence has stopped and the causes that gave rise to the violence have been addressed (such as in comprehensive peace agreements and related follow-up activities).
> This definition implies that the mere ending to violence ("nonwar") or the signing of a truce is not considered enough to speak of peace. It is common to use the terms positive and negative peace to make this differentiation (Matthies 1995). However, the terms were originally introduced by Galtung who used the notion "positive peace" for a condition, in which people are liberated from 'structural violence', which may include acts and systems that are not be linked to the emergence of physical violence (Galtung 1969).
> Another term that is used increasingly is "no war/no peace" indicating that there is a longer period in societies moving from war to peace in which violent conflicts have not been fully resolved and sustainable peace has not yet been established.

---

2   The Harker-Report, a report that contains the results of a Canadian fact-finding commission to assess allegations of forced population removals in the Sudanese oil fields, addressed the role of the Canadian petrol company Talisman Energy Ltd. in the civil war in Sudan. It is one of the most detailed case studies on the role of a company in a violent conflict (Harker 2000).

Although attention was initially paid primarily to the detrimental behaviour of private business actors in zones of conflict, policy-makers, NGO's and academics progressively began to turn to questions of how the negative entanglement of private companies could be avoided and – beyond this – if the business sector has potentials to **promote sustainable peace**. Even if some firms may profit during war, the majority of enterprises are assumed to experience losses during armed hostility. High political and economic risks, limited access to markets and resources and the destruction of production facilities might make companies amenable to act against violent conflict and in favour of peace (for details see chapter 3.1).

Ideas of how private businesses may constructively contribute to conflict prevention, resolution and peacebuilding and of how they may operate in conflict zones without exacerbating political and social tension **began to thrive** in recent years (Champain 2002: 12). International Alert, the Council of Economic Priorities and The Prince of Wales Business Leaders Forum published, for example, in 2000 "The Business of Peace – The Private Sector as a Partner in Conflict Prevention and Resolution" that deals with the idea (Nelson et al. 2000). Virginia Haufler discussed if and where there is a role for business in conflict management (Haufler 2001b; Haufler 2001a). Wenger and Möckli advocated strongly in their book "Conflict Prevention: The Untapped Potential of the Business Sector" for a closer integration of private companies in conflict management[3] and post-conflict reconstruction (Wenger/Möckli 2002). And in the Security Council of the United Nations, the British and the German governments initiated debates on this topic.

The broad consideration of the potentials of private business actors to promote peace is new. Traditionally, conflict resolution and security issues were considered exclusive domains of the state. In recent decades, however, the general quality of the **relationship between state and non-state actors**[4] – private business actors as well as "non-commercial" civil society actors – has changed. Integrating private companies into the hitherto primarily governmental task of conflict management seems entrenched in a global trend of altering relations between non-state authorities and governments, admitting more influence to non-state actors.

Quantitative data on the **size of companies** seem to underpin the hypothesis of an increase in corporate influence. According to *Corporate Watch*, for example, 51 of the 100 largest economies in the world are global companies; only 49

---

3   For definition, see Box 1.
4   Non-state actors or private actors are mostly understood not only as the private business sector, but the terms normally comprise both, NGOs as well as private companies. The increasing number of trisector partnerships (NGOs, private business sector and state actors) makes it sometimes difficult to distinguish between the different players. In the following, the term "non-state actors" will be used with reference to business actors and NGOs.

of them are nations. Ford's economy exceeds South Africa's GDP (gross domestic product) and the combined sales of the 200 biggest corporations in the world are bigger than a quarter of global GDP (Anderson/Cavanagh 2000). General Motors produces in more than 50 countries, is present in about 200 countries and has more than 30.000 suppliers all over the world, establishing an ample web of international relations and connections (Haufler 2001a: 5).

Different terms such as "privatization of politics", "economization of politics" but also "global governance" "corporate social responsibility", and "Public-Private Partnership" indicate to the two sides of the same trend, that there is an alleged shift of power as well as responsibility from political to private actors. Economic globalization and the end of the Cold War seems to have brought about a **rise in corporate political leverage**, which also led to increased accountability for private companies ("with power comes responsibility")[5] (Strange 1996; Bornschier 1997; Braun 2001; Hummel 2001; Bomann-Larsen/Wiggen 2004).

State institutions more often **consider companies as partners** in traditionally exclusively governmental arenas. The number of national and international treaties, for example, that refer to the role of private institutions and Public-Private Partnership, such as in the context of the World Summit for Sustainable Development in Johannesburg in 2002 or the Copenhagen Declaration on Social Development, increased steadily[6]. The World Bank and the United Nations declared their intention to establish strategic alliances with non-state actors that go beyond merely financial contributions to the organizations (Gerson/Colletta 2002: 18-19). The United Nations' "Global Compact" is probably one of the most prominent examples for this trend. The initiative brings together companies "with UN agencies, labour, non-governmental organizations and other civil society actors to foster action and partnership in the pursuit of a challenging vision: a more sustainable and inclusive global economy" (Global Compact: 4)[7]. (For more details see for example Bennis 2001; Paul 2001; Hamm 2002).

---

5   Many may disagree with the premise that non-state authorities gained power and intruded more and more on governmental areas of responsibility with globalization and the end of the Cold War. However, for this context it is not important if private actors have gained more power and restrain the state or if the increase in non-state authority's power was just a "false assumption". Independent of if based on fact or fiction, state authorities seem to be generally more willing to integrate non-state authorities.

6   The World Summit for Sustainable Development in Johannesburg in 2002 is considered a milestone for partnership-building with the business sector. During the summit a broad number of "partnerships for development" were announced, giving new impetus to a development that was ongoing since at least two decades (Raynard/Cohen 2003; Zadek 2004).

7   With regard to relationships that existed between the business community and the UN-System prior to the establishment of the Global Compact, see for instance Hüfner or Zammit (Hüfner 2002; Zammit 2003).

Many tasks such as poverty reduction, environmental conservation and the fight against HIV/AIDS are assumed to only be tackled successfully by joint efforts of private and non-private actors. Partnerships in those areas are considered more effective than attempts by governmental institutions alone, since only with joint resources, knowledge and capacities those challenges can be confronted. But beyond this, partnerships are also considered a way to pursue **common goals** and interest. In countries, for example, with HIV/AIDS infection rates of over 40 percent of the population, the disease is not only a public health concern but vital for the labour market, staffing costs and the availability of employees. Pervasive poverty is not only a governmental welfare challenge but higher purchasing power can also increase markets and sales for private companies. And environmental protection is not only a state affair dealt with in international conferences, but a significant medium and long-term concern for insurance companies and other branches.

Yet, it is not always certain if private companies indeed agree that "doing good", respecting human rights and following social and environmental standards may be compatible with and conducive to profit maximization (e.g. Bennett 2002). The trend towards greater **corporate social responsibility** (CSR) and the increasing attempts to make the business case for "doing good" seem to be a positive signal. Private companies appear to be more willing[8] to fulfil their role of "good corporate citizen". "Meeting the triple bottom line of prosperity, social responsibility and good environmental practices", "strategic philanthropy", "corporate citizenship", and "stakeholder responsibility" have become new guidelines of corporate behaviour that go beyond the narrow concept of corporate shareholder responsibility (see for example Schwartz/Gibb 1999).

The field of human rights, for example, was in the vanguard of corporate social responsibility. In 1991, Levi Strauss & Co. promulgated one of the first ever **Codes of Conduct** as a reaction to continuous public accusations about unacceptable labour practices[9]. Since then, Codes of Conduct and other forms of corporate social responsibility have proliferated and many companies have developed their own code. Corporate social reporting gained importance since the 1970s. Social reporting of companies seeks to shows the degree to which social responsibility is taken seriously and most annual reports of major international enterprise today describe the firm's social or environmental achievements

---

8   Or as some claim, by accepting more and more social responsibility, e.g. due to states lacking capacity or will, corporate actors automatically gain more political power (Belsie 2000).
9   One type of a Code of Conduct are the "Sullivan Principles". Twelve American enterprises operating in South Africa published them in 1977. The signatories committed themselves to e.g. non-segregation, equal and fair employment practices, the education of black employees, the enlargement of numbers of non-whites in leading management positions etc. The initiative derived in part from international pressure and increasing corporate awareness that the politically tense situation in South Africa threatened the national economic system (Man 1992: 251).

(Schwartz/Gibb 1999; Braun 2001: 258; Berthoin Antal et al. 2002; Wenger/Möckli 2002: 111-120).

The voluntary nature of CSR and Codes of Conduct, however and the lack of monitoring give free reign to abuse and many of the ideas for better corporate behaviour meet resistance from business players. Firms are – rightly in many cases – accused of merely paying lip-service to social values, human rights and environmental standards. Companies may implement CSR or participate in initiatives like the Global Compact in order to **improve their public image** but not because they consider it as profitable for their operations (for example Zammit 2003). Critics warn that relying on corporate interest in implementing social and environmental standards without governmental control and supervision may result in an erosion and overall decline of ethical and social standards instead of an improvement (Engels 2000: 41-43; Wenger/Möckli 2002).

The invitations and demands for business engagement in conflict management stand in this tradition of CSR, Public-Private Partnership and changing relations between governmental and non-state actors. As will be shown (see chapter 2.3), the reasoning and the risks for business participation in conflict prevention and post-conflict peacebuilding are similar to the rational for and the critics against CSR and PPP. But before elaborating further how business can or could participation in conflict management, the following chapter explores and defines business in more detail.

2.2 Businessmen, business associations and economic elites: A closer look

This chapter will give some **definitions** of the terms private business sector, businessmen, economic elite, and business association. Since the private business sector, businessmen and business associations are the key actors for this study, a clear understanding of the terms is essential. In addition, this chapter gives some theoretical ideas on business-state relationship in political processes, going beyond the more general assertions made in the previous chapter. Companies differ from other non-state actors in a number of aspects. Getting some clarification about corporate particularities in political and social processes is helpful in trying to understand the potentials and weaknesses of business in conflict management. Special allowance will be given to the Latin-American private sector.

2.2.1 Defining the terms business sector, businessmen, corporations, economic elite and business associations

Social sciences as well as common parlance knows **numerous terms** for business sector, companies and businessmen, including 'corporate sector', 'business community', 'private sector', 'employers', 'managers', 'entrepreneurs', 'capitalists', 'firms', and 'corporations'. In many cases, the different terms convey an ideological implication or are used differently depending on if a juridical, economic or political viewpoint is taken. In the following, the terms are used in a descriptive and not ideological sense, differentiating only between business sector (interchangeably used with business community or private sector), businessmen (interchangeably used with employers and entrepreneurs) and corporations (interchangeably used with firms and companies).

The **"business sector"** is understood as the totality of businessmen and their interest groups in a country. **"Businessmen"** are defined as independent individuals who own and in the majority of cases also run and manage a firm. Some authors distinguish businessmen from landowners (Wagner 1997: 36), but in the following **"landowners"** are subsumed to the term "businessmen", if not indicated differently. **"Companies"** are defined as durable organizational entities in which economic goods and services are produced with the aim of profit maximisation.

The notion "business sector" is often equated with the term "economic elite", in particular in the Latin-American context. Subsequently, however, it will be differentiated between economic elite and business sector. **"Economic elite"** is considered a part of the national elite of a country, which is professionally dedicated to private economic activities. "Elite" again is defined as a socially or politically leading minority within a society. Hence, a private businessman is only considered part of the "economic elite" when he or she assumes a lead function within his or her respective society. A small retailer, for instance, belongs to the private business sector but not necessarily to the "economic elite". The notion "economic elite" resembles the Spanish terms *grupos económicos* or *grupos dominantes*, which are frequently used to describe the biggest, often closely interconnected enterprises and entrepreneurs in a country. Other common terms in the Latin American context are *sector privado* (private sector) that is especially used to distinguish it from the *sector público* (public sector) (Birle et al. 1992: 1).

With regard to "business associations" it should be noted, that the development of a modern system of lobby groups was closely connected to the epoch of industrialization and the emergence of a *bürgerliche Gesellschaft*. Division of labour, social differentiation and the concomitant evolution of different sets of interest brought forth to the formation of **interest groups**. Business associations are one type of interest groups.

Here, they are understood as **associations of business people** that intend to:

- shape political decision-making processes according to the interests of their members, on issues relevant for their members;
- coordinate interests among their associates and influence their behaviour;
- provide (in many cases) services to their members, such as advanced professional training facilities, information services etc.

Business associations function therewith as a junction between the state and individual businessmen, assuming a **mediatory role**. In contrast to governments, corporate interest groups have, however, not the power to enforce the decisions among their members (Schäfers 1995: 373-376; Meier 1997: 33-41; Birle 1999: 181; Kraus 1999: 23).

Business associations can be **organized in various ways**, e.g. according to economic branch, size, region etc. Especially in cases where a concerted performance towards the central government is required and where the business sector is not overly polarized, entrepreneurs tend to found comprehensive umbrella organizations as the chief economic pressure group within a country (Birle 1999: 191-192).

Vital for political leverage of the private sector is often the question how the different business entities can collaborate. Misleadingly, notions such as "business sector" or "economic elite" suggest that entrepreneurs are a homogeneous group. Although entrepreneurs may share a common interest in demanding private property rights and the principal of free markets, the business sector including business associations are not a monolithic bloc. Much rather, **heterogeneous interests** may result in conflictive relations between different business actors. Birle et al., for example, suggest that in Latin America the major dividing line between different business associations runs along the small and medium sized and big enterprises as well as between export-oriented companies and those oriented towards the domestic market (see also Birle et al. 1992: 46; Birle 1999). However, if principle corporate interests are at stake, such as private property rights, individual interests are likely to be deferred.

2.2.2 Influence of entrepreneurs and business associations in the political decision making process: A brief overview

Entrepreneurs and business associations play in many regards an important role as social actors or "**actors of change**". Different academic approaches have studied their influence on social processes, such as on democratization or in the case of dependency and modernization theories, on national development. The new field of the potential role for corporations in conflict management can learn from these debates, in particular regarding the more generalized findings on how business actors shape political and social processes and what distinguishes them from other actors. Above all, in hindsight to those parts of peace processes for which companies' role as social or political players is requested (e.g. peace constituencies) and not so much their philanthropic engagement, their particularities in exerting influence should be considered (see the following chapter for ideas how the business executives may contribute to conflict management).

In principal, corporations can **shape political processes** through economic as well as political means (Payne/Bartell 1995). Economic measures comprise among others the dismissal of employees or the refusal to make productive investments. Political means can be both, formal as well as informal. Formal exertion of influence includes all those areas in which corporate interest groups or individual companies are legally entitled to advocate for their concerns, such as the right to free collective bargaining. Yet all social actors – not exclusively entrepreneurs – exert influence not only in public but also informally, behind closed doors. Strategies to shape political decisions range from personal contacts based on family or professional bonds to bribery and extortion. In those cases, it can be difficult to detect, if exertion of influence occurs and if it has an effect on the final political decision.

Many authors suggest that business entrepreneurs in comparison to most other social actors can more **efficiently exert leverage on political decision making processes** – especially in capitalist systems (Dahl/Lindblom 1976; Lindblom 1977; Dahl 1982). First, the capitalist development logic inevitably results in a **more powerful position of private entrepreneurs**, as they are the key players who control means of production, create wealth etc. This may lead to a "structural dependence of the state on capital" (for a brief summary of the most important literature see for example Przeworski/Wallerstein 1988: 11-14).

Second, unlike workers, entrepreneurs have the choice to either **assert influence on an individual basis or in a more concerted way**, such as via pressure groups. Dependent on the respective size and importance in the national market, contact to the ruling elite and so on, not only interest groups but individual businessmen have leverage in the political decision making process. Workers by contrast can only effectively exert political pressure in joint efforts, as their individual bargaining power is small. For some entrepreneurs, it might even be more efficient not to orchestrate their interests with an association but to apply influence on an individual basis (Offe/Wiesenthal 1980). Austin and Ickis, for example, found in Nicaragua after the revolution that many international companies avoided joint activities through business associations. Major reasons included difficulties in reaching consensus and the fact that: "the government listens to a company on a personal level but does not like to listen to the associations because they apply political pressure and the government does not like to feel threatened" (Austin/Ickis 1986: 107).

However, how meaningful individual or concerted corporate influence on political decision making processes can be, tends to be **conditional on a broader range of factors**, going beyond the national development model (e.g. if it is a capitalist system) and the economic-political set of rules. Additional key factors include the regime type, the macro-economic structure of the country, the legal rights of business associations to influence political processes, the personal contacts between policy-makers and economic actors etc. Indeed, in comparison to democratic regimes, authoritarian regimes concede by definition little room for manoeuvre to private interest groups. However, this does not imply that the (individual) concerns of private entrepreneurs are not at all considered in non-democratic systems. If and how the interests are included in the decision-making process is, nonetheless, much more at the ruler's discretion (Schmitter 1974).

In addition, **internal business factors** such as the membership structure of an interest group, their representativeness, their ability to overcome fragmentation, size, organizational structure, financial capacity, social status and image within the country, linkages to state authorities, position with the national market, economic success and so on determine the power of the private sector (von Alemann 1989: 224-225; Payne/Bartell 1995; Wagner 1997: 43). Thus, corporate influence on political processes is neither equal between different countries nor equal between different private sector actors within a country.

In general, one may argue that **Third World economic systems** tend to function more often to the benefit of a small group of individuals. The economic elite and the political elite are apt to be closely linked with each other and the political system is frequently used as a tool to maintain the dominant position of elites by obstructing access to the political and economic realm for non-elite groups (see also Birle et al. 1992; Meier 1997). If private interest groups exist at all in Third World countries, they tend to be part of the economic elite and be closely affiliated to the existing state system (Croissant et al. 1999: 331-332).

For the **Latin American context**, we know that private business entrepreneurs have traditionally a strong influence on politics, much stronger than in many other Third World regions, such as in Africa or East-Asia. Latin American businessmen conventionally exercised influence not through formal institutions but through informal, clientelist and personal contacts. Corporate leaders are usually stereotyped as a relatively small group of influential businessmen, which used to be dependent on authoritarian states that protected business ventures from detrimental external factors (see also chapter 3.2.2.1). Torres-Rivas, for example, describes this constellation as "deeply unequal societies, in which, both, groups of entrepreneurs successfully realize their demands and the state explicitly protect business interests with their politics" (Torres-Riva 1995: 17)

But the **modes of exerting influence** changed seemingly during recent decades. In the course of democratization, which occurred in the majority of Latin American countries since the 1980s, informal exertion of influence was curbed in favour of formal exertion of influence (Birle et al. 1992: 44-45; Birle 1999). Although many critics argued that these democratic systems are still strongly formed according the interest of the private sector (see for instance O'Donnell 1992; UNDP 2004), others emphasis growing transparency in companies' political exertion of influence (Payne/Bartell 1995).

Payne et al. for example differentiate in their analysis on **entrepreneurs' behaviour in the democratic transition** processes in Latin America, between a politically and economically "weak" and a politically and economically "strong" business sector. A weak business sector varies from a strong business sector in its inferior social status and its uncompetitive products that require governmental protection against global competition (Payne/Bartell 1995: 258). Based on a comparative analysis they conclude that: "if business leaders feel alienated from the political process because of their social inferiority, fed in part by their lack of entrepreneurship or even their own weak ability to overcome the collective action problem, they may attempt to restore their political influence and gain attention from the government in ways that have in the past destabilized governments and political systems" (Payne/Bartell 1995: 276). However, not only can an inferior business sector obstruct political processes by supporting authoritarian regimes, allying with the military etc. but also a strong business sector may undermine any kind of policy initiatives *because of* its strength. Entrepreneurial political power may lead to effective **corporate objections** against political projects, in cases they contradict corporate interests (Payne/Bartell 1995: 276-280).

Payne's findings seem to support for the Latin American context that private business actors are **structurally powerful actors** in politics. No matter if they are officially included in a political process or not, and no matter if it is a weak or a strong business sector, entrepreneurs seem to have significant leverage over politics. This strong position maybe facilitated by the alleged structural privileges of private business actors in influencing politics, the collaboration of business leaders with authoritarian regimes and strong informal relations between (parts of the) business-elites and state-authorities.

2.3 Potential roles for business in conflict management: From conflict prevention to post-conflict peacebuilding

In chapter 2.1 it was argued that the seeming metamorphosis in the relationship between state and private actors, CSR and PPP form the background against which the idea evolved to integrate the corporate sector into conflict management. To date, however, the potentials for business actors to promote sustainable peace have been hardly realized. In the following paragraphs, the specific **demands and ideas** how companies may contribute to conflict management will be presented (for overview, see Table 1). Given the newness of public-private engagement in peace and security, the ideas from academics, governmental as well as non-governmental organizations will be laid out in some detail. Some of these ideas have been implemented, many however were not.

The chapter is an exemplary, not-comprehensive presentation of ideas and practical cases of how the business community can or does partner in conflict management. There are many other ideas for corporate engagement in the different phases of a conflict that are not mentioned in the following pages. The chapter attempts to draw a **generalized picture** of the various proposals for "business and peace", to put these suggestions into a wider context and to give examples where private actors already engaged in conflict management. The largely descriptive chapter will be complimented by a more analytical chapter 2.4.

Box 2: Definition of conflict management and related expressions

> "**Conflict management**", "conflict settlement" and "conflict resolution" are commonly used terms to describe the process of ending an armed conflict. In the following, "conflict management" will be understood as an umbrella term, covering all parts and phases of the process to end an armed conflict. "**Conflict settlement**" means reaching an agreement between the warring parties that enables them to bring an end to the armed conflict. The terms "**conflict resolution**" and "**conflict transformation**" describe that not only that the violence is stopped but that the deep-rooted sources of the conflict are addressed as well. "**Conflict prevention**" describes measures in order to avert an outbreak of violence. The term "**post conflict peace-building**" describes measures implemented after the resolution of a violent conflict (see for example Miall et al. 1999).

The following paragraphs are structured according to the common distinction of violent conflicts into pre-conflict, conflict and post-conflict phases[10]. This categorization entails the risk of a simplistic analysis of armed conflict, but is still the most adequate way of arranging the chapter. It should be kept in mind, however, that the dividing lines between the three phases are often diffuse and that the post-conflict phase is often the pre-conflict phase for the next outbreak of an armed struggle. Correspondingly, different conflict management activities overlap or can be implemented in more than one conflict phase.

From the outset, it should be made clear that the majority of concepts introduced below rest on the assumption that the **main responsibility** for conflict management remains with the governmental sector. The business sector has a special profile that may complement public endeavours, but it cannot replace them (see for instance Carnegie Commission on Preventing Deadly Conflict 1997: 123-125; Nelson et al. 2000; Barnes 2002; Wenger/Möckli 2002: 8, 81).

---

10 Perhaps more accurate are the notions "pre-violence, violence, and post-violence", since it is important to differentiate between conflicts, which are part of all our everyday lives and conflicts that turn into violent conflicts (e.g. civil wars).

2.3.1 During the pre-conflict-phase

The prevention of violent conflicts is the favoured goal of most conflict management strategies. The landmark policy agenda "Agenda for Peace" by former UN Secretary General Boutros Boutros Gali or the UN Report "Prevention of Armed Conflict" by Secretary General Kofi Annan (United Nations 1992; United Nations 1997a), for instance, **prioritized conflict prevention** over conflict resolution. Experiences such as Rwanda and Yugoslavia were palpably key to the agenda setting. Prevention of violent conflict is not only more human, but is also considered as more cost-efficient than conflict resolution and reconstruction (Schnabel 1997).

Conflict prevention is defined as "those factors or actions which prevent armed conflicts or mass violence from breaking out" (Miall et al. 1999: 96). Conflict prevention can be classified as **"light" and "deep" prevention** strategies. Similar to conflict management strategies for the other two conflict phases, "light" and "deep" prevention varies in how they tackle the process factors and root causes of a violent conflict. "Deep prevention" aims to dispel the root causes of armed strife, whereas "light prevention" intends to prevent threshold conflicts from turning into violent conflicts without necessarily tackling the reasons that underpin the eruption of violence in the first place (Miall et al. 1999: 97).

The suggestions on how the private business sector can participate in preventing violent conflicts primarily refer to "deep" prevention. They range from very specific suggestions to rather broad concepts. Some of the more specific proposals suggest that companies could intensify their cooperation with national and local authorities, and hence **"contribute to community stability"** (Carnegie Commission on Preventing Deadly Conflict 1997: 123-125). They could encourage capacity building of local civil society organisations or fund projects that aim to promote diversity, tolerance and civic education (Nelson et al. 2000). Private businessmen are assumed to be particularly capable of fostering these types of activities due to their professional experience in managing and evaluating complex problems (for details see Wenger/Möckli 2002: 86-88).

A broader and often repeated idea is rooted in the private sector's function as the "dominant **engine of growth**; the principal creator of value and wealth"[11]. Economic development is by some scholars considered an important means to reduce violent conflict. More developed societies offer more economic opportunities, may reduce economic grievances and tend to be more stable. Meyer for example argues that there is a link between economic investment, development, respect to human rights and political stability (Meyer 1998). Or in other words, "simply by doing business" and promoting economic growth, private companies

---

11 Kofi Annan in a speech on the World Economic Forum in Davos in February 1997 (cited in Hüfner 2002: 4).

are said to contribute to less conflict-prone societies (Wenger/Möckli 2002: 6, 52-53, 86).

However, contrary to the idea that "simply by doing" business, companies contribute to conflict prevention, there is also evidence that corporate actors **do harm "simply by doing business"**. Similar to development aid projects, corporate investments are never neutral to their environment and companies should implement conflict-sensitive business practices in order to avoid stirring up hostility (Anderson 1999). Even if companies intend to be non-partisan and impartial, business activities shape the social, economic and political fabric they invest in. Obviously, businesses do not inevitably result in detrimental effects for their surroundings. Their positive effects may in fact compensate for most negative consequences. However, various examples show that business activities can aggravate or generate social tension – not always deliberately but often unintended because of ignorance, indifference or unfamiliarity with local conditions.

One side effect of particularly large-scale investments in the **natural resource sector** is that the newly created wealth may lead to social tensions about who gets what. In many contemporary civil wars, the abundance of natural resources perpetuated "greed-motivated rebellion" (de Soysa 2000: 113). Income from oil exploitation for instance, is linked to a number of conflicts in Africa, e.g. in Angola, Sudan, Chad, or Nigeria. Dismantling and trading coltan appears to be a strategic factor in financing the armed conflict in the Democratic Republic of Congo. Revenues from the trade in "blood diamonds" funded armed forces in Sierra Leone, Angola and in the Democratic Republic of Congo[12]. Since private companies very often are those who extract the natural resources, they become easily entangled in potentially emerging violent conflicts (for more details see the following chapter 2.3.2).

In addition, on a smaller scale, imprudent hiring practices, for example, with or without recognition of ethnic groups can generate grievances among the local population. Environmental pollution or a lack of respect for cultural, historical or social values and traditions may **undermine the potentially positive outcomes** of business investments. Missing or insufficient compensation to the local population for damages caused by the investment can reinforce or trigger tension.

Mary Anderson's "Corporate Engagement Project" gives telling **examples** of how companies that tried to "do the right thing" ended up doing "deleterious business". An international company, for instance, that invested in a conflict prone region intended to compensate the local population in a "correct and adequate way". They engaged an anthropologist to scrutinize:

"kinship patterns, indigenous associations and land ownership traditions. [...] The anthropologist reported that there were eight major societal groupings and twenty-three smaller subgroups with distinct identities in the area where the company would need to

---

12 For example Global Witness 1998, Smillie 2002.

provide compensation. [...] The company launched compensation negotiations with all twenty-three of the subgroups and soon, found themselves facing an increasing number of other sub-sub groupings with special claims".

The population had realized that the more groupings there were the more monetary compensation they could gain from the company. By trying to do the "right thing" the firm had in fact generated increasing division and grievance within the communities (Anderson 2002: 41-43; see also Zandvliet 2004).

Although organizations such as the *Carnegie Commission on Preventing Deadly Conflict* argued that the private sector has begun to recognize its responsibilities in helping to prevent conditions that can lead to violent conflicts, it is generally agreed that mainstreaming **conflict sensitive business practices is a neglected issue** in companies (Carnegie Commission on Preventing Deadly Conflict 1997: 123-125). Business projects in which executives actively aim to avoid conflict-aggravating behaviour and unintended side effects still are the exceptions to the rule. Rienstra, for example, found in her research that the majority of companies do not integrate conflict prevention policies, such as socioeconomic impact assessments into their business practices, although the mainstreaming of related issues, such as respect for human rights and community development is much more widespread (Rienstra 2001)[13].

One of the most prominent examples where private business actors became part of a larger scale conflict prevention strategy is an initiative of oil companies operating in **Azerbaijan**. Due to various political, economic and social factors, Azerbaijan is vulnerable to the emergence of violent conflict. Its oil resources, however, have attracted oil companies from all over the world that had to deal with the country's fragile social and political situation. *International Alert* launched a process to bring together various stakeholders such as oil companies, the national bank, UN representatives, local business leaders and the Azerbaijan Entrepreneurs Confederation, seeking to avoid tensions over the use and distribution of the oil-revenues (Killick; Rienstra 2001).

The World Bank started a similar initiative in the context of the **Chad-Cameroon pipeline** project. This initiative (a "tri-sector partnership" that also included NGOs (Davy 2001) sought to minimize the negative environmental and social impacts of the pipeline. It was a pioneering attempt to direct petrol revenues away from corrupt state elites and provide benefits to the general population (Killick; Rienstra 2001). (The initiative failed, however, when the government of

---

13 There is a relatively wide variety on voluntary agreements on business and human rights like the "Human Rights and Business Roundtable" or the "OECD Guidelines for Multinational Enterprises". These agreements can be conducive to conflict management but are not linked directly to conflict resolution or prevention.
Especially in the United States, corporate social responsibility initiatives proliferated. The most advanced are probably the Social Accountability Standard (SA 8000), the Fair Labor Association and the Worldwide Responsible Apparel Production (Braun 2001).

Chad broke the agreement and the World Bank decided to suspend Chad's loans.)

Corporate conflict-prevention, in other words, has two major dimensions. The first one comprises more general and unspecific measures, such as supporting NGOs in promoting tolerance or education. The second dimension is much more business-specific. Since business operations can be "part of the problem", leading to escalating tensions, business and **conflict sensitive business practices** have to become part of overall conflict prevention strategies. "Do no harm" should be the guiding principal for day to day business activities. Private companies should analyse the conflict-related risks and effects of their operations, develop appropriate strategies, mainstream them and enter into a regular dialogue with the affected local population (Nelson et al. 2000; Haufler 2001b). Business guidelines or Codes of Conduct that incorporate conflict prevention measures, the Guidelines for Multinational Companies by Amnesty International or the OECD (ai 1998; OECD 2000) are considered one way to realize these goals.

2.3.2 During the conflict phase

Once violence has broken out, possibilities for corporate engagement are certainly more limited than during a pre- or a post-conflict period. Conflict resolution, probably more than other fields of conflict management, has to remain largely a preserve of state authorities. The risks inherent in escalated violence and the political sensitivity of this stage of a conflict makes it difficult for the majority of companies to be engaged in conflict settlement. Given the volatile ground during a violent conflict, most corporate actors may aim to maintain **political neutrality** and to have as little interaction with the belligerent parties as possible.

But firms can seldom ignore the conflict and their businesses activities may accidentally (or deliberately) have conflict-exacerbating instead of mitigating effects. The line between being **"accidentally" or deliberately involved** in violent conflicts is often diffuse. Companies may deliberately profit from investing in war-ridden societies because it may strengthen their bargaining power and increase their profits. Studies on the role of Shell in Nigeria, for instance, found that the more pressurized the government became due to high rates of political instability, the larger the concessions the government granted the company in order to stay in operation (Khan 1994; Frynas 1998).

Other companies that staid in conflict ridden societies accidentally perpetuated violent conflict by bridging the legal economic sphere with the economies of violence. It was mentioned earlier that economic interests such as greed-motivated violence can sustain or even trigger wars (e.g. Keen 1997; Collier/Hoeffler 1998; Collier/Hoeffler 2001). Corrupt, weakened or collapsed state authorities and the outbreak of disorder during civil wars, can be mis-used by warlords, elite groups, rebels, international trading networks, etc. to pursue their respective economic agendas. Looting, collecting protection money, forced control of trade networks, or stealing aid supplies are just some forms of profiteering from war situations (Keen 1998: 15-17; Jean/Rufin 1999). Easily exploitable "conflict timber", for example, helped uphold war factions like the Khmer Rouge in the Cambodian civil war, and sustained warfare in Sierra Leone and the Democratic Republic of Congo. Those "economies of violence"[14] are dependent on the maintenance of illegality but are at the same time interconnected with legal production circles. Most pillaged products have to be sold on the **legal market** (e.g. diamonds), or money earned in illicit business must enter the "legal circulation" of money (Duffield 2000; Reno 2000). In a number of conflicts, diamond traders purchase raw diamonds that are produced in rebel-held territories or oil companies do business with illegitimate regimes. They therewith perpetuate violent conflict, by providing the warring fractions with financial resources, which flow through the channels that connect the legal market to the illicit sphere.

Although disinvesting is arguably what many (international) companies do, despite the fact that this may be their least favoured option[15], there are often some that stay or start investments in conflict affected countries in order to skim off extra rents, ignoring the potential negative consequences. Many practitioners and academics therefore demand that companies do not invest in conflict-ridden countries and **withdraw** from regions, once violence has broken out. Closing down business operations prevents companies to accidentally perpetuate violence and can be a signal to governments and rebel groups that the violence is not tolerated by the private sector as well as an incentive to reduce or end violence.

International organisations and private initiatives increasingly also consider voluntary **measures that aim to restrict private production and trade** in commodities that finance war. The *Kimberly Process*, for example, brought together NGOs, the industry sector and government representatives in order to de-

---

14 It is important to delimit the term "war economies" from the term "economies of violence" although they are often used synonymously. Economies of violence cover all those income activities that are based on the threat or implementation of violence. Laundering money, kidnapping, smuggling of e.g. drugs, weapons or natural resources such as diamonds are some examples of economies of violence. The notion war–economies should cover here all structural changes that arise due to warfare, e.g. the decline in production or destruction of infrastructure. Another term that is often applied in this context is the term "shadow economy". Shadow economies are "economic activities operating outside of formal or government-controlled structures" (ESSD et al. 1999: vii). Although economies of violence form part of shadow economies, shadow economies are not necessarily dependent on violence.

15 Chevron, for example, left Sudan in 1990 after ongoing attacks against their employees and their installations (Harker 2000: 12). Or, when rebels repeatedly damaged Exxon Mobil's production facilities in Aceh, Indonesia, the government first sent troops to protect the gas field. But when the violence became worse, the company withdrew (Arnold 2001). However, it is obvious that less risk averse companies enter the scene in spite of violent conflicts going on. When Chevron withdrew from Sudan, first the Canadian company Arakis entered and later Talisman.

velop an international voluntary certification system for rough diamonds that intends to stem the flow and laundering of "blood diamonds".

Others, however, invite companies' executives to **participate actively in conflict settlement,** arguing that if companies are staying in conflict-ridden regions, there are numerous positive things business actors can do in order to mitigate violent conflicts and their effects. One can roughly distinguish between two sets of ideas of what the business community can do during a violent conflict:

i. The first approach focuses on **corporate support for humanitarian activities,** including supply of relief products, equipment and services or support of international emergency aid initiatives. In the 1999 Kosovo crisis, for example, the companies British Telecom, Dell, Newbridge Networks, Nortel Networks and Oracle worked jointly to provide satellite telephones and other communication devices to refugees in Albania (Nelson et al. 2000: 108).

ii. The second approach addresses **conflict diplomacy,** asking businessmen to get engaged in conflict mediation and resolution. Some theories of conflict mediation have integrated the business sector into their concepts of conflict management. But also political institutions, such as the Development Assistance Committee (DAC) of the OECD promote the idea of business diplomacy (OECD 2001). They invite business executives to participate in peace initiative, such as in peace delegations or negotiations. Other related approaches ask companies to provide "good services" for official negotiations, such as logistical support or offering secretariat services.

Already at the beginning of the 1980s, US-Ambassador John McDonald included the business sector into his concept of "Track Two Diplomacy". His concept of conflict resolution differentiated between "track one" (official, governmental actions) and "track two" diplomacy (unofficial efforts by non-governmental professionals). "Track two" had the purpose of affecting or changing the orientation of "track one". In 1991, McDonald expanded the model to the concept of **"Multi-Track-Diplomacy",** embracing nine different "tracks" of diplomacy, all interconnected and equally important. The underlying argument of this approach is that protracted conflicts are located within social systems in which conflict has become an integrated part. Only by integrating all parties of a society in a peace process, including the private sector, can a durable peace be achieved (Diamond/McDonald 1996).

Similar is the concept of "peace constituencies", which may also include the private business sector. The principal idea is that a sustainable process of conflict transformation needs to establish alliances between and integrate all those civil actors that are interested in peace. **Peace constituencies** comprise, in contrast to so-called war-constituencies, all those actors that profit more from peace than from war. It thus also embraces those businessmen who need a peaceful and stable environment for their day-to-day business activities (Lederach 1995; Rupesinghe 1995).

Other authors emphasize **particular corporate skills** that are worth harnessing for conflict resolution. Business communities are assumed to have regular contact with other groups of a society. They have established communication channels, for example with politicians and labour unions that facilitate the exchange of ideas and bring them into regular dialogue. Those communication channels can also be utilized during wartime, helping to bring opposing groups together. In addition, companies are said to have decisive influence on politics. Oil companies, for example, often provide a large share of national income and are therefore potential actors with positive leverage over governments (McCartney 2002; Swanson 2002: 9). Allan Gerson and Nat J. Colletta furthermore acknowledge the pragmatic and instrumental way in which the private sector thinks and works (Gerson/Colletta 2002). Ideology and politics would not hamper their position in peace processes and can make the private sector a reliable mediator (see also INCORE).

Table 1: Examples of business activities in different stages of a violent conflict

Pre-Conflict-Phase	**Conflict-Phase**	**Post-Conflict-Phase**
− Contributing to development and wealth creation, "simply by doing business" − Contribute to tolerance building and community stability by supporting NGOs − Mainstream conflict prevention policies in day to day business activities − Conflict sensitive investment decisions	− Supply of relief products, equipment and services − Support humanitarian work − Get engaged in diplomacy, by providing 'good services', use communication channels to social stakeholders, develop ideas of peace etc. − Participate directly in peace delegations and negotiations − National and international lobbying for peace	− Support rebuilding of infrastructure − Investments in the productive sector − Support special reconstruction initiatives such as programmes for the reintegration of ex-combatants − Share business know-how and other skills in support of small-and medium businesses − Support social reconstruction and reconciliation activities, such as truth commissions

Business diplomacy and related measures had already been set a range of more or less successful acid tests. In the context of peace negotiations in **Columbia**, for instance, the insurgency group *Fuerzas Armadas Revolucionarias de Colombia* (FARC), had direct contact with private businessmen. A FARC commander commented on this as follows: "We do not trust the government because there are corrupt and ineffective. We do not trust the army because they believe that they can military defeat us. But we do trust the business community because we know they have self-enlightened interests and can deliver on their promises" (cited in Gerson/Colletta 2002: 32). In 1999, a groups of Columbian entrepreneurs then founded the *"Fundación ideas para la paz"* (Foundation Ideas for Peace), intending to be a 'think tank', able to contribute to reach a lasting peace in the war ridden country (Fundación Ideas para la Paz 1999; Rettberg 2004)[16].

Other prominent examples are "Tiny" Rowland's endeavours in the peace process in Mozambique, the activities of the Sri Lankan Chamber of Commerce, or of South African and Northern Irish companies.

Tiny Rowland, manager of a **Mozambique**-based subsidy of the British transnational corporation *Lonrho* provided good services and embarked on shuttle diplomacy for the national peace-process. His eight years of support were decisive for creating trust between the conflicting parties and for the final signing of the peace accords at the end of 1992. Before Rowland became actively involved in the peace process, *Lonrho* had first attempted to do business with the rebel forces. But the dramatically swelling cost made Rowland strike the diplomatic path instead (Vines 1998).

In **Sri Lanka**, the private business sector, represented by the "Ceylon Chamber of Commerce", participated in peace talks that resulted in a ceasefire agreement in 2003, after 19 years of civil strife. The local business community established a forum, the *Joint Business Forum,* comprising all chambers of commerce, trade and employer associations to address questions related to the peace initiative and to launch peace campaigns such as *Sri Lanka First* in support of the national peace process (de Zoysa 2002).

In **South Africa** in the 1980s, business groups were actively engaged in the political transition from the apartheid regime to a more democratic system, and from violent conflict to a more peaceful society. First, individual business leaders and later an organized group called the Consultative Business Movement (CBM) pressurized for and assisted in political discussions and peace negotiations across the political spectrum. They provided administrative and organisational services for meetings, wrote reports, built relationships between the parties, and became a trusted partner in a process leading to the national peace accord in 1991, and to further democratisation of the country (Charney 1999; Eloff 1999).

Similar, but with stronger emphasis on substantive support was the engagement of the business sector in **Northern Ireland**. The Northern Ireland branch of the Confederation of Business and Industry (CBI) acted as a political think tank, developing economic arguments against the civil war and advocating for anti-sectarian business practices (European Platform for Conflict Prevention and Transformation 1999).

Obviously, not all of these interventions succeeded. The civil war in Sri Lanka, for instance, is still ongoing. Yet, as a generally important actor within

---

16 For more information on business-led activities in favour of peace in Columbia, see Rettberg 2004.

the national society, the position of businesses regarding a violent conflict seem to have some weight for governmental groups as well as rebel forces. They may not be able to determine about peace or war, but can potentially exert some influence.

2.3.3 During post-violence peacebuilding

Countries coming out of war have approximately a 40 percent higher risk of relapsing into violence in the first five years of peace. Only one in five countries manages to maintain peace for a longer period (Collier et al. 2003: 83-84). Insufficient commitment for peace by the negotiating parties, widespread proliferation of weapons, instable and weakly developed governmental institutions, economic frustration etc. are some reasons why countries slip back into armed hostility. Once an armed conflict has ended, **costly reconstruction** measures have to be implemented, the economic structure has to be rebuilt, jobs have to be created, ex-combatants and refugees have to be reintegrated, and if economic issues were at the root of the violence, they need to be addressed when fighting is over.

The issue of how the private business sector could get involved in post-conflict peacebuilding closely ties in with what has already been said for the pre-conflict phase. In principal, corporate contributions in post-conflict peacebuilding can range from providing funds and in kind donations, to strategic philanthropy, or "simply" doing business (Wenger/Möckli 2002: 133-159). Companies are mostly thought to support all kinds of remedies that tackle **economic reconstruction**, including building infrastructure, investing in the productive sector, supporting initiatives to attract foreign investments, engaging in private sector development programs, provide their know-how and skills for economic peacebuilding programmes, or support job-creating programs with a special focus on the reintegration of ex-combatants (Nelson et al. 2000; Wenger/Möckli 2002).

Some NGOs or governmental institutions emphasize in addition to the economic contribution, the significance of **social initiatives**, such as involvement in reconciliation efforts, truth commissions or other measures that seek to rebuild trust (Nelson et al. 2000). But the majority of proposals fall into the economic realm – the genuine field of private business. Wenger/Möckli, for example, stress that:

"the case for corporate action in this field [economic peacebuilding] do not only arise from the ability of the business sector to create value in economic matters. Rather, the reluctance and inability of the international community to comprehensively cover the socioeconomic dimension of conflict prevention makes an active corporate role in this field important. Although there is no best practice in the area of economic peacebuilding, development and/or rebuilding a strong local private sector in conflict-prone countries is certainly key" (Wenger/Möckli 2002: 133).

However, Economic development in general is a difficult task. Economic peacebuilding is like economic development under aggravated circumstances and not likely to bring quick results. Without certain preconditions fulfilled, such as functioning markets, a certain level of social trust and juridical security, infrastructure and basic governmental institutions, corporate investment in a larger scale is not likely[17]. Given the volatile ground in post-conflict settings, some authors have proposed to implement **incentives**, such as tax breaks or specific credit lines in order to establish a more attractive business environment and to encourage firms to do business in those high risk environments (CSIS/AUSA 2002; Mendelson Forman 2002).

An interesting example of business support in a post-conflict period that went beyond a merely economic focus comes from **El Salvador**, where business had launched a voluntary weapons collection programme. Three years after the settlement of the civil war in El Salvador in 1992, common crime rates were extremely high in the country. Although disarmament and demobilization had been important in the post-conflict recovery strategy, studies suggest that about 360,000 military-style weapons were still in circulation.

"In November 1995 a citizens group in El Salvador, including leaders of the business community, alarmed by the impact of this armed violence on the economy of the country formed the Patriotic Movement Against Crime (Movimiento Patriótica Contra la Delincuencia – MPCD). By April 1996 MPCD had decided to conduct a weapons collection program. The organization was formed for three key reasons. First, the Association of Distributors (consumer goods) of El Salvador (ADES) members were continually having their delivery trucks assaulted by men armed with military-style weapons. Second, ADE members ere becoming increasingly concerned with the security of their employees in transit between work and home, Third, ADES was looking to collaborate with government and civil society to reverse the growing violence affecting all Salvadorans." (Laurance/Godnick n.d.: 3)

Thousands of weapons were collected between 1996 and 1999 for a compensation of vouchers for supermarkets, pharmacies and shoe stores and "for contributing to the development of a peaceful and secure future in El Salvador" (Laurance/Godnick n.d.: 4).

---

17 However, in most countries, emerging out of a violent conflict there will be some companies that invest in an early post-conflict stage or while violence is still going on, hoping for a profitable market position. Coca-Cola, for instance, started investments in Angola in 2000, two years before the signing of the cease-fire agreement and a year after the UN terminated its peace mission in Angola. The company expanded significantly since then, expecting large future sales and profits (Wenger/ Möckli 2002: 150).

2.4 Who, how, where and why: A brief analysis of the demand for corporate engagement in conflict management

As was shown in the preceding paragraphs, options of corporate engagement in all stages of conflict management seem manifold. What a company could do, however, may depend on the **particular circumstances**. These circumstances are determined by the type of company (branch, size, ownership, history etc.), the type of conflict (causes, stage, location) as well as the constellation of "other actors", such as governments or international organizations (role, power, relationship, capacity) (Nelson et al. 2000). The approaches to corporate promotion of peace are indeed overall eclectic and little explored. Only few of the suggestions have been implemented, and even less have been analysed.

In the following paragraphs, the current demands and invitations for corporate engagement in conflict management are discussed further, exploring the foci, limits and reasoning of the proposals.

i. Which types of corporate actors are primarily addressed by the invitation and demand to participate in conflict management?

Although most publications and ideas do not exclude any type of enterprise in principal, the focus lays palpably on **international companies**. Wenger/Möckli for instance state: "Which groups of business actors have a stake in conflict prevention? And which of these can make a contribution to international peace and stability? Those that immediately spring to mind are transnational corporations" (Wenger/Möckli 2002: 120).

This focus is little surprising, given that the majority of current research is done on the negative involvement of international corporations in violent conflicts. It ignores, however, the significance of the **domestic business sector** in most developing countries. Domestic firms and not foreign ones are the mayor source of investment and jobs in the majority of Third World states (Mendelson Forman et al. 1998). They are an important political force and perhaps have to carry most of the burdens that come along with violent conflict.

To date only **little light has been shed** on the role of the local private sector and only a few (although steadily more) authors acknowledge the importance of domestic economic groups[18]. Of a more exceptional character are statements such as by USAID (US Agency for International Development) who point out to the essential position local business actors may be able to assume in conflict management (Mendelson Forman 2002: 3, 7, 9). Phil Champain for example in-

---

18 A recent indication for the growing interest in the role of domestic companies in peace is a publication by International Alert on this topic (Banfield et al. 2006). The volume was published briefly before my own study went into print. For this reason the book by International Alert could not be considered here.

dicates: "[...] TNCs [transnational companies] are not the whole picture. In some conflicts they are not part of the picture at all. The local business sector [...] is of particular relevance to conflict transformation, offering opportunities for engagement, given their stake in the conflict, that TNCs do not have."(Champain 2002: 10-11).

The above outlined cases about the activities of the El Salvadorian, Northern Irish, Columbian or Sri Lankan business communities are some concrete examples of how local business engaged in conflict transformation (see also International Alert 2004).

In all three phases of a violent conflict, the role and position of domestic businesses is likely to differ from those of international players. National commitment, different ways to perceive the risks of violent conflicts, different patterns in withdrawal of investments when violence erupts, different ways and possibilities to receive information and influence the political decision making process are just some of the **differences between local and foreign investments**.

Yet, it is not clear how this **influences the domestic companies' attitude** towards war and peace. Virginia Haufler, for example, says in one of the first comprehensive academic articles on the question of whether or not there is "A Role for Business in Conflict Management?": "One final important point to make is the difference in context for local versus foreign companies. Local company leaders are more intimately linked to the political system and may be active "players" in political conflict. This can give them greater influence in promoting reform, as in the case of the National Business Initiative in South Africa, or great but negative influence in a corrupt and illegitimate system" (Haufler 2001b: 670) However, there is still little knowledge on how national business actors perceive widespread and sustained violence and what their particular role in generating, maintaining and ending civil wars may be.

Additional to the question of the national origin of the companies involved, another important issue is the organizational structure of these enterprises. Are **individual companies** addressed in the invitation for corporate engagement in conflict management or **business associations**? The answer is 'both'. Many conflict management activities lay in the immediate sphere of influence of the individual company. The payment of compensations, for instance, or providing funding to post violence peace-building activities are decisions that are made by each individual company. However, business associations have the power to influence individual business decisions and they generally have the role to represent the business community in political decision making processes. Corporate involvement in Multi-Track Diplomacy, for example, or the concept of "peace constituencies" can only be meaningful if the national business community has some form of representative organization. Or in other words, "the private business sector will become a strategic partner in a sustainable prevention effort only if corporations are willing to overcome their fragmentation and pool their resources and know-how" (Wenger/Möckli 2002: 8).

The engagement of business associations in a war-torn country faces, however, a range of difficulties. Many war affected states are characterized by a low level civil organization, including corporate organizations. Especially in third world countries, business associations are only rudimentarily developed. Corporate interest groups often do not exist at all or they represent only the interest of a small minority; they lack organizational and financial capacity, infrastructure, members etc. In the course of a violent conflict, these **organizational weaknesses** may even aggravate.

A mere concentration on corporate interest groups would, in addition, not be appropriate as individual businessmen can be of outstanding importance during a civil war and a peace process (see for example the initiative of 'Tiny' Rowland in Mozambique) and because "individual preventive activities and programs must [...] be the first step for companies to engage in corporate conflict prevention" (Wenger/Möckli 2002: 8).

ii. What are the main areas of conflict management in which current literature sees a role for business?

One can roughly differentiate between economic and social-political activities. The focus in the current ideas on corporate engagement in conflict management is clearly on **economic activities**, including economic reconstruction, private investments, provision of financial resources etc. It was shown earlier that, for example, Multi-Track-Diplomacy and the concept of peace constituencies address the political function of non-state authorities including the private sector. Similar to this include ideas for corporate promotion of sustainable peace also activities such as social investments, engagement in reconciliation initiatives and so on. But many authors plead that private firms should focus on the economic realm. Wenger and Möckli, for instance, argue that:

"corporations must not attempt to play the same role and take up the same activities as other preventive actors because business actors operate in very different ways from public and civil society actors [...]. Because of such differences, business diplomacy should not be regarded as a standard role of corporate conflict prevention. [...] Direct involvement in conflict prevention should remain focused on economic peacebuilding" (Wenger/Möckli 2002: 131, 133).

A focus is also put on **conflict sensitive business conduct**, aiming to prevent that corporate activities contribute to the emergence or perpetuation of violent conflicts. Consideration is given to what the business sector can do additional to avoid their entanglement in violent conflicts, such as by suggesting business support to infrastructure reconstruction, humanitarian activities or business diplomacy. But attempts to prevent a repetition of cases such as DeBeers in Liberia or Shell in Nigeria still arrest more attention. The debate therewith largely focuses on the immediate sphere of influence of private companies and address less vigorously the broader context of business activities in conflict management.

iii. What is the reasoning behind business engagement in conflict management?

The ideas on business engagement in conflict management outlined above are reasoned in two ways; they appeal to **corporate philanthropy** and moral behaviour or to the **corporate self-interest**.

A number of approaches to business engagement underpin their ideas with corporate philanthropy and altruistic impetus. Supporting peace processes with financial resources and knowledge is considered a **social responsibility** and moral duty. Others argue that a mere appeal to corporate philanthropy is neither necessary nor sufficient. Calling on corporate social responsibility is not necessary, since a peaceful and **stable environment is considered economically rewarding** for the majority of private companies. Violent conflicts are chastising, due to the destruction of production facilities, infrastructure, national decline in purchasing power, the emergence of distrust etc. (for more details see chapter 3.1.2). Since the corporate costs of war are high, private companies are assumed to support voluntarily conflict management activities. Richard Holbrooke, former US Ambassador to the United Nations, for example, underpinned his appeal for corporate support to the then ongoing UN peacekeeping missions in East Timor, southern Lebanon, Israel, Kosovo, Sierra Leone and the Democratic Republic of the Congo economically. He claimed that these countries would provide numerous future business opportunities, such as in tourism, communication and the energy sector (UN Wire 5 June 2000; McMahon 2000; Bennis 2001: 144).

An exclusive appeal to corporate responsibility is also considered insufficient since it entails the risk that only those companies that are vulnerable to reputation damages may support conflict management initiatives. Companies, not susceptible to international **reputation damage** in contrast, such as the majority of domestic firms in Third World countries would consequently barely partner in conflict management. The corporate responsibility argument underestimates the fact that companies are driven by making money and not by doing 'social good'. Although there are companies with a 'not-only-for-profit' business philosophy, enlightened economic self-interest' is not the prevalent stimulus of companies in a capitalist market system.

Hence many authors emphasise the necessity of giving evidence to companies that conflict management can benefit the private sector (Haufler 2001b: 673). Similar as in debates on corporate social responsibility in the areas of human rights and environmental protection, **"making the business case"** is an important element to convince the private sector to support conflict management. Jonathan Berman, founder of the Political & Economic Link Consulting (PELC) states, for example: "Arguments about corporate social responsibility will not influence a company to mainstream conflict prevention. However, every company wants stability in the region in which their asset is located. The conflict prevention strategies that managers are most likely to internalise are the ones that work for them by enhancing stability or otherwise improving the business environment" (cited in Rienstra 2001). The debate on the self-interest argument and moral reasoning reveals how little is actually known about the corporate perception on war and peace. The majority of reports on the topic *assume* that the corporate costs entailed by a violent conflict are incentive enough for private companies to welcome or even support a peace process (Wenger/Möckli 2002). Indeed, the argument of economically rewarding peace is plausible. But *de facto*, there is **little systematic research** about how private companies experience violent conflict or peace processes.

Older **literature** about the role of private companies during the First and Second World War focused largely on companies that profited directly from violent conflict by supplying or trading war-products ("merchants of death") (Haufler 2001a: 4). These studies shed little light on those – numerically bigger group of – companies that operated in war shattered countries *without* profiting from war related businesses, such as producers and traders of civil goods. During the Cold War period, then, the issue of links between private business actors and armed conflict was barely of interest, due to the dominance of ideological factors. And the studies that have been undertaken since the end of the Cold War on companies functioning in conflict situations, tend to be anecdotal, highlighting how transnational corporations perpetuated and fuelled armed strife (e.g. debate on Blood Diamonds)[19].

Those who appeal to the business case of corporate support for peace cannot explain why, if the advancement of peace is economically rational, private business actors to date have only in rare cases displayed a clear interest in getting engaged in conflict management endeavours. Is it because prevailing conflict management strategies are still state centric and because the idea of integrating corporations emerged only recently? Is it because the private business sector itself still seems to regard their activities as unrelated to conflict management (Wenger/Möckli 2002: 4-5)? Or perhaps, peace and peace processes are in fact less economically viable for firms than was previously assumed? The following chapters attempt to shed some more light from a general viewpoint on how private companies perceive armed conflict and peace process.

---

19 See for example the publications, such as Private Sector Actors in Zones of Conflict by the International Peace Academy (International Peace Academy 2001) and publications by other academic institutions, NGOs and organizations such as Fafo Institute for Applied Social Science or Global Witness (Global Witness 1998; Global Witness 1999; Global Witness 2002; Smillie 2002; Swanson 2002; Taylor 2002). See also Hook et al. for a academic contribution to this debate (Hook/Ganguly 2000).

3 Corporate Costs of War and Peace

As argued earlier, an exclusive appeal to corporate philanthropy and responsibility does not seem to be sufficient to spur private companies into action with respect to conflict management. One might like to think that human suffering in wars may morally motivate business actors to get engaged in any kind of governmental or non-governmental relief activity – but the moral impulse seems not to be enough.

More has to be known about how private companies perceive armed struggle, peace processes and post-conflict peace building phases. How economically devastating are conflicts for private companies? What effects does a peace process have on business? What prevents them from getting engaged in conflict management and what might stimulate them to do so? Do private business actors regard it as economically viable to get involved in conflict prevention, conflict settlement, and post-violence reconstruction?

The following chapter aims at addressing these questions from a theoretical point of view. It will not be discussed if corporate engagement in conflict management is socio politically desirable. Instead, it will be asked how private companies perceive violent conflict, peace processes and peace building. The following two main hypotheses will be developed and explained further:

i. Violent conflicts are generally harmful for private companies, but qualifications are required, both in terms of the characteristics of conflicts and of the enterprises.
ii. Peace processes as well as war situations may bring about costs for private companies. Whether companies support a peace process or not, is not only influenced by the costs associated with the armed conflict, but also by the costs of peace. The corporate costs of war and peace derive not exclusively from the actual destruction related to warfare, but also significantly from changes in the political and social setting.

Three major strands of literature are taken into consideration:
i. General publications domiciled in peace and security studies, including literature on economic agendas in internal conflicts;
ii. Research dealing with the economic effects of violent conflicts;
iii. Political Risk Analysis (PRA).

Publications in the field of peace and security studies set the stage for the study at hand and the specific literature on economic agendas in civil wars gives some insights into what is economically rewarding in times of war and chastising in peace. Through literature on the consequences of violent conflicts and Political Risk Analysis, a sub-discipline of business administration, one can better comprehend the economic effects of war on companies[1].

3.1 Costs of war

Private companies exist as a system within an environment (Kobrin 1979: 70). In order to explore if private companies may become future partners for conflict prevention and peace promotion, it is necessary to elaborate how a war ridden environment affects firms. The first hypothesis, which assumes that violent conflicts are not per se harmful for private companies is further elaborated in the following paragraphs. Although this chapter focuses largely on negative effects of war for business it should be kept in mind that, as mentioned already earlier, companies can also "do well out of war".

3.1.1 Macroeconomic effects of violent conflicts

Violent conflicts have **negative impacts on welfare** and economic and social development of a country. Scholars such as Cranna (Cranna 1994), Blomberg and Hess (Blomberg/Hess 2002); Elbadawi (Elbadawi 1999), Murdoch and

---

1 Political Risk Analysis is a sub-discipline of business studies. Political Risk Assessment boomed first in the 1970s when the rapidly increasing number of FDIs was confronted by forced divestment and expropriation.
However, Political Risk Analysis focuses largely on FDIs. Domestic entrepreneurs are rarely considered. Although there are significant differences between the behaviour of domestic and foreign companies, e.g. due to different ways of interpreting political events (Thunell 1977), some of the findings of PRA are of relevance for this study. In addition, most of the quantitative studies in PRA that focuses on the link between violent strife and private investments are either very old, dating largely from the mid 1970s to the mid 1980s, or they look at violent conflict only as one indicator for political instability among many others. Contemporary research on PRA, for examples, deals primarily with legal-governmental risks, such as changes in investment law or trade regulations. Those kinds of risks are said to cause globally more corporate financial losses, than revolutions, wars or terrorism (Kennedy 1987: 17).

Sandler (Murdoch/Sandler 2002), Stewart and Fitzgerald (Stewart/Fitzgerald 2001), or Collier (Collier et al. 2003: 13-32) undertook studies on the economic and social consequences of war. Although social and economic costs of violent conflict may vary, depending on factors such as governance response, nature of the conflict or the response by the international community, scholars largely agree on that violent conflicts have negative impacts on the economic and social long and short term performance of a country. Systematic research on the economic consequences of war, however, is difficult and rare due to problems in ascertaining reliable data, comparing different conflicts and estimating the economic development without the effects of war (Debiel 1996: 4).

Macroeconomic costs caused by violent conflicts are manifold. Just to mention some:

- people are killed and displaced, often in large numbers and often with a high percentage of civil population;
- the work of administrative bodies, educational and health systems is strongly affected by destruction, displacement of people and lack of resources, leading e.g. to higher rates in infant mortality and illiteracy;
- transport, communication and electricity systems, as well as other forms of social and economic infrastructure are destroyed – often as part of a fighting strategy of rebel forces, aiming to weaken their enemy;
- public financial resources are channelled from growth-promoting investments to military spending;
- agricultural acreage may be mined and made unusable for a long period of time, resulting in decline in agricultural outputs;
- daily economic activities are confined and markets destroyed;
- foreign direct investments may be diverted to less risky countries;
- international isolation may hamper trade relations.

In general, interstate wars are more **disruptive** than intrastate conflicts, since all fighting occurs within the national territory and largely outside rules attempting to regulate the fighting (e.g. Stewart et al. 1997: 12). In average, GDP per capita declines during civil wars at an annual rate of 2.2 per cent relative to its counter-factual[2] (Collier 1998). At the time an "average" civil war ends more than double of the private wealth is held outside a war torn country, in comparison to when the armed hostility began (Collier et al. 2003: 15)[3]. Stewart, Huang and Wang

---

2 The decline in GDP is caused by a direct reduction in production and by a gradual loss of capital stock due to destruction, dissaving, and the substitution of portfolios abroad.
3 Capital flight can be caused by various reasons: overvalued exchange rates, high domestic inflation rates, differences between domestic and foreign interest rates and political instability and uncertainty. Although not always easy to separate the different motives for capital flight from each other, different statistical analysis confirmed

found in a survey of 18 cases that in 14 countries for which the average annual growth rates of GDP per capita could be calculated that the average annual growth rate was negative at -3.3 percent. For 15 countries they found that per capita income dropped; in 13 cases food production declined and in 12 economies export growth fell (Stewart et al. 2001).

The destruction of economic capital and the erosion of previous economic and social achievements do not only affect the status quo but also risk future development. Rebuilding war-torn societies takes often decades, or they may never "fully recover" (Woodward 2002). After a violent conflict ends, countries do not only have to establish the pre-war standards, but they also have to catch up with the time they lost during the armed hostility. Persistent adverse legacies of war in both the social as well as the economic realm often severely hamper post-war reconstruction and rebuilding. Refugees may not return to the country; capital that was shifted abroad during a war may not re-transferred due to persistently high risk levels; destroyed social capital may take decades to recuperate; and political institutions and policies in post-conflict settings are typically insufficient (Collier et al. 2003: 19-23).

While the disruptive macroeconomic impacts of war are relatively clear, research exploring the effects of violent conflict on firms is rare. The corporate consequences of war will be addressed on more detail in the following paragraphs.

3.1.2 Costs of violent conflicts for companies

Calculations for the civil war in Sri Lanka estimate that the national **private business sector** faced costs of about USD 2.2 billion. In the case of Mozambique, economic losses accruing from the war skyrocketed to USD 15 billion, with the industry sector so seriously damaged that production capacity in the post-war period had declined to 20-40 percent in comparison to the pre-war level (Nelson and the Carnegie Commission, cited in Wenger/Möckli 2002: 109). However, most existing studies focus on the macro-economic and household levels[4]. There is only a limited number of reports that address the issue of how individual companies are affected by war.

Valpy Fitzgerald realized an important analysis on economies during war that gives some more consideration of **how violent conflicts affect business** (Fitzgerald 1997). He found that for companies, wars are decisively different from any other kind of "exogenous shocks", such as natural disasters or trade

---

    the assumption that political instability causes capital flight (e.g. Lensink et al. 2000: 42).
4 Research on companies is rather rare. Studies concentrate mostly on macro-economic and social variables including the effects on GDP, poverty, health services, (child) mortality, employment or they refer to the household level (e.g. Matovu/Stewart 2001).

shocks. Only in wartime situations, decline the existing capital stock, the desired capital stock and the speed of adjustment, which determines the private investment response. In any other kind of external shock, at least one variable is staying the same or is increasing.

The existing capital stock falls due to **destruction**. The desired capital stock declines as a result of **little expectations** for future profitability. And the speed of adjustment that "is determined by the availability and costs of funds and above all by the degree of uncertainty about the future because of the difficulty of reverse fixed investment decisions once undertaken" declines due to the **high rate of uncertainty** and **lack of funding** in war time situations (Fitzgerald 1997: 50).

Table 2: Direct and indirect economic effects of violent conflict

Direct effects	Indirect and long-term effects
– uncertainty (or the inability to plan rationally); – raising transaction costs; – destruction of markets; – destruction of infrastructure and manufacturing facilities; – workforce instability; – raising costs for security and risk management.	– decline in GDP and per capita income[5] leading to declining purchasing power; – loss of market opportunities[6]; – regression of public investments (civil governmental expenditure) resulting in a decline of private investments since public and private investments are generally linked; – higher inflation; – shortage of private finance for investments; – increase of black-market activities; – tendency to more ineffective, weak and corrupt public institutions; – foreign exchange shortage (caused by the destruction of export capacity and interruption of normal trade channels or by sanctions/embargos); – declining levels of education; – 'brain drain' due to the displacement of population; – less confidence in the future;

---

5   Given an average duration of a civil war of 7 years, income is about 15 percent lower after its ending than if the war would not have occurred (Collier et al. 2003: 17).
6   "Expanding peace means expanding markets, and expanding markets translates into greater profits for business" (website of the Institute for Multi-Track Diplomacy http://www.imtd.org/initiatives-businesspeacebuilding.htm).

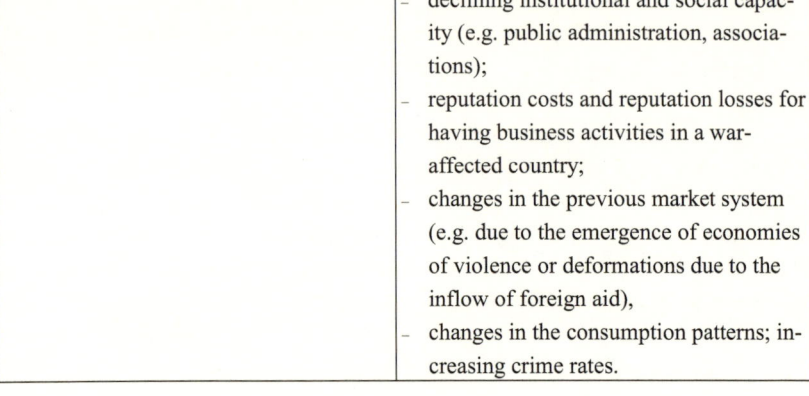
- declining institutional and social capacity (e.g. public administration, associations);
- reputation costs and reputation losses for having business activities in a war-affected country;
- changes in the previous market system (e.g. due to the emergence of economies of violence or deformations due to the inflow of foreign aid),
- changes in the consumption patterns; increasing crime rates.

Various direct as well as indirect (long-term) consequences affect companies (see Table 2). The direct effects lead to an immediate reduction in output. Indirect and long-term effects normally affect the level of production with a certain time delay. By far the greater part of economic effects of violent conflict is indirect. However, **direct and indirect effects** do not exist independently of each other, but they mutually influence each other. The level of destruction of infrastructure (direct effect), for example, influences the economic performance on the long-run. Summarizing some of the literature, the following major effects of war are relevant for companies[7]:

However, not all companies are in the same way and to the same extent affected by violent conflict. Political Risk Analysis (PRA), for example, differentiates between political events, including different forms of violent conflict, that have an impact on private companies and those events that do not affect business. The term "**political instability**" describes accordingly more general conditions and changes in a country. "**Political risk**", in contrast, refers directly to a company. While both terms cover political changes that take place within the constitutional order of a country (e.g. elections) as well as "irregular" changes such as coups or civil wars, political risks cover only those "political events [including different forms of violent conflicts] that cause financial, strategic or personnel losses for a firm" (Kennedy 1987: 3)[8].

---

[7] (Ball 1991; Ohlson 1991; Brück 1996: 17-19; Debiel 1996: 7-11; Fitzgerald 1997; Stewart et al. 1997: 19-21; Collier 1998; Nelson et al. 2000; Wenger/Möckli 2002; Collier et al. 2003).

[8] Most authors in the field of Political Risk Analysis also distinguish "uncertainty" and "political insecurity" from "risk". Uncertainty and risk are generally differentiated according to the level of information that decision makers have at their disposal. The term uncertainty is used in cases in which an actor does not have information about possible outcomes of an event. Risk, in contrast, describes events, when objective information about the likelihood of all possible outcomes is available (Thunell 1977: 4; Balleis 1985: 86-91). Although the differentiation is useful under some circumstances, in the following, the terms are used interchangeably as

One **index on political instability**, for example, assumes that the quantity and intensity of aggressive, politically-relevant behaviour within a society reflects the grade of political instability. The index differentiates between thirty categories of political activity ranging from predictable occasions, such as regular elections, to irregular political changes, including civil wars. The more "destabilizing" the political activity, the higher the weight it gets in the index. Elections receive a weight of zero; civil war a weight of six (Feierabend/Feierabend 1966).

This concept as well as other concepts on political instability such as that developed by Bruce Russet who measures political instability by the number of fatal casualties as a result of political violence (Russett 1964), only have **limited relevance for companies**. The civil war in Guatemala, for instance, has in a Central American comparison the highest number of causalities. But private companies have not been affected by the civil war to such an extent as companies in other countries, such as El Salvador, with a similar or lower level of "political instability", as measured by causality rate.

Political instability of all kinds *can* be associated with political risk for a firm but do not have to. "[...] Political fluctuations that do not change the business environment significantly do not represent risk for [...] business. Political Instability [...] is a separate although related phenomenon from that of political risk" (Robock 1971: 8).

A study examining the relationship between major trend changes in US FDI flow and elite and mass stability in nine countries for the years 1949 to 1967, concluded in this context that: "disturbance often is correlated with changes in investments. But at the same time it has also been found that the level of disturbance [determined by the number of deaths] can be low or high without any change in the investment trend" (Thunell 1977: 64). Although the analysis could not show satisfactorily, under which circumstances violent turmoil adversely affects business, it reveals that even if political instability occurs, it does not have to constitute a political risk for a firm.

Brewer, for example, explicitly excludes in his article on **instability and political risk**, phenomena such as riots and internal wars, arguing that these forms of strife are not likely to entail changes in the national policy that are relevant for business. Riots, coups and domestic warfare constitute in his interpretation, a certain *mode* of change but they do not say anything about the *direction* of the change or if the change is harmful or conducive for business (Brewer 1983: 149)[9].

---

we do not have reliable data on the information companies have on wars and their effects.
9 Entrepreneurs tend to be less nervous about regular or predictable changes in the political structure (e.g. through elections) than about irregular changes, e.g. caused by revolts. This is understandable, just because irregular changes are difficult to predict. However, irregular changes do not necessarily have to have a more adverse

There are numerous potential risks resulting from a violent conflict for private companies. But as this chapter showed, they do not inevitable have to harm business activities. This may to some extend explain, why private companies are reluctant to support conflict management. If companies are not or hardly affected by violent strife, their incentive to actively promote peace may be low. In the subsequent chapter it will be attempted to better understand **what makes conflicts deleterious** to companies and if indeed corporate impacts of war can be so low to undermine the business-case for peace.

3.1.3 Risky and not so risky conflicts: What makes a violent conflict detrimental to a company?

So, if violent conflicts are not per se hazardous for private business, what makes violent conflicts risky for companies? Or in other words: What makes a violent conflict a political risk?

Stewart et al. emphasize in their pioneering comparative analysis on the economic consequences of war on countries, the difficulties in generalizing and predicting the economic effects of violent conflicts (Stewart et al. 1997: 38). This seems to be in a similar way true for companies. The nature of a conflict, the characteristics of a company or even each individual business project, the respective pre-conflict state of the economy, different governmental policies, and the general political environment all influence the way in which firms perceive and react towards armed hostility. The multitude of influencing factors may explain divergences in perception of violent conflict, with some companies being better able to protect themselves from the costs of rebellion than others. Authors in the field of Political Risk Assessment came to similar conclusions and stated that "one cannot discuss the relationship between political conflict and FDI [foreign direct investments] in general" due to the complexity of influencing factors (Kobrin 1978: 114, 115).

However, some tendencies and patterns seem to surface and are outlined below. It will be explored which characteristics of conflicts, characteristics of companies, and characteristics of economies and governments make violent conflict more detrimental to business than others.

3.1.3.1 The varying nature of conflicts

As to the nature of a conflict, the following characteristics are discussed in more detail: Geographical spread, length, intensity, the aims of the conflicting parties, and the government's ability to handle a conflict[10].

---

    bearing on the political and economic structure of a country than predictable changes (Kobrin 1978: 114).

10 There are certainly also other characteristics that can describe the nature of a conflict such as the strength of the parties involved, the war-techniques used (e.g. guer-

The Political & Economic Link Consulting (PELC) found in a survey conducted among 25 managers of different international companies active in war-affected countries that the **geographic scope** of a conflict is the most important aspect for companies, in deciding whether to operate in a war ridden country or not (Berman 2000). They learned that as long as a conflict was restricted to a certain region and relatively stable, companies were willing to run their investments in those areas not directly under attack. Even if the geographical area affected by fighting is large in comparison to the rest of the country, like in Columbia, fighting might still be geographically contained, hence be more predictable, and less risky for firms.

The **duration of a conflict** seems to have an ambiguous bearing on companies. Some argue that short wars have only limited deleterious economic consequences on national economies and that longer conflicts lead to higher economic costs (Debiel 1996: 9). Correspondingly, short wars may not have a serious negative impact on firms but protracted wars may have. However, some authors point out that long-term conflicts provide the opportunity for economic actors to adapt to the conflict situation, which may mitigate some adverse impacts of war (DiAddario 1997: 124).

Referring to the **severity of warfare**, one may assume that firms perceive high intensity warfare as more risky than wars conducted at low intensity. A scorch-earthed civil war that is not contained in a particular geographical region and that leads to pervasive economic, social and cultural disintegration is probably one of the worst scenarios for economic actors. A PELC's survey found correspondingly that low intensity "terrorist conflict is a widely tolerated risk. This can be seen in Belfast and Tel Aviv, as well as in Colombo and Bogotá" (Berman 2000)[11].

The causes of a violent conflict, its **aims and political consequences** are also of explicit importance for the business sector. Violent conflicts waged around structural economic discontent, for example, tend to be more risky for business than most other types of conflicts. Economic discontent, due to for example unequal access to economic resources or poverty, is an important factor in many contemporary violent conflicts. Conflicts such as in Burundi, Malaysia, Namibia or Uganda are prominent examples (Stewart 2004). Economic causes of violent

---

rilla warfare), or the involvement of foreign governments. The characteristics chosen here seem to be those that are of primary importance for private firms.

11 Similarly, compare Michael Harvey's findings on corporate strategies for managing terrorist threats. His article is based on a survey among US-American TNCs on corporate programmes to reduce the impact of terrorism. Harvey reports that less then 50% of the companies had "anti-terrorist programs" – those who had such a programme spend their money mainly on security equipment. Harvey also found that the majority of the companies totally misjudged the geographic distribution of terrorist acts against companies. Furthermore companies very often did not feel threatened by terrorism and they often regarded measures against terrorists acts as too costly or useless (Harvey 1992).

conflicts do often not result from misconduct of individual companies, but are rooted in structural social-political conditions, including discriminatory national labour laws or historically unequal distribution of land. However, in those conflicts, entrepreneurs still are more likely to become a direct target of attacks[12]. In some cases, armed opposition may intentionally attack private companies for ideological or symbolic reasons or in order to weaken the economic capacity of a country. Insurgency groups, such as the African National Congress in South Africa or the majority of left-wing guerrilla movements in Latin-America with an open antagonism against private companies and private ownership of property as part of their ideology, were perceived as particularly threatening by private companies (Berman 2000).

But also those types of conflicts, which in contrast to mainly politically motivated wars, seek to gain income from **pillaging and looting**, may directly harm private firms (e.g. Democratic Republic of Congo, Liberia, Sierra Leone). Extortion via protection money or road tolls, corruption, the embroilment of state authorities in enrichment, or the deformation of traditional market structures due to the flood of foreign aid, all those factors can undermined daily operational business activities.

Another important category that may influence if violent conflicts are deleterious to private companies or not, is the **government's ability** to handle (violent) conflicts. The state's ability includes both, its military strength as well as its civil political capacity to deal with conflicts. Governments can respond to (incipient violent) conflicts either by military actions (e.g. violent repression) or by trying to alleviate the causes of the conflict by civil political means. Both strategies can have adverse effects on the business sector, but they limit at the same time the negative impacts that would result from escalating violence.

In cases where state military force is strong enough to suppress an emerging violent strife, violent repression by the state may have adverse affects on the business sector due to for example destruction of infrastructure. However, at the same time, a quick **repression** by the state may – at least in the short run – curb the negative impacts of escalating violence. Violent strife that the military can easily contain, tend to be less risky for a firm

Likewise, civil political strategies against conflicts can affect firms. In particular, political measures that intend to tackle economic causes of conflicts are apt to have an effect on business. A land reform, for example, that a government implements to mitigate a conflict may have a strong impact on the business sector[13]. However, the implementation of civil political means at an early stage of a

---

12 Some scholar, however, regard the chance of direct attacks against production facilities of private companies in general as "extremely rare" (Berman 2000: 3).
13 Political measures such as granting regional autonomy or special rights to ethnic groups may be less intrusive to companies (Kobrin 1978: 115-116).

conflict may prevent a conflict from escalating and avert high levels of destruction and direct war costs[14].

A **PRA study** confirms this assumption for a broader context. It examined the relationship between decline of FDIs and different types of violent conflicts and found a significant relationship only for one form of interstate conflict – highly focused, covert anti-regime violence that can bring changes in government policy (Kobrin 1978)[15].

The study distinguishes between turmoil, internal war and conspiracy. Turmoil reflects spontaneous mass protest that can be confined comparatively easy through political measures such as the engagement of police forces (e.g. protest, riots, demonstrations). Internal war represents relatively large-scale, organized anti-regime violence that often takes place in rural areas and can be contained by military response (e.g. armed attack, guerrilla war). Conspiracy also represents organized overt anti-regime violence but on a smaller scale and highly specific and covert (e.g. coups, revolutions, assassinations). This form of violence is not easy to repress and may lead to changes in governmental policy. Kobrin concludes that the major risk resulting from violent conflicts is not the direct destruction of business assets and infrastructure, but business relevant changes in governmental policies (Kobrin 1978).

Not all conflicts are, in other words, in the same way hazardous to companies. The intensity of a war is just one factor among many others. Characteristics such as the spatial spread of the fighting are even more relevant than severity of the war. If companies, however, always have the ability to differentiate between a more dangerous and a less dangerous conflict is another question that should be explored further.

3.1.3.2 Different characteristics of companies

The private business sector is very heterogeneous and comprises different types of firms, such as foreign and domestic companies; small, medium and big enterprises; the modern sector, and companies active in agriculture. The consequences of warfare vary for all of them, since the **war-susceptibility seems dependent on enterprise-specific characteristics** (Kobrin 1978; Kobrin 1979: 70). Relevant characteristics are, for example, the economic branch, the geographic location, nationality, dependency on external and internal markets, the market posi-

---

14 Civil policy instruments can also be oriented towards the company itself. Governments of war-affected countries tend to grant preferential terms (e.g. tax incentives) in order to attract companies and compensate for the risks linked with the armed conflict. Under these circumstances, private companies may gain indirectly from violent conflicts, and not loos.

15 The analysis covers a sample of 48 non-socialist bloc least developed countries (LDCs) that gathered more than USD 1 million of US manufacturing FDI by the end of 1967.

tion (e.g. oligopoly), profit expectations (market attractiveness), number of subsidiaries or level of diversification, dependence on preliminary products and so on.

Just to give some examples of how significant company specific characteristics are:
- **High profit-expectations**, a big market, cheap labour costs, first-mover advantages etc. can counter risks of violent conflicts. Companies with high returns on investments may decide to stay in a war-ridden region, regardless of the violence going on around them.
- Firms **dependent on a specific region or resources** and firms with **high investment costs** may tolerate a higher level of risks associated with armed conflicts than other firms may. Investments in natural resource extraction, for example, tend to uphold their assets despite violent conflict because of high investment costs.
- Companies with a high **level of diversification** – either geographically or by product – are less exposed to the adverse effects of violent conflicts. Possible losses in one subsidiary can be cushioned by ongoing production in other subsidiaries.
- Some particular branches have **"by nature" a smaller tolerance for war-related risks** than others. Tourism, for example, or companies producing image sensitive products are normally more conflict risk averse than others (Campbell 2002: 6; Neumayer 2004).

Analysis dealing with the macroeconomic consequences and costs of warfare found that the **modern business sector**, e.g. companies in the manufacturing sector, tend to be more seriously affected by war-related uncertainty. The modern sector is generally more input- and transaction-intensive, than the traditional sector. Due to raising transaction costs in war time situations, the modern sector has more difficulties in receiving its production inputs. Transaction costs rise during violent conflicts owing to the demolition of infrastructure and a decline in trust and other forms of social capital. In case of war related exchange shortages, the modern sector is more affected due to its higher dependence on imported goods.

Consequently, during violent conflicts economic actors tend to switch from the modern sector to **small-scale production, subsistence agriculture or the informal sector**. The modern sector and those sectors, which supply the necessary inputs and transactions (transport, distribution and finance) contract more rapidly than GDP as a whole and sectors not characterised by high transaction costs and input-intensity expand relative to GDP (Collier/Gunning 1995). In addition, small producers are more flexible and can more easily adapt to conflict situations by using unofficial networks to obtain resources and access to markets (Fitzgerald 1997: 50).

Again, other scholars suggest that **firms with big production facilities, a long life span or a high level of specificity** are more vulnerable to conflict than other types of firms. Big firms are more likely to be affected by an armed conflict because they are an easier target than small factories. A long life span increases the probability of being affected by violence over time. And high specificity, describing "the capital's degree of exclusiveness to an economic activity or sector", makes the company a more vulnerable target to military attacks (Brück 1996: 7-9). The extractive industry is thus more vulnerable to violent conflict than e.g. service industry, due to its relatively easy visibility, long life cycle, little flexibility and its propensity to be of structural importance for a national economy. However, it is obvious that this conceptualisation is insufficient. The high vulnerability of tourist industry, for instance, cannot be explained with this concept.

In conclusion, it may be stated that although some patterns of vulnerability for entire branches or sectors may be deduced, more relevant than the branch or the sector seem to be **company-specific characteristics**. Two companies belonging to the same branch may be affected very differently by an armed conflict, because they are located in different areas of the country, have different sizes, or have different subsidiary structures.

3.1.3.3 State of the economy and government

The **state of the economy** is closely linked to market attractiveness briefly mentioned in the previous section. Relevant characteristics for market attractiveness are income level and population as indicators for the size of a market, economic infrastructure, external dependency, dependence on a small number of power plants and flexibility. The flexibility of an economy refers to its ability to adapt to a new situation, e.g. by substituting for imports, locating new markets and especially by the ability to develop substitutes for collapsed economic and governmental institutions (Stewart et al. 1997: 17-19). The less flexible governmental policies are, the smaller the corporate tolerance of war related risks.

Wenger and Möckli for instance write in this context: "A weakened government and ineffective institutions pose major hindrance to the free flow of business" (Wenger/Möckli 2002: 109). Variations in the **flexibility** of war-affected countries may be one crucial factor why wars in developed countries have decisively different consequences for the national economy than wars in developing countries. For example, wars in developed countries often lead to technological advances and improvements in the living standards of the poor due to rise in employment, whereas wars in poor countries tend to increase economic inequality (Fitzgerald 1997: 46).

These factors mentioned in the preceding two paragraphs shape the **attractiveness of a national market** and have consequently an effect on private firms' willingness to stay in a market given the occurrence of an armed conflict. In simple terms this means: the more attractive the market the higher the tolerance for war-related risks.

A study by **Bennett/Green**, for example, found no significant relationship between political instability and the allocation of US investments abroad (stock). They tested for a sample of 46 countries over the period 1948 to 1965 different incidents of political instability and their relation to US foreign investments. They concluded that international managers appear to make their investment decisions on the basis of other overriding factors, such as the size and potential of markets and that political instability, including civil wars and situations with a "mild amount of violence", does not prevent them from investing in a country (Bennett/Green 1972)[16].

3.1.4 Curbing costs while adapting to violent conflicts

In the previous sections, it was concluded that a violent environment does not inevitably expel firms out of a war-ridden region. Some types of conflict are more detrimental and some companies are more vulnerable to armed rebellion than others are. Especially geographically contained, low intensity warfare seems not to stipulate a major hindrance for business activities. In addition to this, companies have measures at their disposal that help them to mitigate the impacts of violent conflict and to **curb the war-related costs**. Some authors go so far as to argue that it is not the violent conflict itself that is dangerous for a private company, but corporate mismanagement of violent conflict (Gladwin/Walter 1980; Austin/Ickis 1986).

How effective these management measures are must be evaluated on an individual basis. Doing business in war-ridden environments not only requires the creativity to implement those measures, but also the **willingness to take risks** and accept related costs. During the civil war in Nicaragua (1962-1989), for example, a surprisingly large number of international companies continued to operate in the country. Despite of price regulations, foreign exchange shortages, petroleum cutbacks, disruption of contacts to the government etc. companies found ways to make profits (Austin/Ickis 1986). Exxon Mobil, in contrast, decided to curtail their operations in Aceh (Indonesia), after more than 24 years. The ongoing hijackings related to the armed conflict finally exceeded Exxon's willingness to look for effective ways to protect their investments (Arnold 2001).

How can a company manage the risks related to armed hostility? Which strategies and measures can be implemented? Moving production facilities away from war affected areas, disinvestment and shifting big proportions of wealth into liquid form (see for instance Collier/Gunning 1995) are certainly common ways of reacting to violent conflicts. In this chapter it will be shown what other **management tools** companies have at their disposal. The first section of this

---

16 Kassicieh and Nassar came to the same conclusion while investigating changes in MNC's activities prior to and during the Iran-Iraq war (1976-84). They found that MNC in the gulf region were not influenced by the war at the time research was conducted (Kassicieh/Nasser 1982; Kassicieh/Nassar 1986).

chapter briefly outlines how companies can "get used to" violence. The second section presents the most important active corporate strategies to mitigate adverse consequences of armed conflicts.

3.1.4.1 Getting used to it

Nordstrom and others have argued that civil populations can get used to a certain level of violence (see e.g. the notion "culture of violence" as used in Nordstrom 1992). This seems to be in the same way true for private firms. Companies learn to accept a certain level of armed hostility, take it as part of the normal business environment and internalise conflict related expenses as additional operational costs when exposed to it.

For some countries, a violent environment is perceived a "regular" part of business life. Thunell, for example, compared foreign direct investments in European and Latin American countries and deduced that in Latin America (in the 1970s) "political violence is [considered] a normal part of political life; managers are used to living with it and do not care too much when it goes up and down" (Thunell 1977: 61). For the case of Nicaragua, Austin and Ickis found that (foreign) business managers learned to better assess the effects of different forms of violent upheavals and political changes, which helped them to deal with violence-related risks (Austin/Ickis 1986: 105, 107).

Becoming inured to a war-torn business climate can imply that the individual entrepreneur misinterprets war related costs. Slowly creeping, indirect, long-term consequences of violent conflicts, such as a decline in purchasing power or level of education, tend not to be fully discerned by business actors as consequences of armed hostility. Companies that are not suffering immediately from war cannot easily compare the war ridden business environment with a peaceful business climate and may assess incorrectly the adverse economic effects of war for their business.

3.1.4.2 Active conflict management strategies

In addition to this more passive way of "dealing" with violent conflicts, companies have a range of active measures at their disposal in order to cushion the deleterious effects of armed strife. The most common strategies are political risk insurances, protection through security forces and the implementation of certain management strategies, such as the establishment of joint-ventures.

i. **Political risk insurances** are provided by private as well as public entities (such as political risk insurances provided by the US Overseas Private Investment Corporation (OPIC) or the German "Hermes-Bürgschaften"). They insure against direct as well as indirect damages caused by political instability (e.g. expropriation, currency inconvertibility). Some, but only a few mainly public insurances include the protection against political violence in their programmes. Most private insurers do not offer protection against this type of hazard. OPIC, for instance used to cover damages and losses:"as a result of violence undertaken for political purposes. OPIC provides coverage against this risk, including the possibility of declared or undeclared war, hostile actions by national or international forces, civil war, revolution, insurrection and, at the purchaser's option, civil strife such as politically motivated terrorism or sabotage." (Perry 1996: 530).

Political risk insurances, covering political violence tends to be costly. It is a type of risk management that is predominantly available for international companies. Some programmes also cover domestic companies although only in rare cases (Fitzgerald 1997: 50; Berman 2000)[17].

ii. Especially in regions where the public security apparatus is weak, the establishment or hiring of **private security companies** (PSCs) is a common form of protection for private corporations. The importance of private security firms in many violent hotspots of the world is for example reflected in the term "privatisation of security"[18]. Private companies seek mostly the services of PSCs, and not of so-called private military companies (PMCs) (although overlaps often occur). Both PMCs and PSCs may use violence in order to fulfil their mission, but PSCs are not supposed to use military forms of violence. However, there is no clear-cut dividing line between PMCs and PSCs. The security company Executive Outcomes, for example, was engaged in both kinds of services during the civil war in Sierra Leone. It protected diamond mines and was also engaged in military fighting against rebel groups (Kaldor 2000: 151; Mair 2004: 261). In some (often criticized) cases such as in Indonesia, private companies support or have supported also **public security forces**. They directly pay the army for their services or provide equipment and infrastructure in order to facilitate public forces to better protect their investments.

iii. Another form of violence-related risk mitigation addresses the **management structure** of a business project. Venture progression, entering into alliances or joint ventures with other companies, attaching investments to multilateral development projects, reducing the pay-back periods on capital investments, trying to keep the revenues and funds abroad so that the belligerent parties have no access, are all mitigation methods (Miller 1992; Berman 2000). Trying to get an international donor on board or to participate in a multilateral development project, for example, has the advantage that in case of a threat to

---

17 (For more details on the history of Political Risk Insurances, including the risk related to wars, see Haufler 1997).
18 The term Privatisation of War/Security is normally used to cover different developments. Münkler, for example, differentiates three characteristics: the growing number of mercenaries and private military companies, the increasing importance of warlords and the growing number of child-soldiers (Münkler 2002b: 220-224).

the investment, the international organization has a better chance to successfully pressurize the host government to increase protection.

Whereas those methods introduced above convey no or limited changes in the modes of production, there are also those cases in which companies decide to shift from one type of investment or the production of one product to another type of investment or product – instead of "simply" shielding the existing production plants, products or modes of production.

With regard to legal business, different studies concluded that, faced with violence-related risks, firms are apt to **shift their investments from a susceptible economic activity or sector into a relatively safer one**. Collier and Gunning, for example, found that businessmen who are active in war ridden environments tend to prefer investments in those assets that are easily removable and reversible. "[…] They [investors] will favour investments such as vehicles over those such as tea estates, even if (abstracting from risk) the return on the latter is considerably higher" (Collier/Gunning 1995: 236).

Similarly, Elizabeth Wood in her work on the violent conflicts in **El Salvador and South Africa** argued that during civil war, the economic elites transferred their investments from the war-vulnerable and traditional labour intensive branches to other, less war-vulnerable and less labour intensive branches. Grievances such as labour-repression and exploitation in the traditional economic sectors were central causes for the emergence of violent conflict. Correspondingly, those branches were key targets in the civil wars. Direct attacks against plantations and high rates of workforce instability were common phenomena during the wars. Rising costs in those "war-vulnerable" business sectors, made businessmen intensify their investments in other branches that were less exposed to war-related attacks, such as the industry sector (Wood 2000). Interestingly, this study showed that the new emerging economic elites (industrialists), which were *less* threatened by war-related risks, cherished a *bigger* interest in peace than the traditional branches (agricultural sector) that faced high war-related costs. The reason for the seeming contradiction might be that the traditional branches were also the most affected by the "negative" impacts of peace (see section below).

With regard to illegal business, its relevance for wars (and especially "New Wars")[19] has already been mentioned in the previous chapters. The **step into il-**

---

19 So called "New Wars" are said to be emerging since the end of the Cold War. The term "new war" is shaped in the Anglophone sphere by Mary Kaldor and in the German speaking sphere by Münkler (Kaldor 2000; Münkler 2002a). Other authors introduced different terms (e.g. low-intensity wars by Crefeld), but they describe a similar phenomena. It is, however, debatable what the "new" characteristics of "new wars" actually comprise. The expanding amount of private actors in wars; the raising importance of economic factors in wars and the loss of salience of political and ideological reasons; the vast number of actors; the low severity and protracted nature and the high number of civil victims are some of the most frequently mentioned characteristics of "new wars".

licit business or into one that is located in the border area between legal and illegal business, is for some entrepreneurs that hitherto did legal business, one way of adapting to war conditions. A lack of alternative sources of income, weak governmental structures, rising corruption and unreliable security systems during war periods, all create fertile ground for an increase in illegal business activities. Illicit markets burgeon during violent conflicts, trade with illicit goods, such as weapons and drugs increase, and new elites emerge that make their living out of these types of activities (see literature on "economies of violence" such as Debiel 1996; Jean/Rufin 1999).

The group of criminal businessmen is often complemented by those, who Collier calls **"opportunistic" businessmen**. Opportunistic business behaviour is not necessarily tantamount to illicit business but may be located in the grey area between legal and illegal business or in fact may be completely legal. As the future is less foreseeable during violent conflicts, entrepreneurs consider future gains resulting from good reputation (social capital) as less secure than any current opportunities to make profits – even if this implies a loss of reputation and more opportunistic behaviour (Collier 2000a: 101-102). An example that supports this thesis is the change in companies in the coltan extraction sector in the Democratic Republic of Congo. When violence broke out, more risk-averse companies withdrew their investments. But new, more opportunistic companies followed and replaced those that had exploited the resource before the beginning of the turmoil (Evangelischer Entwicklungsdienst 2002).

3.2 Costs of peace

Violent conflicts are likely to be harmful for private business. Chapter 3.1 showed how companies are affected by armed hostility, what makes some conflicts more detrimental to private firms than others and how they tend to respond. As important as the understanding of companies' perception of violent conflict, is the understanding of companies' perception of peace, and more specific, of peace processes. The second hypothesis assumes that corporate costs deriving from violent conflicts are a major incentive for private companies to support peace processes and that not only violent conflict but also peace may entail costs for companies. The following paragraphs will provide a better **understanding of the corporate benefits and detriments of peace**.

A **peaceful business environment** provides overall a better possibility for companies to plan rationally. Insecurities that go along with violent conflicts dwindle and "normal" business conduct can be re-established. The danger of loosing production facilities due to military violence is diminished. In particular, international companies do not run the risk of loosing reputation by being accused of immoral behaviour in the context of the violent strife. Goods and labour force can flow more freely, e.g. because international economic sanctions are lifted and road blockages are abolished. Markets and governments can develop without the stress of violent conflicts and the end of a conflict situation may make regions accessible again for business that had turned into no-go-areas during the conflict.

Violent conflicts are seldom the expression of random, unmotivated violence. They rather manifest the existence of **different interests**, values and beliefs, in political, ideological, religious, ethnic, or economic contexts. Dealt with in a peaceful manner, conflicts over different interests are hardly harmful. Much rather, they are a significant and indispensable element for social, political and economic development. If appropriate mechanisms for the peaceful resolution of different interests are missing or insufficient, such as governmental institutions or informal means, disagreements over different interests may turn into violent conflicts. Violence becomes the means to deal with disagreements over different interests.

However, when bellicose violence ends, either through a military victory or through a negotiated settlement, the underlying differences in interests are rarely settled. Licklider stated in this context: "Typically, war or civil violence has not solved the problems that caused it. If two groups of people have been antagonistic toward each other, large-scale killing is unlikely to have improved relations. If maldistribution of economic resources has been a problem, the destruction of the economy will not help" (Licklider 2001: 697).

In the majority of cases, the issues that had elicited armed hostility in the first place, still have to be tackled after the bloodshed has stopped: antagonistic groups have to be reconciled; political differences have to be settled; economic grievances have to be appeased. Given the unsettled state of the conflict itself, it is not surprising that countries are frequently on the verge of war again, just a couple of years after the signing of a peace accord (Licklider 1995; Licklider 2001). Indeed, the absence of violence is not enough to guarantee a stable peace. Much rather, a complex process of conflict transformation is required that addresses the causes of the armed hostility and establishes mechanisms to resolve conflicts peacefully (see for example Matthies 1995). **Conflict transformation** by definition "implies a deep transformation in the parties and their relationship and in the situation that created the conflict" (Miall et al. 1999: 21) (see also Box 2).

In fact, peace accords, as often as not comprise not only *military* but also *political* stipulations. They go beyond military regulations addressing the ending of the actual violence, disarmament measures or reduction of troops. **Political regulations** address issues such as constitutional changes, the distribution of political power and ideally other issues that have been at the heart of the violent conflict (Ohlson/Söderberg 2003: 17). Peace and peace-processes are consequently not politically, economically or socially neutral processes. (Negotiated) Settlements of violent conflicts are always constitutional deals, which require the agreement on a new political order (Waterman 1993).

Some (such as Haufler 2001) link the risk of **changes in the political structure** primarily to violent conflicts and a military victory, arguing that violent conflicts may result in changes in the rule of the game. While this is a worthwhile interpretation, it pays little attention to the fact that conflicts may not end with a military victory over the ruling regimes. The termination of armed hostility through negotiations, is in fact a frequent way of settling conflicts, which in the same way as military victories, might convey changes in the political structure.

In the aftermath of a war, countries consequently have to meet two major challenges simultaneously. The war damages have to be repaired and the root causes of the armed hostility have to be addressed, respectively the political provisions of the peace treaty have to be implemented. Correspondingly there are, by and large, two major **types of costs related to the establishment of a sustainable peace**:
i. direct costs for redressing war damages,
ii. indirect costs resulting from approaching the root causes of violence. Indirect costs of peace should cover here changes and reforms that are implemented in the context of a peace process and their potential (monetary) costs.

The peace expenditures for the reconstruction of infrastructure, civil institutions etc. are primarily monetary costs. The indirect costs, however, are less straightforward: They comprise monetary as well as non-monetary costs and tend to be much more ambiguous and complex.

In the following paragraphs, **direct and indirect costs** of peace will be outlined further. It will be explained what kind of costs emerge in the aftermath of a violent conflict and, most important, how those costs may affect private companies. In chapter 3.2.3.2 further factors will be introduced that may prevent companies from supporting conflict management strategies.

3.2.1 Direct costs of peace

As already mentioned in chapter 2.3.3, rebuilding a war-shattered society is by all means a **costly** endeavour. Return of refugees and internally displaced people, demobilization of soldiers, removal of war damages, reviving the economy, satisfying immediate basic needs such as education, healthcare and access to clean water etc., all requires a large amount of financial resources. Given the urgency of most of these needs and the high expectations of the population in the immediate post-war period, a lack of funds can endanger or thwart a peace processes.

The **difficulties in funding peace** have often been underestimated. Expectations were high regarding the compensating effect of the "peace-dividend"[20], and

---

[20] The "peace dividend" is here understood in a narrower sense as the monetary savings resulting from a reduced military expenditure.

regarding a quick recovery of the economy, the influx of capital and the realization of investments. Peace related expenditures, however, tend to exceed the financial resources saved by a decline in defence spending; the economy recovers usually slowly and requires significant start-up support. Partly due to this, the national tax revenues remain low for a long time (e.g. de Soto/Castillo 1994; Brömmelhörster 2000; Woodward 2002).

In principal, there are two main sources how peace expenditures can be covered: Either through external assistance or through domestic resources (Segovia 1996: 107). Private companies very likely do not oppose an influx of **international grants** since they can benefit from them, for instance through contracts for reconstruction projects[21]. Although external assistance tends to increase notably in the aftermath of a violent conflict (Boyce 1996: 17), most examples show that the average amount of external funding falls short of covering all peace-related expenditures (Wenger/Möckli 2002: 135-136). In any case, countries can barely rely exclusively on foreign donors, but have to raise additional domestic capital.

Governments have a couple of measures at their disposal, of how to **augment their revenues**. They can e.g. privatize state properties, realize shifts in the national expenditure, or implement tax reforms. Expenditure shifting and tax reforms that burden the private business sector almost certainly engender corporate resistance. In countries in which state authorities do not enjoy public confidence – and this is very common for post-conflict situations –, where governments are notorious for corruption and squandering of public resources, corporate antagonism against tax increases will even be worse.

3.2.2 Indirect costs of peace

It is in the nature of things that each peace process and each post-conflict phase is different. Reform priorities are laid according to the respective needs of the country and according to the outcomes of each peace negotiation. Notwithstanding the distinctiveness of each post-conflict setting, it is largely agreed that contemporary peace processes tend to share two **common principals**, which are (1) democracy and (2) the free market principal. For reasons that will be explained later, one more feature should be added: (3) lack of poverty alleviation strategies in most peace processes.

World market-oriented market economies and democracy became the leading paradigms in world politics with the collapse of the Eastern communist bloc. Also the currently prevalent conflict management strategies consider "liberal internationalism", "**liberal peace**" or "liberal democracy" as the surest principles for preventing armed hostilities and for bringing peace after civil as well as inter-

---

21 It will be not discussed in this context that not all types of international assistance are conducive to post-conflict rebuilding. In fact, it is not only a question of the quantity of resources provided but also of the kind of resource provided. For more details, see Woodward 2002.

state wars (Paris 1997; Lipschutz 1998: 7; Paris 2004; Rothchild 2004). The majority of violent conflicts (especially those mediated by third parties) are managed according to those tenets. For example, in post-war Namibia, Angola, Mozambique, Rwanda, Cambodia, Bosnia, Croatia and other countries, attempts were made to construct democratic institutions and market oriented economies. Despite the apparent difficulties in implementing those principals successfully, market economy and democracy are the political and economic tenets likely to shape post-war policies.

As a third principal, the issues of poverty-alleviation should be added to the common characteristics of peace processes. Effective poverty alleviation and a redistribution of wealth is by many authors considered a key element of a successful peace process (Boyce 1996: 2, 5-7; Pastor 1996; Woodward 2002: 186). In the pre- and post-violence phases, poverty in addition to inequality in economic and social opportunities often underlies the (re-)emergence of armed hostility. In fact, 80 percent of the world's poorest countries experienced an internal conflict in the last 15 years. Although **poverty and unequal distribution of wealth** are barely the only elucidators of warfare, they tend to form part of the complex picture of factors that leads to the (re-)igniting of violence (see also chapter 3.1.3.1). In many cases economic grievance are used by local or national elites as a "scapegoat", which – effectively implemented and often combined with ethnic and religious reasoning – makes it easy to mobilise followers (Ball 2002: 70-71).

Strategies for fighting poverty and the unequal distribution of wealth consequently form ideally part of post-violence peace-building efforts. Boyce, for instance, draws from the peace process in El Salvador the following lesson:"Over the long run, the consolidation of peace in countries emerging form civil war often hinges, as in El Salvador, on the forging of a more equitable distribution of wealth and power" (Boyce 1996: 15). And Paris laments that in Mozambique (as in Central America), "the long-standing socio-economic divisions [...] today remain 'the greatest threat to peace'" (Paris 2004: 146).

Despite the recognition of the importance economic recovery and poverty alleviation, peace processes commonly do not tackle these issues. "**Peace agreements**, as a rule, do not address economic reconstruction and development. Economic objectives are often included in a list of concerns, but with little and vague discussion [...]" (Woodward 2002: 184; see also Wallensteen 2003: 147-148)[22]. Most provisions in peace treaties deal with procedural issues and governmental institutions and not with issues of poverty and economic inequality. Even in countries (e.g. El Salvador or Namibia) in which poverty and unequal distribution of wealth are widely acknowledged to be central causes for the civil wars, the topic is not adequately tackled in the peace accords.

---

22 Woodward, however also admits that there are exceptions to the rule like e.g. Bosnia-Herzegovina or Mozambique (Woodward 2002: 184).

The reason why the **absence of strategies for poverty reduction** should be added here to the list of characteristics of contemporary peace processes, is primarily based on the relevance of the issue for private companies in general and on the importance of the theme for the case of Guatemala.

Democracy, liberal market principals and absence of strategies for economic development/poverty alleviation certainly do not describe fully contemporary peace processes. Many aspects have to be observed for the individual case. The three characteristics are, however, key tenets, which are discussed and implemented in most conflict-situations. They are a useful point-of departure for a more generalized discussion. The question is how the business sector perceives and responds to these three tenets of democracy, free-market principal and (absence of) poverty alleviation in post conflict settings. Special focus will be put on the Latin American private sector.

3.2.2.1 Installation or reinforcement of democratic rule

With regard to **democracy**, some scholars suggest that the type of political regime is of secondary importance for the private sector. Key is only if the business actors can safeguard their economic interests (Wagner 1997: 54). Looking at the position of Latin American businessmen towards the type of political regime, there seems to be some truth to it (see also chapter 2.2.2)[23].

The Latin-American corporate sector is historically notorious for *undermining* **democratic rule**. For a long time Latin-American entrepreneurs were dependent on authoritarian regimes that sheltered them against economic decline and popular upheavals. Yet, the business sector experienced in many cases that:

i. authoritarian regimes were incapable of protecting their interests;
ii. business actors became in point of fact politically and economically strong enough to defend their interests also in a democratic system;
iii. private actors incrementally lost influence over the authoritarian regimes. O'Donnell put it this way: "[...] the main lesson for the bourgeoisie from the last wave of authoritarian regime seems to have been that the military may save them from leftist and radical populist threats, but once in government, they are a rather unreliable patron" (O'Donnell 1992: 44).

---

23 Given the wide literature on the corporate position towards democracy, just some key findings from the literature on corporate appositions in processes of democratization with the regional focus on Latin America will be highlighted. For further reading on the influence of the private business sector on politics in general see e.g. (Bottomore 1966; Schmitter 1974; Offe/Wiesenthal 1980; Przeworski/Wallerstein 1988; Birle et al. 1992) and on the process of democratisation with regard to Latin-America in particular e.g. (Cardoso/Faletto 1976; O'Donnell et al. 1993; Schubert et al. 1994; Bendel/Krennerich 1996; Bos 1996; Wagner 1997; Kraus 1999).

In particular since the 1970s, business elites in many countries welcomed or even actively supported a transition from authoritarian regimes to democracy. Today nearly all Latin American countries fulfil the basic criteria of a democratic system, in electoral and political terms (UNDP 2004).

However, some authors are sceptical about the corporate inclination for democratic values. A recent study on the status of democracy in Latin America revealed that a large number of people believe (about 80 percent in selective interviews with decision-makers) that business leader amass "**de facto political power**". Although they do not form part of the political-institutional order, private business's ability to lobby governments, promote their interests and direct political decisions limit democratic political power for the benefit of private actors (see also chapter 2.2.2) (UNDP 2004: 149-159).

In fact, one central reason why business actors may oppose a democratic system or its reinforcement, is the **potential loss of informal political influence**, individual privileges and sinecures (see for example Karl 1990). Individual private companies or lobby groups, in particular big ones with influence on the national income may be able to profit from weak, undemocratic or instable governmental authorities, because it is easier for them to influence the decision making process.

A peace process, promoting democracy and good governance may consequently **endanger the possibility for (individual) companies to protect sinecures and privileges**. Even if an overt (re-)installation of a non-democratic regime does not appear likely at this stage in history, given the broad international recognition of democracy being the preferred political system, business leaders may for economic reasons attempt to obstruct the transformation to a fully-fledged democratic structure.

3.2.2.2 Liberal market-principle and poverty alleviation

With regard to **free market principles** one might expect private companies in general to support the implementation or reinforcement of this tenet. Also Latin American business leaders that are stereotyped as being dependent from state protectionism (see chapter 2.2.2), developed in recent decades – faced with global political and economic liberalization and international pressure – into advocates for less state interventionism (Payne/Bartell 1995).

Yet, some qualification is required. Especially in developing countries, in which an often relatively young economic sector produces goods that are not competitive on the world market, businessmen may tend to plead for more **governmental protection** and state-led economic policies. Entrepreneurs may consequently only advocate for free-market principals if their particular privileges, e.g. subsides and protection for selected products, are not at stake[24].

The promotion of free market-principals can to a certain extent also explain the common lack of comprehensive poverty alleviation strategies in most contemporary peace processes. The endorsement of a reduced involvement of the state in national economic policies, which is part of the liberal market-principal, contradicts certain **poverty-alleviation policies**, such as far-reaching social reforms and aggressive redistribution strategies. In the same way as private business may tend to support the establishment or reinforcement of free markets, they may resist policies aiming for a more equal distribution of wealth and a policy focus on poverty eradication – in particular if those policies encroach on the private sector's privileges, such as through a progressive tax-systems.

Indeed, a number of studies suggest that in part direct or indirect resistance by certain economic groups impeded the recognition of economic redistribution and poverty alleviation in peace treaties[25]. In particular in countries where (segments of) the private sector depends on **unequal distribution of resources** or exploitation of labour, peace treaties that give allowance to poverty reduction and equity seem to manifest a major threat to their interests. Poverty reduction strategies, including rise in wages or land reforms might contradict their interests, constituting a major corporate cost (see also Wood 2000).

In the case of **El Salvador**, for example, the ruling political party (ARENA) agreed to only limited socio-economic reforms in the peace negotiations with the insurgency, in part because it did not want to threaten its constituency among the coffee growers and the business community. The guerrilla's economic claims had originally included a comprehensive land-reform and policies aiming at a more equal distribution of wealth, which contradicted the businesses sector's interests (Wood 2000: 78-91).

The situation was similar in **Namibia**: The thorny issue of economic reforms, including the question of land redistribution was not addressed, partly due to the opposition of elite groups (Howard 2002). In both cases, the incorporation of the economic factors would have jeopardized the signing of the entire peace accords, due to the resistance of particular groups from the private sector.

3.2.3 Costs and risks of participating in peace

Additional to those costs potentially resulting from peace processes for private companies, other types of costs and impediments may thwart a constructive en-

---

24 The effects of rapid privatization and orthodox liberal stabilization policies on the sustainability of peace in general will not be discussed, since the focus here should be exclusively on the perception of the business sector. For a more detailed discussion of those measures, see for example Woodward 2002 and Paris 2004.
25 Not only private economic actors opposed the integration of economic aspects into peace agreements, but also international players hardly prioritized this issue.

gagement of business in peace related activities. Although not strictly speaking "costs of peace", these conditions may shape private companies' propensity to contribute to conflict management. A lack of knowledge among business executive on how to get engaged in conflict management has already been mentioned. In the following sub-chapters two additional issues – organizational factors and the detrimental business environment in an immediate post-conflict situation – will be explored in more detail. It will be shown that in particular an inauspicious business setting encumbers corporate support to post-conflict reconstruction.

3.2.3.1 Unrealistic expectations and persistent risks

In the invitations for corporate engagement in conflict management many view a role for the private business sector, particularly in economic post-conflict reconstruction efforts (see chapter 2.4). Non-philanthropic activities such as job-creation initiatives, productive investments and support for reconstruction measures rank high on the "wish list". But how likely is it that companies invest in an **immediate post-conflict setting**? Although some companies may profit from first-mover advantages and from restoring basic infrastructure, such as water-systems and power supplies, companies are only prone to invest in post-conflict zones if some basic factors are given: "security, infrastructure, financing, post-conflict planning and visible progress" (UN Security Council Press Release 2004).

In the following paragraphs, the typical conditions of countries evolving from violent-conflict are illustrated. It is argued that although fighting has stopped, the political and social milieus are in most cases still **inauspicious for business** and that "economic conditions usually worsen after the civil war ends" (Woodward 2002: 184). The following parameters will take centre stage: the level of violence and political, social and economic risks/insecurity.

Paradoxically, violence often does not stop after the signing of a peace agreement. Many war-ridden societies are notorious for an upsurge in criminal violence, after war related violence has ended. Weak and badly trained police forces, a powerless judiciary, widely proliferating small weapons, an insufficient job-market that cannot absorb the labour force, all seem to contribute to a favourable climate for increasing rates of common crime (e.g. Kurtenbach 2002; Woodward 2002: 187). **Violence and physical insecurity**, consequently more often than not prevails, such as for example in El Salvador. For the private business sector, this implies that they are obliged to maintain or establish safety measures similar as during war-situations, including private security forces or insurances.

Conditions are similar in hindsight to **social, economic and political security**. After the signing of a peace accord, countries have to take a vast number and complex set of smaller and bigger political, economic and social decisions. As stated earlier, the political order and constitution have to be (re-) established;

laws have to revised; a new role for the security forces has to be found; capacity in governments have to be re-established; contacts with the international community have to be revived; mechanisms to finance the peace-building related costs have to be developed, and so on (see for example Kühne 1998; Ball 2001; Carbonnier 2001: 37; Ball 2002). The common employment of verbs appended by the prefix "re-" makes one easily believe that post-conflict rebuilding "only" requires the revival of pre-conflict conditions. But the reforms necessary to establish a lasting peace are more pervasive and contain a high level of political insecurity and risk for any kind of planning (see e.g. Ball 2001: 724). Indeed, the overall political risks for companies tend to remain high after fighting stops.

Also **peace-agreements** barely provide political or juridical security for companies to develop long-term plans. Peace-agreements frequently do not address key issues for a successful transition from war to peace, either because the negotiating parties could not reach consensus in the peace-negotiations, or because the issues were not considered relevant during negotiations. In other cases, key political, economic and social issues are addressed, but without the details being mandated (Ball 2001: 723). Bargaining and negotiations consequently have to carry on also after the signing of the peace accords – yet, presumably on a lower political level and often with weakly consolidated governments that do not have adequate social and political legitimacy and structures. Some decisions taken in the post-conflict phase may even contradict the objective of the original peace-agreement (Ball 2001: 722).

In addition, war experiences such as death and expulsion, loss of property, violent disruption of everyday life, constant insecurity and propaganda-stereotypes about "the foe", have **undermined trust and entrenched prejudices**. Individual war experiences strongly influence everybody's personal attitude towards peace or war. In this regard, private businessmen – in particular domestic entrepreneurs – do not form an exception to the rule. They are part of the civil war affected population who lost friends and family, property and the basis of living. An entrepreneur who has lost his belongings or members of his family may reject peace negotiations with the group he holds responsible for his individual losses – regardless of the possible economic advantages a quick settlement of the violent conflict may entail.

Yet, most peace models are based on the assumption of **rational actors**. They assume that according to a cost-benefit calculation the conflicting parties either support or reject a peace process. For private businessmen, this is particularly true (e.g. Gerson/Colletta 2002). In keeping with common wisdom, businessmen epitomise rational behaviour. Little regard is given to subjective factors that include not only personal war experiences, but also political and ideological convictions. Especially with the end of the Cold War and since the emergence of economistic conflict interpretations such as by Collier/Höffler (Collier/Hoeffler 1998), these seemingly irrational factors have found relatively little recognition (Matthies 1995: 13).

Altogether, **post-conflict situations tend not to be a secure**, stable and safe environment for doing business. Adverse war consequences often endure after a violent conflict has come to an end (Collier et al. 2003: X) and future political, economic and social development is uncertain. Although a rapid attraction of private capital is one of the priorities of the World Bank's and the IMF's post-conflict economic policies, it is not surprising that conditions in post-conflict situations barley attract private capital (Woodward 2002: 184). Or as an author in political risk analysis put it in the 1970s: "A level of mass political violence makes the companies decrease their investment relatively fast, but a low level of political disturbance is not enough for them to increase their investment" (Thunell 1977: 60).

3.2.3.2 The price of participating in peace

It was assumed that high corporate costs of war in comparison to corporate costs of peace may spur private companies into supporting conflict management. However, not only the actual violent conflict respectively peace process might lead to costs for companies, but also **engaging in peace related activities might cause monetary or non-monetary expenses** for companies and influence their decision of weather or not to participate in conflict management.

First, given the volatile ground in conflict situations and the political sensitivity of peace processes, companies may run the risk of **loosing neutrality, appreciation and recognition** through supporting conflict management than actually gaining credit. To date, there is no clear checklist of "dos and don'ts" for corporate contribution to conflict prevention and settlement. Corporate activities may be interpreted as the company taking sides in a conflict and becoming part of it, or as if the company tries to unduly profit from what is actually intended to be beneficial for the population. As long as companies may not have clear backing by national or international agencies, they may be reluctant to lay itself open to this kind of criticism.

Secondly, costs arise e.g. from joining meetings, making donations or getting involved in "business diplomacy". Peace and stability, however, are **public goods**, featured by non-rivalry in consumption and by non-excludadbility of benefits. They are therefore easily subject to free riding. To bear the expenses of getting involved in a peace process may imply a **competitive disadvantage** for those businessman who get engaged, in comparison to the competitors who free-ride.

Enabling "collective action" for the common goods "peace and stability" is consequently difficult. In chapter 2.4, it was argued that the private sector can gain particular influence on a peace process if a national business community is well organized (Wenger/Möckli 2002: 8-9). But like any other social movement, business organizations face **organizational challenges** and "collective action" problems. In other words: Even if individual entrepreneurs may be inclined to get engaged in a peace process, motivated by whatever targets, organizational impediments may prevent them from doing so.

Furthermore, it should be kept in mind that the private business sector is **not a homogeneous group**. As was argued earlier, the size of a company, its relationship to the state, market orientation, personal convictions and experiences etc. have a bearing on which position each individual entrepreneur takes towards certain policies. Different political issues can therefore generate different (informal) communities of interests within the business sector that may even cross cut existing formal business associations (Wagner 1997: 52-53). Depending on a business association's ability to maintain unity, internal interest divergences may lead to a disruption of the interest group or to maintenance of cohesion.

With regard to a peace process, we may assume that only if the peace related policies at issue affect the majority of entrepreneurs, they will overcome the collective action problem. This is particularly likely if the war has pervasive negative impacts on business or when a peace process **challenges principal corporate interests,** such as the right for private property.

3.3 Is there a role for business participation in conflict management? Some conclusions

The previous chapters gave a brief overview of the potential roles private companies can assume in violent conflicts and peace processes. Many ideas have been discussed since the end of the Cold War. Governmental as well as non-governmental institutions have alluded repeatedly to the advantages of corporate support to conflict management. But there is still **little common ground and knowledge** on what the business sector should do and in particular also on what they are willing and likely to do.

One line of argumentation in favour of corporate engagement in conflict management justifies the demands with the negative entanglement of private companies in the emergence and perpetuation of civil wars. Since companies are frequently part of the problem, they therefore have to be part of the solution. An increasingly better understanding of how companies contribute to violent conflict, such as through support of rebel groups or inappropriate consideration of affected communities made it relatively easy to develop concrete suggestions what companies should do. Guidelines for conflict-sensitive business practices, codes of conduct, legal regulations as well as initiatives such as the Kimberly Process for the trade of diamonds have been established in this context (see for example International Alert 2005). Although the implementation of those ideas is frequently obstructed by lacking regulations of responsibilities or deficient corporate awareness, there is a relatively clear framework for the role of companies in conflict management.

However, demands such as business diplomacy, support to post-conflict reconstruction or reconciliation activities are more difficult to justify. Although the ideas are well laid out, with seeming potentials for effective public-private partnerships, implementation seems less likely than for those ideas based on the entanglement of firms in violent conflict. This second set of ideas can normally not be rationalized by the negative consequences of bad corporate behaviour in conflict zones, but other reasons have to be found. They are generally based on normative and moral arguments as well as on the argument of corporate self-interest in peace.

The self-interest argument seems compelling since there is much evidence that support the assumption that violent conflicts have by and large a detrimental effect on private businesses. Although business executives have measures at their disposal to mitigate the consequences of armed conflict; although companies differ in their vulnerability to armed hostility; and although not all forms of violent conflicts are in the same way hazardous for business operations, violent conflicts seem to take long- or short term, immediate or indirect **tolls from the private sector**.

One major shortcoming of the appeal to corporate self-interest in peace, however, is the disregard of potential detriments of peace. A military ending of a conflict or an armistice may only bring about an end to the violence and an end to destruction and physical insecurity. But in a negotiated settlement changes in policies, laws and governmental behaviour may occur, which may be negative for companies (Kobrin 1979: 77). Licklider stated in this context: "A negotiated settlement to a civil war is likely to result in veto groups that will not surrender power for social change whose impact on them is uncertain" (Licklider 1995: 685). If the private business sector is willing to actively support conflict management, depends among others on how the social changes that accompany a negotiated settlement affect their interests.

Economic factors are among the most likely to trigger a veto from the private sector. Economic factors, in general, can assume a *function* in a violent conflict (**economic function of violence**) or they can form a *cause* of the violence (**economic causes of violent conflicts**). In cases such as Liberia or the Democratic Republic of Congo, for example, violence assumed a major economic function because it facilitated the control of natural resources. In other cases such as El Salvador, economic factors were instead primarily a *cause* of the violent conflict. Distributional inequality and poverty in combination with other sources such as ideological differences and political exclusion were considered major roots for the civil war.

In addition to this, there is also an area where **the causes and the functions of economic factors overlap**, adding another dimension to the issue of economic factors and violent conflict. Systematic political and economic exclusion of segments of the population, economic inequality and pervasive poverty (the *causes* of the violent conflict) are often also a function for those social groups in a country that benefit from maintaining inequality and exclusion (Preti 2002). The major threat in the peace process for the private sector may be located in this area where economic functions and causes of violence overlap, implying a social change that is harmful for business interests.

Other elements that are often neglected when dealing with the demand for positive corporate involvement in conflict management are the potential organizational and political costs firms may be exposed to when dealing with peace and security issues; the bad business conditions in post-conflict settings and the lack of understanding among firms how they may be able to contribute to a more stable and peaceful environment.

Companies can play a role in conflict management – and they probably have to when they are part of the problems leading to violence. But the newness of the idea makes it difficult for the business sector, governmental and non-governmental alike to find the right mode of cooperation. State institutions and NGOs should not expect that firms know what best to do and of being able to do it alone. Guidance must be given to firms and methods have to be developed that are feasible for companies and beneficial for peace. Firms, in return, should be willing to assume a new role in conflict management and not to dismiss it as an exclusive state task. Without concerted activities among the major stakeholders, it is not likely that private business will find and assume their role in establishing a more peaceful environment.

II Case Study

The civil war in Guatemala began in 1960 and lasted for 36 years. Political factors such as ideological differences; economic issues including unequal distribution of wealth; social-political aspects such as a systematic exclusion of the Mayan people, injustice and anti-democratic institutions, as well as historic developments linked to the Cold War, were the main factors that gave rise to the violent conflict. The civil war was characterized by extreme atrocity against the civilian population including massacres against the indigenous population, high rates of internally displaced people as well as forced disappearances.

This second part of the study explores the role of the private business sector in the context of the armed conflict and the peace process for the case of Guatemala. The hypothesis and assumptions made in the theoretical part of the study are explored empirically. The chapter is largely structured chronologically. After a brief introduction into the economic structure of Guatemala and an overview of the private business sector, the role and perception of the private sector regarding the civil war (1960-1996), the peace process (1986-1996) and the post-conflict phase (1996-2002) are elaborated.

It is important to keep in mind that the concept of corporate engagement in conflict management started to thrive significantly only after the formal ending of the Guatemalan civil war. The idea of civil society integration into conflict prevention and settlement was discussed for quite some time (e.g. the approach of Multi-Track Diplomacy), but only in the late 1990th, the public debate on business engagement broadened. The Guatemalan case can consequently not fully explore corporate participation in conflict management as it is discussed today, but it can shed some light on corporate perception of violent conflicts and peace process and can serve as a basis to discuss the potentials and limitations of the concept.

4 The Economic and Social Structure of Guatemala

The following chapter on Guatemala's economic structure and development is divided into two major parts. The first part gives a brief overview of Guatemala's geographic conditions and most important macroeconomic features. The explanations fulfil two purposes: first, building the basis for an analysis of the private business sector in Guatemala (chapter 5); and second, providing essential economic background information to better understand how economic factors were linked to the civil war.

In the second part, this chapter explores the macroeconomic impacts of the armed conflict on the Guatemalan economy. This part complements information from the first part of the chapter, illustrating the corporate costs of war.

4.1 The Guatemalan economy and the dominance of coffee

Guatemala is **located** in Central-America and is with about 110,000 square-kilometres a small country. Its neighbouring countries are Mexico in the North and North West, Belize in the North East and El Salvador and Honduras in the South-East (see map 1). It has access to the Pacific in the West and the Caribbean Sea in the East.

Guatemala belongs to the **tropical zone**. Due to variations in altitude, however, the country has a wide variety of climatic conditions. It embraces areas belonging to the *tierra caliente* (up to 600 meters in Peten and the coast), the *tierra templada* (between 600 and 1,800 meters, in particular in the centre and the South East) as well as the *tierra fría* (between 1,800 and 3,000 meters in the Cordilleras in the West) (Kurtenbach 1998) (see map 1).

Three major natural regions dominate the country:

i. More than half of the size of Guatemala is covered by the sparsely populated tropical **lowland** in the North. The lowlands cover the area of Peten, the Caribbean littoral near Lake Izabál and a strip ranging from the northern Huehuetenango to Alta Verpaz, known as the *Franja Transversal del Norte*. The lowland areas are rural regions, though the Caribbean area holds Guatemala's most important port, *Puerto Barrios*.
ii. In the West and the centre, the country is covered by **highlands**, the foothills of the Central-American Cordilleras coming from Mexico. This region is home for about a third of the population. It is often divided into the western highlands that are largely populated by indigenous population, living in small villages or towns, and the eastern highlands that are flatter and predominately populated by ladinos. The highland areas reach in the West altitudes of over 4,000 meters and comprise more than 30 in part active volcanoes. Partly deep canyons and gorges characterize the landscape.
iii. The highlands fall away to the South to a 50 to 60 kilometre wide coastal area, the **Pacific lowlands**. The Pacific lowlands are divided into two zones, the higher *boca costa* and the lower Pacific littoral. The *boca costa* has a temperate climate and rich soils, stemming from volcanic aches; the Pacific littoral has hotter and more humid conditions with less fertile soils.

Guatemala is overall a **rural country**, with around 60 percent of the 11 million population living outside the urban centres, primarily the capital Guatemala City and the second biggest town, Quetzaltenango. The majority of the population lives today in the central highlands, with about a third living in the capital of Guatemala City. The western highlands are the main settlement area for the indigenous population, specifically in the departments of Quiche, Solola, Totonicapan, San Marcos and Huehuetenango. The areas of Zacapa, El Progreso, Julapa, Chiquimula and Jutiapa are largely populated by the Ladino population (Kurtenbach 1998).

Some of the geographical zones provide excellent **conditions for agriculture**. Especially the *boca costa* and the Verapazes between the highlands and the tropical lowlands provide at an altitude between 600 and 2,000 meters good climatic conditions for the cultivation of coffee and cocoa. Further south in the hot costal areas, the natural conditions allow the cultivation of sugar cane, bananas, cotton and fruit. Cattle find good conditions in the eastern region of the country.

The **agricultural sector dominates** the economy of the country: almost 23 percent of the GDP is produced in (1980: 24,8 percent, 2000: 22,8 percent) and about 40 percent of the labour force is absorbed by this sector (UNDP 2001: A74; World Bank 2003b). The most important crops today are coffee and sugar, followed by bananas and cardamom. In addition, Guatemala is considered to have a comparative advantage for the cultivation and export of flowers, fruit, and vegetables due to its proximity to the North-American market and the low labour costs. In the past, also other agricultural products such as cotton, cochineal[1] and meat were cultivated in Guatemala but lost relevance, mainly due to developments on the global market.

Coffee is the most important agro-product for Guatemala. It maintained its dominance in the national economy since the 19th century. Similar to other Central-American countries, the impact of **coffee** on the economic, social and political development of Guatemala was outstanding[2]. Robert G. Williams for example wrote for Central-America:

"A key element that changed the day-to-day material lives of Central-Americans and accompanied the construction of national states was the rise of coffee as the region's most important export. Along with the expansion of coffee came changes in trading networks, international financial connections, patterns of immigration and investment, and international political relations, but coffee also reached back into the structures of everyday life of ports, capital cities, inland commercial centers, and the countryside, altering the activities of merchants, moneylenders, landowners, shopkeepers, professionals, bureaucrats, the urban poor, and the peasantry." (Williams 1994: 9)

And the World Bank concluded for Guatemala: "In fact, past policies greatly contributed to an exclusionary pattern of development in Guatemala, particularly for land, labor and education. All of these spheres were interwoven with each other. They are all also immediately connected with the development of coffee, Guatemala's primary export crop." (World Bank 2003b: 33).

Coffee set out to conquer the Guatemalan economy in about 1840, taking the place of cochineal. With the "liberal reform" in Central America in 1871 (see chapter 5.1), coffee perpetuated its dominance in the national economy. In the early 20th century, Guatemala had developed into one of the world's leading coffee exporters. Although Guatemala attempted to diversify away from the dominance of coffee, for example, with the introduction of the first banana plantations at the beginning of the 20th century, or with the increase of non-traditional agricultural products, such as fruits and vegetables particularly in the 1950s and 1980s, coffee remained a **principal export crop** (Graph 9). In the year 2000, coffee still generated about 12 percent of the national GDP, accounted for about 21 percent of Guatemala's total export earnings and about 48 percent of export earnings from traditional export products, followed by sugar, bananas, petrol and cardamom (UNDP 2001: A72).

Guatemalan coffee is renowned for its high quality. About 50 percent are cultivated in regions between 1200 to 1600m, about 25 percent in the lowest regions between 600 and 900 meters. Although about 250 companies dominate the **culti-**

---

[1] Cochineal is a red dye obtained from insects. The market for cochineal collapsed in the early 19th century, due to replacement by chemical products.
[2] For more details on the origins of the modern plantation economy in Guatemala, see for example Cambranes (Cambranes 1985).

vation of coffee in Guatemala, there are also a vast number of smallholders (about 59,000) (COVERCO 2000). It is estimated that more than half a million workers are directly dependent on the coffee industry, in particular in the form of unskilled, seasonal workers (Boot 2002). Coffee is mostly exported as green coffee in particular to the US-American and the European market, providing little value added for the Guatemalan national economy (see Graph 1).

Graph 1: Area planted with coffee and production between 1961 and 2002

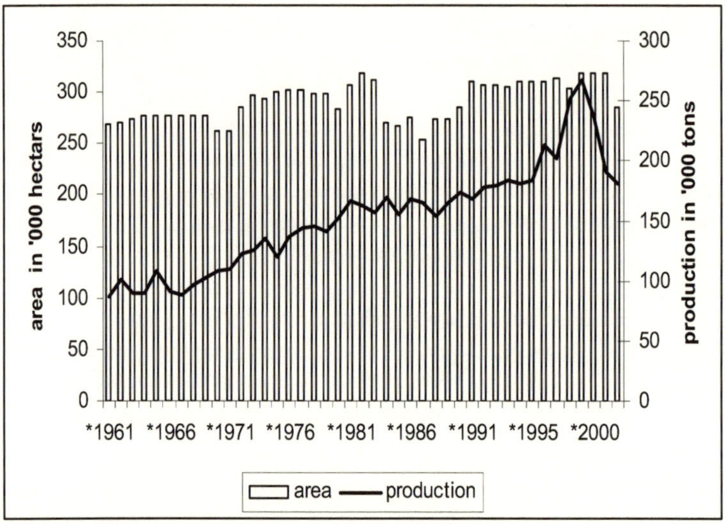

Source: FAO. FAOSTAT [online database] http://faostat.fao.org, accessed at 23 November 2004

In contrast to coffee, the cultivation of **sugar cane** as the now second-most important agro-product in Guatemala began already in colonial times. But only in the 1960s, sugar became an export good, being then considered (together with cotton) a non-traditional agro-product. Cultivation and production of sugar expanded since the 1970s and in particular in the 1980s (see Graph 2). Guatemala is today the biggest sugar exporter in Latin America, after Brazil and Cuba and number sixth in the world market.

The leading position of the Guatemalan sugar producers in the world was largely achieved by repeated efforts to **modernize** the sector, both with regard to management as well as cultivation and production technologies. The cultivation of sugar cane and production to sugar in sugar mills (*ingenious*) is closely linked, making it easy to reach economies of scale and low prices. In addition and in contrast to the coffee sector, the number of sugar cultivators and sugar mills is very small (17 sugar mills), simplifying sector-wide agreements (Oglesby 2002).

The **banana** as Guatemala's third most important export crop is probably the most stable product of the three main crops, undergoing less fluctuations over the last 15 to 20 years (1985 to 2002) than coffee or sugar. The variations that occurred were largely due to the detrimental effects of weather-related events, disputes, crop diseases, raising production costs and declining prices for bananas (see Graph 3). The area planted as well as productivity remained relatively stable, although the area under cultivation expanded more rapidly. In particular in recent years, areas planted were shifted to former sugar-land closer to the West Cost for easier access to the US West Coast market. In contrast to sugar and coffee that have seasonal peaks during the harvest season, the cultivation of bananas is a year-around activity. It provides relatively constant employment and income, accounting for 9 to 11 percent of Guatemala's total agricultural exports (FAO 2003).

Graph 2: Area planted with sugar cane and production between 1961 and 2002

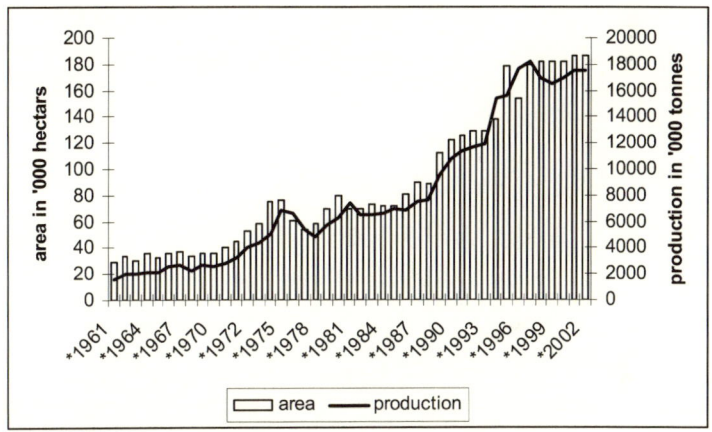

Source: FAO. FAOSTAT [online database] http://faostat.fao.org accessed at 23 November 2004

The agricultural sector in Guatemala and its dominance within the national economy could at no time be challenged by the **industry sector**. Although industrial production increased over time, it is with approximately thirteen percent still low (see Table 3 and Table 4). The manufacturing sector developed primarily around consumer and alimentary goods, such as the chemical and plastic industries in the area of Guatemala City and the region of Amatitlán, south of the capital of Guatemala City. Currently, the most important industrial products are textiles and clothing, furniture, chemicals and rubber, overall products with low value added and low levels of technology inputs.

Graph 3: Area planted in with bananas and production between 1961 and 2002

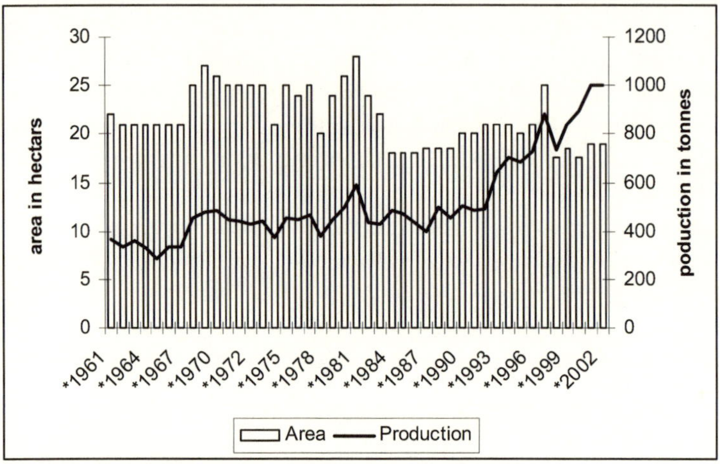

[Graph showing area in hectars (bars) and production in tonnes (line) from 1961 to 2002]

Source: FAO. FAOSTAT [online database] http://faostat.fao.org, accessed at 23 November 2004

Table 3: Growth rates of the industrial production

1950-60	1960-70	1970-80	1980-85	1986	1987	1988	1989	1990
4.6	7.7	5.6	-1.4	0.7	2.3	2.4	2.4	2.4

Source: CEPAL, Base de Estadisticas e Indicadores Sociales [online database] http://websie.eclac.cl/sisgen/badeinso.asp, accessed at 9 December 2003

Table 4: Share of the industry in GDP

1950	1960	1970	1980	1985	1990	2000
10.7	11.7	13.5	13.6	13.6	12.9	13.2

Source: CEPAL, Base de Estadisticas e Indicadores Sociales [online database] http://websie.eclac.cl/sisgen/badeinso.asp, accessed at 9 December 2003

The industrial sector experienced its pinnacle from the 1950s to the end of the 1970s, when the share of industry in the Guatemalan economy increased significantly due to positive impacts of the **Central-American-Common Market (CACM)**. The CACM facilitated the development of industrial branches with products mainly produced for Central-America through isolation of the region from the world market. In the 1980s however, the breakdown of the CACM resulted in a process of deindustrialisation. Guatemala became again more dependent on its traditional agriculture products and on the United States as a main trading partner (Minker 1990: 21)³. Although Guatemalan economic policies targeted industrial development also after the 1980s, due to traditionally protectionist economic policies, the Guatemalan industrial products still face difficulties to compete on the world market (Minker 1990).

The *maquila* **sector**, in particular producing textiles for the US-American market, was one of the few industrial branches that grew notably after the CACM crisis, specifically since the midst 1980s. Between 1985 and 1992 alone, the number of employees in the *maquila* sector swelled by 52% to about 80.000 people (Minker 2000: 41-42).

Certainly a disadvantage for Guatemala's industrial development is the low exploitation of the country's **mineral resources**. Deposits of antimony, gold, iron, lead, nickel and oil are known throughout the country. Oil, for example, has been found in the northern regions of the country, primarily in Peten. But only in the midst 1990s, Guatemala began to exploit its oil resources in a noteworthy scale. Although still a net energy importer, Guatemala's oil production raised from five thousand barrels per day in 1980, to approximately 19 thousand barrels as of 2001 (Doan 1999). Similarly, the exploitation of nickel in eastern Guatemala was stopped in the early 1980s and is now considered to be reassumed. Other, smaller-scale mineral production includes gold, iron ore and lead.

The **service sector** in Guatemala, comprising among others commerce, tourism, finance and other activities, produced about 45% of the GDP (average between 1990 and 2003). In particular tourism, has an important share in the Guatemalan service sector.

Tourism did hardly play a role in the 1970s, became, however, an increasingly important factor in the 1980s and declined again significantly in the late 1980s due to the civil war (see details Graph 7 and Graph 8). Tourism in Guatemala is largely concentrated in two destinations: In the picturesque colonial city of Antigua Guatemala in the highland areas close to the capital and in the area of Peten around the Mayan ruins. A large part of the population in the tourism sector is employed in restaurants and hotels, while employment in the production of handicrafts is still of notable, but in relation to the service elements of declining importance (Minker 2000).

Foreign capital plays a particular important role in two branches, in the manufacturing sector and in the cultivation of bananas. Foreign ownership dominates, for example, the *maquilas*, the beverage, tobacco and food industries, and also the modern industrial sector, such as the production of tires, steel or petro-

---

3   Guatemala's major trading partners are the United States, followed by Mexico, the European Union, and countries in Central-America such as El Salvador, Honduras, Nicaragua and Costa Rica. About 40 to 50 percent of Guatemalan exports go to the Central-American region. The value was declining in the 1980s, in particular as a consequence of the violent conflicts in the region. Recent developments for the establishment of a US-Central American Free Trade Agreement (CAFTA) may revitalize the trade relations with the neighbouring countries.

chemicals. Similarly, the banana plantations are largely in the hands of multinational companies such as the Dole Food Company or Del Monte. The coffee sector, in contrast, is largely in the hands of national owners.

The share of **foreign investments** changed notably in the course of the last six or seven decades: The Arbenz-Administration (1951-1954), for instance, favoured an economic policy that aimed to make Guatemala less dependent on foreign capital, but the subsequent regimes strongly fostered the inflow of foreign capital. In 1968, foreigners (primarily from the US) were in control of about 62 percent of all major manufacturing firms. However, the effects of the "lost decade" in Guatemala resulted in a significant decline in the share of foreign capital (Jonas 1991: 47, 59).

Table 5: Income from principal exports, tourism and remittances (in USD millions)

Year	Non-traditional Agricultural	Coffee	Sugar	Maquila	Tourism	Remittances
1990	108.5	323.4	139.5	67.6	185.5	96.5
1991	136.4	286.2	137.5	106.6	211.3	122.6
1992	151.4	248.9	156.1	134.5	243.2	172.4
1993	167.2	267.4	162.6	147.2	265.4	198.8
1994	206.3	317.7	232.7	211.5	258.0	255.1
1995	282.5	538.7	207.0	238.8	276.6	379.7
1996	292.0	472.4	264.2	280.1	284.3	362.8
1997	321.0	588.8	308.3	212.2	325.2	387.5
1998	320.8	586.3	177.8	284.9	322.5	423.2

Source: Oglesby 2002: 53

This brief description of the Guatemalan branches and economic structure already suggests some of the countries major economic **challenges**: Dependence on a few primary export commodities and with low value added for the national economy. The large-scale dependence on the products coffee, sugar, bananas makes the country especially vulnerable to price changes on the world-market. The recent coffee-crisis, for instance, that started in the year 2000 is a telling example (see Graph 1). In addition, the agricultural products require only a low level of processing. The available workforce can hardly be absorbed, being reflected in high unemployment and underemployment rates (around 50 percent). Guatemala therewith remains an overall small economy with a small market and little purchasing power. This makes trade and capital inflow from abroad in the form of foreign direct investments, foreign aid as well as remittances very important. Especially remittances expanded significantly in recent years and became one of the major sources of income for the country (Table 5).

Graph 4: GDP growth rates in Guatemala between 1971 and 2003

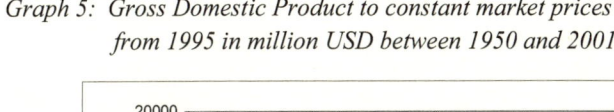

Source: CEPAL, Base de Estadisticas e Indicadores Sociales [online database] http://websie.eclac.cl/sisgen/badeinso.asp, accessed at 12 December 2003

Graph 5: Gross Domestic Product to constant market prices from 1995 in million USD between 1950 and 2001

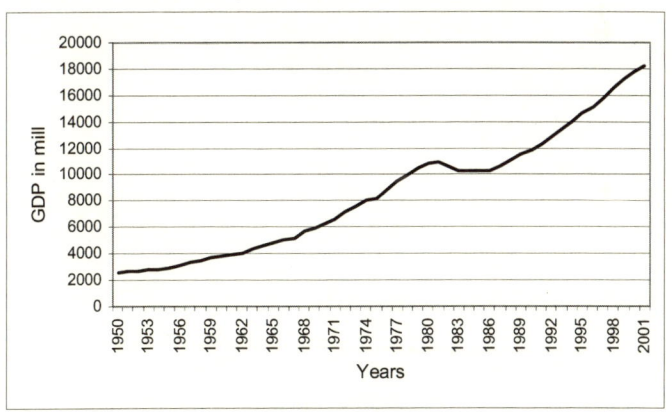

Source: CEPAL, Base de Estadisticas e Indicadores Sociales [online database] http://websie.eclac.cl/sisgen/badeinso.asp, accessed at 12 December 2003

Despite the structural problems of Guatemala's economy, Guatemala is the largest economy in Central America, with a GDP of about USD18,000 million in

2001[4]. It has enjoyed reasonable **growth rates** (average 3.4 percents) and relatively low rates of inflation (see Graph 4 and Graph 5). This comparative economic prosperity, however, does not translate into positive social indictors.

Indeed, **poverty rates** in Guatemala rank amongst the highest in the whole of Latin America, as some basic figures show (UNDP 2001: A82; World Bank 2003b):

- Over half of the Guatemalan population lives in poverty (1989: 62 percent; 2000: 56 percent) and about 16 percent lives in extreme poverty, having an income of less than one USD a day.
- Guatemala's ranking in the Human Development Index is far below what would have been expected given the level of GDP per capita (for 2002 rank 121 out of 177 countries; for 1993 rank 112 out of 174 countries).
- Guatemala ranks among the worst in Latin-America for malnutrition. Life expectancy is the lowest in Central America. Literacy rates are far below the average in a Latin American comparison.
- 30 percent of households still do not have access to clean water and electricity although coverage of basic services has increased significantly in recent years. Many households do not have access to motorable roads.
- At least half of the population is either under- or unemployed.

The pervasive poverty and the bad social indicators are by many interpreted as a consequence of the **unequal distribution** of wealth and land (for example Barry 1992: 81). In fact, Gini indices for 2001 using consumption and income for Guatemala are 48 and 57. These figures indicate a level of inequality, higher than for most other Latin American and Caribbean countries (LAC) – a sub-continent, which as a whole has higher inequalities than other regions in the world (World Bank 2003b: 13). Although poverty is a national phenomenon, poverty rates are significantly higher in a belt including the northern and north-western regions of the country, comprising Huehuetenango, Quiche, Alta Verapaz, San Marcos, Totonicapan and Solola and among the Indigenous population.

With regard to the **distribution of land**, the last agricultural census in Guatemala from 1979 shows that about two percent of the population possesses about 65 percent of the land and over 78 percent of all farms accounted for only ten percent of the land (Palma Murga 1997). Alongside, the share of indigenous communal lands (*ejidos*) dropped considerably: In the late 19th century about 12 percent of total land were communal lands; in 1950 the figure had dropped to less than five percent and in 1964 to about one percent (World Bank 2003b: 33).

The extreme economic inequality in Guatemala became rooted soon after the Europeans began to colonize the continent and persisted in the economic and social structure ever since. The mostly **European colonizers** and their descendents

---

4   Cost Rica: USD 17.5 billion; El Salvador: USD 14.5 billion; Honduras: USD 6.9 billion; Panama: USD 12.9 billion; Nicaragua: USD 4.1 billion.

formed an elite class that enjoyed large rents and was able to protect them. Their economic and political influence have mutually reinforced themselves, securing economic and political institutions that favoured their interests and excluded large segments of the population from equal access to economic and political resources (World Bank 2003a: 171-189). The unequal distribution of land, for example, has its origin in large scale land expropriation from the indigenous population, in particular in the course of the coffee boom in the late 1900s (McCreery 1994).

In fact, the dividing line of the dualistic social and economic structure in the country is particularly sharp between the **indigenous population,** the descendants of the colonizers and the ladino population. Indigenous people are over half of the national population, but account for more than 70 percent of the extreme poor. The majority of the Indigenous live from subsistence agriculture and more than 75 percent cannot produce enough to cross the poverty line. Life expectancies are lower for the indigenous population than for the white or ladino population. Whereas about 50 percent of the entire Guatemalan population cannot read and write, illiteracy rates among the indigenous population have been estimated to be up to 75-80 percent (Sieder 1997).

The division of the country in ethnic groups, which largely coincide with economic groups as well as a severe lack of **social welfare** is not an unusual phenomenon. Recent studies, for example, have shown that societies, which are strongly stratified along ethnical lines, tend not to support an improvement of general social welfare (World Bank 2003a: 233-235). This may in part be based on racial prejudices but is also grounded in economic reasoning: an increase in the welfare status of the underprivileged may jeopardize the rents of the elite.

Economic inequalities, the unfair distribution of land and ethnic division seem also to account as underlying factors for the **civil war** in Guatemala. Landau for example states that one of the roots for the rebellion "was the skewed division of wealth and property in the country, which, for centuries deprived the majority of access to land or social justice" (Landau 1993: 148). Other point to the socio-economic, historical and political factors, including the domination of a small economic and political elite group, the systematic exclusion of large parts of the population from political power and wealth, and the repressive political regimes that developed against the background of the Cold War (Smith 1990b; Weaver 1994; Booth/Walker 1999)[5]. This link between economic factors and the civil war will be discussed further in the following chapters.

---

5   Stoll found in his study on the civil war in the area of Ixil in Quiche that the major reason for the indigenous population to join the guerrillas was not the attempt to increase their access to economic resources but was mainly a reaction to government repression. However, he admits that grievances over land, labour and other economic issues were an important topic addressed by the insurgency (Stoll 1993).

4.2 Economic impacts of the war

The following paragraphs provide a brief description of the major **economic effects of the civil war** in Guatemala. The explanations take a primarily macroeconomic stance and do not consider the enormous damage the war inflicted on subsistence production in large parts of rural Guatemala (for more details on the effects for subsistence production see for example Washington Office on Latin America 1988; Smith 1990d). More details on the economic consequences of the strife will be provided in chapters 6 and 7).

With more than 201,000 killings and disappearances, 150,000 refugees, and 36 years of warfare, the armed conflict in Guatemala is the longest conflict and the conflict with the highest number of casualties in Central America (see Table 6 and Table 7)[6].

Table 6: Estimated killings and disappearances between 1960 and 1996

Year	Approximate number of killings and disappearances
1960-1967	5,000
1968-1969	5,000
1970-1977	12,000
1978-1996	132,000
Other regions	7,500
Disappearance	40,000
Total	**201,500**

Source: CEH, Indice: 73

---

[6] Different estimations on the causalities of the Guatemalan civil war came to different results: ODHAG for instance estimated 200,000 killings and 50,000 disappearances. A study by CIIDH that only considered a selection of documentary sources, used the number of 36,906 killings and disappearance between 1960 and 1996. However, CIIDH mentions that this number presents only a fraction of the deaths attributed to the Guatemalan State during the years of armed conflict (Ball et al. 1996).

Table 7: Central-American war affected countries, where over 0.5% of the population died, 1970s and 1980s

Country	Deaths, '000s		As percentage 1990 population		Percentage civilian	
	1970s	1980s	1970s	1980s	1970s	1980s
Nicaragua	50	30	2.3	0.8	50	50
El Salvador		75		1.4		67
Guatemala		140		1.5		71

Source: F. Stewart et.al., 1997: 18

Major macroeconomic consequences of the civil war included lower growth rates of GDP, capital flight and reduced saving rates. The *Comisión para el Esclarecimiento Histórico* (CEH – Historical Clarification Commission/Guatemalan Truth Commission) calculated that killings, flight, expulsion, and resettlement reduced the economically active population by about 101,000 individuals annually between 1980 and 1989. This is equivalent to a loss in national production of about 4.1 percent on average. The intensified military expenditure in particular in the 1980s implied significant opportunity costs for the country, since funds spend on the military sector could not be spent elsewhere. Capital flight and other war-related factors lead to a reduction of the national saving rate to 18.1 percent of GDP between 1976 and 1981 and 9.6 percent between 1981 and 1985. In addition, enormous social costs emerged from the civil war (e.g. due to the killing of community leaders, leaders of popular organizations, loss of trust) that are not easy to quantify, but had an significant detrimental effect on the Guatemalan economy and society (CEH 1999c: §4445-4504).

Table 8: Estimates of cumulative GDP loss for Nicaragua, El Salvador and Guatemala

	GDP growth, percentage per annum		Loss in growth compared with region, percentage per annum		Cumulative loss as GDP 1965-90 as percentage 1965 GDP
Country	1965-80	1980-90	1965-80	1980-90	
Nicaragua	2.6	-2.2	-3.4	-3.8	-113.4
El Salvador	4.3	0.9	-1.7	-0.7	-38.1
Guatemala	5.9	0.8	-0.1	-0.8	-9.9

Source: Stewart et al, 1997: 38

However, in comparison to other war-ridden countries, Guatemala experienced remarkably **modest macroeconomic war-related economic losses**. Despite a decline in national growth rates, Guatemala still experienced a positive trend during the war period. A comparative study on the economic and social consequences of countries most affected by war from 1970 to 1990 showed that Guatemala was the only country in the sample, with a GDP per capita that grew during the conflict. For the period 1966-1990, a GDP growth of 0.6 percent per capita per annum was recorded (a calculation of the average growth rates for the period between 1960 and 1996 also showed positive growth rates of about 1 percent). By comparison, Nicaragua experienced a drop of 4.4 percent annually, according to this data set (Stewart et al. 1997). Furthermore, whereas other Central-American countries experienced cumulated, war related losses of up to 113.4 percent, Guatemala's shortfalls of less than ten percent during 1965 and 1990 were relatively moderate (see Table 8).

Two factors are key for this phenomenon[7]:
i. the geographic spreading of warfare;
ii. the largely low intensity of the armed conflict.

It was argued earlier that the **geographic scope** of a violent conflict is crucial for its economic consequences. Guatemala's armed conflict occurred predominately in poor, rural areas, outside the economic centres of the country. Indeed, killings in rural regions outnumbered those in cities for most years. Although the leading protagonists of the armed conflict resided and were from the capital, more than 80 percent of the killings happened outside the cities (see Graph 6). During some periods of the civil war, armed hostility spread also into urban regions but war-related violence was a primarily rural phenomenon. Specifically, indigenous peasant communities "became a convenient battleground for the struggle for state power" (Ball et al. 1996). More than 83 percent of the war victims were indigenous people, and therefore among those who tend to be economically disenfranchised.

The **department** most affected by the armed conflict during the 1970s and 1980s was Quiché. Nearly half of the infringements reported by the CEH occurred in this highland department, followed by Huehuetenango, Alta Verpaz and Chimaltenango (see Table 9 and map 2 as well as 3). Quiché as well as Huehuetenango and Alta Verapaz belong traditionally to the poorest departments of the country. Quiché, for instance is characterized by a high rate of indigenous population, infertile mountain soil with a large percentage of minifundias and only a few bigger *fincas* in the more fertile valleys (e.g. the *finca* La Perla or the *finca* San Francisco). From the three major agro-export products, coffee, sugar and banana, only coffee plays a somewhat important role in Quiché (see map 2). Whereas the centres of coffee cultivation in Guatemala were Santa Rosa, San Marcos, Quetzaltenango, Suchitepéquez, Huehuetangno, Chimaltenango and Alta Vera Paz, the share of Quiché in national coffee production rarely com-

---

7   Other factors, including the role of the Guatemalan military as protectors for private business installations, will be explained in later chapters.

prised one or two percent[8]. Hence, while coffee cultivation declined in Quiché in the early 1980s (CEH 1999c: §4482), only a few entrepreneurs were affected in a national comparison.

Graph 6: Percent of killings and disappearances occurring in rural areas by year, 1960-1995

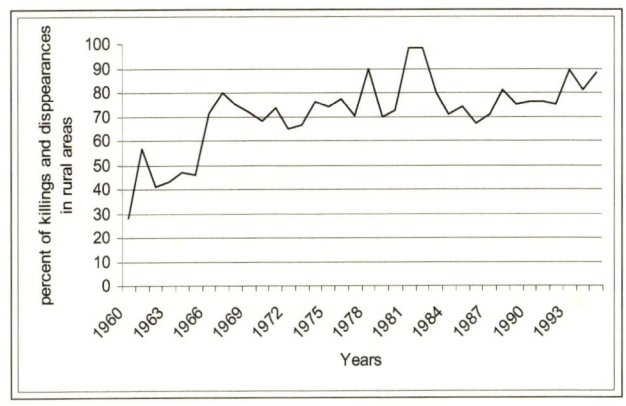

Source: Ball et al., 1996

As to intensity of armed strife, it was suggested in chapter 3.1.3 that low intensity warfare tend to cause comparatively little economic harm. Despite Guatemala's high absolute number of casualties, a closer look at the dispersal throughout the 36 years of warfare reveals a very pronounced peak of killings, for the year 1982 (CEH 1999a: 209). Thus while the army murdered tens of thousands of civilians in 1982, war related deaths barely exceeded 500 cases annually during the other years of civil conflict (for more detail on annual variations, see the following chapters).

In addition to these factors that mitigated the economic consequences of the violent conflict, attacks against infrastructure remained relatively limited (appendix 3). For the period between 1980 and 1995, CEH counted 19 destroyed bridges, 53 electricity pylons, some attacks against petrol installations, electricity installations and plants, telephone lines etc. In El Salvador as well as Nicaragua, for instance, attacks against infrastructure were much more pronounced and resulted in sever obstruction of economic activities (see also annex 2, with an incomplete listing of attacks in Guatemala).

---

8 Seven out of sixteen departments produce 75 percent of total coffee in the country: 51.4 percent in the south-west (comprising the departamentos San Marcos, Quetzaltenango, Sololá, Retalhuleu and Suchitepéquez) and 17.3 percent in the South-East (Santa Rosa, Jutipap and Jalapa) (Roux/Nassar 1992).

Table 9: *Ranking of human rights violations and acts of violence in percent according to department*

Departamento	
Quiché	45.52%
Huehuetenango	15.6%
Alta Verapaz	9.45%
Chimaltenango	6.72%
Baja Verapaz	4.54%
Petén	3.09%
San Marcos	2.89%
Guatemala	2.74%
Sololá	2.22%
Quetzaltenango	1.92%
Izabal	1.45%
Escuintla	1.03%
Suchitepéquez	0.97%
Totonicapán	0.55%
Retalhuleu	0.17%
Santa Rosa	0.12%

Source: CEH, Anexo 3: 234

In a sectoral comparison, the economic branches most negatively affected by the insurrection were the coffee sector and tourism industry. The tourism industry was the sector most severely hit. Tourism in Guatemala generated a significant amount of foreign exchange in the middle and late 1970s (CEH 1999b: §4494), but the armed conflict caused a rapid decline in the number of visitors with concomitant financial losses (see Graph 7 and Graph 8). In 1979, tourism was the third most important branch for generating foreign currency, generating USD 200.6 million. By 1984 the income had dropped to USD 47.5 million (Mersky 1988: 8).

Graph 7: Number of visitors for the years 1973-2000

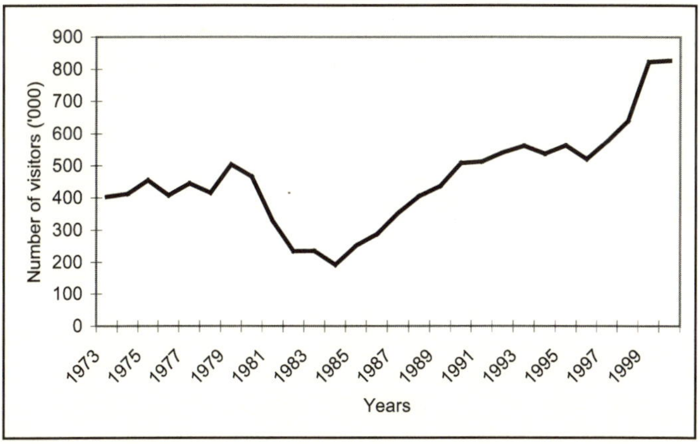

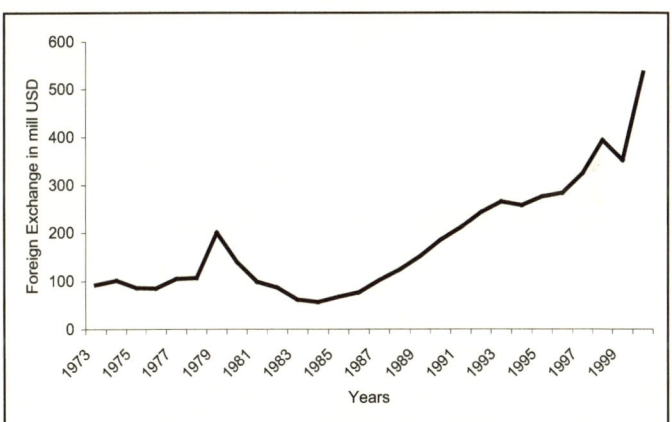

Source: Chamber of Tourism. No title [data received from the Chamber of Tourism in Guatemala, 16 May 2002]

Graph 8: Foreign exchange from tourism in million USD from 1973-2000

Source: Chamber of Tourism. No title [data received from the Chamber of Tourism in Guatemala, 16 May 2002]

Likewise to the zones of sugar cane and banana cultivation, the industrial branch was also concentrated in areas where little belligerent activities occurred. However, there is some strong indication that the war precluded some investments in the **industrial sector**, especially larger-scale projects in the resources sector. It became, for instance, apparent that only in 1996 after the signing of the final peace agreement, the Guatemalan government opened the oil region in Guatemala for bidding from private companies. The dramatic jump in oil production (see earlier chapter) and the increase of business's interests also in other areas of resource exploitation suggests that investors were reluctant to realize projects while the country was still in war. Although data is not available, it is likely that similar opportunity costs affected also other industrial branches.

Despite this example of increased investments in natural resource extraction for the **time after the signing of the peace accords**, macro-economic development did overall not improve significantly. In particular, abating world coffee prices hit Guatemala hard. Coffee export declined drastically since the year 2000, while other traditional and non-traditional export products increased slightly or stagnated (see Graph 9), but could not compensate for the losses in the coffee sector. Average growth rates of the gross domestic product between 1996 and 2003 lay with 3.3 percent below the average growth rates of the previous ten years (1987-1995: 3.9 percent) and are for only two out of these eight years above the regional average for Central-America (2001 and 2002). In addition, national gross internal investment rates varied significantly between 1995 and 2003. There is not a clear positive trend for the post-conflict period, making it difficult to make assumptions for the midterm trend of economic investments (see Table 10).

Graph 9: Export value of main traditional product between 1995 and 2002

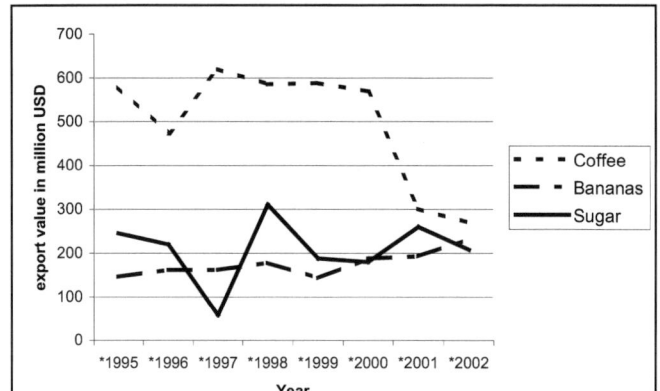

Source: CEPAL, Base de Estadisticas e Indicadores Sociales [online database] http://websie.eclac.cl/sisgen/badeinso.asp, accessed at 7 December 2003

Table 10: Gross internal investment in percent between 1995 and 2002

Year	1995	1996	1997	1998	1999	2000	2001	2002
Gross internal investment in percent	-1.2	-15.0	20.1	36.3	-0.4	2.5	6.4	14.3

Source: CEPAL, Base de Estadisticas e Indicadores Sociales [online database] http://websie.eclac.cl/sisgen/badeinso.asp, accessed at 7 December 2003

4.3 Excursion: The indigenous population in Guatemala

For a better understanding of the Guatemalan social and economic structure as well as history, it is of central relevance to get a better understanding of the indigenous population. The indigenous people account for more than half of the national population of Guatemala. They belong to the poorest in the society with limited access to political and economic resources. The indigenous population took the brunt of the warfare since they were identified by the military as the major mobilization basis for the insurgency. Questions of ethnicity, indigenous rights and indigenous leadership in the armed conflict were much debated subjects amongst Indians, scholars and politicians alike, exploring if and in which way the civil war in Guatemala was an "ethnic conflict". **Indigenous issues** shaped the political discourse in Guatemala also in the post-conflict period. Unresolved challenges such as nation-building and ethnic identity will shape the future development of the country and influence if the peace process can be considered a success. Given the relevance of the indigenous population for Guatemala's overall social fabric and for the civil war in particular, this excursive chapter gives a brief introduction into the indigenous population.

Guatemala is one of the few countries in Latin America in which indigenous people form the majority of the national population. Only in one other country, Bolivia, are the **quantitative relations** between Indian and non-Indian population similar. More than 50 percent of Guatemala's inhabitants are of indigenous descendent (depending on the source, the figures vary between 40 and 80 percent). They form 21 Mayan linguistic groups (seeTable 11), in addition to two other indigenous groups, the Xinca near the Salvadoran border and the Garifuna on the Caribbean coast (Sieder 1997).

As described above, the **indigenous population** belongs to the poorest in Guatemala (see chapter 4). The majority of them are small farmers in the western highlands, supplementing their income with earnings from migrant work on plantations. They live mostly in rural areas, although an increasing number moved to the urban centres, in particular as an effect of the war (Plant 1998; Plant 1999: 323).

Deep-rooted **discrimination** against the indigenous population and a strong dichotomy is characteristic for the relationship between the indigenous and non-indigenous population. Being Indian is considered by many as a sign of backwardness. However, Indians are not to be distinguished from the ladino population through their physical appearance. Or as Smith put it: "At no time in Guatemala's history has a color bar prevented people who are phenotypically Indian from being accepted as ladino in Guatemala" (Smith 1990c: 4). More important elements for the indigenous identity are language, history, religious practices, and clothing.

Table 11: Mayan language groups

Language	Number	Language	Number	Language	Number
K'iche	1,500,000	Ch'orti	60,000	Awakateko	16,000
Mam	700,000	Poqomchi'	50,000	Mopan	6,000
Kaqchikel	500,000	Popti'	32,000	Sipakapense	3,000
Q'eqchi'	400,000	Poqomam	32,000	Teko	2,500
Q'anjob'al	112,000	Chuj	29,000	Uspanteko	2,000
Tz'utujil	85,000	Sakapulteko	21,000	Itzaj	300
Ixil	71,000	Akateko	20,000		

Source: Kurtenbach 1998: 23

The conflictive relationship between the indigenous and non-indigenous population has its roots in **colonial times**. In the first decades after the arrival of Europeans, the indigenous population was decimated by approximately 80 percent, either through killing or as a consequence of diseases. Disruption of the existing political system, proselytisation to Christianity, forced labour, introduction of the *ecomienda*[9] to the region further transformed the cultural, economic social and political lives of the Indians. However, the Spanish culture did not replace indigenous traditions. Instead, the cultures partly mixed, becoming evident for instance in religious practices in which Mayan myths and customs were integrated into the catholic belief system.

During the colonial period, the **village community** became the central place for indigenous identity. Most villages were founded as *reducciones*, as a means by the conquistadores to better control the Mayan population. Indigenous communities were granted relative autonomy for most of the time. State presence was generally weak, giving a relatively high level of influence to traditional authorities, such as the *principales* (elders), council of elders (*cofradías*), or Mayan

---

9 Through the ecomienda, the Spanish Crown promised mostly conquistadores sovereignty rights in exchange for converting the indigenous population to Catholicism.

priests. The reduction of the indigenous pre-colonial social structures to the village level led to a revaluation of the community. Indigenous identity began to be largely perceived in the context of village life. Communities were the place where indigenous customs and traditions could be lived. *Communidades* became on the one hand the only safe area for indigenous practices, on the other hand this was concomitant to a rather strict limitation of indigenous life to the local level (Garbers/Heckt 2000).

Attempt's by the state in the colonial as well as in later periods to encroach on the Indian's relative autonomy frequently led to revolts. More than forty cases of **Indian rebellions** were counted between 1780 and the late 1800 alone (Smith 1990a). In the early 19th century, for example, the introduction of new forms of tax and other forms of duties (e.g. agricultural products) resulted in high levels of indebtedness among the indigenous population. They were forced to sell their lands or to work on plantations. The threat to the traditional indigenous form of living resulted in one of the few joint protest of indigenous people and impoverished ladinos under the lead of the ladino Rafael Carrera, who after a second revolt became president of Guatemala (1839-1965).

The coalition between the indigenous and the ladinos was however only temporary. Once in power, Carrera established gradually closer relations between the Ladinos and the white descendents of the Spanish conquistadores, facilitating thereby that the formerly also excluded Ladinos got access to political and economic resources. Whereas during the colonial period the dichotomy between Spanish and Non-Spanish (including ladinos and indigenous) shaped the social structure, during Carrera's presidency this was modified into a **dichotomy between indigenous and non-indigenous** (including ladinos and Spanish).

Despite the history of indigenous resistance, indigenous people in Guatemala did not have a strong tradition of *common* **indigenous activism**. The vast number of lingual groups as well as the role of the community as the main anchor for indigenous identity arguably worked against a joint struggle. During the civil war, for example, indigenous issues were considered less relevant than other issues, such as economic concerns. Despite the high level of Indian involvement in the armed conflict, indigenous identity issues were subordinated to class-terms. Indigenous and impoverished ladinos were jointly considered by the guerrilla organizations as the proletariat that has to fight against the capitalist elite. Once the economic problems were solved, ethnic questions were assumed to become insignificant.

Only in recent decades, a **strengthening of ethnic identity** led to stronger integration amongst the different lingual groups. Most Indians today aspire to preserve their distinctive traditions, while taking a position of economic and political equality with others in a modern multicultural nation. The "new way of being indigenous" (Jonas 1991) dawned since the 1960s and 1970s. In the early 1970s for example the *Asociación Indígena Pro Cultura Maya-Quiché* was funded by a small group of Maya intellectuals. Another landmark was the creation of the

Academy of Mayan Languages of Guatemala (ALMAG) founded first in 1986 and recognized officially in 1990. Strong military repression in the 1980s interrupted the first movement for a Mayan identity of the 1970s, but the late 1980s with the beginning of the political opening provided new room for strengthening Indian identity through various indigenous groups and organizations. Events such as the 500th anniversary of the "discovery" of the Americas (500 Years of Resistance Campaign), the award of Rigoberta Menchu with the Nobel Prize for Peace and the signing of an indigenous accord in the context of the peace process further vitalized the indigenous movement.

Indigenous identity was since then not only seen in the context of the villages but also outside, on a national level, leading to a palpable decrease of the importance of communities for the indigenous identity. One central sign for the changing self-perception was the re-definition of the term "Maya". The notion **Maya** was originally only used in a historic-archeologically context. In common parlance, the Mayas were considered the historic population of Central-America that had 'disappeared' already before the arrival of the Spanish. But in the late 1980s, the indigenous population commenced to describe themselves as Mayas, moving away from the often condescendingly used notion of 'Indio'. The term was, for example, more frequently utilized for indigenous organizations, such as the Council of Mayan Organizations of Guatemala, COMAG. On the basis of this new "Maya-identity" political, economic, cultural and social demands were made to the state.

The *Acción Católica* was central for the strengthening of the indigenous movement. They supported alphabetization and education in the formal school system, assisted in improving agriculture techniques (e.g. introduction of chemical fertilizers), encouraged the establishment of *campesino* and indigenous organizations etc. They therewith not only increased the ability of the indigenous population to make political, social and economic demands to the state but also brought the indigenous population closer to a cash crop system and monetary income and weakened the influence of the traditional indigenous leaders.

The growing ability of the Indians to organize themselves and to turn into an increasingly more vocal **political force** is crucial for the social, economic and cultural development of Guatemala as a whole. The significance of indigenous issues – and the strong resistance against it, in part from the private sector – was for example reflected in one of the peace agreements that dealt explicitly with the Indian population. It will be shown in the following chapters, how the private sector in particular was affected by the changes, which the indigenous population underwent since colonial times.

5 Structure and Role of the Private Business Sector in Guatemala

Corporate interest groups can play potentially a crucial role in conflict management (see chapter 2.4). They can function as representative for the business community in peace negotiations, encourage or discourage corporate engagement in conflict management. In fact, in the Guatemalan case, different business associations and not individual entrepreneurs were the most important corporate actors in the peace process.

The purpose of this chapter is to give a brief characterization of the Guatemalan business sector and to provide an overview of the most important business associations in the country. The key private business actors that were involved in the peace process are introduced, their history and background, their relationships to one another and their position in the Guatemalan society are outlined. Understanding, how the different organizations function and interact is crucial for the understanding of their respective positions in the peace process[1].

---

1 This chapter will concentrate on the domestic private sector. Foreign corporations influenced, however, key periods in Guatemala's history. The involvement of the United Fruit Company in the overthrow of president Arbenz, for example, was notorious for the influence single foreign companies had for a long time. Yet their political influence declined. International companies today normally keep a low profile. Some authors claim that firms under foreign ownership are closely tied to national organisations and capital (Jonas 1991: 58; Harten 2000), whereas others emphasis that (first of all for the case of) the US business community exists apart from the domestic economic elite. Although the foreign owners formed economic partnerships with Guatemalan oligarchs, they neither integrated into the domestic elites by marriage nor by joining professional associations. Through the US business associations AMCHAM or through their embassies, they lobby for various economic political issues such as tax-increases, but they do not form a concerted action group with domestic capital (Dosal 1995: 142).

5.1 The private business sector in Guatemala – its characteristics and historic political role

Like in many other Latin American countries (see chapter 2.2), the economic elite in Guatemala has considerable **influence on politics**. The roots for this were laid in colonial times (1524-1821) when the export oriented, (semi-)feudal structure of the economy, based on the exploitation of indigenous labour and land, was constituted. During the colonial period, colonists acquired vast estates of land that were largely self-contained, with the landowners holding not only power over land but also holding political and social authority over the (indigenous) people. The "landed elite" also filled the majority of positions in the central public administration, which further advanced its political leverage.

The expansion of coffee cultivation since the middle of the 19th century, the liberal revolution in 1871, and the persistence of a system that is often described as semi-feudal (rule of *caudillos*) that endured until the October Revolution in 1944, allowed the economic elite to consolidate its position. During the **liberal period** (1871-1944), the economic structure of Guatemala underwent crucial changes, largely in favour of the economic elite. The tenure system was reformed at the expenses of the indigenous population, and the state system and its legislation was moulded to the benefits of the plantation owners, privileging their interests over the interests of large segments of the population. Numerous discriminatory politics to combat "labour and land shortage" were implemented, the two major impediments for the expansion of coffee cultivation. Laws were, for instance, enacted that facilitated the expropriation of indigenous land and the indigenous population was – directly or indirectly – forced to work on coffee plantations (Jonas/Tobis 1976; Jonas 1991; Paige 1997; Martínez Peláez 1998; Wiarda 2001; Wiarda/Kline 2001). Williams wrote about the time of the liberal revolution:

"In the 1850s and the 1860s, [coffee] growers came to dominate department governments in the coffee zones and were able to influence some of the policies of the national government, but when the Liberals came to power in 1871, coffee growers finally had a national state of their own." (Williams 1994: 56).

Coffee producers remained the politically most influential economic group for quite a long time. Indeed, in almost all Latin American countries the traditional elite groups – the church, the military and the economic oligarchs – revealed a similar capability to protect their power and privileges. But whereas in other Latin American countries, emerging industrial elites tended to displace the landed elite from political power and weakened the feudal legacy, lack of industrialization in Guatemala resulted in a **persistent influence of the agro-elite**.

Only the "October revolution" of 1944 that brought an end to the caudillo leadership weakened – for a short period of time – the strong link between the economic elite and the political rulers. In the **ten years of democratic rule** that followed the October revolution of 1944, the two presidents, Juan Jose Arévalo (1945-1951) and Jacob Arbenz Guzmán (1951-1954), realized a range of social reforms that ran contrary to the economic and political interests of the economic elites. The introduction of basic rights for workers, the formation of peasant and labour unions, an increase in social welfare, Arbenz's political coalition with the communist party *Partido Guatemalteco de Trabajo* (Guatemalan Labour Party – PGT)[2] and in particular the beginning of an agrarian reform alienated the private sector[3].

Subsequently in 1954, significant parts of the private business sector supported the **overthrow of the democratic system**, which was initiated by the CIA together with the US-American United Fruit Cooperation[4]. The reforms had not only threatened the business sector's leverage over political decision making processes, but also their immediate economic interests, such as low wages, low tax rates etc. Together with the middleclass, the economic elite feared a radicalisation of Arévalo's and Arbenz's social reforms, leading to labour and peasant organizations gaining influence and to a concomitant restriction of their own privileges.

The **military regimes** that were established in the aftermath of the 1954 counterrevolution, repealed most of the reforms implemented in the previous decade and largely restored the private business sector's political influence (Lizano 1995: 137). Labour and peasant unions were suppressed, the communist party forbidden and the land reform emphatically annulled (Dunkerley 1988). Nonetheless, not all reforms of the democratic period were reversed. In fact, various elements of the strategy for economic development were upheld. Increased efforts towards economic diversification and industrialization (primarily based on foreign capital) that were established in the late 1940s, persisted until the end of the 1970s (for example Borrell 1995: 21-23). A small industrial elite

---

2   The PGT was de facto of only minor importance. None of the ministers was from the PGT and only some positions in the administration were held by members of the PGT (Molkentin 2002).
3   There is a large amount of literature dealing with the period between 1944 and 1954. See for example: (Jonas 1991: 43; Centro de Estudios de Guatemala 1995; Booth/Walker 1999: 46) (Flora/Torres-Riva 1989; Castellanos Cambranes 1996)
4   In the midst of the 20th, century foreign companies, in particular the US-American enterprise United Fruit Company controlled vast parts of Guatemala's economy. The United Fruit Company held a monopoly on the banana export, owned extensive areas of land, employed directly or indirectly about 40.000 people (significantly more than people employed in the entire industrial sector at this time), and controlled important elements of the national infrastructure. Their empire comprised the only significant harbour at the Atlantic coast, the majority of the railway system, as well as Guatemala's telephone and telegraphy network. Arbenz and Arévalo's reform programme in particular the land reform threatened the US-American interests in the country and lead to American support for the putsch against Arbenz in 1954.

emerged, although it rarely challenged the interests of the agro-elite (for details see later in this chapter).

During these first years of the military regimes, the Guatemalan business elite developed **close links with the military rulers** and became once again, one of the most influential players in Guatemala (Weaver 1970; Molkentin 2002). Weaver, for example describes how in the early period after the coup in 1954, the military governments and the economic elites entered into a symbiotic relationship in which the support of economic elite provided legitimacy to the military government, while the military regimes granted economic privileges to the economic elite (Weaver 1970: 69-79).

Yet, describing the **relationship between the private business sector and the state** in Guatemala before and after the democratic decade, 1944-1954, as unanimously harmonic would be drawing a wrong picture. In fact, Guatemala's history is rife with examples in which the state passed legislation that went against the interests of the economic elite. Already in the liberal period, for instance, president Manuel Estrada Cabrera (1898-1920) "did not hesitate to 'undermine the economic base' of opponents among the coffee oligarchy by seizing their properties and redistributing them to political allies'" (Mahoney 2001: 139). Also during the military regimes (1954-1982), the private business sector had repeatedly fundamental discords with various rulers. The disputes became more over time, as for instance during General Rios Montt's administration, escalating in a de facto break between the two (for more details see the following chapters). Many of these dissonances emerged as a consequence of the private business sector's claim to power, its self-image as an essential political actor and the widely spread rejection of governmental involvement in many fields of economic life. Those areas include, for example, taxes, agricultural policies or a comprehensive welfare system.

Today, in most of the literature (for example Dosal 1995; Valdez/Prado 1998; McCleary 1999; Jonas 2000) a "standard" **characterization of the Guatemalan private sector** is that it is:
- politically influential;
- very unified;
- anti-state/anti-government, conservative in its political views.

Those characterizations are, of course, **broad generalizations**. They give little allowance to differences between branches or within sectors or chambers, which – without doubt – exist. They are however helpful for a general understanding of the private sector and to better comprehend variations between the various business actors.

Power and influence: Vinicio Cerezo Arévalo (1986-1990), the first democratically elected president of Guatemala after more than 30 years of military regimes, argued in an interview that he only held 30 percent of his potential political power. More than 50 percent would be concentrated in the business sector (Holiday 1997: 70). Cerezo's statement reflects a common assessment on the entrepreneurs' influence in Guatemala's political decision-making process. Many interpret the country's notoriously low tax rates and minimum wages as the most obvious signs of the business sector's traditional right to a political veto. The widespread term **"Economic Oligarchy"** (for example Jonas 1991; Dosal 1995) probably describes most clearly the magnitude of political influence ascribed to the entrepreneurs. Dosal for instance writes in this context:

"In the original definition of Plato and Aristotle, oligarchy means 'rule by the few', a concise definition that is still widely accepted. Those who rule do not necessarily govern, for they may control governmental policy without actually administering the state. The [economic] oligarchs do not have to administer the state institutions to maintain their authority; at times the oligarchy has delegated a part of its power to either the church or the military, but **it has 'ruled' since the conquest.**" (Dosal 1995: 3 Emphasis by author).

Maria Casaus Arzú counted in a study on Guatemala's elite 46 **oligarchic families**. The clans base their political power on the control of economic means of production, particularly land and labour. However, this does not imply that oligarchic families are tantamount to the wealthiest families in the country. "A minority of people certainly control the nation's wealth, but any attempt to identify the oligarchy within this 15 percent is speculative" (Dosal 1995: 4). In other words, a small group of economically wealthy people has and had enormous influence on Guatemala's political and economic decisions, although it is not always clear who they actually are.

The difficulties that result from this, may at least in part explain why some of the more detailed studies on corporate influence in Guatemalan politics have such different results in defining who holds economic and political power in the country. Although there is little doubt that the private business sector is a politically important player, opinions vary significantly with regard to how corporate **influence changed over time** and which **branch** took the lead role among the business community. Some authors argue, for instance that the private business sector lost much of its historical leverage with the democratic opening of Guatemala in 1982 (for example McCleary 1999), whereas most conclude that they managed to safeguard their interest in the democratic era (Sarti 1989: 153; Palencia Prado 1996). Similarly controversial is the discussion to which degree the coffee sector lost political power in favour of the industrial sector. It is largely assumed that the industrial and service sector gained influence over the last two to three decades without, however, being able to surpass the agriculturalist in terms of political influence. Not clear is to which extent the agricultural sector lost leverage.

Unification and cohesion: The Guatemalan business sector has the reputation of being one of the most unified business sectors in Latin America (see for example Cardenal 2000). Throughout decades, the private business sector largely managed to overcome internal dissensions that evolved out of different interests of different branches[5], building up a close front against the state as well as society. Even if conflicts between competing interests erupted, such as in the 1980s over state intervention (Mersky 1988), the private sector mostly managed to overcome the differences for the sake of a common position. In fact, the private business sector's political authority could only develop due to this marked cohesion.

Close family ties, racism against the indigenous population (Casaus Arzú 1992), the hostile experiences during the democratic decade (1944-1954) (Dosal 1995), and the limited diversification of the economy (Cardenal 2000) are common **explanations for the unity** of the entrepreneurs. Dosal (similar to Torres-Rivas 1989; Robinson 2000), for example, argues that the origins of industrial entrepreneurs in the landed gentry meant that "they [industrial elite] will not likely destroy the *finqueros* by enacting an agrarian reform". Or in the words of Lizano: "New strategies in Guatemala's political economy made the traditional agro-oligarchy into an industrial-oligarchy as well" instead of developing into a separate group, focusing on their particular interests (Lizano 1995: 139). Largely excluded from this group of entrepreneurs are, however, the majority of more recently developing small and medium enterprises, which do not have (family) links to the traditional economic elite (Escoto/Marroquín 1992: 85).

Probably the most obvious symbol of the strong unity among the Guatemalan entrepreneurs is the umbrella business association **CACIF** (*Comité Coordinador de Asociaciones Agrícolas, Comerciales, Industriales y Financieras* – Coordinating Committee of Agricultural, Commercial Industrial and Financial Associations). Later on, it will be explored in more detail how CAFIF managed to remain *the* representative of the private business sector in Guatemala. Different, for example, to El Salvador, where the emergence of non-traditional economic activities fragmented the private sector, CACIF kept the unity and overcame for most of the time internal disputes over ideology or economic interests.

Anti-state/anti-government, conservative political views: The close unity among the economic branches as well as the long-lasting dominance of the agricultural sector, made the Guatemalan business sector seemingly more conservative in its political views than most business sectors in other Latin American countries (see for example Sarti 1989). Recalcitrant economic elites, most of them part of the

---

5   "Although not part of the traditional oligarchy, commercial elites have existed in Latin America since independence; one of the early political conflicts was between those who wanted free trade – the commercial elites and allied landed interests producing crops for export – and those who wanted protection of nascent industry – the industrial elites with allied landed groups not producing for export" (Wiarda/Kline 2001: 89).

traditional agricultural sector, could maintain their political influence for a long time and have hampered the emergence of more modernist ideas. Political convictions such as strong anticommunist sentiments, deeply ingrained scepticism against a democratic system, which only dwindled in the early 1980s, and the fear that the government expands its influence into what the entrepreneurs consider "their domain" are common features (Sereseres 1985b: 104-105; Mersky 1988; Oglesby 2002).

In deed, many consider strong "(neo-)liberal political convictions" characterized by a dominance of the free market principal without state-intervention as a major trait of the Guatemalan business sector (Mersky 1988; Jonas 1991; Jonas 2000). In the view of the entrepreneurs, *"la libre empresa"* is regarded the driving force for social development and should hence not be restricted by taxes, qualifications in the right to private property or other confining state laws. Since the 1980s, this "neo-liberal discourse" has started to replace the anticommunist arguments of earlier decades and has developed into a key connecting piece between the different economic branches and interests.

5.2 Business organizations in Guatemala

A high level of organisation is distinctive of the business sector in Guatemala and fundamental for its political influence. Today there are more than one hundred different **business associations**, representing various branches and groupings of the private sector. The first business organization was founded in 1894 (Guatemalan Chamber of Commerce) to become the first organized non-governmental interest group in Guatemala. About 50 years later, after the private sector had experienced the disadvantages of being fragmentized and weakly organized in the context of the October Revolution of 1944, businessmen intensified their efforts to coordinate their interests and more organizations were founded. (e.g. Weaver 1970; Dosal 1995: 104; Molkentin 2002: 111).

In the following, the most important business entities will be briefly introduced. In this context it is important to keep in mind that the different economic branches in Guatemala are closely connected through family ties and that entrepreneurs often are active in more than one economic branch. Correspondingly, many **executives are being associated in different business organizations**: Representatives of the Chamber of Agriculture are actually more active in software distribution, and affiliates of the Association of Sugar Producers in Guatemala (*Asociación de Azucareros de Guatemala* or ASAZGUA) are at the same time influential bankers and organized in the Chamber of Finance. In addition, the activities of many business chambers overlap: the Chamber of Commerce has a *gremial* for tourism although there is a specialized Chamber of Tourism; nearly all big business associations offer services for small and medium enterprises, although there are specialized interest groups for these entrepreneurs, and so on.

This chapter largely focuses on domestic interest groups, since **foreign business associations** did hardly participate in the Guatemalan peace process. However, it should be mentioned that a number of foreign countries have their own business representations in Guatemala. The American Chamber of Commerce (AMCHAM) for example, was established in the late 1950s and represents US firms doing business in Guatemala. The German *Aussenhandelskammer* has an office in Guatemala City that covers the whole Isthmus and Spanish firms have a similar representation tool. Most of the foreign chambers are members of CACIF's *asamblea ampliada* (see below) but are generally not linked further to Guatemalan business groups.

5.2.1 Comité Coordinador de Asociaciones Agrícolas, Comerciales, Industriales y Financieras (CACIF)

Without doubt, CACIF is the most influential business entity of the organized private business sector in Guatemala. Jonas even called CACIF the "political party of the bourgeoisie" (Jonas 1991: 58). This business association functions as an **umbrella organization** for different Guatemalan business chambers. Its principal objective is to give the corporate sector a unified voice against the government.

CACIF's membership structure distinguishes between organizations *cotizantes* **(paying) and** *invitados* **(invited)**. Paying members disburse a fee to CACIF, have the right to vote in the *junta directiva* (board of directors) and by turns chair and preside over CACIF. Invited organizations in contrast do not pay a membership fee but also do not have the right to cast a vote in the decision making process. Invited organizations can only take part in CACIF's weekly meetings and designate members to the different working groups (see below). They have a voice but do not have a vote (*"Tienen voz pero no tienen vota"*).

The *junta directiva* is CACIF's most important organ. It is integrated by the directors and vice-directors of the affiliated business organizations. Until January 2002, the presidency of the *junta directiva* was supposed to change every six months, rotating among the associated chambers. In reality however, the nomination of the president was an *elección convenida* or "a gentlemen agreement". Since beginning of the year 2002 however, CACIF has changed the nomination procedures and the tenure to a formal election and a 12-month long incumbency. The old procedure and in particular the short term in office had been considered a major stumbling block to allowing presidents to take more far-reaching decisions.

The **decision-making process** within the *junta directiva* is by consensus. In cases where no consensus can be yielded, the members either continue to discuss the issues until they can come to an agreement or, if possible, they delete the issues from the agenda – temporarily or permanently. It is part of CACIF's operational tradition that the member associations do not fight in public over issues on which CACIF intends to take a public stance. CACIF's different member associations can act and lobby for their particular interests, but CACIF's role as the consensus organ of the private business sector is safeguarded. These mechanisms are essential to assure CACIF's high level of unanimity.

Hierarchically superior to the *junta directiva* is the **asamblea general** (general assembly) or *asamblea ampliada* (broader assembly). The general assembly is formed by CACIF, its direct member organizations, and a large number of other non-member business organizations, like the American Chamber of Commerce, the *Cámara Guatemalteco/Alemana* (Guatemalan-German Chamber of Commerce), the *Asociación de Amigos del País* (Association of Friends of the Country) or the Guatemalan development organization FUNDESA (*Fundación para el Desarrollo de Guatemala* – Foundation for the Development of Guatemala). Only in the 1980s was the general assembly integrated into CACIF's bylaws, as part of broader structural reforms of CACIF. Central aim was to assure close communication with private entities that did not form part of CACIF in order to create stronger links between the various business entities.

Currently, about 28 different corporate entities participate in the assembly. Although the broader assembly formally constitutes the organ "at the top" of CACIF hierarchy, it does not play an important role in the umbrella association's decision-making process. The assembly meets only once or twice a year and has limited power and influence.

In order to formulate public positions and develop strategies, CACIF commonly forms **comisiones de trabajo** (working groups). Working groups are founded as and when required and according to subjects. The president of CACIF has the right to dissolve these working groups and their advice is not binding to the board of directors. The working groups' principal task is to pool knowledge and to develop proposals for CACIF's public positions. To date working groups have been formed on labour issues, on political themes, or for security issues and strategic topics. The Business Commission for Peace (*Comisión Empresarial para la Paz*, CEPAZ) that came (formally) into being in 1994, was also a working group in this sense. The nomination process and the members of the working groups vary from group to group. In the case of CEPAZ, the members were former presidents of CACIF's affiliated organizations, aiming to increase the working group's weight and influence. In other commissions, such as in the commission for labour issues, the participants are mostly representatives from below the level of ex-presidents.

CACIF was established in 1957 with three founding member organizations: the *Cámara de Industria y Comercio* (Chamber of Industry and Commerce), the *Asociación General de Industriales* (Association of Industrialists), and the *Asociación General de Agricultores* (General Association of Growers – AGA). Since then CACIF underwent two major organizational reforms and extended the number of **members** significantly. Currently CACIF embraces seven business cham-

bers, each of them representatives of different sub-chambers or regional divisions:
- the Cámara Guatemalteca de la Construcción (Chamber of Construction);
- the Cámara de Comercio de Guatemala (Chamber of Commerce);
- the Cámara de Finanzas de Guatemala (Chamber of Finance);
- the Cámara de Industria de Guatemala (Chamber of Industry);
- the Cámara del Agro (Chamber of Agriculture);
- the Asociación de Azucareros de Guatemala (Sugar Association);
- and the Asociación Gremial de Exportadores de Productos No Tradicionales (Non-Traditional Products Exporters Association).

Since December 1999, the *Federación de la Pequeña y Mediana Empresa Guatemalteca* (Federation of the **Small and Medium Enterprises** of Guatemala, FEPYME) is (the only) invited member of CACIF.

According to its own information, CACIF represents through these chambers about 60,000 enterprises. The majority of members belong to the coffee sector. About 70 percent are small enterprises that generate less than 20 workplaces. Since there is little information on the total number of enterprises in the country, it is difficult to assess CACIF's national **representativeness**. Vinicio Cerezo Arévalo president of Guatemala between 1986 and 1990, once stated: "[…] not all entrepreneurs belong to CACIF. But an investigation to assess the scope of their power is missing. I would be of immense utility for the government and all politicians to elucidate this. […]" (Monteforte Toledo 1998: 126)

In addition, despite the numeric dominance of **small and medium enterprises** in the membership, CACIF is reputed to be de facto ruled by the traditional economic elite or "oligarchy". This study cannot give a thorough analysis of the underlying structures of interest in CACIF[6]. It can be clearly stated, however, that in historic retrospect (see following chapters for more details), small and medium enterprises often did not feel represented by CACIF's decisions. That said, there is a seemingly increasing number of leading members in CACIF that do not form part of the traditional elite, as identified by Dosal or Casaus Arzú (e.g. Luis Reye Mayén from the coffee sector, Jorge Briz Abularach and Juan Francico Reyes López from the commercial sector). This suggests that change is in progress and that a "new" economic elite can expand influence (Casaus Arzú 1992; Dosal 1995).

CACIF's political leverage is in part manifested by its role as a formal representative of the private business sector to the government. CACIF is the **legally announced representative** of the Guatemalan business sector for a large number of governmental entities. The most important ones are the National Salary Commission, the Monetary Board, the Guatemalan Social Security Institute (Instituto

---

6   The interrelations between CACIF and those families identified as members of the oligarchy are not explored systematically.

Guatemalteco de Seguridad Social – IGSS), and the Council for Urban and Rural Development.

5.2.2 Interest groups in the agricultural sector

The agrarian sector has experienced waves of fragmentation since the 1970s, resulting in a **growing number of agriculture related business associations**. The diversity of interest groups does not only ground in the diversity of agricultural products cultivated in Guatemala but origins also in discords over (economic) political convictions[7]. In the following paragraphs, the most important agricultural business associations will be introduced briefly.

5.2.2.1 *AGA – Asociación General de Agricultores* (General Association of Growers) and the *Unión Nacional Agropecuaria de Guatemala (*National Agricultural Union of Guatemala – UNAGRO*)*.

The AGA is the oldest – and generally considered one of the most conservative – private business association in Guatemala. It was established in 1920 as a loose **amalgamation of individual businessmen**. And still today, the AGA differs from most other business associations in particular by representing individual entrepreneurs, and not sub chambers.

Historically, the AGA played a decisive role in Guatemalan politics. In recent decades, however, it has lost members as well as influence[8]. Despite of being one of its founding members, the AGA **left CACIF** in 1984, when a younger generation of entrepreneurs, in particular representatives of the Chambers of Commerce and Industry, launched organizational reforms within CACIF. The reforms aimed at expanding the number of members, "eliminate the practice of clientelism be-

---

7   In the middle of the 1990s, the agricultural sector attempted to re-unify the different groupings by founding the Consejo Agroindustrial (Agro-industrial Council) under the auspices of the CAG. The council is an informal amalgamation of various agriculture-related interest groups such as the gremial of the Banana sector that had left the Chamber earlier due to internal disputes or the sugar associations. Critics, however, claim that the Council does not work properly and could not coalesce the agrarian sector.

8   In the literature on Guatemala the AGA is mostly described as a kind of prototype ultra-conservative agricultural business organization. AGA's vehement opposition against the land- and labour reforms during the Arévalo and Arbenz administrations established their reputation. In his influential work on power-structures in Guatemala, Richard Adams portrayed the entity as a discordant and un-unified group of individualistic entrepreneurs with little understanding for structural political changes (Adams 1970: 191-192, 335-337). By the year 2001/2002, when field research was being conducted for this study, AGA encompassed only about 40 members. There where discussions to dissolve AGA completely but a couple of younger members of the AGA decided to reorganize the entity.

tween the public and private sector individuals, to introduce fundamental market principals [...], to promote industry as the priority of national economic policy, and to unify the private sector's voice for effectively lobbying government" (McCleary 1999: 57)[9].

The AGA opposed to the changes, worrying that they might lose their influence on the government. Yet, the AGA **rejoined CACIF** in 1985, although this time indirectly. A former splinter group of the AGA, the *Cámara del Agro* (CAG) decided to merge with the AGA in a loose alliance, the ***Unión Nacional Agropecuaria de Guatemala*** (National Agricultural Union of Guatemala – UNAGRO). For a short period of time, UNAGRO represented the AGA and the *Cámara del Agro* in CACIF (McCleary 1999: 58). A dispute over tax reforms, however, re-ignited an already smouldering discord between the AGA and the CAG on the one hand, and between the AGA and Chambers of Industry and Commerce on the other hand and lead to the disbandment of UNAGRO. The AGA again withdrew from CACIF and has since than not rejoined the umbrella organization (McCleary 1999: 79).

5.2.2.2 *Cámara del Agro (*Chamber of Agriculture – CAG*)*

As just said, the *Cámara del Agro* (CAG) emerged in 1973 from the AGA, as a **splinter group of younger agriculturalists**. At the beginning, the chamber could not assert itself against the AGA as the main representative of the agricultural sector against the government (Dosal 1995: 134). But throughout the last 20 years the Chamber has extended its political stance and is – at least since the final renunciation of the AGA from CACIF – considered one of the most important interests groups representing the agricultural sector.

The CAG represents different agricultural sub-chambers. These are currently:
– the *Consejo Nacional del Algodón* (National Cotton Council),
– the *Asociación de Productores de Soya* (Association of Soya Producers),
– the *Unión de Cañeros del Sur* (Union of Sugar Cane Producers of the South),
– the *Asociación de Azucareros de Guatemala* (Association of Sugar Producers of Guatemala, ASAZGUA)
– and the most influential member, ANACAFÉ, the *Asociación Nacional de Café* (National Coffee Association).

Two members of the CAG have a special standing and should be highlighted: the sugar association ASAZGUA and ANACAFÉ.

---

9 The reforms brought about, among others the creation of the above-mentioned "broader assembly of presidents" in CACIF.

5.2.2.3 Asociación de Azucareros de Guatemala (ASAZGUA)

ASAZGUA is the **organization of the sugar producers** in Guatemala, founded in 1957. The organization represents all 17 existing sugar factories in Guatemala and therefore forms a national sugar-cartel. ASAZGUA's main task is to define annually together with the sugar-cane planters the price of sugar cane. Although ASAZGUA builds a joint group together with the Sugar Cane Association that represents the planters, the members of ASAZGUA are largely dedicated to the production of sugar and not to the cultivation of sugar cane.

While being the organ of an agro-industrial branch, ASAZGUA is a member of the Agricultural Chamber as well as a member of the Chamber of Industry. Additionally, it has a direct representation within CACIF. Although ASAZGUA is "three times represented" in CACIF, the organization only has **one vote** in CACIF's decision-making process.

5.2.2.4 ANACAFÉ (Asociación Nacional del Café; National Coffee Association)

ANACAFÉ was founded in 1960. In contrast to the other corporate interest groups in Guatemala, membership in ANACAFÉ is obligatory for all coffee producers in the country. ANACAFÉ acts as a private interest group, but is de facto a **semi governmental institution** (for more details on the history of Anacafé, see for example Weaver 1970). The coffee law of 1969 (*Ley de Café; decreto 19-69*) sets the main regulations for ANACAFÉ, including a one percent levy on coffee exports, which finances the organization.

ANACAFÉ's *junta directiva* has 20 members: Four representatives of the big *cafetaleros,* four representatives of the median size coffee growers, four representatives of small producers, four representatives of coffee cooperatives and four representatives named by the government. The representation of government officials in ANACAFÉ's managing board origins from the time when the state still owned coffee *fincas*. Although the governmental sold all its estates, the state is still represented in the *junta directiva*.

The **Consejo de Política Cafetalera** (Council for Coffee Politics) is the maximum authority of ANACAFÉ. It stipulates the national coffee policy and ANACAFÉ has to execute it. The council is formally dominated by state officials and consists of four governmental envoys[10], one representative of ANACAFÉ as well as the president of the *junta monetaria* and the president of the central bank. Notwithstanding the numeric dominance of governmental officials in the Council, ANACAFÉ itself considers the state's influence as small: the four governmental representatives in the Council are mostly suggested by ANACAFÉ and

---

10 Representatives of four ministries: ministry of agriculture that presides the council, the ministry for external relations, the ministry of economy and the ministry of finance.

are in the majority of the cases coffee growers themselves (Roux/Nassar 1992 and interviews with representatives from the coffee sector).

Additional to ANACAFÉ, as a national organ, various **regional coffee associations** exist. The individual members of these regional groups are – by law – also member of ANACAFÉ, but the groupings themselves are not associated in ANACAFÉ. In fact, they sometimes interfere – independently of ANACAFÉ – in public political discussions. There are for example the *Asociación de Caficultores del Oriente de Guatemala* (Association of the Coffee Cultivators of Eastern Guatemala; ACOGUA), the *Coordinadora de Asociaciones Regionales de Caficultores Organizados de la República* (Coordinator of Regional Associations of Organized Coffee Cultivators of the Republic, CARCOR), or the ACU, *Asociación de Caficultores Unidos* (Association of the United Coffee Cultivators). CARCOR and ACU, for instance, embrace *fincas* exclusively from the area of San Marcos. The regional coffee organizations have the main task of supporting the *finqueros* in their respective regions, for example, by organizing meetings to inform about particular issues.

CARCOR is one of the most influential regional associations. In the 1960s, it was very powerful within ANACAFÉ ("ANACAFÉ belonged to them [members of CARCOR]" as one representative of the coffee sector put it; see also Adams 1970). CARCOR forfeited influence over time. In the 1980s, the organization was accused of personal enrichment at the expense of ANACAFÉ, leading to the segregation of CARCOR members in ANACAFÉ. To this day, CARCOR is by repute one of the hard-line conservative business entities in Guatemala, and has been closely linked to the MLN (*Movimiento de Liberación Nacional* – National Liberation Movement)[11].

With regard to membership as well organizational characteristics, CARCOR is highly similar to another agricultural business entity, CONAGRO (*Coordinadora Nacional Agropecuaria* – National Agricultural Coordinating Office).

5.2.2.5 Coordinadora Nacional Agropecuaria (CONAGRO)

CONAGRO, founded only in 1994, was strongly involved in the last phase of the Guatemalan peace process. The organization represents the hardliner fraction of the Guatemalan private sector that split from the rest of the business sector over fundamental differences regarding the peace process. Similar to CARCOR, CONAGRO's number of members is small. At the time of its foundation, the organization counted only about 25 individual members. Although exact figures are missing, it is generally assumed that since then it has not significantly extended the number of its members.

---

11 The MLN was the leading party after the putsch against president Arbenz in 1954. It was the party of Castillo Armas invasion group that emerged out of the anti-communist crusade and called itself the "party of organized violence" (Trudeau 2000).

The central figure in CONAGRO is **Gustavo Anzueto Vielman**. Although an architect by training and originally not part of the landed elite, he held various influential positions within a range of private sector interest groups, which made him one of the most well-known players of the agricultural business sector. Among others, he was member of the AGA (and UNAGRO), spokesman of CARCOR, founder of CONAGRO and with respect to his political life, minister of communication during the administrations of General Arana Osorio (1970–1974) and General Kjell Laugerud García (1974–1978) and presidential candidate in the 1982 elections for the *Central Auténtica Nacionalista* (CAN – National Authentic Centre Party). CAN is an extreme rightist and anticommunist party founded in 1979 by General Carlos Arana Osorio after dissociating from the *Movimiento de Liberación Nacional* (MLN) (Rosada-Granados 1992: 94; Gramajo Morales 1995: 324, 334).

Numerous incidents associated Anzueto with the right-wing **extremists' movements** of Guatemala. In the late 1980s, for instance, Anzueto was accused together with five other civilians of having staged an attempted coup d'état against the then president Vinicio Cerezo Arévalo (Prensa Libre 1988; Schirmer 1998: 218, 219)[12]. Some, e.g. the influential military official General Hector Alejandro Gramajo Morales, linked Anzueto in this context to the *Oficiales de la Montaña*, a clandestine group of hard-line right wing, anticommunist militaries and private businessmen. The group surfaced first in 1966 and again during the Cerezo administration (see also chapter 7.1.3) (Schirmer 1998: 207-209).

Another important pillar for Anzueto, besides the private business sector, was the military. By being a lieutenant in the army reserve and allegedly connected to the *Oficiales de la Montaña,* it is not surprising that CONAGRO is also **linked to militaries**, especially members of the military with similar political believes as Anzueto. Thus within CONAGRO, rightist hardliners from the military and the private business sector joined forces. The most well-known military figure within CONAGRO is probably ex-general José Quilo Ayuso, co-founder of CONAGRO, ex vice minister of the National Defence and the colonel in charge during the massacre at El Aguacate, Chimaltenango, in 1988 (Schirmer 1998: 60).

In some publications Anuzeto is portrayed as a key representative of CACIF. The **relationship between him and the umbrella organization** is however, conflictive. Although the bond between Anzueto and the organization never broke entirely, Anzueto resigned from CACIF (as representative of the AGA in UNAGRO) in 1987 because of internal disputes over tax issues (Prensa Libre 1987b). However, since both parties maintained for most of the time the façade of unity, only little is known about their quarrels.

---

12 Rachel Mc Cleary claims in her book "Dictating Democracy" that various interview partners informed her, that not Anzueto Vielman was responsible for the coup d'état, but the son of Roberto Castañeda Felice (McCleary 1999: 213).

5.2.3 *Cámara de Industria* (Chamber of Industry) and *Cámara de Comercio* (Chamber of Commerce)

Until the late 1950s, the industrialist and the commercialists were organized in one business association, the Chamber of Commerce and Industry. Only in 1959, the organization split in two separate business entities, the Chamber of Industry and the Chamber of Commerce. The **organizational structure** of the two associations is still very similar: A General Assembly of Members (*Asamblea General de Socios* or *Asamblea General*) elects the president, the vice-president and the board of directors. Both chambers embrace a wide range of *gremials* and *filiales*, representing different branches (e.g. chemical industry, textile industry and metal-processing industry) and regional sub-entities. The Chamber of Commerce comprises the biggest system of regional branches, expanding their representations in particular since 1996.

No thorough information is available on the **number of members** and their representation. The Chamber of Industry counts approximately 1,700 associates and therefore – according to its own estimations – assembles about 10 to 15 percent of all industrial enterprises in Guatemala.

Besides the CAG the Chambers of Industry and Commerce are the most prominent corporate interest groups in Guatemala. They have expanded their influence gradually in the last few decades, although neither of the two could clearly prevail over the other.

5.2.4 *Cámara de Turismo* (Chamber of Tourism)

The Chamber of Tourism was founded in 1974, emerging from the *Asociación Guatemalteca de Turismo* that had been established 20 years earlier. Currently the chamber has about 439 affiliated members[13]. The **organizational design** of the Chamber is similar to the structure of the Chambers of Industry and Commerce: the association has a general assembly, a board of directors and is divided into various *gremiales* according to branches.

The Chamber of Tourism never gained the **authority and weight** one may expect, given the economic relevance of tourism in Guatemala. Weak organizational structures, pronounced economic setbacks since the late 1970s, and a traditionally weak lobby for tourism are main reasons for this. For most of the time, the Chamber of Tourism was not even a full member of CACIF, but only had the status of an invited associate. Only in 1995, it became a paying member, but had to leave CACIF again three years later due to financial constraints that impeded that chamber to pay their member fee.

---

13 The 439 members embrace about 1200 different firms, as some of the members are fusions of several enterprises.

5.2.5 AGEXPRONT (*Asociación Gremial de Exportadores de Productos no Tradicionales;* Non-Traditional Products Exporters Association)

AGEXPRONT (formerly GEXPRONT) was founded in 1982 as part of a strategy by USAID to organize the **"modernizing fraction" of the Guatemalan business sector** and establish a counterbalance to the traditional corporate groups in Guatemala. The creation of AGEXPRONT was therewith the USAID's second attempt to assist liberal business forces. In 1981 – likewise to similar approaches in El Salvador or Costa Rica – USAID funded the *Cámara Empresarial de Guatemala* (CAEM – Business Chamber of Guatemala). But CAEM was inadequately equipped with financial resources and could not develop into an independent business association. In 1985, four years after its foundation, CACIF integrated CAEM and unified – once more – the corporate sector under its umbrella (Barry 1992: 152-154; Escoto/Marroquín 1992: 117-121; McCleary 1999: 35-37).

The foundation of AGEXPRONT had a similar background, but was far more successful. Its establishment aimed at supporting younger entrepreneurs, foster the production of non-traditional export goods and establish a business association with a **strong development-related mandate** (Dosal 1995). Besides seven *gremiales* for different products (for example VESTEX for apparel and textiles, mainly *maquilas,* Guatemala Apparel and Textile Industry Commission) the entity comprises also a "development division", responsible for the realization of development projects. At the beginning, AGEXPRONT was established as part of the Chamber of Industry. But due to its growing membership and success, AGEXPRONT became fully independent in 1997. In 1999, the organization joined CACIF. Some interpret this as yet more proof of CACIF's power, whereas others argued that AGEXPRONT's entry might weaken the influence of traditional fractions within CACIF.

5.2.6 *Federación de la Pequeña y Mediana Empresa Guatemalteca* (Federation of the Small and Medium Enterprises Guatemala; FEPYME)

FEPYME, the business association of the **small and medium enterprises**, was established for similar reasons as AGEXPRONT. Although FEPYME did not operate as well as AGEXPRONT, the organizations played a particularly interesting role in the peace process and should therefore be introduced briefly.

FEPYME was founded in 1987 with the technical and financial support of the German *Handelskammer Düsseldorf* (Chamber of Commerce from Düsseldorf) and the German foundations Friedrich-Ebert and Konrad-Adenauer. Key motivations for the establishment of FEPYME were defending the particular needs and interests of the small and medium business sectors and building up a counterweight to CACIF. In particular during the years when Roberto Ayerdi, founding member of FEPYME, presided over the organization, the **relationship between CACIF and the new interest group** was taut. CACIF argued that FEPYME was not a fully-fledged private interest group, since president Cerezo (1986-1991) had supported its foundation. However, in recent years and after Ayerdi's withdrawal CACIF and FEPYME converged and in December 1999, FEPYME joined CACIF as an invited member.

FEPYME's **membership** has oscillated since its establishment. Starting with about 200 members, it grew to about 1,000 members in the early 1990s and lost members again in following years. Today FEPYME only counts about 400 affiliated enterprises. The associates belong mainly to the industrial, service and commercial sector, with virtually no representatives from the agricultural sector. In the first year after FEPYME's foundation, the organization established small branches in the interior of the country (for example Quetzaltenango, San Marcos, Retaluheu) but with the decline in membership, these regional branches were eventually closed.

6 The Private Business Sector during the Civil War

Guatemala experienced a phase of democratic rule between 1944 and 1954. The period ended in a violent overthrow, organized by conservative Guatemalans in close cooperation with the Central Intelligence Agency (CIA) and the United Fruit Company (see e.g. Schlesinger/Kinzer 1992).

The governments installed in the aftermath of the 1954 coup, were predominantly military regimes. After the interim government of Carlos Castillo Armas (1954-1957), Miguel Ydígoras Fuentes assumed power (1958-1963). He was ousted by military official Coronel Enrique Peralta Azurdia (1963-1966), followed by President Julio César Méndez Montenegro (formally elected in 1966). The military putsch in 1963 against Ydígoras Fuentes marked the **beginning of the military regimes** in Guatemala for the following 23 years. Although Méndez Montenegro was formally elected, he was forced to sign a pact with the army, securing the ascendancy of the armed forces. The pact guaranteed among others, the autonomy of the military and the continuation of the "fight against communism".

The military regimes in the aftermath of the coup in 1954 largely re-manifested the political, social and economic conditions Arévalo and Arbenz had attempted to reform. In 1960, only six years after the 1954-coup, a group of military officers who opposed the re-established sustained unjust social and political conditions, launched a violent attempt to remove the corrupt and despotic regime from power. This first attempt to overthrow the regime was the **prelude for the thirty-six year long civil war,** lasting from 1960 to 1996.

The civil war in Guatemala is formally divided into **two phases**. A first phase lasted from 1960 to 1968 and a second phase from the end of the 1970s to 1996. The following chapters will illustrate the Guatemalan civil strife in chronological order. They will describe and analyse how the private sector perceived the armed conflict and reacted towards it. The first sub-chapter will outline the first phase of the civil war. The central aims of the emerging guerrilla groups will be outlined.

It will be argued that the first war-period manifested mainly a **political threat** for the business sector. Direct economic destruction was only a secondary concern. As a means to mitigate and manage war related threats, the entrepreneurs primarily sought to intensify their relationship with the military rulers. The links between the private sector and the army that emerged in consequence had both an institutionalized and a clientelist character and covered security issues as well as economic policy issues (Weaver 1970: 75).

6.1 The war begins:
The period between 1960 and 1970

November 13, 1960 is generally considered the **first day of the civil war** in Guatemala. On this date, a group of military officers attempted a coup against the ruling president, Ydígora Fuentes. The officers' primary motivation for this uprising was strong discontent about the political and social conditions in Guatemala. Large parts of the military opposed US involvement in domestic political affairs and vehemently denounced the increasing levels of corruption, personal enrichment and a state policy, which favoured the interest of the *latifundists* (Schlesinger/Kinzer 1992).

The officer's rebellion was suppressed immediately, but laid, nonetheless, the foundation for the first guerrilla organization, the ***Movimiento Revolucionario 13 de Noviembre*** (November 13 Revolutionary Movement – MR-13) that was created in 1963. Soon after the establishment of the MR-13, a second guerrilla group emerged, the ***Fuerza Armada Rebelde*** (Rebel Armed Forces – FAR). The FAR was an armed group that developed out of the communist party, PGT, which had to go underground after its prohibition in 1954.

Both guerrilla groups were strongly inspired by **communist political ideas**. Whereas the FAR had a clear communist agenda, the MR-13 held a more moderate political view (Wickham-Crowley 1991: 39)[1]. In a statement from 1964, the FAR declared, for example, that their goals were: "…the seizure of power of the working class allied with the peasant population, the intellectuals and other revolutionary sectors of the petit bourgeoisie, the establishment of the dictatorship of the proletariat in a worker-campesino state, for fulfilling the anti-feudal and anti-imperialist goals and the realization of the socialist tasks of the revolution" (CEH 2000: 66-67)[2].

---

1   The MR-13 joined the FAR for a time but operated independently again a couple of years later.
2   One should however emphasis that neither the FAR nor other, late emerging guerrilla organizations were supported significantly by the leftist Cuban government.

The MR-13 in contrast aimed at re-establishing democratic norms and a more equal spread of wealth. In an early document they even appealed to "progressive industrialist and commercialists" to explain to their colleagues that only a more equally distribution of purchasing power assures bigger markets and higher sales (CEH 2000: 217).

The armed struggle of the two early guerrilla groups was largely **contained geographically** and focused on the rural, eastern regions of Guatemala, in particular the districts of Izabal and Zacapa (see map 3). A number of armed attacks were committed in the capital, but the epicentre of the fighting was in the eastern regions. Izabal and Zacapa had at this period in time high proportions of impoverished ladino people, "pressured by cattle ranchers and foreign investors" (Jonas 1991: 65). The guerrilla forces anticipated a broad mobilization basis among the local peasants, but the support held off. Already by 1968, the guerrillas were dispelled from the mountain areas of Izabal and Zacapa.

Several reasons lead to the **early defeat of the first guerrilla movement** in Guatemala. Firstly, since 1966 the number of military forces was massively expanded in the region. Intensified counterinsurgency and terror emerged, including the foundation of more than 20 paramilitary death squads, e.g. *MANO Blanca (Movimiento Anticomunista Nacional Organizado)* or *Ojo por Ojo*[3]. Secondly, the guerrilla movement itself lacked experience and suffered from internal fragmentation. And thirdly, the tactic to largely restrict the mobilization base to the ladino population turned out to be a strategic error. The guerrilla movement could not count on sufficient support from this part of the population and was doomed to failure.

For the **private business sector**, this first phase of guerrilla fights posed a serious threat, although it never gravely endangered their interests. Companies suffered from destruction, insecurity and more difficult working conditions, but direct war losses remained limited for the largest part of the business community. The private sector successfully implemented strategies to confine war related risks and profits were generated despite the guerrilla attacks due to the generally positive economic conditions (for more details see later in the chapter)[4].

The corporate risks that resulted from armed conflict were both, the risk of political changes as well the risk of physical attacks and destruction of production facilities. But the **threat of detrimental political changes**, namely the implementation of a left-leaning political regime, with an overt anti-corporate discourse was at all points in time significantly higher than the physical threat. The principal reasons for this were:

Some guerrilla leaders and warriors received training in Cuba, but little further support had been accepted by the Guatemalan leaders (Wickham-Crowley 1991: 89).
3   Between 1966 and 1968, about 4,000 Guatemalans were killed and names appeared constantly on death-lists; in 1967 alone over 500 (McClintock 1985: 86, 95).
4   Economic growth occurred among others, due to the positive effects of the COMECOM, increased foreign direct investments and growing industrialization.

i. The conflict was geographically contained in the areas of Izabal as well as Zacapa and it was quickly repressed by the military.
ii. The insurgency committed attacks mainly against military bases. Sabotage against civil, economic targets, such as installations against the United Fruit Company in 1962 (McClintock 1985: 50), and kidnappings of leading entrepreneurs, occurred but were relatively rare.
iii. Neither the FAR nor the MR-13 had in mind to enter into long-lasting guerrilla warfare. Their main objective was to (quickly) overthrow the ruling government and establish a new regime according to their political objectives.

The risk of an unfavourable political change for the private business sector was even more real since the emergence of the guerrilla movement in the early 1960s was embedded in **mounting public demonstrations** and strikes. A broad coalition of students, workers, the church, and labour organizations protested against the unreliable political system, electoral frauds, degrading living-conditions as well as low minimum wages on *fincas,* and demanded the implementation of agrarian reform and the restoration of the constitution (Molkentin 2002: 116). The riots assumed alarming proportions and even lead to a disruption of production in the commercial and industrial sectors (CEH 2000: 64).

The Guatemalan private business sector responded to these political and physical threats that resulted from the guerrilla rebellion as well as the open public discontent by strengthening its relationship to those institutions that promised to be most effective in the fight against communism in general and guerrilla forces in particular: the military-government. Indeed, during this first phase of the civil war the private business sector's **relationship with the state rulers** gained new momentum. Links between the businessmen and the post-1954 governments became closer and the private business sector developed into an even more important partner for the military rulers (Adams 1970: 194-195; Jonas 1991: 52; Molkentin 2002).

General Héctor Gramajo, senior military official and defence minister under president Vinicio Cerezo (1986-1990) stated in this context later in an interview:"In 1954, groups from the economic elite and the Army overthrew the government with a counterrevolution. A new Army was created and joined forces with the right wing. With the rise of the insurgency in the 1960s, this alliance drew even closer together, such that between 1970 and 1978 they were almost one and the same" (Schirmer 1991: 13).

After the military-putsch of 1963 against Ydígoras Fuentes, representatives of the private business sector and leading military officials met regularly to discuss political and economic issues. A State Council was created, in which representatives of different business chambers participated in order to advice the Chief of Government (Weaver 1970: 75).

Anticommunist sentiments as well as the conviction that the best way to deal with the guerrillas was through military means, were strong ties that kept the military government and the businessmen together for a long time. **Anticommunism** grew into the Guatemalan state ideology since the coup in 1954. But in following years, external events such as Castro's victory in Cuba in 1959 or the US anticommunist 'witch hunt', and the upsurge of large-scale, internal popular demonstrations and the formation of a left-wing guerrilla opposition radicalized anticommunist ideology. The oft cited close link between a landowner faction and the MLN, an ultra-rightwing political party that directly developed out of the anti-communist crusade of Castillo Armas, is one telling example for this.

In the 1950th, the passing of a law about the "defence of democratic institutions" anchored anticommunism in Guatemalan law. Protected by statute, anticommunism flourished, leading to human-rights violations, "disappearances", the killings of labour leaders and political opponents, as well as a further economic and political exclusion of large parts of the population thorough the deprivation of popular and peasant organizations. Anticommunism, thus not only functioned as an governmental ideology, but also worked as an instrument for politicians, militaries, the church and private businessmen alike to **resist all kinds of unpalatable social reforms** (CEH 2000: 37, 41-43) (see also the following chapter).

In particular, landowners were accused of having **violently suppressed peasants**' demands for improved labour conditions (CEH 2000: 79), e.g. by financing, supporting or even indirectly commanding paramilitary forces and death squads under the cloak of fighting against communism (Weaver 1970; Sereseres 1978: 187-193). Although allegedly rare events, those activities remind of reports about human rights violations committed by companies in contemporary violent conflicts (e.g. Harker Report on companies in the Sudan mentioned in chapter 2).

The close contacts between the government and the private sector furthermore facilitated the adaptation of **public security systems** according to the needs of the private business sector, in particular the agriculturalists. It was mentioned earlier that the military intensified its presence and counterinsurgency activities in the regions under guerrilla attack. For the entrepreneurs in this area the enhanced fighting strength of the army was certainly the most important protection measure against the immediate threats and costs related to the rebellion. In addition, amendments in the Guatemalan law, such as the passing of decree 332 in 1965 as well as changes in the function of so called *comisionados* (military commissioners) further improved the security situation of the private business sector.

Decree 332 assigned the newly founded Mobile National Police (*Policía Militar Ambulante, PMA*) to also assist *finqueros* in labour disputes and to provide for a fee, security services to landowners, financial institutions and major industrial plants (whether in domestic or foreign-ownership) (Sereseres 1978: 183). The decree stipulated among others: "[The PMA shall] lend assistance, in cases of emergency, to the owners or administrators of estates, haciendas, agricultural lands, forests and all rural properties.... [and] observe all activity that tends to inflame passions among the peasant masses or in the rural communities and, when necessary, repress through licit means any disorder that should occur." (cited in McClintock 1985: 64-65).

At the end of the 1960s, *finqueros* obtained the legal right "to consider themselves authorities of the law and to shoot 'guerrilla suspects'" (Jonas 1991: 63). A similar law had existed during the presidency of General Jorge Ubico (1931-1944). It allowed *finqueros* to bear arms, make arrests and assume other police responsibilities. Arbenz had abandoned the law during his presidency (McClintock 1985: 23), but with the flourishing of the relationship between landowners and the government in the aftermath of the coup in 1954, the law was revived in a similar form.

Comisionados originally – in the late 1930s and thereafter – had the role of a more symbolic representation of the military in the countryside. After the military putsch in 1963, their function, however, changed significantly. Among a wide range of different tasks they became responsible for reporting insurgents, political and labour organizations and to (if necessary forcibly) secure a sufficient seasonal workforce on the plantations (Weaver 1970: 73-74; McClintock 1985: 65-68). McClintock for example writes: "In the more than 4,000 settlements located entirely within the boundaries of large private agricultural estates [...] military commissioners and PMA contract guards alike were likely to be employees of the farmowner, since vis-à-vis counter-insurgency, the interest of the army and the large landowners were considered identical."

Although PMAs and *Comisionados* are hard to compare to contemporary Private Security Companies (PSC) (see chapter 3.1.4.2), given their close links to the government and give their additional task to "secure the labour force", one basic function of PSC and PMA's/Comisionados is identical: Providing protection to private entrepreneurs against direct violent threats.

Notwithstanding the overall close coalition between the private business sector and the government on security issues, it is important to mention that with regard to other issues this relationship was occasionally contentious. Parts of the private sector opposed economic and political decisions by the military governments (McClintock 1985: 70) and **mutual distrust** about expanding influence of the other at the cost of ones own influence overshadowed the bond. In the midst of the 1960s, for example, the discrepancies within the coalition became obvious on a discussion about the role of ANACAFÉ in representing the national interest of the coffee sector. The business association, together with other business groups vigorously resisted a threatening nationalisation of their institutions, whereas parts of the government argued against the expanding scope of corporate influence (Weaver 1970: 75-77).

The **first phase** of the Guatemalan civil war was, as described, a manageable threat for the business community. Although the guerrillas had identified the business elite as part of the structural conditions that motivated them to take up arms and fight against the regime, direct attacks against private targets were limited. However, the open antagonisms of the insurgency against the private sector, combined with their communist demands were certainly fundamental factors, why the entrepreneurs considered a military victory as the only way to cope with the rebellion. The close partnership with the army clearly followed this rational. Besides, it helped to take care of the public protests that were an additional threat to the entrepreneurs' interests and helped to provide favourable economic conditions through e.g. securing labour force and repressing labour-unions (see also next chapter for more details).

6.2 A violent interlude:
Low-intensity warfare as a business climate

The time between the late 1960s and the late 1970s was a bloody interlude between the two guerrilla upheavals. Although guerrilla activities remained limited in this period of time, the **military consolidated their political dominance** through overt repression and fraudulent elections. President Julio César Méndez Montenegro's (1966-1970) three successors in office (Carlos Manuel Arana Osorio, 1970-1974; Kjell Laugerud García, 1974-1978; Fernando Romeo Lucas Gacía, 1978-1982) were all military officers and former ministers of defence.

In 1970, Col. Carlos Arana came into power, a man also known as the *"Butcher of Zacapa"* due to his responsibility for the killing of thousands of civilians in Zacapa in 1964. During his presidency, Arana **institutionalized counterinsurgency terror** into the state apparatus. Disappearances and killings, above all, of members of trade unions and student organizations, censorship of the press and curfews became routine. In 1974, Gen. Kjell Laugerud assumed presidency. He headed the MLN and in an openly fraudulent election, stole victory from General Efraín Rios Montt, who at this time advocated a comparatively reformist policy. Although repression and terror abated slightly during Laugerud's tenure, violence continued.

6.2.1 Economic prosperity during the military regimes

For the private sector, the period until the emergence of the second guerrilla wave was relatively calm, and even economically prosperous. Protected by the counterinsurgency policy of the military rulers, physical threats from insurgency attacks remained limited.

The 1970s were characterized by overall **positive economic growth rates**. Stimulated by the CACM and successful government economic development plans, the national economy grew and diversified significantly. *Finqueros* invested into industrial agricultural products such as sugar, meat and cotton and modernized their means of production. Industrial production increased to 15-20 percent of national GDP and the number of workers in the industrial sector expanded by 50 percent (CEH 2000: 91).

However, as suggested already in chapter 4, this positive economic trend did not translate into economic wellbeing for the majority of the population. Only about one third of the national population benefited from this economic growth (Sereseres 1985b: 107). More than 70 percent of the **population remained poor**, and about 40 percent extremely poor. High population growth rates (about 3 percent annually) and low wages, partly consumed by high inflation rates (15 percent in 1974) deteriorated the living conditions of the majority of the Guatemalan population. President Laugerud's anti-inflation initiative that included an increase in the national minimum wage as well as Aran's attempt 1973 to increase taxation rates on export products, failed. This was in part due to vehement resistance by the private business sector (CEH 2000: 96-97). In addition, an earthquake in February 1976 that killed 22.000 people, injured more than 77.000 and made more than 1 million people homeless meant further economic setbacks for the poor population.

In the 1970s, parts of the business sector – as well as the military – increasingly **harnessed the weak state structure**, the insufficient governmental control mechanism and the clientelist system between the military and the entrepreneurs for their personal enrichment. In particular, since the administrations of Arana and Laugerud corruption, nepotism and misconduct all flourished in a political regime that continued to seek legitimacy through its fight against the insurgency.

In addition, through the **massive suppression of labour unions** and peasant organizations, private entrepreneurs could relatively easily circumvent social and economic minimum standards and preserve exploitative economic relationships. Education in rural regions, for example, remained deficient, in part because many *finqueros* did not comply with their legal duty to establish schools on their estates. The union on the Coca Cola bottling plant, for instance, has sought legal recognition since 1975. Managers of the plant had repeatedly attempted to exclude organized workers from the workforce and until 1980, more than 80 workers had been killed.

Throughout large periods of the civil war the business sector, above all the **agricultural sector and the manufacturing sector benefited** from this preemption of meaningful political organization of workers through violent repression by the army. Wages remained low and the economic privileges grounded in the exploitation of cheap labour were protected. Large parts of the Guatemalan economic elites, in other words, did not profit from the war itself (such as for example weapon producers would) but they benefited from the preservation of the social economic status quo through violent and authoritarian means, such as through the disappearance and torture of labour activists or prohibition of certain unions.

The Guatemalan **military profited** more directly economically from the power gained during the period of the armed conflict. Their entanglement in organized crime, such as stolen car or weapon traffic was (or is) one form (e.g. Keen 2003). But the military as individuals as well as an institution, also spread out into the legal economic area that was formerly left largely to private entrepreneurs.

A prominent example of the military's enrichment at the individual level was the exploitation of the *Franja Transversal del Norte* that commenced in the 1970s. The *Franja Transversal del Norte*, also called "the Zone of the Generals", is a sparsely populated region[5] of about 3,500 square miles stretching from the Mexican border to Guatemala's Caribbean coast. In an infrastructure plan for this area, it was originally envisioned to develop the region and to distribute the land among landless population. Instead, the growing world market for agricultural products as well as the presence of deposits of valuable resources (oil, nickel) made this region attractive for military officials. They quickly took possession of the majority of the region, making significant profits from the exploitation of nickel and oil, from the establishment of hydroelectric power stations and from conducting extensive cattle breeding.

The Guatemalan army as an institution **extended its economic activities** into a wide range of different branches. George Black describes the Guatemalan military as a "financial monster with active capital of USD 119.2 million in 1981" (Black 1989). Painter counted more than 40 governmental and para-governmental enterprises, including an airline and a telecommunication-network (Painter 1987: 47). Other estimates are lower counting although still significant, comprising for example about seven larger investments in the banking, security and finance sector, in industry (Maya Químicos, Sociedad Anómima) and transport (airline AVIATECA) all held by the *Insitituto de Previsión Militar* (IPM), a social security organ for military associates (Brenes/Casas 1998: 70). The *Banco del Ejército* is certainly the most significant among these investments due to its financial volume.

More controversial than the quantity of the army's economic possessions, is the impact that the intrusion of the military into the formal economic sphere had on the **relationship between the private business sector and the army**. Some suggest (Black 1984; Molkentin 2002) that the corporate sector perceived this development as a threat to their interests. Yet interviews conducted with both military associates as well as private business representatives allege the opposite for two reasons. First, at this time landowners did not intend to invest in the *Franja Transversal del Norte*, due to the violent resistance of the local population (see footnote 3: 127). Secondly, the army deliberately invested in branches in which private business interests were not threatened (Brenes/Casas 1998: 71). Very likely, a smaller number of entrepreneurs considered the enhanced eco-

---

5 Although sparsely populated, the north-eastern zone of Guatemala was a retreat for indigenous farmers. When the military "developed" the area, massive violent strife occurred and hundreds of people were killed (Black 1984: 25-35; Handy 1989: 218).

nomic activity of the army as threatening (Brenes/Casas 1998: 82), but the military was not largely considered an immediate competition[6].

6.2.2 The emergence of the second wave of the civil war

Increasing poverty rates, as described above, were probably a central reason why, despite persistent repression during Arana's and Laugerud's tenures, **civil interest groups as well as the guerrillas experienced a unique surge in popularity** in the 1970s (Jonas 1991: 123-129).

Membership of trade unions increased and new unions were formed, in urban as well as rural regions. Indigenous peasantry joint these **organizations and unions** emerged representing the growing seasonal workforce (McClintock 1985: 127-130). Amongst others, important labour unions and peasant organizations, such as the *Comité Nacional de Unidad Sindical* (CNUS – National Committee of Trade Unions) and the *Comité de Unidad Campesina* (CUC – Peasant Unity Committee) were founded during this period.

The foundation of the CNUS and the CUC are of special relevance since it reflected increasing unity among workers. The **CNUS**, a coalition of PGT and Christian Democratic Forces, organized a series of important strikes in the 1970s and early 1980s and developed into a central player at this time. Even more important was probably the foundation of the **CUC**, a coalition of social groups that traditionally did not work together. The CUC became one of the most important national (indigenous) peasant organizations, advocating for agrarian reform, improved labour conditions etc.

These popular organizations gathered momentum only just before the re-emergence of armed guerrilla groups in Guatemala. Indeed, in many cases the popular organizations were closely **linked through ideological as well as personal ties** to the newly developing guerrilla organizations (Wickham-Crowley 1990; Molkentin 2002). In addition, both groupings, guerrilla as well as popular organizations, found their main support basis in the same regions: the highland areas of Guatemala, the home of the growing army of impoverished migratory workers population (see for example Paige 1983)[7]. The constant but fruitless protest in the 1970s, deteriorating living conditions, and ongoing state terror made

---

6   David Keen argued in an article that the enrichment by the military as well as the insurgency contributed to the prolongation of the violent conflict in Guatemala (Keen 2003). Although this argument should not be ignored completely, the quantity of individual enrichment does not seem to be sufficient to explain the continuation of the civil war.
7   The army of seasonal, migrating labourers grew in the 1970s due to the modernization of modes of production and the expanding cultivation of sugar cane, cotton and cattle. 300,000 to 600,000 peasants migrated annually from the highlands of Guatemala – providing at this time the largest proportional stream of migratory labour in the world (Wickham-Crowley 1990: 235).

many members of these popular organizations becoming radicalized and gave them incentives to join or support the idea of an armed struggle.

Three guerrilla groups come to light in the period between 1972 and 1979: the *Ejército Guerrillero de los Pobres* (EGP – Guerrilla Army of the Poor), the *Organización del Pueblo en Armas* (ORPA – Organization of People in Arms), and the revived FAR.

The **Ejército Guerrillero de los Pobres** was founded in 1972 by a nucleus of 15 former FAR members and later developed into the strongest of the three Guatemalan guerrilla organizations. Already, their first public attack made clear that the guerrillas considered the business sector as one of their central foes: On 7 June 1975, the EGP killed the *finquero* Luis Arenas Barrera on his *finca* "La Perla" in the area of Ixcán. Arenas Barrera was also known as the *Tigre de Ixcán* (Tiger of Ixcán), due to his despotic behaviour against the labour force[8]. The autocratic conduct of many landowners had nourished a deep sense of abhorrence and hostility among the peasant population. By assassinating the "prototype" of a tyrannical *finquero*, the EGP clearly laid out its aims (Handy 1989: 117; Le Bot 1992). "Arenas was a symbol: A latifundist with semi-feudal methods, active collaborator of the regime since 1954, for a time director of the organisation responsible for the distribution of land in El Petén; a representative of these 'rich ones' against which the 'Ejército de los Pobres' wanted the population to rebel" (Durocher 2002: 69).

In the following years, the EGP **executed a number of *finqueros*** and plantation administrators, among others, dependants of the second biggest *finca* in the area of Ixil, the *finca* San Francisco owned by the Brol family. The Brol family was frequently used in the rhetoric of the emerging EGP as a symbol of a system that stole the land from the indigenous people, exploited the population and took advantage of the economic inequalities. Enrique Brol, the owner of the *finca* in the 1970s, was moreover known for allegedly having raped numerous indigenous women on his *finqua*. He was killed by a female *guerrillera*, making a statement against inhuman treatment (Stoll 1993; Durocher 2002: 69-70).

The EGP concentrated their military activities in the areas of Quiché, Huehuetenango, Verapaces and Chimaltenango. On the South coast, the EGP only committed occasional acts of sabotage against agricultural production facilities (Molkentin 2002: 153).

The **Organización del Pueblo en Armas** (ORPA) was the second guerrilla organization that emerged in the 1970s. Only a nucleus of eleven people worked clandestinely for more than eight years, before the ORPA appeared in public in 1979. ORPA's foci were educational work in the rural, primarily indigenous regions of the country and collaborating with labour unions and peasant organiza-

---

8   Stoll claims that the name "Tiger of Ixán" was create by the EGP and not by the local population (Stoll 1993).

tions. But ORPA also directed its first public activity against a private target: the violent occupation of *Finca Mujulia* in Quetzaltenango.

Also in the early 1970s, **FAR** re-emerged [9]. The first military activities of FAR since their defeat at the end of the 1960s were attacks in the region of El Péten as well as enhanced collaboration with labour unions and popular organizations in urban areas. FAR was again suppressed very quickly, although it surfaced once more at the beginning of the 1980s.

For the private business sector, the **intercessional period** between the two war-peaks brought about ambivalent developments. On the one hand and in particular in the early 1970s, the economic development was largely positive. Physical attacks went down for a couple of years and the continued suppression of labour unions, social minimum standards etc. was in the interest of most entrepreneurs.

On the other hand, these developments foreshadowed the rising number of selective **attacks against private properties**. Although it was already obvious in the first phase of the civil war that the insurgency was antagonistic towards the private sector in general, and large landowners in particular, attacks such as by the EGP in 1975 against *finqueros* were clear signs for the persistent or even augmented hostility against the private sector. In 1982 the then newly-created guerrilla umbrella organisation *Unidad Revolucionaria Nacional Guatemalteca* (Guatemalan National Revolutionary Unity – URNG) stated that its intention was to "guarantee the provision of the basic needs of the majority of the people by eliminating the political domination of the repressive rich, both national and foreign, who rule Guatemala" (Sereseres 1985b: 111).

Although the military reacted immediately by intensifying their presence in guerrilla hotspots and by establishing military installations directly on threatened private properties (including the *fincas* La Perla and San Francisco), the guerrilla struggle gained remarkably in force (Camacho Nassar et al. 2003: 235).

---

9 The FAR broke with the PGT in 1968.

6.3 The second war peak: The business sector between fleeing the country and developing new conflict management strategies

Between 1978 and 1983, the civil war escalated to unprecedented levels. So far, the armed conflict was characterized by low intensity but in the late 1970s and early 1980s, its strength increased significantly: The guerrillas fought vigorously and managed to control more and more regions of the country. The military responded with systematic terror, developing into genocides. At the same time, the country underwent growing political fragmentation and economic decline.

The following paragraphs first describe the course of the armed conflict during this period, before analysing the impacts on and the strategies of the private business sector. It will be argued that the period between the end of the 1970s and the early 1980s was the most destructive period of the armed conflict for the business sector. Violence raised and took its toll from business in form of high levels of insecurity as well as direct destruction of production facilities, infrastructure etc. At the same time, the relationship with the military rulers deteriorated, primarily over economic and political issues and in part concerning the counterinsurgency strategy. The business sector reacted on the one hand with increased capital flight but on the other hand with a political campaign, tackling the political threats resulting from the success of the leftist popular as well as guerrilla movement.

6.3.1 Rise and fall of the second guerrilla movement: The course of the civil war during Lucas Garcia's and Ríos Montt's administration

With General Fernando Romeo Lucas Garcia assuming presidential office in 1978 through fraudulent elections, Guatemala fell into **one of its darkest eras**. Random, massive counterinsurgency policies and intensified guerrilla activities pushed the country into a spiral of violence. By 1982, there were an estimated 6,000 or more guerrilla combatants and about 250,000 supporters. Two key events, the massacre in the region of Panzós and the burning of the Spanish embassy in 1978 and 1980 marked the opening of Lucas's brutal regime.

The massacre in Panzós, one of the key events during the Lucas regime, occurred in May 1978 in a village in Alta Verapaz, located in the *Franja Transversal del Norte*. More than 150 Indian peasants who resisted land expropriation were machine-gunned in the village's main square. About two years later, in 1980 a group of CUC members from El Quiché peacefully squatted the Spanish embassy in Guatemala City, in order to draw attention to the violence committed by the army in their home region. According to Indians interviewed by Amnesty International, the four dominant landowners in the region had called the military to their villages because the peasant population had refused to work for the *fin-*

queros for wages below the statutory minimum wage (Handy 1989: 118). The Guatemalan army burned the Embassy and killed all its occupants including embassy employees' apart from two. Both incidents, the ***Panzós* massacre** as well as the **burning of the Spanish embassy**, happened against the background of an increasingly vocal and organized indigenous and *campesino* movement, demanding economic, political and cultural rights. They became for many Guatemalans – and in particular for many indigenous – symbols of the ineffectiveness of a peaceful struggle and drove many to take part in the guerrilla movement (Arias 1990: 248-255).

Massacres committed by the army in the primarily Indian area of Ixil[10], Sololá, Chimaltenango and other highland areas followed in the coming years. The **military fortified** their presence in these regions, establishing military headquarters among others in Quetzaltenango, Quiché and Sololá and extending the intelligence apparatus throughout the country (McCleary 1999: 44). In addition, the Lucas government intimidated the civil population in such a way that all the room for manoeuvre that the popular organizations had obtained in the 1970s, was nullified in a few years.

The **guerrillas intensified their fighting** since the end of the 1970s, concentrating their activities first in the highland areas. The insurgency attacked military bases, intercepted traffic to collect "war taxes" on the important Pan American Highway, kidnapped and executed *finqueros,* politicians and people suspected of collaborating with the military regime. In 1979, for example, the EGP launched an offensive, directed against military and economic targets, and in particular against the agricultural sector (ODHAG 1998: 115). Amnesty International estimated that only in spring 1979, thirteen leading entrepreneurs were kidnapped (ODHAG 1998: 94). By early 1980, guerrilla forces controlled or had significant support in eight of twenty-two *departamentos* (Schirmer 1998: 41) and started to increase their attacks in the capital (ODHAG 1998: 115). The country "was on the verge of collapse" (Schirmer 1998: 18).

A military associate described the situation at this time as follows: "We were up against the wall because the guerrillas were as close as Chimaltenago. I mean, you couldn't even drive out on a Sunday to Antigua without running into guerrillas at Amatitlán!" (in Schirmer 1998: 42). And a *finquero* stated in an interview: "The late 1970s were the worst. You could not go to your finquas anymore or to your estates in the countryside. It was simply too dangerous because of the guerrilleros."

Lucas' inability to win the war against the guerrillas, the high death toll the army had to pay in combat against the insurgency, in addition to mounting corruption amongst high ranking army commanders antagonized large segments of the military. In March 1982, a group of 950 junior army officers, lead by General

---

10 Ixil was considered the heartland of the EGP and was as a result a main target for the army's counterinsurgency strategies.

Efraín Ríos Montt, staged a **coup against General Lucas**. After a short interim period in which a military junta governed the country, Ríos Montt assumed office for the following one and a half years, from March 1982 until August 1983.

Ríos Montt surpassed Lucas with regard to brutality in the fight against the guerrillas. Montt's **military plan 'Victoria 82'** peaked with the destruction of more than 440 villages, the killing of more than 100,000 civilians, and the displacement of more than one million people in a period of little more than a year. He introduced Civil Self-Defence Patrols (*Patrulla de Autodefensa Civil –* PACs)[11] and developed model villages with the aim to utilize the civil population for the governmental counterinsurgency campaign. More than one million people were organized in PACs. This was allegedly on a voluntary basis, although membership was de facto compulsory for most people.

Ríos Montt's military government underpinned its scorched earth counterinsurgency policy with new, **socioeconomic strategies**. Programmes such as *Fusiles y Frijoles* (Rifles and Beans) and *Techo, Trabajo, y Tortilla* (Shelter, Work, and Food), or the implementation of *polos de desarrollo* (development poles) attempted to address the miserable living conditions of the highland population, aiming to "win their hearts". Montt's "two-track" anti-guerrilla strategy was part of newly developed military doctrines, the ***Plan Nacional de Seguridad y Desarrollo*** (National Plan of Security and Development) of 1982. In the new plan, the army gave allowance to the fact that the war could not be won with military means alone. Younger army officials had recognized that poor socioeconomic living conditions in rural areas, made large parts of the population susceptible to the guerrillas' "communist propaganda". In order to win the war, it was important to tackle the economic conditions and to improve the economic well being of the population (see for details Schirmer 1991; Schirmer 1998; McCleary 1999: 47)[12].

The tactic soon proved to be successful. Weakened by internal quarrels, the **insurgency was militarily defeated by 1983**. Despite continuous skirmishes and the unification of the three guerrilla groups under the umbrella organization *Uni-*

---

11 Among others, PACs were forced by the military to participate in massacres and members of the PACs were trained in torture methods. (Molkentin 2002: 173).

12 In early 1980, about 80,000 plantation workers participated in a strike in the South coast. This massive strike brought the sugarcane harvest and the preceding processing to a standstill and is regarded a highlight within the Guatemalan labour movement. The workers protested for better salaries and working conditions. After longlasting altercations, the government increased the minimum wage from Q1.20 for each tonelada of cut sugarcane to Q.3.20 (the workers originally had demanded Q5). But many finacas did not pay the new minimum wage (ODHAG 1998: 125). About this strike, the CEH writes: "The power to convocation, that was shown by the CUC was perceived as a strong threat by the army and the private sector, not only for the quantity of persons that they mobilized but because they represented a dangerous alliance between ladinos and mayas, with the participation of religious people and with influence and links with insurgency groups" (CEH 1999d: §613).

dad Revolucionaria Nacional Guatemalteca (URNG) in 1982, there was little doubt that the guerrilla forces did not pose a grave threat to the state anymore.

Ríos Montt's military success could not prevent him from being putsched out of office. His eccentric religious behaviour (he was a born-again Christian) and contentious economic policies alienated large parts of the army as well as the private business sector. In August 1983, General Oscar Humberto Mejía Victores staged a **coup against Montt** and assumed office.

Mejía Victores was Guatemala's third president within eight years. His major achievement was in launching the **first steps towards a democratic opening** of Guatemala: a constituent assembly was installed in 1985 that developed a new constitution. At the end of 1985, the first free elections since 1944 were held and Marco Vinicio Cerezo Arévalo became president.

6.3.1.1 The business sector feels the war: The corporate consequences of the second war peak

Without doubt, for the private business sector the period between the late 1970s and early 1980s was the most intimidating phase, with the highest war-related costs during the entire insurrection. The costs that were caused through the civil war for the private sector resulted from overall insecurity and the political threat of a leftist takeover, as well as from direct attacks against corporate and infrastructure targets, workforce instability etc. In contrast to the first phase of the civil war in the 1960s, the second phase differed significantly in terms of higher direct costs and a much more sever threat of an actual victory of the guerrilla forces. The agricultural sector remained the sector that suffered most, although other branches felt the civil war as never before.

Many entrepreneurs feared that the Marxists would take over the state and that the government would not be able (and willing) to defend them[13]. A number of factors made a leftist overthrow appear likely in Guatemala. From a regional perspective, the majority of countries in the Isthmus underwent severe political crisis: in 1979, the Sandinistas overthrew dictator Samosa in Nicaragua, and attempted to install a left-leaning government. In El Salvador, a bloody civil war began between Marxist guerrillas and the ruling regime. And in Honduras, a military junta assumed power. National as well as international observers predicated a domino like expansion of Marxist governments throughout the Central American region, starting with Nicaragua, and then to El Salvador and Guatemala.

---

13 Some authors, however, argue that the indigenous population forming the major source of combatants and supporters for the insurgency forces, would "have little taste for Marxism; rather, they are champions of private property. They want their own land, an end to cultural discrimination, and a large degree of autonomy" (Gleijeses 1985: 68).

Nationally, a number of factors gave the impression that Guatemala would experience the same political fate as its neighbours. To these belonged among others:
- ongoing popular demonstrations, assuming the nature of riots at the beginning of the Lucas administration;
- the strong support for guerrilla organizations and socialist ideas in general among large parts of the Guatemalan population;
- the military success of the Guatemalan guerrillas until 1982;
- rampant military violence;
- governmental corruption;
- and changes in the military's security strategy since 1982 and a deteriorating relationship between the military government and the private business sector.

Fincas were certainly the most common **corporate targets for guerrilla attacks with related direct costs**. Assaults against industrial and commercial facilities occurred, as mentioned earlier, but were still comparatively rare. Especially in those cases in which *fincas* accommodated military unites, they became a preferred objective for guerrilla attacks. A report by ANACAFÉ about the war period between 1960 and 1996, counted more than 60 registered attacks of private property on *fincas* (primarily burning of agriculture machines) and about 100 cases of blackmail on *fincas*. The actual numbers are possibly higher. The attacks peaked in 1981 and 1982 (CEH 1999c: §4462)[14]. In addition, during the second war-peak, "war taxes" (*impuestos de guerra*), which were collected by the insurgency from *finqueros* became more and more common (for more details see chapter 7.3.2).

Acts of sabotage against **infrastructure targets**, including power poles, streets, and patrol stations, committed in particular by the EGP and the FAR, increased as well and had a detrimental effect on every-day business activities. A study by ANACAFÉ counted approximately 183 attacks against infrastructure facilities between 1960 and 1996.

Both, infrastructure and private property were **strategic as well as symbolic targets** in the guerrilla tactics. Assaults against infrastructure made it possible to hit various enemies at the same time: it affected the economic interests of the state, the economic interests of the productive sector, and hampered army activities (CEH 1999b: §3855). An informant to the CEH stated:"[…] To interrupt the free circulation on the streets, to break the communication system of the enemy, destroy bridges, paralyze sugar refineries and harvesting machines, are some of the tasks that our compañeros have to realize".

In addition, private companies and *fincas* as prominent "symbols of capitalism" that led to the exploitation of workers, and discrimination against indige-

---

14 The FAR counted 58 attacks against infrastructure and 37 against production facilities (CEH 1999b: §3836).

nous people, were forceful targets in guerrilla strategies. Direct attacks against private property were, for example, explained as follows:

"[...] our Frente guerrillero Otto René Castillo realized, among many others, acts of sabotage in the capital, directed against luxury buildings that serve as places for business and business associations of the big rich exploiters ... our principal activities against the big millionaires were the virtual demolition [21 December 1981] of three sumptuous buildings: the Chamber of Industry, the tour Panamaericana where the Banco de Café is, and the Centro Financiero where the Banco Industrial is located. [...]" (CEH 1999b: §3858).

And with regard to fincas: "[...] they directed against the machinery and the means of production of the finqueros who displace workforce, condemn labour families into unemployment, sabotage against the plains that spray pesticides, which poison the workers and their families, sabotage against the helmets of the fincas utilized as operation and training centres for the army and repressive bodies [...]" (CEH 1999b: §3865).

Another threat to the interest of the private business sector, additional to damages of production facilities was the risk that insurgency forces **infiltrate companies**, in particular through labour organizations. In particular the EGP and the ORPA attached some importance to this part of the guerrilla strategy and established close links to labour and popular organizations. The insurgency approached labour unions in their search for new members and support. The entrepreneurs, however, feared that closer links to the guerrillas could radicalize as well as destabilize the workforce.

6.3.1.2 Changes in the conflict management strategies of the business sector

How did the **private sector** react, faced with these intensified, war-related costs and threats? Until this period in time, the private business sector had very much relied on the military to protect them against any kind of war-risk, political as well as direct threats. But since the Lucas administration and given the unprecedented success of the insurgency and high levels of violence, the majority of the private sector lost some confidence in the effectiveness and ability of the military as the main way to "manage" and adapt to the war-related risks (for more details see the following chapter).

Corporations started to **lower their economic activities** and **capital flight** raised to record levels. ODHAG (*Oficina de Derechos Humanos del Arzobispado de Guatemala* – Archbishop's Human Rights Office in Guatemala) estimated that between 1980 and 1984, USD 2,000 to 2,500 million were transferred abroad (Mersky 1988; ODHAG 1998: 121). Moreover, private investments declined between 1975 and 1981 by about 20 percent (Gallardo/López 1986: 57)[15]. In some regions, most affected by the civil strife, such as the area of Ixil in El Quiche, *finqueros* decided to abandon their land or put it on the market. Direct attacks by the guerrillas, discrepancies with the army and increasing labour instability made the business too risky. With the arrival of the EGP in the region, *finqueros* were increasingly confronted with seasonal workers not showing up despite advance payments or "contracts". Stoll found that between 1980 and 1991 from 43 *fincas* in this region 24 changed owner (outside the family) (Stoll 1993: 233). Among others, the Herrera, Brol, Arenas and Hodgsdons patronal families, the most important in the area, handed over their estates or parts of their estates to the government or former workers, including the *fincas* La Perla and San Francisco (Durocher 2002: 82).

Despite the mounting levels of capital flight, the Guatemalan private business sector still claimed that they – in contrast to for example entrepreneurs in El Salvador – **maintained broad swathes of production**. Indeed, growth rates in El Salvador during the peak of its civil war (1979-1982) dropped much more dramatically than growth rates during the second peak of the armed conflict in Guatemala (1978-1982)[16].

Common **security remedies** by those who stayed in Guatemala included the hiring of additional private security companies and to a much lesser extent – due to the enormous costs – insurance. Some individual businessmen, primarily those from the agricultural sector, sought to protect their properties by intensified collaboration with the army. ODHAG found that at the end of the 1970s, some *finqueros* increased their support for the military by lending the army private planes or helicopters, or by allowing the military to use their facilities on the *fincas* (ODHAG 1998: 108).

However, this collaboration should not belie the fact that many landowners refused to host military units on their property. Some of them feared – rightly in many cases – that hosting army divisions on their land might heighten the risk of being attacked by the guerrillas. Others simply wanted to remain neutral. Rodrigo Asturias, one of the founding members of the ORPA and a leading figure in the URNG, for instance, estimated that this type of **direct contribution of businessmen to military** activities was insignificant. Likewise, General Mejía Víctores, president from 1983 to 1986 and Minister of Defence during the Ríos Montt administration claimed in this context that entrepreneurs gave very little support. "Proper support, no, they [private entrepreneurs] were interested in being able to produce in their fincas; in some zones, the only thing, more or less, were permissions and authorizations, sympathy, nothing that economically would

---

15 The breakdown of the CACM and the globally deteriorating economic situation had also asked for its toll.
16 Percent growth rates in per capita GDP for El Salvador between 1979 and 1982: -5.9; -11.7; -9.6; -6.5. In Guatemala the percent growth rates in per capita GDP between 1978 and 1982 were: 2.4; 1.9; 0.8; -1.8; -6.1.

have been of support, as they did in El Salvador where the industrialists said [to the government] ... 'see, here you have money so that you can buy materials.'" (Valdez/Prado 1998: 54).

Apart from these individual measures to manage war-risks, CACIF as a business association organized the *Campaña de los mil días* (Campaign of the Thousand Days) at the beginning of the 1980s. As mentioned earlier, the private business sector was severely alarmed by the strong support that socialist ideas and the guerrillas had found among the Guatemalan population. The *Campaña de los mil días* was a political campaign with the principal aim to spread alternative political ideas to the leftist model among the Guatemalan people. The campaign started 1,000 days before the planned elections at the end of 1982 and was supposed to end with the Election Day[17]. Easily presented liberal, anticommunist political messages were widely distributed throughout the country, for example with the help of cartoons in national newspapers, TV and radio spots, or with the help of individual campaigns in different enterprises, including for example *Pollo Campereo,* a Guatemalan based fast-food chain.

It is without doubt remarkable that in the middle of the civil war, the business sector overcame potential organizational impediments and agreed to **launch a political campaign**, targeting political threats. Their focus was not so much on direct, war related damages and physical risks. Much rather they tried to weaken the insurgency and other leftist groups by counterpropaganda, seeking to undermine the ideological arguments of the left in Guatemala. Several reasons may explain this: First, the majority of the entrepreneurs considered a leftist political changes either through rebellion or (similarly immediate) through the ballot box, a higher risk than the threat of physical war damages. Second, they did not want to further intensify their relationship with the army and get involved in the "bloody business" of the military (see following chapter). Third, they figured that the army would be able to cope with the insurgency militarily, but not politically.

The second, significantly less important aim of the *Campaña de los mil días* was to improve Guatemala's political image abroad. The task included missions to foreign governmental officials and businesses abroad, in order to improve Guatemala's image and lobby against the guerrillas. Already since the middle of the 1970s, ongoing (war related) human rights abuses had turned Guatemala into an **international pariah state** (e.g. Sereseres 1985b: 97). Protests by governments as well as NGOs such as Amnesty International visibly distressed the country. The guerrillas had at this point in time already established close diplomatic relations to various countries (e.g. the United States and in Europe) and lobbied successfully for their concerns and for Guatemala's international isolation (Central American and Caribbean Program 1985: 9; Sereseres 1985a: 34-37). The international political strategy of the URNG, was however, not chal-

---

17 Due to the coup by Ríos Montt in March 1982, the campaign did not end as envisaged.

lenged by similar efforts from the Guatemalan government. The Guatemalan businessmen aimed to mitigate this deficit.

In 1977, for example, US-president Jimmy Carter withdrew military and economic aid from Guatemala and set up a trade embargo, followed by the first travel warning (Travel Advisory) for Guatemala, emitted in 1981. The **corporate economic hardships** of those measures were even more severe, since the breakdown of the CACM in 1980 and the massive decline in tourism had taken its toll on the Guatemalan economy.

Although the private business sector feared the impact of international condemnation, their activities in the international arena remained limited at this point in time. Apart from activities in the context of the *Campaña de los mil días*, the only measure information is available for is about corporate support for Ronald Reagan's presidential campaign: A number of Guatemalan entrepreneurs considered Carter ("Jimmy Castro") a communist in the White House who threatened to harm the economic relations between the two countries. In consequence, individual Guatemalan businessmen **supported Ronald Reagan's election campaign** with about USD 2 million (Escoto/Marroquín 1992). In subsequent years, after Reagan's victory, he carefully eased the US-embargo and by 1982 the US erased Guatemala from the list of human rights offenders (Black 1984: 160; ODHAG 1998: 106; Molkentin 2002: 157).

6.3.1.3 Changing relations between the military and the private sector

It was argued earlier that end of the 1970s, beginning of the 1980s, the relationship between the Guatemalan business sector and the military started to rift. Since the beginning of the 1960s, the majority of the **private sector** held the position – although never expressed in public – that the army should defeat the guerrillas militarily. Both the military and the private business sector alike, considered the guerrillas as a national threat. Or as one businessman has put it "the guerrilla was our enemy". Also the amplified war damages in the late 1970s and early 1980s did not prompt the corporate sector to suggest alternative, peaceful solutions to end the civil war, as one may expect following the argument that the private sector has a self interest in peace.

At the beginning of the Lucas regime the relationship between the private sector and the military, based around the idea of having a common foe, was still functioning well. The army "was in charge" of **controlling the war and guaranteeing a favourable business environment**, a strategy that included the control of popular movements (Schirmer 1998: 37). Also the massacre in Panzó, for example, was interpreted by some as a result of this liaison. Augilera argued that this massacre was part of the overall military strategy to provide private enterprises (including "military businessmen") with safe and stable working conditions: "This 'creation' of conditions involves not only infrastructural works, labor mobilization, etc, but also creation of the necessary 'social peace', i.e., preventing the development and mobilization of popular organizations which could hamper the project of capitalist development"(Aguilera Peralta 1979: 22).

However, the relationship between the army and the private sector lost much of its original quality with the mounting levels of corruption (CEH 1999d: §598), insurgency success and quarrels over economic and political topics. During the Lucas regime a downward trend in their relation began, which continued in the subsequent administrations.

The second peak of the civil war can be considered an interface in which the business sector still needed the army for security reasons, but at the same time grew more independent from the military rulers. **Breaks in the relationship** did initially not develop so much because of differences over the counterinsurgency strategy, but much rather over political and economic questions. The defeat of the army over the guerrillas in 1983 made the close coalition between the corporate and the military sector largely unnecessary for the private sector from a security point of view. Quarrels over economic and political issues loomed ever larger and the private sector had hardly any incentive to compromise with the army.

The **contentiousness** between the private business sector, represented by CACIF and the military administration reached its first climax in 1981 with disputes over raising export tariffs, personal enrichment by army officials, land confiscation and repatriation of capital (McCleary 1999: 46). Some (e.g. General Gramajo) even conjectured that private business actors were responsible for the coup against Lucas that replaced him with Ríos Montt "who then brought his own people and the two split apart once again" (Schirmer 1991: 13).

Regardless of if (parts of) the private business sector directly supported the coup, Ríos Montt's takeover was originally widely welcomed by the Guatemalan business community. From the outset, Ríos Montt promised to eliminate corruption, defeat the insurgent forces and reduce violence. **The business sector welcomed Montt's** counterinsurgency strategy, including the *Plan Nacional de Seguridad y Desarrollo*. They appreciated the military activities as well as those parts of the Plan that attempted to improve the rural living conditions by for example, cultivating new agro-export products in the indigenous highlands. Those activities seemed necessary and had the further advantage of not challenging the private sector's interests.

Still, already some months after Ríos Montt assumed office, not only his economic policy but also his counterinsurgency policy became a major **stumbling block for the relation between the private business sector and the military regime**, leading to the second climax in the worsening relationship with the military rulers. In March 1982, still before the defeat of the insurgency, the military junta published the *Plan Económica a Corto Plazo* (Short-term economic plan). The plan aimed at bringing the country out of the economic crisis, solving the financial problems, reactivating productive activities and reducing unemployment rates. However, the plan failed and the economic situation even deteriorated.

Following this, the finance minister invited 14 individual Guatemalan entrepreneurs who – in his perception – were representatives of the private business sector and submitted the ***Propuesta de Acción Conjunta*** (Proposal for Joint Action). The *Propuesta de Acción Conjunta* triggered a public dispute between the private business sector and the military government, directly related to the counterinsurgency strategy.

Similar to the current demands by national and international agencies for corporate engagement in conflict management "simply by doing business", Montt's Proposal for Joint Action asked the Guatemalan business community to increase production and to accept economic sacrifice so that the country could escape the economic and political crisis. In addition, it requested direct financial support from the entrepreneurs for the governments counterinsurgency strategy. In detail, the requests included:

- Repatriation of USD 100 million in 1982 and USD 200 million in 1983. This money had been transferred by Guatemalan businessmen to foreign bank accounts during the climax of the armed conflict. It was hoped that this money would help reactivate the national economy.
- Direct financial support for the army's counterinsurgency campaign (Q15 million in 1982 and Q45 million in 1983).
- Increase of the level of private, national investments.
- Accept and support decree 502-82 that would regulate the spending of foreign currency for different kinds of products according to national priorities.
- Acceptance and support for press censorship.

It was suggested that if the entrepreneurs would agree to grant funds to the counterinsurgency approach, the businessmen could decide where and for which particular elements of the army's strategy the funds should be used. In return, the military government would intensify the counterinsurgency plans until the defeat of the guerrillas; establish a special credit system for agriculture business; hold steady the level of state employees; privatize some state companies and – most importantly – would not undertake an agrarian reform (Figueroa 1991: 197-199; Memorándum reprinted in Valdez/Prado 1998: 56-57).

The fourteen invited executives forwarded the proposal to different business associations. None of the military's suggestions were accepted by the interest groups. In March 1983, CACIF explained that they would not be interested in collaborating, neither with respect to a **contribution to the national counterinsurgency campaign**, nor regarding the reactivation of the economy. Businessmen did not repatriate their capital; capital flight actually even increased due to Guatemala's precarious financial situation, related to the persistently instable political and difficult economic situation (Figueroa 1991: 200; McCleary 1999: 49-54). The request by the military regime was the first time that the Guatemalan private sector was asked to systematically support the ending of the violent conflict but similar demands should be made again in future. However and despite of the civil war, which at the time the army came forward with its proposal was not decided yet, the private sector rejected any kind of support leading to less conflict-aggravating conditions and a quicker end of the armed conflict. Their negative response was clearly not rooted in a rejection of a military solution in principal. But the corporate groups considered the suggestions as "non of their business" and as an interference into their liberty as independent entrepreneurs. In addition, the private sector did not acknowledge that their business operations were part of the problem contributing to the insurgency's success. Instead, they considered the violent conflict and its endings first of all as the army's responsibility, outside the realm of the private economic.

In the course of the subsequent **quarrel**, Ríos Montt argued that the private business sector would foster the civil war, e.g. by paying "*impuestos de guerra*" to the guerrillas and by not paying the statutory minimum wages to their workers. This would lead to greater impoverishment of the rural population and consequently to a higher propensity of the rural population to join the guerrilla. The new military doctrines had already contained this argument in principal, when it stated that an improvement of the economic situation was precondition to a defeat of the guerrilla, but now it was used in the context of open antagonism against the private sector[18] (Figueroa 1991: 203-204).

Differences over tax issues and an impending agrarian reform worsened the relationship even more[19]. The Ríos Montt administration was in severe need of monetary income, in part in order to cover the costs for the counterinsurgency campaign. This had become a particularly acute need since the US-government cut off military aid. But **tax increases** remained anathema for the private sector. The private sector and the government finally reached an agreement to increase value added tax (VAT). But shortly afterwards, it became public that Ríos Montt planned an **agrarian reform** (July 1983). Based on a study by USAID, Montt intended to reform the land tenure structure – an overt offence against the business sector. Just a couple of weeks later, Mejía Victores putsched himself into power and neither the tax nor the land reform were realized.

Under Mejía Victores the *pugna* (meaning 'long-lasting quarrel') between the private business sector and the military rulers continued and deepened the gulf between the army and the economic elite (Gramajo Morales 1997). Since the guerrillas had been militarily defeated, civil war related issues were of little relevance and provided little potential for conflict. Disputes continued to erupt above all over socioeconomic questions and tax issues. The ongoing difficult financial situation had already prompted the IMF into action during the Ríos Montt administration, demanding a significant increase in governmental tax revenues.

---

18 Many of the officers that had been entangled in the coup against Lucas, had served in military outposts in rural areas and had witnessed the impoverished living conditions of the population.
19 For more examples on Ríos Montt's 'fire and brimstone' speeches against the private business sector, see McClintock 1985: 235.

CACIF continued to oppose vehemently and suggested in contrast to privatize state enterprises and to reduce public spending. The government finally failed to comply with IMF's requests and the monetary organization suspended payments (CEH 1999d: §656-659; McCleary 1999: 57-60).

In 1984/1985 constitutional changes that were proposed in the context of a broader constitutional reform, added more oil to the fire. The argument ignited on paragraph 39, which stipulates the role of private property in society and the rights of the state to intervene. The private business sector successfully opposed the introduction of the term **"social function of private property" in the new constitution**. The entrepreneurs feared that this expression would be the beginning of an agrarian reform and the introduction of communist ideas. The Chamber of Industry wrote for example in a *campo pagado*: "Private property not only refers to the big capital. Also your lot, your house, your car are private property [and they are in danger]." (ODHAG 1998: 227).

The third **nadir of the confrontation** was reached in spring 1985. Repeated power breakdown, a quarrel about a consumer protection law, shortages of foreign currency and petroleum, the reorganization of popular organizations in addition to heated strikes resulted in CACIF declaring a work stoppage (*paro*) (McCleary 1999: 60-62). The government tried to master the aggravating situation by establishing a National Dialogue between CACIF, popular organizations, government representatives etc., however, with little success.

Despite severe disagreements between the military rulers and the private business sector, the entrepreneurs supported Victores **move towards democracy**. Having experienced in recent years increasing self-confidence of the military and poor performance in the realms of economic policy and reliability, the private business sector welcomed the transition to a procedural democracy[20].

With the seeming military defeat of the insurgency, the private sector was lulled in a certain **sense of security** and war-related risks lost much of its volatile nature. Although they staid sceptical as to the economic recovery of the country (see next chapter), other political issues moved into the centre of attention. Those threats that still radiated from the guerrilla (see next chapter) were considered minor. The private sector was used to a level of uncertainty and the violent conflict was widely interpreted as under control.

---

20 The Chamber of Tourism, for example, considered the democratic election of president Cerezo as a significant improvement of Guatemala's international image that would generate raising numbers of visitors (Prensa Libre 1986).

7 The Costs of Peace: Entering the Peace Process

The de facto military victory over the guerrillas in 1983 did not bring an immediate halt to the civil war. Instead, fourteen more years of low-intensity war passed, before the Guatemalan government and the insurgency formally ended the armed conflict with a peace agreement in 1996. In 1986, the peace process formally began. A conducive international environment and the democratic opening of Guatemala in the 1980s facilitated the possibility of a negotiated settlement of the civil war.

It was suggested earlier that not only a violent confrontation may result in costs for business, but that also peace can bring about corporate losses. In the following chapter, this idea will be analysed within the context of the Guatemalan peace process. It will be argued that the majority of the entrepreneurs opposed the peace process, though with variations over time and among different groups. Overt rejection occurred first, before acceptance (though not support) for the peace process began to prevail, paired with a strong attempt to influence the outcome of the peace negotiations according to the interest of the private sector. Variations between different groups of the private sector were largely based on ideological convictions (closely linked to generational differences), and not so much in terms of economic differences, such as branches or geographical location.

It will be shown that the measures the private sector assumed largely against the peace negotiations were primarily lobbying as well as political and legal campaigns. In accordance to what was suggested in chapter 3 the Guatemalan business sector was clearly most concerned about the economic and political consequences of the peace talks and the risks of physical attacks was used as an argument *against* the peace process instead of in favour of it.

7.1 Negotiating interests: The business sector during the commencement of the peace process

7.1.1 Guatemala enters the road of negotiations

In November 1985, Vinicio Cerezo from the Christian Democratic Party won the first democratic and free elections in about 40 years. His victory was welcomed by the business sector. But similar to previous governments, the initially good relationship did not persist for very long. Soon after he assumed office, the **new president and the private sector** entered into a relationship that accelerated towards confrontation. Being aware of the political influence of the entrepreneurs and their necessity for the economic recovery of the country, Cerezo repeatedly attempted to build alliances with the business community. He, for example, nominated prominent businessman Rodolfo Paiz Andrade as finance minister in his cabinet and set up a national consultation processes (*concertación nacional*) in which the private sector could bring its position to the table. But Cerezo's attempts to ease the relationship with the business sector failed.

Major stumbling blocks included structural questions over taxation, equity and democratization. While the armed conflict itself had lost much of its immediate political urgency, the **structural challenges** that gave rise to the civil war in the first place were still present and formed potential sources for violence to rekindle and intensify.

In particular, the military pressured to tackle those issues. The **army**, although not formal governor of the country anymore, was still a prominent player in the Cerezo administration. They had safeguarded various privileges in the constitutional amendment made in 1985 and secured significant influence on the civil government. Of particular impact during the Cerzo administration was the newly developed military Thesis on National Stability (*Tesis de Estabilidad Nacional*). The thesis formed a continuation of Ríos Montt's "National Plan of Security and Development" of 1982. It intended:

i. to turn the Guatemalan army from an "army of occupation" to a "national army", emancipating itself from the US-implemented Cold War national security doctrine as well as the Guatemalan private business sector;
ii. to tackle the massive social problems that yielded the guerrilla movement (Jonas 1991: 166). "The key elements of the Thesis, military fundamentalism, exhorts officers to prepare justification for military actions both towards their troops and domestic elites, as well as toward Washington and Geneva. At the same time it rejects its historically subordinated role vis-à-vis the ultra-right latifundistas who, for the most part, see no need to justify the use of the military for a 100 percent solution to dissent and insurgency" (Schirmer 1998: 238).

President Cerzo supported the concept. Making the military de facto independent of the private sector was considered a must for democratizing the country as well as the army (Schirmer 1998: 189, 204). General Héctor Gramajo, defence minister under Cererzo and a key leader in the development of the *Tesis de Estabilidad Nacional,* tried to **dissolve the clientelist entanglement of the *finqueros* and the army** by prohibiting for example "the army from guarding private property or accepting food and lodging from *finqueros* as compensation for 'killing the union leader organizing his workers'" (Schirmer 1998: 208).

In addition, the army proclaimed, very similar as during the Rios Montt administration that it had saved the private sector from communism in recent decades and that now, in return, the private sector should support the social agenda of the Plan of National Stability. The military and Cerezo demanded that the **businessmen pay their "social debt"** in the form of increased taxes, appropriate salaries for workers and productive investments in order to prevent violence from rekindling (Schirmer 1991: 12; Gutiérrez 1995). This resembles in many ways the idea of private business sector participation in conflict management, as it was introduced in chapter 2 – although the idea of corporate engagement in conflict prevention was not systematically developed yet. The request by the Guatemalan military based essentially on the reasoning that the private sector is part of the problems leading to the emergency of the violent conflict, and should therefore be part of the solution and take responsibility.

On one key event during which the new military doctrine was presented, a conference entitled 27 Años de Lucha por la Libertad (27 Years of Struggle for Freedom), the military lobbied for the corporate sector's support and recognition for the new counterinsurgency strategy. In detail, they requested their acceptance for an increased tax burden that would reduce Guatemala's fiscal deficit and finance the counterinsurgency policy. The military emphasised that injustice, poverty and social problems were the breeding grounds (caldo de cultivo) for the guerrilla movement and that the private business sector had to contribute to combating this (Anderson/Simon 1987: 9-11; Prensa Libre 1987c; Prensa Libre 1987a; Jonas 1991: 166-167).

General Gramajo stated in the daily press in the context of the *Foro 27 Años de Lucha Por la Libertad* that the private sector: "has to consider the social economic priorities of the country. If they do not pay the social debt, the subversion will grow and Guatemala will have three debts to pay: the social debt, the political debt and the military debt. You have to increase this in order to fight the subversion." (Prensa Libre 1987a).

The entrepreneurs refused. Instead, the private sector rejected any responsibility for the emergence of the armed conflict, and made the army responsible for poverty and for the "killing of innocent people" (Schirmer 1998: 238). Moreover, it blamed the Christian Democratic government and the institutional line of the military for advocating communist ideas. In particular, UNAGRO **feared leftist tendencies in Cerezo's politics**, leading ultimately to an agrarian reform.

Indeed, since the democratic opening of the country, **popular organizations** regained strength and pressured for social reforms, which undermined the private sector's trust in the government. To give some examples:
- Beginning of the year 1988, the *Conferencia Episcopal de Guatemala* (CEG – Guatemalan Episcopal Conference) published a *carta pastoral* entitled *Clamor por la Tierra* (Clamour for Land). The church therein took a clear stand for the need of an agrarian reform – also as a requirement for a stable peace (Palencia Prado 1996: 11). The *carta* triggered immediate resistance by UNAGRO, publishing statements against the church's involvement in the issue (UNAGRO 1988; Rosada-Granados 1999: 201).
- The church, union and *campesino* organizations increasingly supported and organized invasions of *fincas* in various occasions. Occupation of private land increased in many parts of the country.
- In the early 1990s *campesinos* striked in the sugar plantations and factories on the south coast in demand for higher wages[1]. Representatives of ASAZGUA affirmed that the strike did not originate in their factories, where the workers were content with their working conditions, but instead claimed that the work stoppages were stirred up by outsiders (Prensa Libre 1990e; Prensa Libre 1990a). However, the strike worsened. The *campesinos* negotiated with UNAGRO and CACIF but a favourable outcome for the workers was not obtained (CEH 2000: 220).

In order to handle the "*pro-tierra*" movement, Cerezo decided (among other elements) to distribute state *fincas* among landless families[2]. UNAGRO conjectured that Cerezo was inclined to make more far reaching concessions to land and labour organizations, opening a Pandora's Box, leading to a fully fledged land reform (Schirmer 1998: 208).

Throughout Cerezo's presidency no agreement was reached between the two elite groups on these structural questions. Instead, the relationship oscillated between heavy **disputes and attempts at reconciliation**. In 1988, for example, Gramajo accused the private sector of being involved in the attempted coup against president Cerezo. Shortly afterwards, he partially retract his accusation, qualifying that also within the agrarian elite exist modern businessmen, willing to assist in the development and democratization of the country (Crónica 1988b; Crónica 1988a). Likewise, Cerezo attempted to integrate the private sector into the development of his national development plans (e.g. the *Programa de Reordenamiento Económico y Social de Corto Plazo* or the *Plan de Reorganización*

---

1 In 1988 the major Guatemalan labour unions consolidated their increasing influence with the foundation of the umbrella organization Unidad de Acción Sindical y Popular (Jonas 1991: 181; McCleary 1999: 83).
2 Cerezo's initiative remained a timid attempt that due to a lack of technical, financial and social support was doomed to fail (Inforpress Centroaméricana 1987: 4, 55; Jonas 1991: 184; ODHAG 1998: 246).

Nacional, known as PREN)[3] and to accomplish agreements on national economic policies[4]. But in autumn 1987, the **relationship** escalated over tax issues and CACIF organized its second *paro* (work-stoppage) (McCleary 1999: 75-80).

The lack of trust in Cerezo's administration was aggravated by globally difficult **economic circumstances**, increasing crime rates, homicides (e.g. the murder of the president of the Chamber of Industry, Ramiro Castillo Love), kidnappings, drugs trafficking and sporadic guerrilla attacks (Prensa Libre 1989d; Prensa Libre 1989e). Consequently, the business sector only modestly intensified its business activities. General growth rates, private investment rates, "non-traditional exports" and investments in construction only increased modestly since 1987. Unemployment and underemployment rates increased, exchange rates deteriorated and inflation rates raised. Although the civil war was not a severe threat anymore, entrepreneurs remained sceptical about the economic situation and continued to send money abroad (Jonas 1991: 83). Abating war related violence did consequently not bring about the anticipated economic recovery. Employment and investment rates remained low with little signs of a change in the near future.

7.1.2 The agreements of Esquipulas I and II

The Guatemalan guerrillas had lost most of their fighting vigour by 1983. But Victores as well as Cerezo **maintained counterinsurgency remedies** (e.g. *Operación Fin de Año* 1987, *Fortaleza* 1988), even if on a significantly lower scale than Ríos Montt or Lucas (Jonas 1991: 190-191; Molkentin 2002: 201). However, with Vinicio Cerezo assuming presidential office, the armed conflict entered a new stage. In his election campaign, Cerezo had promised to search for a political settlement to the conflict, and indeed, during his presidency he took the first, modest steps towards a peaceful solution of the civil war.

A misunderstanding in the Guatemalan press is generally considered the **beginning of the national peace process**. In February 1986, shortly after Cerezo assumed office, the URNG announced that they would not impede the new president's promise to establish democracy and peace in the country. Although misinterpreted by Guatemalan newspapers as a ceasefire offer, URNG's announcement is still perceived as the beginning of the Guatemalan peace process.

---

3   Cerzo's Economic and Social Reordering Program originally intended to increase salaries for teachers and social workers, subsidising medicine and different agricultural goods, fuel etc. and the creation of jobs in rural public services. In large parts due to objections by the private sector, only public wages were raised. Neither the job program, nor subsidies were implemented and the educational program was reduced substantially. In return the commercial sector withdrew from insisting of privatisation of state firms and accepted moderate public spending for social programs (McCleary 1999: 76).
4   In 1986 CACIF published for the first time "their" national vision in the document "Guatemala: Pasado, Presente y Futuro" (CACIF 1986).

At this very moment, however, none of the key players were ready to enter into a serious dialogue over a peaceful settlement. Neither the civil government, nor the military, nor the insurgency were prepared or willing to look for a nonviolent solution of the armed conflict. President Cerezo made direct negotiations with the URNG contingent on URNG's surrender – a demand the guerrillas rejected until 1995. The military claimed victory over the insurgency and rejected negotiations with the guerrillas. And the URNG for their part doubted that the government was really inclined to realize a comprehensive democratization process due to Cerezo's alleged predisposition to the economic "oligarchy" (Morán 2002: 63, 65-67). For all parties, there was in addition **no real need to enter into negotiations**: the guerrillas did not impose an immediate threat to the state and the insurgency could persist on a lower scale, without being at risk of being eradicated entirely. Beyond this, 1986 was still a year of cold war reality. Although the constitution of 1985 allowed communist organizations (Azpuru 1999: 102), anticommunism and ideological oppostion still influenced official decision making processes and made it hard for the government and the URNG to begin peace talks.

The Guatemalan peace process gained slight impetus when Central-American countries entered into a **region-wide peace initiative**. In May 1987, the presidents of Central American countries met in the Guatemalan town of Esquipulas in order to discuss the issues of armed conflicts and potential peace processes in the Isthmus. The so-called *Esquipulas I* meeting did not bring concrete results for a peace process, but gave rise to a follow-up meeting in August 1987. Initiated by the Cost Rican president Oscar Arias, the second round ended with the signing of the document "*Procedimiento para establecer la paz firme y duradera en Centro América*" (Proceeding for the establishment of a firm and lasting peace in Central America), better known as the contract of *Esquipulas II*.

In eleven paragraphs *Esquipulas II* outlined the principals for national peace initiatives in the region. It obligated from the signatory states to continue with the process of democratisation, realize free elections, enter into a dialogue with the insurgency groups, stipulate an amnesty law, and establish a national reconciliation commission (*Comisión Nacional de Reconciliación*, CNR). The CNR was considered a central tool to launch a dialogue of the governments "with all disarmed groups of the internal political opposition and with those [groups] that sought sanctuary in amnesty" (reprinted in INCEP 1987).

The **reactions** towards *Esquipulas II* were mixed. Some considered the declaration as a "real peace accord" (Inforpress Centroaméricana 1995: 19), whereas others criticized its unbinding nature and its restriction to dialogue only with *disarmed* opponents (Dietrich 1990: 279-280). The URNG embraced the agreement in various *campos pagados*, but General Gramajo publicly raised doubts about whether or not the contract would be executed in Guatemala.

The private business sector, similar to other popular organizations, barely got involved in this phase of the peace process. One major reason for this was that the negotiations for *Esquipulas I and II* did not provide room for civil society engagement. Apart from a more general paper ("philosophic paper" as one business executive put it), expressing CACIF's hope for a quick settlement of Central American civil wars, the Guatemalan private **business sector did not engage in this early stage of the peace process**. Some had speculated that although Guatemala's entrepreneurs may resist a domestic peace process, they may advocate for more stable external conditions: Guatemala was at this time the biggest inter-regional exporter in the Isthmus. The industrial sector in particular had experienced severe setbacks in their exports due to the war related collapse of markets in its major regional trade partners. Between 1982 and 1986, regional exports of the industrial sector declined from USD 654 million to USD 303 million (Dietrich 1990: 251). Although the private business sector was in principal interested in peace for the region, little was actively done at this stage.

7.1.3 Implementing Esquipulas II: The private sector begins its resistance

Cerezo did not show much commitment in fulfilling the agreement of *Esquipulas II*. Indeed, until 1990 the **government's activities remained rather halfhearted**. In order to comply at least formally with the accord, Cerezo launched a meeting with the insurgency in the autumn of 1987. Low ranking government and military delegates met with representatives of the URNG in Madrid. Deliberately planned as a mere conversation and not as an initial dialogue, there were no further encounters between the government and the URNG in the following years. Instead, fighting between the guerrillas and the military intensified again.

Additional to this, Cerezo complied with a second provision of the Esquipulas agreement, the formation of a national reconciliation commission. In September 1987, the vice president, members of the church (Rudolfo Quezada Toruño as chair, and Juan Geradi), officials of different political parties and representatives of civil life, including the future president of Guatemala, Jorge Serrano, formed a **national reconciliation commission**, CNR. At the end of 1987, the CNR and the URNG held several meetings and in October 1988 the CNR convened a National Dialogue (*Diálogo Nacional*).

The first session of the **National Dialogue** was held end of February 1989. Although not a large success, it opened the peace process to a wider audience. The creation of a National Dialogue was certainly far away from the concepts of multi-track diplomacy or peace constituencies as introduced in chapter 2. However, it was a move into this direction. As will be outlined below, the business sector represented by CACIF, decided (although invited) not to participate in this initiative. This position foreshadowed CACIF's recalcitrant standpoint towards the peace process that they kept nearly unrestricted throughout the next seven years.

More than 80 representatives of nearly 50 **civil society organizations participated**, representing labour unions, the churches, media and press, the business sector and political parties. The Dialogue formed 15 working commissions, discussing major social, economic and political topics (e.g. commissions on indigenous rights, on socio-economic topics, the process of democratization and the role of the military in the country) (Palencia Prado 1996: 11; Alvarez 2002b). Bitterness resulted from those organizations that did not participate in the Dialogue, including CACIF and the military[5].

After long-lasting internal debates, **CACIF had decided not to join the National Dialogue**. The organization argued that they were neither a "disarmed group of the internal political opposition" nor a group that "sought sanctuary in amnesty", as stipulated for the composition of the CNR in *Esquipulas II* (reprinted in INCEP 1987). On 23 February, CACIF announced: "Its important to maintain a attitude of caution and responsibility in the participation of an event of national significance in which neither the proceedings and final propositions nor the representativeness, legality and legitimacy are still clear" (Prensa Libre 1989b).

Two days later – three days after the beginning of the dialogue – CACIF stated in the press that still no definite decision had been made on their participation in the National Dialogue. Only 3 May, Juan Luis Bosch, than president of CACIF, declared that they would not take part (Prensa Libre 1989b; Prensa Libre 1989c).

Probably more than any other organization that had chosen to boycott the dialogue, **CACIF was criticised for its absence**. Monseñor Quezada Toruño, coordinator of the CNR and various other delegates lamented CACIF's decision. Some argued that a National Dialogue, without CACIF as one of the most prominent civil organizations in the country, would undermine the entire forum (Prensa Libre 1989a). Others conjectured that exactly this – a destabilization of the initiative – was part of CACIF's strategy to enfeeble the peace process.

This speculation was additionally nourished by CACIF's participation in the ***Centro de Estudios Estratégicos para la Estabilidad Nacional*** (Centre of Strategic Studies for National Stability – ESTNA). ESTNA was a military based institution, founded at the end of 1988 by Defence Minister Gramajo and supported financially over several years by USAID[6]. The centre intended to promote the "Theory on National Stability" and aimed at achieving national security in a democratic system by consensus building and dialogue.

---

5 The URNG was not allowed to take part because of resentments by the president and the military. They argued that the insurgency was a group of only about 700 individuals, "not representing anybody in Guatemala", politically as well as militarily stalemated and desperate for negotiations.

6 Two prominent private sector representatives, Juan Luis Bosch and Ramiro de Castillo Love, were members in ESTNA's board (McCleary 1999: 74-75).

At the end of September 1988, ESTNA organized its first round table with about 70 participants from different sectors of Guatemalan society, including amongst others, individuals from the private sector, such as Edgar Heinemann, president of CACIF and Arturo Pellecer, former president of CACIF and president of the Chamber of Tourism (Inforpress Centroaméricana 1995: 34). ESTNA's foundation, its activities and CACIF's participation were largely interpreted as an attempt to build a **counterweight to the CNR** (e.g. Jonas 1991: 166). In addition, this was also seen as a sign of persistent suspicion on the part of the military and the private sector towards popular organizations in general. Even though the relationship between the army and the business sector had deteriorated in recent years, the private sector could rely on a much stronger bond of trust with the army, than between the business sector and popular organizations.

In the case of Guatemala, the private sector was not, as assumed by some (see chapter 2.3.2), the neutral actor with vibrant **communication channels** to numerous civil society groups. In contrast, CACIF as the main representative of the business community was neither impartial nor was it provided with close contacts to other non-state groups. In the following years, CACIF started expanding their links to those players but in the late 1980s suspicion regarding popular organizations and relative closeness to the military characterised their position.

In this early phase of Guatemala's peace process, more **vehement resistance** than from CACIF emerged from another grouping of Guatemalan society, a clandestine group of ultra-rightists entrepreneurs and army officials in the form of the so-called *"oficiales de la montaña"*. The appearance of such as fundamentalist grouping suggested already at this stage that the business sector was divided over the issue of the peace process: the hardliners who categorically rejected it and those who opposed the peace process but were willing to compromise.

Prompted by the Madrid meeting between the URNG and governmental officials, the *"oficiales de la montaña"* re-surfaced in October 1987. Although there is no accurate information on the exact compilation of the *oficiales*, they are conjecturally a fusion of ultra-conservative individuals from the military and the business community, held together by a deep sense of anticommunism (Schirmer 1998: 208-212) (see also chapter 5.2.2.5). According to General Gramajo, one of the leading figures from the private sector is Gustavo Anzueto Vielman (see chapter 5.2.2.5).

The *oficiales de la montaña* appeared for the first time in 1966, during the government of Julio César Montenegro, accusing the president of being a communist (Schirmer 1998: 208). In 1987, the *oficiales* published *campos pagados* in daily newspapers, criticising the government vehemently for the meeting with the insurgency and apprehending the state already in the grip of the communists (Crónica 1988b). Later in 1988, the *oficiales* were linked to an attempted coup d'état against president Cerezo. A civil court prosecuted Gustavo Anzueto, together with five other civilians (including Nicolás Buanofina, a *finquero* and economic adviser to Ríos Montt) for being responsible for the attempted overthrow (Prensa Libre 1988). The *oficiales de la montaña* were the first group apart from the MLN that emphatically and publicly objected Cerezo's peace initiative[7].

7.1.3.1 A turning point? CACIF meets with the URNG

In 1990, Guatemala's peace initiative made a significant step forward. Although the progress made in Guatemala in this year was still less courageous than those in other conflict ridden parts of the Isthmus, they went far beyond what many had expected would be possible after the clumsy start of the peace process with the National Dialogue.

A global political easing of tension due to the end of the Cold War, advances in the peace processes in neighbouring countries (in particular Nicaragua), and above all enhanced international pressure, forced Guatemala's government to put more emphasis on the pacification of the country. In particular, rising human rights violations (e.g. a massacre in Santiago Atitlán) (Jonas 1991: 163) and the killing of an US citizen in the department of Petén impaired the relationship between the USA, the European Community and Guatemala. The international community subjected aid money to compliance with certain conditions such as an improvement in the human rights situation and progress in the peace process (Dunkerley 1994: 81-82). At the same time, the URNG gained more and more international recognition and influence (e.g. ODHAG 1998: 282).

In addition, official statistics for the years 1989 as well as 1990, counted a rising number of assaults against targets like road tankers in Nebaj, Quiché or Petén or attacks against pylons in Antigua y Sacatepéquez (Inforpress Centroaméricana 1995: 45). CACIF warned the public that a further deterioration in the situation would have negative economic consequences, resulting in increasing unemployment and capital flight, a decline in investment and a negative influence on the tourism industry. It directed its criticism primarily towards the government, complaining about its inability to cope with the threats.

The key achievement of the peace process in 1990 was a meeting between the URNG and CACIF. Early this year, the CNR and the insurgency met in Oslo, resulting in the signing of the Acuerdo Básico para la Búsqueda de la Paz por Medios Políticos ("Basic Accord for the Search of with Political Means" or "Accord of Oslo"). The agreement stipulated the initiation of a series of direct meetings between diverse groups of Guatemala's civil society and the URNG (known as the "Oslo Consultations").

---

7   In the beginning of president Serrano's presidency the oficiales de la montaña reoccurred, yet less often than during Cerezo's term in office. Similar to their emergence during the Cerezo-administration, they appeared in 1991 after Serrano had realized his first step in favour of a peace process and threatened to destabilize the peace process (CERIGUA 12-18 May 1991).

The first meeting of the "Oslo Consultation-Series" took place in El Escorial, Spain in June 1990, when the URNG met with political parties. Even the MLN participated and returned positively from the encounter. Four further meetings followed: a meeting with CACIF in Ottawa, Canada in August; a meeting with the religious sector in Quito, Ecuador; with the popular sector and trade unions in Metepec; and a final meeting with a heterogeneous group of corporate interest groups, cooperatives, academics and intellectuals (the Instancia Multisectorial) in Atlixco, Mexico.

The meeting between CACIF and the insurgency was probably the most unexpected one of all. CACIF only decided to accept the invitation after protracted internal discussions within the umbrella organization. Still at the end of June, only a month before the actual meeting occurred, CACIF had not yet decided definitively whether or not they would participate in a meeting with the insurgency (Bolanos de Zarco 1996: 496).

CACIF was split in two over the question of the Oslo-meeting. A group that wanted to boycott it, opposed a faction in favour for the encounter. Jus to give some examples of the differences in opinions: At the beginning of June, for example, a former president of CACIF, Roberto Cordón Schwank, rejected publicly a dialogue with the URNG until the insurgency laid down their weapons[8]. On the same day, Víctor Suárez, president of the Chamber of Industry, proclaimed that he welcomed a dialogue with the guerrilla organization (Prensa Libre 1990c). Two days later an individual agriculturalist from the South Cost published a campo pagado, arguing against the Socialist-Leninist worldview of the URNG and rejecting the meeting (Anonymous 1990). A similar opinion was expressed by Adolfo Boppel, president of UNAGRO and former president of CACIF. A couple of days before the journey to Ottawa in which he participated, he stated the insurgency had based their economic ideas on Marxist-Leninist ideology, but that this model had failed throughout the world and that the guerrillas had to look for an alternative political agenda (Prensa Libre - Domingo 1990).

The arguments in favour of and against a dialogue with the insurgency were numerous. Those who supported the meeting pointed out that although the insurgency had lost most of their military strength, they still would have the capacity to seriously harm the Guatemalan economy. Guatemala's road infrastructure, the dependence of the country on only two power stations made Guatemala extremely vulnerable to internal attacks. Entering into a dialogue with the insurgency would be the only feasible option to curb this risk. Those against the meeting argued that the insurgency was an illegal force, and overall, militarily defeated. Talking to them would be tantamount to legitimize this small group of "terrorists" and strengthen the leftist enemy.

---

[8] Although, Cordón emphasised in an interview that he would not talk as a CACIF representative, it was clear that his opinion was common within the umbrella organization.

The debate was contentious and opponents accused the "pro-peace" faction of traicionar a la patria (betraying the native country). Contrary to what one might expect, the gulf between the opponents and advocates did not run along the different business chambers. Although voices against the meeting and the peace process came more frequently from the agricultural sector, members of the other business associations also opposed the meeting.

The major challenge for CACIF was to find a compromise that bridged the gap between the opponents and the advocates. Finding a joint position was even more essential, since internal cleavages within UNAGRO overshadowed and weakened the unity of the organization. CACIF decided to commission a study on URNG's chances in future elections, before taking a final decision on the Ottawa meeting. The business sector was well aware that the Oslo consultation was the prelude to a political process, leading to the recognition of the URNG as a political party, and legitimatising the insurgency as a negotiation partner in peace talks. CACIF had closely observed the course of the peace processes in neighbouring countries, in particular in El Salvador. The prevention of URNG from gaining long-term political influence was a major concern for CACIF before the Ottawa-meeting.

The result of the analysis was positive for the private business sector. In contrast to the late 1970s and early 1980s, when the guerrillas enjoyed much support among large segments of the Guatemalan population, CACIF's "election forecast" revealed that the URNG would come off badly in the case of elections. Indeed, the end of the Cold War as well as the increasing number of acts of sabotage against civil infrastructure targets had undermined its popularity.

Between July 1989 and August 1990 alone, the number of guerrilla attacks against primarily civil targets, including infrastructure facilities in cities, bridges, transport ways and electricity pylons increased from about 289 to about 314 (Inforpress Centroamericana 1995: 56). Despite the economic harm of these attacks, CACIF was aware that these assaults had the positive side effect of diminishing popular support for the URNG and leftist ideas in general.

However, CACIF remained careful. Before the meeting with the URNG in an attempt to get the support of all members of the organization, CACIF decided behind closed doors to meet with the insurgency, but not to sign a joint declaration with the insurgency. All other bilateral meetings of the Oslo Consultation resulted in a joint statement. The encounter between CACIF and URNG was the only one that ended with two separate declarations.

Between 30 August and 1 September, 16 delegates of the private business sector met with nine representatives of the URNG in Ottawa. The corporate delegation included, Jorge Briz, than president of CACIF and president of the Chamber of Commerce; Víctor Suárez, president of the Chamber of Industry; and directors and presidents of UNAGRO, the Chamber of Finance and the Sugar Association.

The insurgency acknowledged that the delegation of the private sector consisted of representatives of a younger generation of businessmen, "with a different vision about events, adopted to our times"(citation by Víctor Suárez in Bolanos de Zarco 1996: 132). But after the first day, the discussions came to a standstill over ideological divergences. The delegations decided to form a smaller group, integrated by three members of the comandancia guerrillera and three member of CACIF. The talks went on, but as agreed internally by CACIF in advance, the meeting ended with two separate declarations.

However, both statements as well as a series of internal communications concur surprisingly in many respects: both sides assured their disposition to search for political ways to end the armed conflict, acknowledged the necessity to tackle root causes of the war, and to promote a democratic system with respect for human liberty in all its manifestations. Divergences were rooted primarily in structural issues. The URNG explained in a press conference after the Ottawa meeting that discords ignited above all on different perceptions of what had given rise to the armed conflict, such as the unjust economic system. CACIF in turn declared that: "[…] during the conversation, that developed in an atmosphere of respect and goodwill surfaced discrepancies, which as the private sector repeated have to be solved and overcome peacefully and within the framework of the Constitution".

In the same way as throughout the coming years of the peace process, CACIF stressed two of its principal demands: that the insurgency should lay down their weapons (as stipulated in Esquipulas II) and respect the constitutional order by becoming incorporated into civil political life (Prensa Libre 1990d; Prensa Libre 1990b; Inforpress Centroaméricana 1995: 51). The demands guaranteed a halt to corporate war damages, while minimizing the risk of leftist changes in the political system due to URNG's estimated small chances of success in future elections, as the study commissioned by CACIF showed (Inforpress Centroaméricana 1995: 51; Bolanos de Zarco 1996: 133-134, 517).

Neither the discords during the meeting nor the lack of a joint declaration could however obscure the significance of the encounter. For the first time ever the organized private business sector met with the guerrillas to talk about a peace process. Just a couple of years earlier this would have been unthinkable. CACIF therewith dissociated publicly from dissolving the armed conflict with military means.

The meeting of the URNG with CACIF was followed by dialogues with the religious sector, trade unions and, finally a last meeting with a group in which some corporate interest groups were again represented.

The so-called Instancia Multisectorial that met with the insurgency in Atlixco at the end of October 1990 embraced three business associations: FEPYME, the Chamber of Exportation (Cámara de Exportación) and the General Association of Guatemalan Commercialists (Asociación General de Comerciantes Guatemaltecos, ACECOGUA, General Association of traders in Guatemala)[9].

Internal quarrels between CACIF and the other three corporate interest groups, in particular with FEPYME, impeded a joint meeting with all Guatemalan business associations in Ottawa. FEPYME considered itself an interest group, established to form a counterbalance to CACIF and to represent especially those enterprises whose interests were not sufficiently respected in the umbrella organization (see chapter 5.2.6). By participating in the meeting of Atlixco (and later on in the Asamblea de la Sociedad Civil, ASC), FEPYME intended to strengthen its political stance within Guatemala. Being politically comparatively insignificant, the peace talks were considered an opportunity for the interest group to lobby for their economic-political ideas. Although FEPYME's vision, political and economic arguments in the context of the peace process, did not diverge significantly from those of CACIF, it was a political question and a question of long-term influence as to why FEPYME participated in Atlisxco and the ASC (Asamblea de la Sociedad Civil – Civil Society Assembly).

7.2 Progress and setback during the government of Serrano

The meeting in Ottawa at the end of August in 1990 crowned the corporate involvement in the peace negotiations for the following four years. During Serrano's presidential term (1991–spring 1993), who followed Vinizio Cerzo in office, the private sector hardened its positions again, showing nearly any willingness to enter or accept a dialogue with the insurgency, in particular not about those issues that gave rise to the armed conflict.

7.2.1 Increased willingness to make concessions: Serrano's first Peace Initiative

At the end of 1990, Jorge Serrano Elías unexpectedly won the presidential election. He was candidate for the *Movimiento de Acción Solidaria* (Movement of Solidarity Action – MAS), a comparatively unknown political party founded by Serrano himself shortly before the elections. His election promised **fresh impe-**

---

9 The Chamber of Exportation and ACECOGUA only joined this meeting in Atilsxco and did not contribute to any further events related to the peace process. FEPYME however, also participated in the Coordinadora Civil por la Paz (Civil Coordination for Peace, COCIPAZ) that had the task of supporting the peace process (Alvarez 2002b) and in the Asamblea de la Sociedad Civil (Civil Society Assembly). The members of COCIPAZ were more or less identical to those groups and organizations that met in Atlixco. (For more details on COCIPAZ see Ponciano Castellanos 1996: 76-85).

tus for the peace process: Serrano was not only a former member of the CNR, and had, as the only presidential candidate, emphasised the importance of the peace process in his election campaign (McCleary 1999: 86), but he was also the first president after the ending of the Cold War.

In his inaugural in January 1991, Serrano announced that his peace policy would comprise an armistice as well as negotiations aiming at **addressing the "root causes"** of the conflict – a commitment that went clearly beyond what Vinicio Cerezo's had been able or willing to achieve. In spring of the same year, Serrano published the document *Iniciativa para la Paz Total de la Nación* (Initiative for Total Peace of the Nation). Among others, the plan stressed the significance of the national constitution, the importance of ending armed hostility, and proposed to meet (*in camera*) with the insurgency. Up to then, the Guatemalan government had conditioned a dialogue with the URNG to a prior (unilateral) cease-fire, arguing that negotiations with armed and illegal forces would infringe the constitution. Serrano emphasised his standpoint by maintaining military measures against the guerrilla, claiming that he would demand from neither the army nor the insurgency to lay down weapons[10]. Indeed, both sides – the military and the guerrilla – intensified the armed struggle during Serrano's presidency and the Guatemalan military launched an intense offensive against the guerrillas (Misereor 1999: 306).

Serrano's peace initiative was well received amongst the Catholic Church, labour unions and parts of the private business sector. The Chamber of Commerce, for example, published a *campo pagado* in the daily press (Cámara de Comercio 1991), welcoming Serrano's plan. Other entrepreneurs and military officials, however, strongly **disapproved of the peace plan**. In fact, Serrano's peace initiative in various ways went against the actual ideas of the private business sector. The private sector had made clear in the statement after the Ottawa meeting and in other occasion that they rejected talks between the government and the insurgency and any kind of concessions to the guerrillas without a prior cease-fire. In fact, the previous government had followed this strategy. The business sector interpreted Serrano's plan as a surrender to foreign and international pressures, violating the constitution by accepting negotiations with an illegal group that did not even have broad support among the Guatemalan people (Palencia Prado 1996: 15).

---

10 Another initial sign that Serrano may have sought to choose a path different from his predecessor was his strategy towards the military. Whereas Cerezo closely collaborated with the army, Serrano intended to forestall the army's influence on his politics. For instance, he dismissed his first defence minister Colonel Luis Enrique Mendoza García who had publicly demanded the URNG's surrender as the basis for negotiations and replaced him and other members of the army in leading positions with officers more familiar with and more in favour of the peace process (Inforpress Centroamericana 1995: 85; McCleary 1999: 86-87).

In a consultation that Serrano's government organized for CACIF and the managing boards of the different chambers[11], a corporate representative even proposed to the governmental delegates to intensify their military activities against the insurgency: "One of their representatives said to me that there would be 1200 guerrilleros and why we would not finish with them. And why we would not ask for economic help from CACIF, from the private sector, in order to make a war and to finish with 1200 who where in the mountains." (Interview by author with representative from the governmental peace commission).

Seemingly as a response to the corporate resistance against the Plan, the "Initiative for Total Peace" dedicated some lines, explaining the economic advantages of peace: "Reaching total peace will be the point of departure for our country. You will see this in what we will this receive in terms of international cooperation, in foreign direct investment and in tourism inflow."

Despite the discontent among large parts of the corporate sector and the military, Serrano started an initial round of dialogue with the URNG at the end of April 1991. The first meeting was held in Mexico. The newly created governmental peace committee, *Comisión de la Paz* (COPAZ), which functioned as the main state-organ for the peace process and incorporated military executives as well as civil delegates, represented the government. The negotiations resulted in the signing of the first of thirteen peace accords between the government and the guerrillas: the *Acuerdo del Procedimiento para la Búsqueda de la Paz por Medios Políticos* (**Initial Framework Agreement**).

The agreement stipulated eleven issues that should be negotiated in the peace process and differentiated between **substantive and operational themes**. The substantive themes under point one to seven comprised issues such as democratization and human rights, constitutional reforms, socio-economic aspects and the agrarian situation. The operational issues under point eight to eleven included topics such as the integration of the URNG into civil life, or a definite armistice. The order of the themes stipulated the chronological sequence in which the issues should be negotiated: the substantive themes first, followed by negotiations on the operational issues (Aguilera Peralta 1996: 4). Serrano thereby continued to clearly act against the key demands of the private sector, which had always insisted on reaching a cease-fire first. The signing of the Agreement of Mexico was in this respect crucial for the future negotiations: it determined the future course of the peace negotiations and stole the thunder of those factions within Guatemalan society (including parts of the private business sector) that opposed negotiations with the guerrillas.

In June 1991, overshadowed by continued guerrilla attacks against infrastructure targets (e.g. oil installation, pipelines, telephone poles and electric towers)

---

11 During the Serrano-administration COAPZ had a number of meetings with different business organizations.

and political murders[12], the URNG and COPAZ met again for a second round of negotiations. On the agenda were the first themes of the Initial Framework Agreement: **democratization and human rights**. The meeting was more difficult than the first one. The parties reached an agreement only after a second encounter in Querétaro, Mexico. In July 1991, the *Acuerdo Marco sobre Democratización para la Búsqueda de la Paz por Medios Políticos* (**Accord of Querétaro**) was signed. Due to opposing concepts on the topic of human rights, the accord only covered the issue of democratization. Human rights issues were postponed to a later stage. The Accord of Querétaro agreed on basic, but important democratic principals, including the acceptance of the existing constitutional order[13], the precedence of the civil society, the recognition of the identity and rights of the indigenous people, the subordination of the military forces under civil powers and the resettlement of the displaced population.

The core achievement of the accord was certainly the **formal recognition of the constitution** by the URNG. But the signing of the agreement triggered little public debate. There was a broad acceptance among nearly all sectors of society, including the private sector for a formal democratic system in Guatemala. The reinforcement of these values in an accord with the insurgency was important, but not contentious.

The **issue of human rights** was by contrast much more sensitive. Negotiations continued but remained fruitless. The URNG attempted to include highly sensitive issues that complicated the negotiations, including an amnesty for human rights violators, the establishment of a Truth Commission or the dissolution of the PACs. In several meetings, no consensus could be reached. Tension between the parties accelerated into a public disputes and at the beginning of the year 1992, the peace negotiations came to a standstill.

---

12 The cases of the murder Michael Devine and kidnapping and torture of Dianna Ortiz, both US citizens, as well as the homicide of the Guatemalan anthropologist Myrna Mack were and the killing of José Miguel Mérida Escobar, an official of the National Police who investigated the homicide of Mack were some of the human rights cases that triggered massive national and international discussions on the general human rights situation in Guatemala.

13 The accord did however not exclude the possibility to propose constitutional reforms within the constitutional framework. This will become important later on, in the context of discussions about changes of paragraph 39.

7.2.1.1 Increasing rifts between the private sector and the URNG: A public dispute over war and peace in spring 1992

At the end of April 1992, the URNG launched an **attempt to revitalize the stagnated peace talks**. In a *campo pagado*, entitled "Guatemala, a Just and Democratic Peace: Contents of the Negotiations" (*Una paz justa y democrática: contenido de la negociación*), the guerrilla organization analysed the origin of the insurrection from their perspective and plead for renewed negotiations. They suggested finding first an agreement on the still pending human rights issues, followed by negotiations on the other themes stipulated in the Initial Framework Agreement.

URNG's statement triggered a **lively discussion** within the Guatemalan society. Numerous civil organizations, political parties, as well as the government responded with their own public announcements. The business sector belonged to those sectors who got most strongly involved in the debate (for reprints of the different campo pagados see Molkentin 1993).

The first public statements came from the AGA, followed by a *campo pagado* by CACIF (see Table 12). Already a couple of weeks before the publishing of the *campo pagado*, guerrilla commander Rodrigo Asturias (ORPA) had argued that "obstinate sectors and big landowners had hardened their position" (Inforpress Centroaméricana 1995: 95). The CACIF's and the AGA's reaction to the guerrilla's document indeed revealed **widening disparities** between the entrepreneurs and the insurgency.

Table 12: Timetable of the different statements regarding the peace process between May and June 1992

May 1992	Campo Pagado by the URNG entitled "Guatemala, a Just and Democratic Peace: Contents of the Negotiations"
29 May 1992	Statement by the AGA
08 June 1992	Statement by CACIF
11 June 1992	Statement by a group of civil society organizations
29 June 1992	URNG response to CACIF's statement from 08 June
30 June 1992	Statement by the government

In the guerrilla's initial *campo pagados,* the URNG had made **numerous references to the role of the corporate sector** in the emergence as well as in the potential solutions of the armed hostility. Among the most important were:
- accusing "small economic interest groups" of having contributed to the militarization of the country;

- making "egoism of a few" responsible for pervasive social injustice;
- declaring extreme land concentration and labour exploitation as a fundamental source of poverty.

However, the insurgency did not advocate for the abolishment of market principals. They recognized the necessity of reasonable profit rates, but argued for a more equal distribution of economic rents. Correspondingly, the URNG demanded:
- the introduction of a new development concept;
- improvements in labour legislation and an increase in minimum wages;
- adequate housing facilities for the workers on the *latifundas*;
- the dissolution of the close relationship between the military and *latifundistas*;
- a comprehensive promotion of exports, foreign direct investments and small and medium size enterprises and cooperatives;
- the amendment of paragraphs 39 and 40 in the constitution "so that the *social function of property* comes to effect";
- measures against fallow land and an "amendment of the current agricultural laws, investigation and the revision of the allocation of state land and the restitution of property rights which have been withdrawn or usurped";
- the introduction of specific laws in the constitution, considering the rights of the indigenous population.

Obviously, although the insurgency backed off from some extreme leftist ideas they had held in the 1970s and 1980s, the majority of the URNG's demands and interpretations were **incompatible with the private business sector's point** of views and interests. Increases in the minimum wages or measures against fellow land were diametrically opposed to what the private sector lobbied for.

The **AGA's response** to URNG's statement left little doubt about their opposition and deep distrust. The agriculturalists characterized the URNG as "the visible face of a subversive movement" that manipulated the Guatemalan population. Alike to previous discussions[14], the AGA categorically rejected any sort of constitutional amendment including changes in paragraphs 39 and 40, defending the existing laws as adequate to solve the national defects and emphasising that

---

14 Shortly before this campo pagado, the AGA had published another statement, in which they condemned in more general terms the grievances prevailing throughout the country, in particular rising crime rates, corruption and economic and social deterioration. They blamed politicians and "extremists groups" for being responsible for the "national crises" (AGA 1992). The background for the first statement were ongoing bombings and violent attacks that had wracked the country since the beginning of 1992. Nobody claimed responsibility for the attacks. The army blamed the URNG, who denied any involvement. Others made political parties and the business sector responsible for the assaults who allegedly intended to obstruct the peace process.

the guerrillas' continued attacks violated these laws. The AGA's involvement in peace process related issues, independent from CACIF, was certainly a consequence of AGA's withdrawal (respectively UNAGROs separation) from the umbrella organization in February 1991. The agriculturalists were worried about losing political ground and leverage. URNG's public statement did not only touch one of the AGA's core concerns, but provided a possibility to get involved in public discussions.

CACIF's response to the URNG's *campo pagado* was published about a week after AGA's statement, in 08 June 1992, and supported a similar view. CACIF's *campo pagado* came down to a hard-line political offence against the URNG. In the introductory historical analysis, they equated Jacobo Arbenz Guzmán's presidency (1951–1954) with a totalitarian regime, which was allegedly massively supported by the PGT. The guerrilla movement itself was characterized as antidemocratic, influenced by Marxist and Maoist ideas that intended to imply a totalitarian regime. They were made responsible for Guatemala's miserable living conditions and economic status, the destruction of infrastructure and the militarization of the country. In addition, CACIF repudiated URNG's reproach of labour exploitation in rural areas and objected to any kind of land reform or constitutional amendment. They vehemently opposed URNG negotiating substantive themes of the peace process and continued to limit their ideas of a peace process to an instant cease-fire. URNG's demand to stronger integrate civil society organizations into the peace process was rejected as well, on the grounds that this would undermine the authority of the government.

One central intention of CACIF's declaration, additional to articulating their views, was to discredit the URNG politically, weaken their position at the negotiation table and to undermine their political support basis. The private business sector (as well as the army) had underestimated the relevance and magnitude of the **national (as well as international) political support** for the URNG. They were becoming more and more aware that while the insurgency had lost the war on the battlefield, they were about to win it politically. Throughout Serrano's presidency and also before, the insurgency commandants and their political-diplomatic team advocated for their positions. They regularly visited, for example, European and American governments and NGOs (e.g. URNG's "Europe Tour" at the beginning of 1992) as well as international organizations in order to campaign for their ideas (see also below). When the European Parliament, for instance, blamed Serrano for being responsible for the slow advancements in the peace process due to his lacking will to "make firm commitments to improving respect for human rights" and when the United Nations showed their supported for URNG's demand to dissolve the PACs, this was interpreted as the fruits of URNG's diplomatic success.

The **URNG replied** to CACIF's *campo pagado* about three weeks later. Likewise as CACIF in its *campo pagado*, the URNG lapsed back into stereotypes, blaming the business association as "the privileged minority" that was resistant to structural changes in order to uphold its power position. Moreover, the URNG made CACIF responsible for the outbreak of the armed conflict:

"It seems to be illusory and unlikely to expect that CACIF could overcome its traditional mindsets and approaches. Social forces, like those CACIF represents – in order to say this very frankly here – are the most responsible persons for the ruling inequalities and injustice in the country that finally led to the confrontation and polarisation among the Guatemalans. Traditionally they always vehemently resisted against changes that the country needs, in the interests of all Guatemalans and not only in the interest of a few – and they sill oppose against these changes persistently. [...] CACIF ignores and denies Guatemala's history in order to justify the enforcement and maintenance of his own interests against all other positions and forces that automatically are ostracised or if necessary are even eliminated with violence, like it occurred in 1954. Therewith it is responsible for the backwardness and permanent political and social instability." (URNG 1992: 87).

The URNG also proposed a meeting with CACIF but the proposals remained without response.

CACIF's continued rejection to assume **responsibility** for conditions that contributed to the civil war was understandable from a strategic point of view. Realizing and admitting to be "part of the problem" would probably have resulted in a stronger integration of the business sector and economic factors in the settlement of the violent conflict – something the private sector was not interested in, given the costs. Although a rather different set of factors, the Guatemalan entrepreneur's position reminds of examples from contemporary violent conflicts. DeBeers, for instance, initially denied contributing to the perpetuation of civil wars, partly due to ignorance about the consequences of their operations. Only after they understood and admitted their entanglement, they began to participate in conflict prevention and management strategies. The private sector in Guatemala, however, never recognized that issues such as poor labour conditions or inequalities were part of the web of factors propagating the violent conflict. They instead made the government and the insurgency responsible for the civil war.

At the end of June, about one month after the publication of URNG's initial document, the government responded. They **revealed a disposition to continue with the peace negotiations**, but excluded very contentious themes, including the role of the military, constitutional reforms[15] and an extended influence of

---

15 Serrano dedicated several paragraphs in the declaration, explaining that constitutional reforms cannot be stipulated in the peace accords as the congress or the constitutional assembly was by law the only institution that can enact changes in the constitution. Yet, throughout the peace process, the insurgency insisted on discussing constitutional changes.

civil society organizations in the peace process[16] from the agenda and postponed them to future negotiations.

7.2.2 Serrano's second peace initiative and the issue of human rights

The government and the URNG resumed negotiations over human-rights issues but the peace process could not recover. The negotiations started with debates over the **role of the PACs**, a central sub-issue of the human rights topic. In late summer 1992, an agreement was reached. The government consented to refrain from the formation of more PACs "as long as nothing happens to motivate such actions [to further the establishment of PACs]". The agreement was to come into force as soon as an accord on the other sub-themes of the human rights topic was signed. The PACs had been a key security measure during the armed conflict, created during the administration of Ríos Montt (see chapter 6.3.1). But private business organizations did not comment on the agreement. The main reason for this was that PACs had only assumed security and defence functions in regions, where no *fincas* or plantations were located. In other words, the security situation of private business estates in rural areas was barely affected by the dissolution of the PACs.

Negotiations on the human rights accord dragged on through the rest of 1992 without reaching a final agreement[17]. At the beginning of 1993, Serrano took the initiative once more and presented nationally and internationally, the "**Proposal for the Quick Signing of a Firm and Lasting Peace in Guatemala**" (*Propuesta para la pronta firma del Acuerdo de paz firme y duradera*). The ambitious proposal aimed to achieve the signing of a final peace accord within 90 days: the government would agree to an immediate verification of a human rights agreement (including the establishment of a Truth Commission) and negotiate subsequently any topic pending. In case a final peace agreement could not be accomplished within the 90 days timeframe, a cease-fire would be declared and the guerrillas would be concentrated in areas determined by the Guatemalan government and under supervision of the United Nation. Negotiations on the still unsettled substantive and operational themes would then continue, at two parallel negotiation tables.

Serrano's suggestion triggered varying reactions. Critics argued that it would be impossible to negotiate the open substantive issues in 90 days. Serrano's pro-

---

16 In the course of the debate, popular organizations also published their opinions on URNG's campo pagado.
17 Rumours emerged about an attempted coup against the president and about "intransigent sectors" composed of hardliners of the military sector (cofradía), drug dealers, right-wing politicians and agricultural entrepreneurs, who opposed the continuation of the peace process from behind closed doors (Inforpress Centroamérica 1995: 100).

posal was considered (also by the URNG) tantamount to attaining an armistice without addressing the substantive issues, let alone integrating civil society groups in the consultations. Others appreciated the chance of a formal end to the violent conflict in the near future. Notwithstanding the justified criticism, the URNG surprisingly agreed on a bilateral cease-fire, provided that some amendments would be incorporated in Serrano's plan. Amongst other things, the URNG requested the involvement of civil society groups in the negotiations. Serrano rejected the insurgencies counterproposal and the **initiative failed**.

The international community belonged to those who received the plan more positively. The United Nations in New York and the UN Human Rights Commission in Geneva welcomed the initiative. Both before and at the time Serrano developed the strategy he was under strong pressure from international and bilateral agencies to deal with the **persistent human rights violations** and Serrano's peace plan has to be interpreted as a response to this pressure (see for example Misereor 1999: 305-306)[18]. Soon after Serrano presented his initiative, for example, a new session of the UN Human Rights Commission in Geneva commenced (CERIGUA 7-13 March 1993). At the commission, countries are denounced for human rights abuses, according to different categories. Category "12", for example, is reserved for countries in which human rights have been systematically and gravely violated. Serrano, afraid of a cutback in international economic assistance, endeavoured successfully to prevent his country from being classified under category 12. The Human Rights Commission acknowledged that "the internal armed conflict is a fundamental factor affecting the human rights situation in Guatemala". Serrano's attempts for further peace talks were interpreted as a way of curbing war-related human rights violations in the future (UN High Commissioner for Human Rights 1993).

Also the private business sector was aware of what was at stake economically through continued human rights violations. Threats by the US government, for example, to suspend duty free trading privileges under the General System of Preferences had shown the potential **economic consequences of severe human rights violations** (CERIGUA 4-17 April 1993). In January 1992, CACIF had appealed publicly for Guatemala not to be condemned by the UN-Human Rights Commission as a major human rights violator. According to the corporate sector's perspective, human rights abuses only occurred occasionally and were committed to a significant part by: "groups that operate on the brink of the law, particularly armed insurrectionists. [...] It always exist the danger that some bad Guatemalans and some interested foreigners can create with inexact accusations a negative environment for the economic activity of the country [...]" (Statement by Luis Reyes Mayen in Siglo XXI 1992).

---

18 The Guatemalan indigenous leader Rigoberta Menchú won the Nobel Peace Prize in December 1992. This and the intensified fighting directed again more international attention to the human rights violations in Guatemala.

Making the insurgency responsible for the human rights violations was part of the private business strategy to discredit the guerrillas internationally. But the entrepreneurs were not willing to tackle the economic costs resulting from (civil-war related) human-violations through the means of a peace process[19].

In line with their persistent rejection of peace talks, the private business sector also opposed Serrano's second peace plan. Shortly after Serrano's proposal was published, CACIF's president Mario Granai Fernández sent a letter to Serrano, expressing **CACIF's concern** about the course of the peace process: "We ask that no document be signed that does not exclusively lead to a firm and clear commitment for a cease-fire, the demobilization and disarming of the URNG" (cited in McCleary 1999: 94).

CACIF also rejected a proposal by Serrano to send delegates to a **government mission** that sought to present Serrano's plan to the United Nations in New York. Serrano aimed to compile for this mission a committee of representatives from different sectors of society, including political parties, labour unions and the press, as a show of broad national support for his new peace strategy to the international community. However, CACIF and the different business chambers refused to appoint representatives, due to their lack of approval for his peace-politics. Serrano tried to convince influential, individual members of the corporate sector with a more supportive attitude towards the peace process, such as Luis Reyes Mayen[20] to join him on the mission. But the entrepreneurs refused.

Since Serrano assumed office and presented his first peace initiative, the private business sector had become **more and more suspicious and opposed** to Serrano's peace policy. His strong personal will and "ambition to become the next Nobel Peace Winner" and the raising international pressure let the private business sector fear that Serrano would be willing to make far-reaching economic

---

19 CACIF had repeatedly demanded the implementation of a UN-verification commission (the later MINUGUA, Misión de las Naciones Unidas en Guatemala, that started its mission yet not before November 1994), as stipulated in the human rights accord of April 1993. Luis Reyes Mayen and Juan José Gutierrez, representatives of CACIF, for instance expressed the need for a quick implementation of the commission, hoping for an improvement of Guatemala's international human rights image. A newspaper cited Mayen in the following way: "The businessman believes in the functioning of the Commission, and continued, ' [the commission] will dismantle once and for always all those tendencies and permanent assertions of groups of Guatemalans and foreigners, who sustain that in Guatemala exists a systematic violence of the human rights'. [...] the commission will bring an objective point of view to a theme that was manipulated by the guerrilla and its support groups and that had provoked a serious damage for the country" (Siglo XXI 1994a). (For more details, see for example Siglo XXI 1994d; Siglo XXI 1994b; Siglo XXI 1994c). CACIF considered the verification commission as an internationally renowned organ that would publicly denounce URNG human rights violations and violations against the already signed peace agreements.

20 Reyes Mayen was member and ex-president of the CAG.

and political concessions to the insurgency and relinquish the national agenda just to get a peace agreement signed.

Whereas during the government of Vinicio Cerezo the risks and costs of a potential peace seemed limited, **under Serrano the risk increased that peace would imply significant cost to the private sector.** Cerezo himself did not prioritize the peace process and the close coalition between Cerezo and the army that shared similar views regarding a peace process as the private sector, made it unlikely that a peace process (if it would happen at all) would lead to detrimental outcomes for the business community. In the Serrano government, however, the army played a much smaller role (see footnote 10: 165) and Serrano seemed willing to discuss and compromise over highly sensitive issues, such as land reform and private property rights. The private sector's hardening position with respect to the peace process during the Serrano administration was largely due to their fear that their interest could be disregarded in peace talks with the insurgency, resulting in significant costs for them

7.2.3 The Serranozo and Instancia Nacional de Consenso

Despite the setback for Serrano's second peace initiative, negotiations continued. But in May 1993, after long and fierce discussions over human rights issues and the order of the pending negotiation issues, Bishop Quezada Toruño declared an **impasse in the negotiations**. The government responded with the announcement to intensify their war against the guerrillas, intending to eradicate the URNG through military means.

However, the abrupt ending of Serrano's presidency prevented this threat from being realized. Almost simultaneous to the rupture of the peace talks, the Christian Democratic Party and the National Centrist Union dissolved their coalition with Serrano's political party, the MAS[21]. Social unrest by students and teachers, tensed the situation in the capital. Serrano Elias popularity hit rock bottom. On 25 May, Serrano suspended – supported by parts of the military – the constitution and dissolved the congress and the supreme court. He reasoned that this measures, which later came to be known as the ***Serranozo*** or ***auto-golpe***, was justified on the basis of pervasive corruption in all state institutions, the lack of credibility of the congress and the entanglement of some members of congress in drug trafficking.

---

21 The weak results of the MAS in the national election in 1990 had forced Serrano to build coalitions with other parties in parliament. Serrano initially entered into an alliance with the Party of National Advancement (PAN), a party with close relations to the private business sector. The coalition with the PAN floundered in 1992 and Serrano entered into a new coalition with the Christian Democratic Party (Democracia Cristiana – DC) and the National Centrist Union (Unión del Centro Nacional – UCN).

Serrano's coup was confronted, what for Guatemala was a very unusual opposition: a unified civil society. The day Serrano staged the coup, he asked for backing from CACIF. But the umbrella organization rejected any cooperation and appealed for an immediate reimplementation of the full constitutional order. Subsequently, CACIF searched for like-minded organizations and established the **Instancia Nacional de Consenso**[22], an amalgamation of diverse civil society groups, all demanding the return to the constitutional order. The temporary coalition of such a large range of groupings was widely praised as one of the rare occasions in Guatemala's history in which organizations that for decades had been hostile and suspicious to one another, suddenly cooperated in order to fight for a common cause: the reinstallation of democratic rule.

Indeed, a couple of days after Serrano staged the coup, the *Instancia* managed to bundle together diverse civil society organizations (and later also the military), and **forced Serrano to resign** from office. Mainly due to pressure from the *Instancia,* the national congress decided to elect an interims president: former human rights ombudsman, Ramiro de León Carpio, who assumed office in June 1993.

Yet, more detailed analysis of the *Instancia* revealed that "leftist" organizations and those with direct or indirect relations to the URNG[23] either did not participate in the *Instancia* (although they had occasional contact) or their participation made finding a **consensus "extremely difficult"** (McCleary 1999: 138). Some of the popular groups that aligned with the *Instancia,* blamed CACIF for having misused the *Instancia* for its peculiar interests. Decisive meetings between the private sector and (parts) of the military, for instance, had been arranged without including the popular organizations[24]. Furthermore, some of the popular groups saw the *Instancia* not only as an opportunity to reinstall the democratic order and to support the process of cleaning the congress and govern-

---

22 CACIF appointed on the 25th of May seven members of the organized private sector who formed a Strategic Committee, named El Foro Multisectorial. Five days later, 30th of May, after a wide range of social sector groups had coalesced with the Foro Multisectorial, they changed the name into Instancia Nacional de Consenso.
23 For details on the connections between the for example the CUC and the Acción Católica and the guerrillas (primarily the EGP), see for a example Arias (Arias 1990: 252-256).
24 The coup was likely to bring about negative economic consequences and the private business sector was aware of it. Rachel McCleary summarized the expectations of the corporate sector as follows: "Because of the political crisis, the private sector predicted that there would be an immediate surge in demand for U.S. dollars, that prices would increase, that foreign credit would be suspended, and that investment coming into the country would slow down if not stop altogether. [...] In sum, the closing of foreign markets, freezing of international financing, scarcity of U.S. dollars, speculation on and rise in the exchange rate leading to the erosion in reserves, and the drastic reduction in tax revenues would set Guatemala back, placing it in a situation that would tale tremendous effort and time to overcome." (McCleary 1999: 121).

ment of corrupt politicians[25], but also as a chance to reach national agreements on the "substantial themes" of the peace process. These organisations complained that the private business sector had impeded the broadening of the *Instancia* into an ongoing national dialogue (McCleary 1999: 156-187).

Similar to what has been shown for other organized private sectors in Latin-America, CACIF proved in the *Instancia* that it had a **commitment to a democratic system** (see also chapter 7.2.3). But in the peace process more was at stake for them than the question of a formal democratic government and the businessmen did not intend to compromise with organizations close to the URNG on issues such as economic policy or property rights. Although in the coming period, the corporate sector softened its positions slightly, the peace process remained problematic.

The *Instancia* existed until October 1993. Between the *Serranazo* and the disintegration of the *Instancia* some members finally also dealt with national issues not directly related to the *Serranazo*, amongst others the peace process (see below). But increasing disputes and internal division lead to its **break-up**.

7.3 The business sector gets more involved: The peace process during the De León-administration

The newly elected interims president Ramiro de León Carpio initially enjoyed widespread support and confidence, nationally as well as internationally. Yet, this backing dispersed soon after he assumed office. Persisting human rights violations, a lack of social investments, his controversial peace policy, the way in which he purged congress, and his fiscal policy triggered **discontent and opposition** among nearly all sectors of society.

The **private sector** disagreed with de León in particular about fiscal issues and changes in the tax policies. Despite attempts to increase national revenue, the governmental fiscal income decreased at the beginning of de León's term due to massive tax evasion (CERIGUA 8 July 1993). Corruption-scandals in the context of the privatization of state companies (e.g. the Guatemalan phone company GUATEL) further undermined de León's political credibility among the corporate sector.

The **peace process** entered into its formative years and made significant progress in the two and half years of de León's presidency. After a difficult start, seven accords were signed. However, although differences emerged, the peace

---

25 McCleary claims in her analysis of the establishment of the instancia that one of the objective was to „consolidate the peace process" (McCleary 1999: 138). Yet, my own research and interviews with various entrepreneurs revealed that the peace process played no role when CACIF decided to form a joint movement against the Serranozo.

initiatives were only of minor importance for the ruptures between the government and the private sector. Given the progress in the peace negotiations, increasingly more businessperson began to accept the peace talks as a process they could not prevent from happening. Instead of boycotting the negotiations, CACIF increased its capacity to influence the talks in their interests. However, those groups within the business community that maintained a more hard-line as a consequence, splintered off from CACIF and pursued their own agenda.

7.3.1 The beginning of the peace process under de León

At the beginning of July 1993, de León presented his first governmental peace plan, the *Propuesta para el Reinicio del Proceso de Paz* (**Proposal for the Recommencement of the Peace Process**). The plan was also called *La Initiative Rosada* (Rosada's initiative), according to the proposal's lead author, Héctor Rosada, de León's adviser to the peace process. The major contents of the plan were:
- invite the UN to become mediator for the peace process;
- create a permanent Forum for Peace (*Foro Permanente*) in which the substantive themes of the peace process should be discussed *together* with civil society organizations;
- grant permission to the URNG to travel to Guatemala so that they could participate in the peace talks, including the Forum for Peace[26];
- and start the peace talks from scratch, without considering the previous peace agreements.

The **proposal was rejected** by the majority of the Guatemalan society – although for different reasons. The URNG and popular organizations were not willing to ignore the earlier agreements; some did not want to get the UN involved, and CACIF for their part again declared that de León's plan would infringe the constitution by granting immunity to criminals. CACIF would support the peace process, but only provided it complied with the national legal framework (Prensa Libre 1993b; Prensa Libre 1993a).

In the following months, different proposals were presented – and all of them rejected. In the midst of August, for example, the ***Instancia Nacional de Consenso*** – still in close cooperation with CACIF[27] – published its suggestion for the peace process. The plan was in many ways similar to the governmental proposal: It envisaged negotiations in two tables, one for the substantive themes (equivalent to the *Foro permanente*) and a second one for the operational themes. The dilemma about the participation of the URNG in the *Foro* and in negotiations

---

26 The URNG commanders lived abroad, many in Mexico and were not permitted to enter Guatemala.
27 In particular Peter Lamport and Víctor Suarez were closely involved in developing the proposal.

about substantive themes was to be solved by only inviting the insurgency's diplomatic team to the negotiation table, and not the commanders themselves (Aguilera Peralta/Ponciano 1994; ODHAG 1998: 331-332). Although there was little reaction to the proposal and it was not followed up further, the initiative heralded that the private sector was about to assume a more engaged position vis-à-vis the peace process.

Equally unsuccessful was the first proposal developed by the new governmental peace committee, COPAZ, that was formed in August. Similarly composed as Serrano's peace commission the group comprised representatives of the military as well as the civil sector and was headed by Héctor Rosada Granados, a renowned Guatemalan academic. COPAZ developed a second governmental peace plan, the *Plan Nacional De Paz* (**National Plan for Peace**). Like the previous proposal, this initiative suggested negotiations in two tables, but demanded in contrast to the earlier plan, URNG's surrender as a basis for negotiations. Particularly emphasised in the plan was the fight against the miserable living conditions as a part of the peace process. De León and Rosada had stated already earlier that they sought to build peace in the society and not with the URNG and that "by waging war against poverty" they "want to take away the guerrillas' reason for being" (CERIGUA 2-16 September 1993). But also the National Plan for Peace was received with a lot of scepticism. The URNG, for example, repudiated the plan because it would adopt the private business sector's and the military's ideas (Inforpress Centroaméricana 1995: 203-206; CEH 2000: 227).

Increasing external and internal pressure finally brought COPAZ and the URNG together for direct negotiations in Mexico City in January 1994 – the first direct peace talks since the impasse at the end of Serrano's presidency. The two parties concluded the meeting with the signing of the *Acuerdo Marco* (Framework Accord for the Resumption of the Negotiation Process). The agreement reaffirmed the eleven-point negotiation agenda of the 1991 Mexico Accord and agreed on a continuation of the bilateral talks. In so doing, the government retreated from their earlier demand of a prior cease-fire. In addition, the agreement decided to request that the United Nations mediated the peace process and to establish the so called *Asamblea de la Sociedad Civil* (Civil Society Assembly, ASC). In contrast to the original idea of a *Foro Permanente*, in which civil society organizations were sought to sit at the negotiation table, the ASC was only given the right to develop recommendations to the negotiating parties and to endorse the agreements. Yet, neither the recommendation nor the endorsements were binding for the official negotiators.

In the following weeks, two **further agreements were passed**: the Comprehensive Accord on Human Rights (*Acuerdo Global sobre Derechos Humanos*) and the Accord on the time table for the negotiations (*Acuerdo de Calendarios de las Negociaciones para una Paz Firme y Duradera*). The Human Rights accord agreed that the URNG as well as the government would respect human rights as stipulated in the constitution. Different from all other agreements, the Human

Rights treaty should come into force immediately, and not with the signing of a final peace agreement. The second accord stipulated the time table for the negotiations: It anticipated a cease fire in August or September and the signing of a final peace agreement in December of the same year. Observers immediately criticized the agenda as unrealistic and popular organizations were afraid that the dense schedule would impede a meaningful participation of the ASC (Inforpress Centroaméricana 1995: 212-215).

Despite this positive intermezzo, the peace talks sunk to a new low. The organized private business sector did not take a public stand to the agreements. In the following months, however, they became more engaged in the peace process.

7.3.1.1 The establishment of the Asamblea de la Sociedad Civil and the Comisión Empresarial para la Paz

In spring 1994, Monseñor Quezada Toruño formed and inaugurated the **Civil Society Assembly** (ASC) as stipulated in the Framework Accord from January this year. The ASC aimed at bringing together representatives from all those sectors that had participated in the Oslo consultations in 1990, plus representatives of the Mayan population, women's organization etc. In other words: a wide range of diverse political, popular, religious and university organizations, labour unions and business associations[28]. CACIF, however, decided not to join the ASC.

Similar to many government officials, **CACIF** feared that the ASC would develop into mouthpiece for the insurgency. They held the view that Monseñor Quezada Toruño and many of the participating organizations had a biased position in favour of the URNG. The CUC and a number of labour organizations, for example, were known for having close connections to guerrilla groups. Beyond this, CACIF was afraid of losing, instead of gaining influence over the peace process if they participated in the ASC. First, CACIF would have been considered *the* only representative for the Guatemalan business sector. On a par with numerous small popular organizations, several labour unions, indigenous groups etc., which CACIF in many cases viewed as "illegal and unrepresentative façade organizations", it would have been granted only one voice in the ASC (Alvarez 2002a). Furthermore, the ASC was to reach all agreements by consensus. Given, however, the expected proximity in points of view between the URNG and many member organizations of the *asamblea*, CACIF considered it unlikely that joint decisions could be reached, and expected the assembly's work to be inefficient (for a more detailed analysis of the ASC see Ponciano Castellanos 1996: 85-125).

In the months to come, Quezada Toruño, president Ramiro de León, the URNG and different popular organizations repeatedly called on CACIF to join the *asamblea* (La República 1994a; La República 1994c; Prensa Libre 1994a;

---

28 For more details on how the ASC was organized and functioned, see for example Alvarez (Alvarez 2002a).

Aguilera Peralta et al. 1996). But the corporate organization **rejected the invitation** persistently and rather unanimously. The ASC was concerned that CACIF's absence would undermine the *asamblea's* political leverage, and more importantly, wanted to avert that CACIF's position carried more weight in the negotiations by holding separate meetings with the government, the URNG and other stakeholders.

Indeed, not only was CACIF historically an influential player but it additionally enhanced the organization's institutionalized capacity for peace process-related matters in 1994 and made ASC's concerns about the influence of the private sector on the peace process a tangible risk. More or less since the beginning of the peace process a group for this topic had existed in CACIF. But only in 1994, the group was established more formally and its financial capacity was boosted. The so-called *Comisión Empresarial Para la Paz* (CEPAZ) was an organizational tool in form of a working-group within CACIF with the main tasks to prepare CACIF's strategies on the peace process, collect information, participate in official meetings etc. (see also chapter 5.2.1 on working groups in CACIF). CEPAZ was not, as described in some publications (e.g. Azpuru 1999), a coalition of those in CACIF who had a more favourable view on the peace process. It was, however, a clear singe that CACIF moved from a position of rejecting the peace talks to a position of acceptance, and from a strategy of predominantly boycotting the negotiations to a strategy of lobbying for their interests in the context of the peace process.

A number of factors were certainly conducive for the set up of CEPAZ in 1994:

- With the passing of the *Acuerdo Marco,* the invitation of the UN to mediate the peace process, the continued international pressure and the formation of the ASC, the **peace process became irreversible**. At this stage of the peace process, the question could not be anymore "yes" or "no" to the negotiations, but how to shape their results. Aware of this, CACIF recognized the necessity to establish adequate organizational structures to better influence the outcome of the peace process.
- With the positive course of CACIF's engagement in the *Instancia Nacional del Consenso* in the context of the *Serranazo,* a **group of younger entrepreneurs had gained trust** within the Guatemalan business community. Many of those businessmen, who assumed lead roles in the *Instancia*, also held chief functions in CEPAZ and had an overall more constructive attitude towards the negotiations.
- CEPAZ was the corporate **twin to the ASC**. Whereas with the ASC, popular organizations had established an institutionalized framework for bringing their views to the negotiation table, CEPAZ should be – in the view of CACIF – the corresponding organ for the private business sector. CACIF never agreed that the ASC should be the only organ for civil society groups to

influence the peace negotiations, although a second, separate organ additional to the ASC was not provided for in the Framework Accord.

CEPAZ was largely composed of ex-presidents of the different member-chambers of CACIF in order to lend the working group more weight within the business community and outside. Amongst others Peter Lamport (Chamber of Commerce), Victor Suarez (Chamber of Industry), Carlos Vielman (Chamber of Commerce), Luis Reyes Mayen (Agricultural Chamber) participated. But also other entrepreneurs were **members of CEPAZ**. Gustavo Anzueto Vielman, for instance, who at this time was not even a member of CACIF anymore, was invited to CEPAZ for strategic reasons. CACIF was aware that Anzueto Vielman and the group of businessmen he informally represented, held a much more disapproving and hard-line view on the peace process, than most members of CACIF's *Junta Directiva*. To prevent the faction around Anzueto Vielman unleashing its own political strategy for the peace process and in order to give the private sector a united public face, CACIF attempted to incorporate and fasten Anzueto Vielman to CEPAZ and its position.

Other business organizations and entrepreneurs such as ANACAFÉ often represented through Max Quirin, also collaborated closely with CEPAZ without being formal members. However, some business associations did not incorporate at all in CEPAZ. The Chamber of Tourism, for example, did not join despite its assumedly high interest in a peaceful business climate. Traditionally a rather weak business association, the heavy losses in the tourist branch caused by the armed conflict, further impeded the Chamber's organizational capacity and impaired its participation in CEPAZ. It is not certain if the tourism chamber would have pushed a more progressive and peace-inclined agenda within CACIF, given the close links with the other business groups, but in a number of independent statements the Chamber made clear that they were aware of the relevance to end the civil war in order to increase their business activities.

One weakness of CEPAZ was certainly that it did not manage to closely integrate business executives from outside the capital. Peace process related matters were predominantly **negotiated in Guatemala City**. The central organs of the organized business sector in Guatemala decided basically on all moves and strategies – more often than not without consultation of entrepreneurs in the areas outside the capital. Even those businessmen and corporate interest groups in the second biggest city and upcoming economic centre of Guatemala, Quetzaltenango, have barely been involved in the decision making process. Consequently, those entrepreneurs had little or no knowledge about the peace process and its contents and their views were hardly considered.

7.3.2 Continued dispute between the URNG, CACIF and the AGA

In spring 1994, CACIF and the AGA entered independently from each other into a renewed **dispute with the URNG** about direct guerrilla attacks against private property, specifically about war taxes. The dispute showed clearly that the private sector intended to further weaken the guerrilla organization politically. The URNG, in this case, lost clearly the battle.

In May 1994, the **AGA published a** *campo pagado* in the national press, accusing the URNG of violating human rights and infringing the peace process by collecting war taxes from *finqueros*, threatening them with death and burning down private property. In four direct questions, the AGA demanded that the guerrilla organization take a public stand with respect to the accusations and justify its activities (AGA 1994).

Indeed, in the months previous to AGA's accusations, the guerrillas had again **intensified their attacks against civil targets**. Similar to earlier periods before the beginning of the peace process, bridges and pylons were destroyed, business buildings and commercial centres in the capital bombed, and numerous businessmen kidnapped and assassinated (see newspaper and CERIGUA for this time)[29]. The attacks against economic targets were considered a sign to the "wealthy and well-connected so that [...] they would understand that they cannot control the armed and the powerful" (CERIGUA 21 October 1994). The EGP and the FAR committed the majority of attacks. ORPA deliberately limited its encroachments against civil targets to a minimum, being aware of the political cost of "economic warfare". In fact, attacks against civil targets generated more and more public discontent. They impaired the every-day life of ordinary civilians and *campesionos* accused the guerrillas of mining their fields (Aguilera Peralta et al. 1996: 38, 45). AGA and CACIF for their parts new from earlier experiences that those types of attacks would rather weaken the insurgency among the population than strengthen their position (see chapter 7.1.3.1). Drawing particular attention to those types of attacks would destabilize the URNG politically.

In addition, the press reported increasingly about deteriorating security conditions in rural regions and about **war taxes** (*impuestos de guerra*) being collected by the insurgency, in particular from private *fincas*. Albeit not a new practice (there are reports about the extortion of war taxes dating from the 1960s and 1970s, see also chapter 6.3.1), the guerrilla – and in particular the ORPA – augmented the collection of war taxes since the late 1980s (Holiday 1997: 70-71; CEH 1999b: 489). For the guerrillas the collection of war taxes was not only a measure to finance combat activities, but also a way to make recalcitrant landowners more aware of the armed conflict, hoping that this would lead to a change in their resistance towards the peace process (see for example Inforpress Cen-

---

29 In many cases, it remained, however, unsolved if the insurgency, the army or criminals committed the attacks.

troamericana 1996: 99)[30]. The *Cámara del Agro* spoke about extortion in the order of millions (Aguilera Peralta et al. 1996: 275, 294). The army estimated that the guerrillas had gained approximately 42 million USD between 1978 and 1984 from war taxes, extortion and kidnappings (Prensa Libre 1993c)[31], and CACIF later claimed that in the South coast alone, the insurgency had collected about 2 million Quetzal from *finqueros*.

About one week after AGA's initial *campo pagado* the **URNG responded** with two announcements in the newspapers. In the first, it did not make direct reference to AGA's statement. The URNG criticised CACIF's intransigent position in the peace process and justified the continued armed struggle as a necessary lever, ensuring that the substantive themes are negotiated adequately (URNG 1994a).

In the second *campo pagado,* the URNG directly accused the AGA and big landholders (in the same way as in other occasions), for being accountable for the outbreak of the civil war by violating labour rights, allying with the repressive military regimes and impeding a democratic participation of the Guatemalan population. "They are, thus, one of the principal responsibles of the upsurge of the armed conflict" (URNG 1994b). But beyond this – and certainly more importantly at this stage of the negotiations – the URNG **admitted that they had in fact collected war taxes** and damaged *finquas* of those landowners that refused to pay. In addition, they announced that they did not intend to halt this practice in the near future.

Although nobody would have seriously refuted that the Guatemalan guerrillas extorted money from businessmen, a public confession was a clear victory for the private business sector. Instead of making *finqueros* more responsive to the peace process, with this admission they turned the weapon against themselves. Corpo-

---

30 In 1996 the comandancia guerrillera claimed publicly that members of the business sector had affirmed during the Ottawa-meeting in 1990 that the civil war would not affect their businesses. Allegedly, because of this statement the guerrillas increased the collection of war taxes, hoping to make the finqueros also feel the war in their "own house" (Siglo XXI 1996b; Rosada-Granados 1999: 222). A week later, 10 April 1996, the topic appeared again in the Guatemalan press, this time in a slightly different version. In an article in the daily newspaper Siglo XXI the URNG explained that they had introduced the collection of war taxes after the coup of Serrano in 1993. CACIF had allegedly explained in the context of the auto-golpe that "the war would not affect them and that from their perspective it could go one another 30 years". Furthermore, the guerrilla claimed that the war taxes had a primarily political function, intending to change the position of the finqueros.
It is highly doubtful that the guerrilla only started to collect war taxes in the year 1993 and that it was merely an instrument to assert political pressure. It is much more likely that the different guerrilla organization were depended on the money to finance their fight and that they started long before 1993 – although there are no reliable information when the guerrilla collected war taxes for the first time (Siglo XXI 1996d).

31 Yet, more and more evidence emerged, indicating that many kidnappings were not committed by the insurgency but by the members of the army.

rate war-related costs were now used not as an argument in favour of the peace process as one may expect based on the principal argumentation introduced in chapter 2.4, but as an **argument *against* the peace talks**. Businesses did not argue that because of the costs inflicted through the conflict they favoured a quick negotiated settlement, but they used the costs argument exclusively against the insurgency. All other Central-American guerrilla groups that had been confronted with similar accusations, had disclaimed any responsibility. The accusations against the insurgency not only hit the nerve of a war-weary population, but also the church, the prosecutor for human rights, Mario García Laguarrdia and ODHAG had to take a public stand against the URNG. Later on, also UN Verification Mission in Guatemala MINUGUA (*Misión de Verificación de las Naciones Unidas en Guatemala*) also criticized publicly the URNG for extorting war taxes and for intransigently rejecting a truce (Aguilera Peralta et al. 1996: 51-57, 266; Jonas 2000: 49). Defence Minister General Mario Enríquez, even suggested that *finqueros* could arm their workers and defend themselves against guerrilla incursions. CACIF's president Arturo Guiola Batres, turned down Enríquez's proposal, however, demanded that the army itself should better protect the landowners (Prensa Libre 1994c)[32].

Although it is difficult to evaluate in detail the effect URNG's confession had on its **position at the negotiation table**, it was clearly not conducive. The AGA and CACIF took advantage of their political-diplomatic triumph and interpreted the guerrillas' statement as proof for URNG's limited commitment to the peace process. For the AGA the move had the positive side-effect of improving its stance and position within the organized private business sector and to re-gain closer links to CACIF.

Shortly after the AGA had launched its political crusade against the URNG, CACIF as well attacked the insurgency. Followed by a number of public statements, in which the umbrella organizations had appealed for an immediate cease-fire, a stop to human rights violations and an accelerated peace process[33], the dispute between CACIF and the URNG culminated. In 20 May 1994, it became public that CACIF requested from the public prosecutor to take **legal action against the guerrilla** commanders. In an open letter to the public prosecutor, CACIF asked to launch a lawsuit against Rodrigo Asturias Amado, Jorge Ismales Soto, Ricardo Ramírez de León and Ricardo Rosales Roman for 38 crimes against the national penal code. In detail, the charges included trespassing, duress, threatening behaviour, predation, incendiaries, and depredations.

The political explosiveness of this demand was intensified by the fact that the URNG and CACIF had scheduled a **direct meeting** for the same day, aiming at discussing the peace process bilaterally. The encounter would have been the first

---

32 For a long time, the private sector held the position that the army should assume also tasks of internal security.
33 See Aguilera Peralta et al. 1996.

since the meeting between the URNG and the private sector since Ottawa in 1990[34]. Alienated by CACIF's contradictory manoeuvres, the guerrilla organization did not attend the meeting (Prensa Libre 1994b; Prensa Libre 1994h).

Interview respondents explained that the timely proximity of AGA's and CACIF's move as well as the timely overlap of the planned meeting with the URNG and the attempted law suit were not so much a coincidence or the result of a concerted manoeuvre, but much rather a reflection of two different **factions within the private sector**. The intended meeting with the insurgency had stirred massive discussions within CACIF between the wing that wanted to be more engaged in the peace process and those that were sceptical about any further involvement. It was mainly members in CEPAZ who had convinced CACIF's *junta directiva* of the advantages of another direct meeting with the URNG. However, inspired by AGA's success on the war-tax-admission, another group within CACIF (supported by the AGA) proposed to request legal proceedings against the guerrilla commanders. The suggestion was approved within CACIF, despite the upcoming meeting with the URNG.

CACIF's petition against the guerrilla leaders was turned down about a week later (Prensa Libre 1994f). However, the move drew public attention to the private sector's interpretation of the violent conflict.

7.3.3 The private sector's stance towards the accords for the establishment of a Historical Verification Commission and the return of the displaced population

On the agenda of the peace talks were the next substantive topics, the **resettlement of the uprooted population** and the issue of the **establishment of a truth commission**. COPAZ met various times with the URNG, but only by end of June 1994, the two accords were signed (*Acuerdo para el Reasentamiento de las Poblaciones Desarraigadas por el Enfrentamiento Armado*; *Acuerdo sobre el Establecimiento de la Comisión para el Esclarecimiento Histórico de las Violaciones de los Derechos Humanos y los Hechos de Violencia que Han Causado Sufrimientos a la Población Guatemalteca*).

The accord on the historical clarification commission agreed on the formation of a type of "truth commission" (Historical Clarification Commission – **Comisión para el Esclarecimiento Histórico**; CEH). Heavy disputes among popular organizations, the military and the government preceded and followed this accord. The organized private business sector barely got involved. Only some individual entrepreneurs, such as Jorge Briz form the Chamber of Commerce (Prensa Libre 1994e) or Alfredo Stephenson from the Chamber of Tourism (Prensa Libre 1994d) welcomed the accord. Stephenson declared, for example, that Guate-

---

34 The corporate umbrella organization declared with regard to the planned meeting with the URNG in Mexico that they wanted to have a direct dialogue with the insurgency, although they were not part of the ASC.

mala's image as a tourist destination has suffered a lot from the civil war and expressed his hope that the formation of the commission would contribute to the consolidation of the peace process and an improvement of Guatemala's image.

The organized business sector was more involved in the **treaty on the resettlement of uprooted population** that was signed about a week prior to the accord on the historical clarification commission (June 1994). It laid down the major guidelines for the resettlement of the population internally displaced by the civil war as well as for the population who sought refuge abroad, in particular in Mexico. The provisions of the agreement included that the return process would occur in respect of human rights and that the government would support equitable and sustainable development in the resettlement zones, including the provision of infrastructure. In this context, the agreement stated that the government was to return land abandoned by the uprooted population and acknowledged the significance of land and land tenure. The accord however, left it to the socio-economic agreement, which was scheduled to be negotiated later to stipulate details and tangible solutions.

In numerous meetings between COPAZ and different business associations before the signing of the accord, the private business sector expressed its concern about the potential consequences of the return of the uprooted population[35]. Their concerns were primarily related to **land issues** and relate to the **potential political effects** of the resettlement process. Although the accord on the return of the displaced population postponed many delicate and conflictive matters to the negotiations on the socio-economic agreement, it still mandated e.g. a revision of the existing land register and therewith touched upon land tenure and property rights, an overtly sensitive issue for the private sector. Even these careful concessions were eyed sceptically by some businessmen, who foresaw in a revision of the land register a possible violation of the constitutional right to private property (for more details on this issue see chapter 7.4.1) (La República 1994b; Rosada-Granados 1998: 97).

As to political consequences of the returning process, entrepreneurs were worried about the potential boost in URNG's popularity. According to estimations of the United Nations High Commission for Refugees (UNHCR) about 10,000 refugees came back to Guatemala between 1993 and 1994, and another 100,000 exiled Guatemalans were at this time still living in Mexico. Many Diaspora groups had established close links to the insurgency and formed a signifi-

---

35 Luis Reyes Mayen stated in different occasions in the daily press his support for the return of the population uprooted by the war (Prensa Libre 1994g). Yet interviews with members of the governmental peace commission as well as entrepreneurs revealed that the organized private business sector was very nervous about the return. Entrepreneurs also declared in interviews that some businessmen were personally shocked of the living conditions of the people uprooted by the civil war, when they visited a refugee camp.

cant constituency as well as a pressure group for the URNG[36]. A large scale return of URNG supporters implied a threat to the delicate conditions at the negotiation table as well as the longer-term political developments in Guatemala. The entrepreneurs feared that the returning population became a forceful political pressure group in favour of the URNG, increasing the bargaining power of the URNG in the peace talks and increasing URNG's chances in elections. As was discussed earlier, **augmenting political influence** of the URNG was one of the private sector's major worries. Already in the early 1980s in the "Campaign of a Thousand Days", CACIF had focused on the insurgencies' political impact (see chapter 6.3.1.2). With CACIF's study on URNG's potential election chances prior to the Ottawa-meeting, CACIF had dealt with the same set of threats and had maintained this concern in the following years. The large scale return of refugees threatened to increase URNG's popularity and political power.

7.3.4 The indigenous agreement: A sensitive issue for the private sector

After the signing of the two accords, it became clear that the final peace accord would not be passed by December. The government continued demanding an armistice, which the URNG rejected. A renewed wave of violence flooded the country and both parties accused each other for being responsible. In summer 1994, the peace talks came again to a standstill until finally, after nine months of negotiations, the **accord on the rights of the indigenous population** was conceded end of March 1995.

The accord on "Identity and Rights of the Indigenous People" was generally considered a **milestone for indigenous rights** in Guatemala. Given the high level of racism, discrimination and exclusion of the indigenous population and its relevance for the emergence of the civil war, the accord is one of the most important of Guatemala's thirteen peace agreements.

Major achievements were:
– an agreement to encourage the national congress to pass constitutional reforms that would define Guatemala as a multiethnic, multicultural and multilingual nation;
– a range of detailed activities aiming to overcome racism, discrimination and exploitation of the indigenous population;
– an agreement to develop legislative and administrative measures to ensure the recognition, awarding, protection, recovery, restitution and compensation of land rights to the indigenous population;
– the recognition of communal land and collective land ownership;

---

36 At this time, it was still not clear if the URNG would participate in the next elections end of 1995. Ramiro de León considered in public URNG's participation in the elections but in late summer 1995 it became obvious that the URNG would not be able to participate in the vote (Aguilera Peralta et al. 1996: 352-353).

- a reform of the Municipal Code to promote and acknowledge indigenous customary law;
- and the ratification of Convention 169 (Indigenous and Tribal Peoples Convention) by the International Labour Organization (ILO).

Many of the provisions in the indigenous agreement required **constitutional amendments** or changes in the national legislation. The peace accords, however, could not mandate constitutional revisions, but could only ask that the government promotes in Congress constitutional reforms. All those elements of the peace accord suggesting constitutional changes would not be able to be implemented before the signing of the final agreement and would be put again on the national agenda in a referendum in May 1999 (see chapter 8.4).

The indigenous agreement was probably the most relevant agreement for the business sector, in particular the agricultural sector, after the socio-economic accord. Large parts of Guatemala's economy were based on cheap, primarily indigenous labour and land. The recognition and **empowerment of indigenous rights** entailed the risk of losing both, the easy access to a cheap workforce as well as to land. The Guatemalan business community, for example, was highly sceptical regarding communal lands (see for more details chapter 7.4.1) and feared far-reaching changes for landowners and *finqueros* with the recognition of indigenous customary laws.

Similar, the **ILO convention 169**, which was suggested to be ratified in the indigenous agreement touched upon the immediate interests of the private sector. The convention lays down principals, aiming to eliminate racial discrimination and to establish the official and juridical recognition of indigenous people. Amongst others, the convention deals with land rights, rights to natural resources and relocation of peoples (articles 13 to 19). The Guatemalan private business sector was concerned that ratifying the convention would form the legal basis leading "to invasions on private property" and to more expensive labour. Article 14, for instance, stipulates: "The rights of the interested peoples to ownership and possession of the lands they traditionally occupy should be recognized. And in appropriate cases, measures should be taken to safeguard the rights of the interested peoples to use lands they do not exclusively occupy but to which they have traditionally had access for traditional and subsistence activities."

Guatemala finally **ratified ILO Convention** 169 in March 1996 – but only with an additional amendment, stipulating that the ILO convention was to be subordinate to the national constitution, in which the right of private property was to be assured (Siglo XXI 1996a). In the run-up to ratification, the private business sector (e.g. through communiqués by AGA, AGA 1996) vehemently opposed it, but were reassured when the proviso was added. According to critics, however, this modification waters down convention 169, since it impedes that indigenous people can recuperate their property (for more information on ILO

No. 169 and its links to the indigenous accords see for example (Plant 1999: 328-329, 334).

7.3.5 The first round of negotiations for the socio-economic accord

The momentum the peace talks had gained with the signing of the indigenous accord was short-lived. With the **beginning of the negotiations on socio-economic issues**, the peace process staggered into a new impasse that could not be overcome during de León's term in office. A number of compromises for the socio-economic agreement could be reached, but no final agreement[37].

The numerous cross-references in earlier peace agreements, in particular in the indigenous accord and in the accord on displaced populations, had forecasted the **importance assigned to the socio-economic accord**. The socio-economic accord was, firstly, the most relevant peace agreement for the Guatemalan business sector. The majority of potential direct and indirect costs of peace for the private sector were negotiated in the context of the socio-economic agreement. Second, many considered the issues at stake in the socio-economic agreement as the main issues that had caused the civil war in the first place, including unequal access to land and exploitation of the labour force. And third, the socio-economic accord was for many equal to a start towards future wealth and prosperity in the country. A survey conducted by ASIES (*Asociación de Investigación y Estudios Sociales* – Research and Social Science Association), for instance, found that the Guatemalan population expected from the peace process first of all positive changes in the number of jobs available and in the general economic conditions of the country, before positive changes in the security situation. The same study found that Guatemalans believed that economic aspects were the biggest obstacle for reaching peace (ASIES 1993).

The **environment** to negotiate such sensitive issues was however **unfavourable**. Neither the government nor the URNG showed much interest in quickly finalizing the peace process. The URNG was hesitant to negotiate such a crucial treaty with an interims government, and the government continued to insist on a cease-fire (for more details Inforpress Centroaméricana 1996: 16-17).

In addition, the **relationship** between the private business sector and the URNG **deteriorated** significantly, as the negations on socioeconomic issues approached. The continued collection of war taxes by the guerrilla organizations remained an important issue. The daily newspapers published frequent stories about assaults against *fincas,* including about those that were burned down when the landowners refused to pay *impuestos de guerra.* An attempted murder of the president of

---

37 According to Gustavo Porras, in the negotiations with the de León administration, the URNG had insisted on a number of extreme demands in order to avoid the conclusion of the socio-economic agreement. As stated earlier, the insurgency had little confidence in the de León administration.

the Chamber of Commerce in May 1995, a mounting number of kidnappings and attacks against infrastructure further increased an already tense situation (for example Inforpress Centroaméricana 1996: 43)[38].

Related to this seemed to be a renewed upsurge of **land conflicts** that shook the country. In April 1995, more than 80 *fincas* were occupied. The situation climaxed when the private business sector halted a dialogue with the *campesinos* that was installed to address the problem. The Agricultural Chamber accused the URNG of spurring peasants into occupying private property in order to increase pressure on the peace process and demanded from the army "to do something about the problem" (for example Aguilera Peralta et al. 1996: 157)[39]. Previous to these events, in September, President de León had disbanded the *comisionados militares*. About 24,000 people who were responsible of supporting the national security system stopped working, and it is likely that this contributed to the deteriorating situation in rural areas (Aguilera Peralta et al. 1996: 352; Molkentin 2002: 226). In some, few cases however, the army and the *Policía Militar Ambulante* continued to protect *fincas,* which were directly threatened by the URNG (La República 1995c).

The increased tension between the main players at this point of the peace process was not surprising, given what was at stake for all of them. For the private business sector, the core concern was to diminish the insurgency's credibility and to bring forward their ideas for the socio-economic agreement.

7.3.5.1 Corporate strategies for the first discussions on the socio-economic agreement

Although the private business sector had been engaged in the peace process more or less since its beginning, its **involvement augmented** significantly at the time the indigenous accord and the accord on socio-economic issues were on the agenda. The number of meetings held between the governmental peace organization COPAZ (as well as the UN mission in Guatemala, MINUGUA) and the organized private business sector grew steadily, reflecting how concerned the private sector was about the agreement. Hector Rosada, for example, described that in the months from April to December 1995, COPAZ had nearly twice as many meetings with CACIF than with the URNG or any other organization (Rosada-Granados 1998: 43, footnote 10: 58).

About at the same time, CEPAZ (on behalf of CACIF) published the document *Guatemala: Reflexiones del Pasado, Consideraciones del Presente y Recomendaciones para el Futuro* (Guatemala: Reflections about the Past, Consid-

---

38 The Asociación de Caficultores Tumbador (Association of Coffee Cultivators from the Area of Tumbador), for example, released a campo pagado, complaining about ongoing attacks against private property (Asociación de Caficultores Tumbador 1994).
39 See for example El Gráfico 1995; La República 1995a; Prensa Libre 1995g.

erations about the Present and Recommendations for the Future)[40] (CACIF 1995b). The document was a consensus paper by CACIF and its member organizations, summarizing their **visions and proposals for Guatemala's future development**. Although the document was based on an initiative by CEPAZ and made some references to the peace process, it was not presented as CACIF's position-paper to the peace process. Instead, the more general nature of the document sought to demonstrate CACIF's fundamental disposition for national reforms, but made clear at the same time that CACIF saw these reforms largely independent from the peace process, and therefore out of direct reach of the URNG. The document has to be interpreted as a sign of the private sector's interest in shaping the outcome of the peace process, as a process that was about to influence the future orientation of the country. CACIF had rejected any formal invitation to join the peace process such as through the ASC, but they had found other and for them more effective ways to make their views considered.

In detail, the document dealt with national economic as well as social challenges. It considered aspects such as monetary and fiscal policy, tourism, infrastructure, agrarian or labour policy, social security, health, education and private property. Most of these issues were also on the agenda for the socio economic accord. The overriding tenor of the proposals was CACIF's support for a **democratic system, the rule of law and a liberal market economy**.

The document also calculated the approximate costs for the proposed reforms: 66.3 million USD for a 25 years period[41]. CACIF proposed in this context to establish a *Fondo Privado para la Paz* (**Private Fund for Peace**) as a private support mechanism for the reforms. The fund was obviously thought as the equivalent to the already existing *Fondo Nacional para la Paz* (National Fund for Peace), a governmental finance mechanisms for the peace process. Likewise, CACIF had proposed a couple of weeks earlier to create a "peace tax", which aimed to contribute to the pacification of the country.

CACIF's suggestion to support national reforms with a Private Fund for Peace or **"peace tax"** is very much in keeping with the demands introduced in chapter 2 on business engagement in conflict management, specifically for post-conflict peacebuilding. It was a tangible suggestion of how business could participate in Guatemala's long-term peace process. CACIF's proposals, however, were never realized or put in concrete terms, mainly because it was expected that this would facilitate that CACIF could even more shape the contents and direction of the reforms. The "peace tax" remained an advocacy tool for the organiza-

---

40 Different, although very similar versions of the document circulated beginning of the year 1995. The first one appeared in February and the final version was published in May 1995.
41 At this time, various numbers on the costs of peace circulated. The government estimated costs of USD 45 million; others assumed the costs would accumulate up to USD 120 million (Inforpress Centroamericana 1996: 51).

tion to show its willingness for reforms – at least as long as the changes were in compliance with their interest.

The Guatemalan government had also developed first concrete post-conflict peacebuilding plans and the international community had made financial pledges for the national reconstruction efforts. The Swedish government, for example, held out the prospect of 103 million USD (ODHAG 1998: 331) and the Consultative Group of Donor Countries (primarily the USA, EU and international lending institutions such as the World Bank) offered about 150 million USD in donations and 400 million USD in credits, if a peace agreement would be signed (ODHAG 1998: 333). The expected **inflow of financial resources** as a result of the peace process made many former corporate opponents be more receptive for the idea of a negotiated settlement. The funds held out the prospect of an economic revitalization of the country that was not possible in this form without a signed peace treaty. Or as one entrepreneur put it: "The costs of the peace process were the major argument for the peace process" (see chapter 2 for the theoretic underpinning, which suggested that the inflow of capital in the immediate post-conflict phase is considered positive by business actors).

Despite slightly increasing acceptance of the peace process in general, the business community kept its overall recalcitrant position towards the negotiations. Pablo Monsanto and other guerrilla commanders, Hector Rosada and president de León accused the organized business sector of **impeding the progress of the peace talks**, and in particular, the socio-economic agreement[42]. Indeed, a number of corporate activities reflected this and made clear that some entrepreneurs considered the costs of a negotiated settlement with the URNG as too high despite the expected inflow of financial resources:

i. In June 1995, CACIF rejected vehemently the United Nations' proposal on the socio-economic accord. Although the negotiating parties had agreed on keeping the proposal in secret, CACIF acquired a copy and declared emphatically that 90% of the UN plan was against the constitution and unrealistic (Prensa Libre 1995a)[43] (For more details on those issues that CACIF rejected most in the context of the peace process see chapter 7.4.1).

ii. End of July 1995, CACIF threatened to sue the guerrilla commanders for the second time. CACIF again argued that the collection of war taxes, sabotage, kidnapping, extortion etc. violated the law and infringed the peace agreements that had been signed already (Prensa Libre 1995d; Prensa Libre 1995i; Prensa Libre 1995b).

iii. A couple of weeks later, CACIF (under the lead of the agricultural sector) demanded from the government to withdraw from the negotiation table, until

---

42 See newspapers between June and December 1995.
43 Unfortunately, it was not possible to get a copy of the UN's proposal. Neither CACIF nor MINUGUA were willing to admit access to the document.

the guerrillas stopped extorting war taxes and violating private property rights.
iv. At the same time, a group of individual *finqueros* joined forces and demanded the guerrilla commanders' extradition – again due to the collection of war taxes.

The government rejected all demands and the URNG declared that it would not suspend the collection of war taxes (Prensa Libre 1995c; Prensa Libre 1995h; Prensa Libre 1995j).

Simultaneously, CACIF launched an **international campaign against the URNG,** aiming to diminish URNG's support from abroad. A delegation of the organized private business sector (including Enrique Neutze, Juan José Urruela, Humberto Preti) travelled to various European and South American governments[44], informing these states about URNG's breaches of law. At the ILO, for example, CACIF submitted reports on URNG's human rights violations and collection of war taxes (Prensa Libre 1995e; Siglo XXI 1995c). URNG's continued active "foreign policy" and pressure from international NGOs had created a very positive picture of the insurgency abroad. CACIF's intention was to "rectify" this image and to draw attention to URNG's illegal activities in order to weaken the guerrillas bargaining power in the peace negotiations – in particular before the negotiations about the socio-economic agreement would develop further[45].

Another strategy of the organized business sector was to **build up alliances with popular groups**. In September 1994, for example, a representative of CACIF (Peter Lamport) participated in the Ecumenical Consultation for Peace. The Ecumenical Consultation was a series of meetings, intending to facilitate an informal multi-sector exchange outside the official peace process. The meeting in September 1994 was the third of its kind, but the first with a delegate from the business sector. In the official declaration published after the meeting, the organizers emphasised the importance of Lamports's participation. Furthermore, CEAPZ started to meet with the ASC and other popular organizations. In August 1995, for instance, the ASC had a first meeting with CEPAZ (Siglo XXI 1995e) and more informal meetings followed, many of them in ANACAFÉ's offices.

Those meetings offered a) the opportunity for CACIF to present their ideas for the peace agreements to popular organizations, to look for allies, and b) the

---

44 The representatives of CACIF primarily visited the Países Amigos, among others Norway. The Norwegian government played an important role in the Guatemalan peace process, e.g. by offering "good services" or by pressurizing on the negotiating parties to continue with the negotiations.

45 Earlier this year, Defence Minister Mario René Enríquez Morales had claimed that CACIF financially supported an international campaign to improve Guatemala's image abroad. CACIF denied this, although they in principal would be in favour of any campaign that would balance out those voices that attempted to harm Guatemala's image abroad (Siglo XXI 1995d).

chance to develop closer contacts with those social groups that were expected to become politically more influential (e.g. the *Coordinadora Nacional de Viudas de Guatemala* – CONAVIGUA – National Coordinating Committee of Guatemalan Widows) (for more details on the encounter see Consejo Latinoamericano de Iglesias et al. 1994). Some interview partners claimed that the meetings between the ASC and the organized private business sector had been strongly **supported by the UN**. The United Nations allegedly interpreted the insurgency's uncompromising position in the negations as a result of strong pressure from radical groups in the ASC. The UN hoped that meetings between CACIF and the ASC would weaken these voices.

Also during this period after the signing of the indigenous accord end of March 1994 and before the end of de León's term in office end of 1995, the second official, direct **meeting between the URNG and CACIF** took place. After the first attempt about a year before had failed (see chapter 7.3.3), the two parties finally met in Mexico City at the beginning of May 1995, based on an initiative by the UN (Siglo XXI 1995a). The results were disappointing: Previous mutual (verbal) attacks and hardened political positions on both sides impeded a substantial rapprochement between the two groups.

Some months later, however, probably predominantly end of 1995 and beginning of 1996 in the context of the second round of negotiations for the socio-economic agreement some more meetings occurred between representatives of the URNG and CACIF, although clandestinely. Very little is known about these meetings. Similar **secret meetings** also took place between the military and the URNG. But in contrast to the meetings with the army, which had been discussed publicly after the signing of the final peace accord, there is nearly no information available on the meetings with the business sector. At least two or three meetings were held. Peter Lamport, Victor Suarez and very likely Humberto Preti met with Rodrigo Asturias (alias *comandante* Gasper Ilom) from the ORPA and probably other members of the URNG. In interviews with both members of the URNG as well as the business sector it was stated that the purpose of the meetings was to establish trust and to get to know each other better, after the contentious relationship in previous years.

There is no information about whether any further arrangements were made that influenced the agreements in the socio-economic accord. It is however apparent that the private sector was sufficiently concerned about the outcome of the negotiations on the socio-economic treaty to overcome their earlier patterns of not relating to the insurgency and popular organizations. At the same time, however, the meetings with the insurgency could not be held in public because this would have undermined CACIF's official position, which did not recognize the URNG as a negotiation partner without them having laid down their weapons. CACIF's **strategy** basically entailed two fundamental and related elements: To influence the outcome of the agreements such as through meetings and public communiqués, but without showing explicit support and recognition for the negations.

7.3.6 Splits in the unity: Differences in corporate approaches to the peace process

One aim of the study was to explore the **differences in position between branches** and economic sectors vis-à-vis the peace process. It was assumed that some branches would be more affected by the violent conflict than others and would therefore react differently, arguably being more inclined to support a peace process than those, which were harmed less. The following chapter explains the main variations in positions and strategies within the Guatemalan business sector. The major reason for placing this chapter in the context of the negotiations of the socio-economic agreement is that differences between economic groups erupted largely during this phase of the peace process.

Already in the previous parts, some attention was paid to hardliners and more moderate groups within the Guatemalan business community as well as to small and medium companies. In fact, in the course of the peace negotiations, the various business branches in form of associations entered into different formal or informal **alliances** in order to present and lobby for their respective positions. The most publicly visible coalition was the one built around CACIF, comprising their member organizations and a range of groups around them. Another one was the alliance built by FEPYME in the context of the ASC.

Those alliances and coalitions were, however, not stable. They in fact changed over time, were sometimes loose and sometimes closely united. In the following paragraphs, the most important alliances and breaches in those alliances will be described and analysed in order to illustrate corporate differences with regard to the peace process.

7.3.6.1 The hardliners leave the coalition: The establishment of CONAGRO

CACIF as an **umbrella organization** does not represent the interests of a particular branch, but seeks to stand for the private sector as a whole. Aiming to explore the discrepancies between economic sectors consequently requires looking into the tensions that occurred *within* CACIF. Certainly, the unusual unity of the umbrella organization (see chapter 5.1) makes it more difficult to draw a clear and thorough picture on the internal cleavages. It became, however, clear that the main rifts did run between different economic branches, but rather between hardliners and more moderate groups within CACIF.

Indeed, the most important breach in the alliances around CACIF occurred after **CONAGRO** was established. CONAGRO had been founded only in 1994, in the height of the negotiations for the socio-economic agreement, and was at this time a small group of mostly older and radical rightist businessmen, grouped around the two public figures of Gustavo Anzueto Vielman and the ex general and landowner Quilo Ajuso. It stood for the traditional, rightwing, extremely anticommunist fraction in the Guatemalan entrepreneurship with close connections to CARCOR[46] and radical wings of the army.

The cleavage between CACIF and CONAGRO reached its pinnacle when CONAGRO filled two **lawsuits against the peace process** in October and November 1995. The first one (affected directly by CONAGRO) was addressed against the president of the governmental peace commission, Hector Rosada, for having committed criminal offences in at least eight cases. The charges included violations against the integrity and independence of the state, abuse of office, resolutions against the constitution and illegal association (Inforpress Centroamericana 1996: 63). The second lawsuit was established by a group of lawyers, which represented CONAGRO, accusing COPAZ, CNR and FUNDAPAZ (*Fundación para el Desarrollo en Justicia y Paz*) for violating the national constitution, since the law prohibited negotiations with illegal groups[47]. CONAGRO's lawsuits directly attacked the Guatemalan government, seeking to derail the peace negotiations.

Many times before, business actors had raised questions about the illegality of the guerrilla groups and their actions, such as for example when de León published his first peace plan or in the context of the war-tax debate. CACIF had applied or threatened to apply legal measures, in particular against the commanders of the insurgency, seeking to weaken their bargaining position. But in contrast to CONAGRO's lawsuits, no other organisation had used the legal discourse directly against the government and therewith the peace talks as such. CONAGRO's charges **questioned for the first time the entire peace process**. A positive court decision would have voided all peace agreements since *Esquipulas II* ("totally illegal and void") (La República 1995e; La República 1995b; La República 1995d; Prensa Libre 1995f).

---

46 Although two of CARCOR's presidents had been killed in the course of the civil war, the organization did not get very involved in peace process related matters, apart from occasional public statements. Their opinions were similar to CONAGRO's. For example: Again, the Guatemalans are able to see, how the executive through Dr. Rosada from COPAZ negotiates situations in our homeland. At the moment, we do not know how and for how much they will sell us again. […] It is a lie that we will have a long and sustainable peace, when we know that these tiny terrorist groups continue to seed destruction, terror and death, the only thing they know to do. […] I think, as Guatemalans we have to oppose firmly the betrayal of the COPAZ of the current government, whose only interest is to sign the peace in order to get a place in the history books" (Rodríguez 1995).
47 In addition, CONAGRO opposed vigorously any kind of international involvement in the peace process, such as by MINUGUA. They interpreted MINUGUA's work as interference into domestic affairs and accused "some foreign countries and organizations" of being responsible for the violence in Guatemala, since they had allegedly granted economic support to the insurgency (Siglo XXI 1995b).

CONAGRO's indictments were **condemned vehemently** and unanimously by nearly all sectors of the Guatemalan society. The population, governmental officials, and foreign observers criticised CONAGRO's move. The constitutional court followed suit and dismissed the action. Also CACIF dissociated publicly from CONAGRO's manoeuvre, implying an unusual split in the unity of the business community[48]. Although CONAGRO tried to clarify later that they were not against "peace", since they "represented" the sector most affected by the civil war, all other Guatemalan business groups disapproved publicly with CONAGRO's initiative (CONAGRO 1995b: 427; Aguilera Peralta et al. 1996).

CONAGRO was nearly **unknown** at the time they filed the lawsuits. Although the organization had appeared in public already before October 1995 (for instance with campos pagados, CONAGRO 1995c; CONAGRO 1995a), there was some confusion regarding what CONAGRO was and whom it represented. Many mistook CONAGRO for a business association related to the CAG or even equated CONAGRO with CACIF (see the press reports at this time). CACIF and the CAG published declarations and convened meetings with MINUGUA, in order to clarify that CONAGRO was not formally linked to CACIF or CAG, but represents independently a small groups of hardliners in the Guatemalan business community (see chapter 5.2.2.5) (e.g. CACIF 1995a)[49].

Until CONAGRO's foundation and beyond, CACIF had tried to integrate the extremist wing of the private sector into the umbrella organization in order to have a unified bloc against the government. Gustavo Anzueto, for example, had contributed to CACIF's document *Guatemala: Reflexiones del Pasado, Consideraciones del Presente y Recomendaciones para el Futuro* and the more moderate factions of the business sector had tried repeatedly to convince the radicals of the necessity and inevitability of the peace process. But the hardliners remained antagonistic against the peace negotiations and felt less and less represented by CACIF. The **rift between the umbrella organization and the group around CONAGRO** grew steadily over time and culminated when the socio-economic agreement was on the agenda for the peace process.

Just to give some examples how the hardliners first attempted to work through CACIF: Anzueto, for instance, organized lectures within CAFIC, aiming to prove scientifically that the indigenous population in Guatemala did not descend from the Mayas, which (in his view) made large segments of the indigenous accord invalid. Still in November 1994, CONAGRO had tried to work

---

48 During the second round of negotiations for the socio economic accord under the new administration of Alvaro Arzú, Anzueto Vielman from CONAGRO threatened again to sue the new governmental peace commission, but the threats remained unfulfilled.

49 CACIF and the CAG had repeatedly criticised MINUGUA for not being able to protect private entrepreneurs from encroachments by the URNG and invasions on private fincas. The relationship between MINUGUA and the private sector was tense by the time CONAGRO filed its lawsuits.

against the peace process **through CACIF** by attempting to get a more powerful position within the umbrella organization. In the context of the annual elections for the president of ANACAFÉ, the radical group of the coffee-sector tried to bring about victory for their hard-line candidate by launching a massive internal campaign, aiming to convince members of ANACAFÉ to vote for their nominee. Given ANACAFÉ's overriding weight in the *Cámara del Agro*, controlling ANACAFÉ would have been tantamount to controlling the *Cámara del Agro* and gaining thereby a veto right in CACIF. In so doing, the hardliners would have achieved a position within CACIF that could have impeded a continuation of CACIF's engagement in the peace negotiations. An internal counter campaign, however, undermined the support for the radicals and prevented them from taking over ANACAFÉ.

One of Anzueto's and other hardliners main accusation against CEPAZ was that the group would put the interests of the commercial and the industrial sector first and disregard the particular concerns of the agricultural sector. Although **other agriculturalists** such as members of ANACAFÉ agreed to some extent that the interests of the agricultural sector were often not fully considered in CEPAZ's strategies, they decided not to split from CACIF but to collaborate. ANACAFÉ, for example, was concerned that the collection of war taxes, which was primarily a problem of the coffee sector, was insufficiently considered and ineffectually used in CACIF's approach. As a result ANACAFÉ under the than presidency of Max Quirin got more engaged in the internal discussions and began to assume a lead role in organizing meetings with different sectors of society, outlining public statements and increasingly using the collection of war taxes as an argument against the URNG.

The foundation of CONAGRO in the time of the peace process and CACIF's public dissociation from CONAGRO showed primarily three things. It revealed

i. that the main **cleavages were between hardliners and more moderate groups**. Although CONAGRO was largely compiled by members of the agricultural elite, the majority of the agricultural sector supported CACIF's more moderate position. Furthermore, the tensions that existed between branches, in particular the agricultural sector and the industrialists/commercialists, were largely about the strategies concerning the peace process and not about the position and goals in general. Interviews also revealed that not only the agricultural sector was split in two over the peace process but that also in the other branches such as the industry and the service sector, opinions varied. Although smaller in number and not as organized, hard-line positions against the peace talks were also uttered by representatives from the non-agricultural branches. In other words, the fragmentation concerning peace talks did not ran along branches but much rather along ideological as well as generational lines.

ii. that the hardliners were a **minority** within the organized private sector, in large parts coinciding with generational breaches.

iii. the **relevance of the peace process** for the business community as a whole, even impelling the foundation of a new business association.

It is worth mentioning in this context that even the **AGA** – a group that was in the past closely linked to Gustavo Anzueto – did not support the lawsuit against Rosada. In fact, although the AGA was not member of the Chamber of Agriculture at this time, it participated in the Chamber's internal consultations on the peace process and overall supported CACIF's approach[50].

7.3.6.2 FEPYME's position: The political rift with CACIF

It was shown earlier that the **establishment** of FEPYME as a business association for small and medium enterprises and their participation in the ASC was of primarily political and strategic nature (chapter 7.3.1.1). The following chapter will further elaborate on this point. It will reveal that FEPYME's opinion on the peace process did not diverge massively from CACIF's point of view, although the organizations participation in the ASC and other initiatives may suggest otherwise.

With FEPYME's participation in the Oslo Consultation of 1990 and their participation in the ASC, the lobby group showed an overall more constructive attitude vis-à-vis the peace process than CACIF. However, at the end of June 1996, FEPYME decide to **leave the ASC**. Altogether four members withdrew at this point in time from the ASC. The major reasons for their resignation were disputes with other members of the assembly, in particular over the socioeconomic agreement. The relationship within the diverse ASC was difficult since its foundation, but during the discussions on the economic agreement, fundamental discrepancies surfaced more vehemently.

A couple of months before FEPYME left the organization, the ASC submitted its recommendations for the socioeconomic accord (see next chapter). The ASC was supposed to submit consensus documents, but the ideas on some of the issues were so diverse that no compromise could be reached (El Gráfico 1996d; El Gráfico 1996c). Supplemental paragraphs were added instead to the main document, summarizing the positions of those members that diverged from the main agreements. FEPYME, together with the "Group of Atlixco" (see chapter 7.1.3.1) added, for example, a paragraph on social security arrangements, demanding a profound reconstruction of the governmental institutions. The corporate interest group had furthermore advocated for a more affirmative attitude towards privatization and de-monopolization but could not convince the other members (Ponciano Castellanos 1996: 128). By the time FEYPME left the ASC,

---

50 Close personal links between Luis Reyes Mayen, member of the agricultural chamber, and Arturo Gandara, influential member of the AGA, facilitated AGA's participation.

it had accepted that its pro-private-business **ideas were incompatible** with the left-leaning convictions of most ASC-members[51]. Further interviews with members of FEPYME also showed that the business group held overall rather similar views towards the peace process as CACIF such as on issues of the role of the state in society or tax issues. FEPYME's weak political stance in Guatemala and their general rivalry with CACIF, however, made it difficult for them to ventilate their view on the peace process, other than through the ASC.

CONAGRO's dissociation from CACIF as well as the fact that FEPYME's position regarding the peace process largely coincided with CACIF's views, indicates that only the benefits and costs of war and peace cannot explain why different groups assumed different strategies vis-à-vis the peace process. It does not seem likely that the members of CONAGRO experienced fewer losses from the war or experienced higher costs from the peace treaties. Similarly FEPYME: Although there is no secured data on whether or not small and medium companies were more affected by the violent conflict or were supposed to gain more from the peace process, it does not seem likely that these were the reasons why FEPYME assumed originally a seemingly more peace inclined position. FEPYME's withdrawal from the ASC and an analysis of CONAGRO's political background show that **other reasons** shaped their positions and strategies. In the case of FEPYME these were primarily strategic-political and organizational motives; in the case of CONAGRO ideological and generational aspects.

7.4 The private sectors concurrence: The peace process comes to an end

De León's presidency ended without the socio-economic agreement being signed. At the end of 1995, in the election run off against the FRG (*Frente Republicano Guatemalteco* – Guatemalan Republican Front)[52], the *Partido de Avanzada National* (Party of National Advancement – PAN) with presidential candidate Alvaro Arzú, emerged victorious. The outcome of the elections was decisive for the peace process: with the PAN, a political party came to power that enjoyed **trust and support within the private sector**. With "having one of them as president" the business community was confident that even sensitive issues such as the socioeconomic agreement would be negotiated in their interests.

---

51 FEPYME, FUNDAPAZ, the Chamber for Journalism and the Central General del Trabajadores de Guatemala (Head Office of Guatemalan Workers – CGTG) decided to establish a new organization, the so-called Foro Cívico Democrático por la Paz (FOCIDEP – Civil Democratic Forum for Peace). FCOIDEP never became an important player in the peace process.
52 The FRG, headed by the former military ruler Efrain Rios Montt, used a strongly populist law-and-order rhetoric and found its main constituency among the rural population.

Arzú had ambitious plans for the **peace process** and the national security situation. During his election campaign, he promised to sign the final peace accord within eight months and to significantly reduce the crime rate within six months. Some observers feared that the close links between Arzú and the private business sector would hamper instead of foster the course of the peace process (Molkentin 2002: 245). But the opposite was the case and Arzú complied almost completely with his election promises.

Already before Arzú assumed office, he and his representatives had held secret meetings with the URNG[53]. The major purpose of the meetings was to create a **trusting climate** for the peace process. Indeed, when the official negotiations between the new governmental peace commission and the URNG commenced in February 1996, they were described as "surprisingly cordial" (CERIGUA 29 February 1996).

In addition, Arzú appointed a **peace-inclined cabinet** and a **new peace commission**. The cabinet included Dr. Eduardo Stein, a guerrilla-sympathizer as Foreign Minister; General Julio Balconi, a central figure in the reform wing of the army and earlier representatives of the military in COPAZ as Minister of Defence; the pro-peace businessmen Luis Reyes Mayén, ex president of the *Cámara del Agro* and of CACIF and member of CEPAZ as well as the *Instancia Nacional de Consenso* as Minister of Agriculture; and, Mauricio Wurmser, member of the *junta directiva* of the Chamber of Industry and participant in CEPAZ as Minister of Economy.

The **new peace commission**, COPAZ, varied slightly from the forerunner commissions. Arzú selected four individuals, each of them as contact person and representative for one particular sector in society. Richard Aitkenhead, a widely trusted entrepreneur although not member of CACIF, became contact for the private business sector. Rachel Zelaya (former finance minister) became contact for churches and popular organizations, and General Otto Perez Molina, who belonged to the reform wing in the army, became contact for the military. COPAZ was headed by Gustavo Porras Castejon, a former member of the EGP[54]. Arzú had therewith composed, similar to his cabinet, a strongly pro-peace, centre-left commission.

During the first year of Arzú's presidency, the five pending peace treaties were passed and end of December, only four months later than envisaged, the signing of the **final peace accord** concluded formally 36 years of violent conflict in Guatemala.

---

53 The meetings were initiated by the Community San Egidio. In February 1996, the secret meetings were made public in a communiqué by the government and URNG.

54 Porras was not only an intimate expert on the Guatemalan guerrillas but also a personal adviser to Arzú for two years standing, and furthermore an old school friend.

7.4.1 The socio-economic agreement: The second round

The first agreement on the agenda was the accord on *Socioeconomic issues and the Agrarian Situation*. Arzú decided to renegotiate the compromises attained during de León's tenure. Leaving behind the protracted and deadlocked negotiations of the de León administration was certainly a precondition for reaching a settlement only after two months of negotiations.

The URNG crowned the beginning of the negotiations with **declaring a temporary cease-fire** and with announcing a couple of weeks prior to the signing of the socio-economic accord, a **halt to the extortion of war taxes** as soon as the agreement was signed (see newspapers between the 1 and 11 of April 1996). The end to the collection of war taxes, which had developed into such a politicized issue for the URNG, the private sector and the government, was a clear "offer of conciliation" to the business community and the Arzú administration.

On 6 May 1996, after altogether a year of negotiations, the governmental representatives and the URNG signed the **accord on socioeconomic aspects and the agrarian situation** (*Acuerdo sobre Aspectos Socioeconómicos y Situación Agraria*). The nearly 40 pages long accord included an introductory plus four substantive parts on democratization and participation, social development, the agrarian situation and rural development as well as the modernization of public management and fiscal policy. The following Table 13 gives an overview of the most important agreements.

Table 13: Overview of the content of the accord on socioeconomic aspects and the agrarian situation

Democratization and Participation	– to foster mechanism for citizen participation, dialogue and consensus building among social and state actors – advance decentralization e.g. by "development councils" and by training programs for local government officials
Social Development	– acknowledged both the need for a rapid economic as well as social development – acknowledge that the land problem in Guatemala is a result of a historic, political process and that land distribution and poverty reduction are fundamental for the establishment of a sustainable peace in the country – "Overcoming the historical social inequalities that Guatemala had experienced and the consolidation of peace require a determined policy on the part of the government as well as the entire society." – increase of GDP by at least 6 percent annually – increase public spending for education and health by at

	- least 50 percent by the year 2000, using GDP in 1995 as a baseline
- increase the literacy rate to 70% (from about 55%) by the year 2000
- to reform the Instituto Guatemalteco de Seguridad Social, IGSS
- spent at least 1,5 percent of the annual tax income on house building programs
Agrarian Situation and Rural Development	- create a land trust fund to purchase land and distribute it at low cost amongst the landless population and tenant farmers to facilitate land ownership. The fund would at first procure: idle state land (tierra nacionales); state land in the Petén and in the Franja Transversal del Norte, that was irregularly occupied during the civil war; and fallow land, that can be expropriated according to the constitution (§ 40)55
- create mechanisms to provide a "dynamic land market". In other words the accord did not provide for direct expropriation.
- establish measures for the efficient resolution of land disputes, the return of or compensation for misappropriated land
- protection of municipal and communal lands (ejidos)
- realize a national land survey and a national land register
Modernization of Public Management and Fiscal Policy	- raise the ratio of taxes to GDP by 50 percent by the year 2000 – or in other words to increase the tax rate from under 8 percent to about 12 percent
- establish a land tax on underused and idle land
- establish measures to punish tax evasion and to close tax loopholes

National daily newspapers, the UN and international financial institutions **welcomed the agreement**. The majority of the private business sector, namely CACIF, ANACAFÉ and other business associations also reacted very positive and praised the accord as a significant move to provide legal certainty for landowners and ensure productivity (Prensa Libre 1996).

Yet, the **ASC** and the majority of its members were **sceptical**. ASC's recommendations, in particular those on the landholding structure had not been adopted by the official negotiation committee. Only after two months of internal

---

55 "This article refers to land expropriation and appropriate compensation, although it does not mention under-utilisation of land as a justifiable cause for expropriation" (Palma Murga 1997)

debate, the ASC finally endorsed the agreement. Peasant and indigenous organizations such as CONIC, CUC or CNOC (*Coordinadora Nacional de Organizaciones Campesinas*; National Coordinating Office of Peasant Organizations), viewed the accord at best as a first step towards an improvement of structural, national challenges, and at worst as a minimum agreement that did not at all tackle Guatemala's most explosive problems. Some even questioned whether or not the outcome of the socio-economic agreement was worth 36 years of fighting (Inforpress Centroamericana 1996: 105).

Without doubt, the **socioeconomic agreement fell short** of what the URNG had envisaged and promised. The insurgency had repeatedly reasoned its armed struggle with the aim of achieving fundamental socioeconomic changes. The accord on socioeconomic aspects and the agrarian situation did hardly provide for this type of deep-rooted changes. The treaty did for example, not entail a full-fledged land reform or a ban on the privatization of state companies. No provisions were made on a comprehensive job-creating programme and many had expected a more comprehensive role for the state in promoting equity and social development. The function of the state, however, was reduced to a minimum as frequently requested by the organized private sector and only a few measures aimed at contributing to a redistribution of wealth. The agreement was therewith very much in line with what the private sector had hoped and lobbied for. In fact, only view provisions went against the interest of the business sector. It did not entail significant costs for the entrepreneurs, despite the risks the negotiations with the URNG originally implied for the business community.

Still, the mere fact that socio-economic issues were addressed at all is exceptional. Dunkerly, for example, compared the peace process in Guatemala and El Salvador and concluded:

"[…] the rebels [in EL Salvador] continued to insist on a full set of economic demands that were plainly unacceptable to the capitalists. This, it might be remembered, was before the FMLN [Farabundo Martí Front for National Liberation] had entered into serious talks with the Salvadoran regime and reduced their focus to transitional political arrangement and the question of human rights. By contrast, the Guatemalan guerrillas insisted throughout on retaining a set of substantive economic demands on their agenda despite their weak position." (Dunkerley 1994: 82-83).

It was argued in chapter 3.2 that contemporary peace agreements as a rule advocate for **democracy** as well as **liberal market principals** and do commonly not comprise **poverty alleviation strategies**. The Guatemalan agreements also followed overall liberal economic principals, fostered democratic rule and did not entail a full-fledged plan to tackle the poor living conditions in the country. But some significant concessions were made, addressing issues such as improved labour conditions, increased wages, support for labour unions and a market-led land-reform.

During the negotiation process for the socioeconomic accord it had loomed ever larger that three (interlinked) issues were the most contentious – and the most **critical for the business sector**:
i.   changes in the constitution, primarily article 39 and 40,
ii. agrarian reform and land issues in general,
iii. and fiscal policy.

For the private sector, those issues threatened to be the most costly of the peace process. For the guerrillas and their allies, these issues, however, would have made the difference between a more socially oriented and a rather liberal peace agreement, between a peace process that truly addressed the root causes of the violent conflict and one that does not.

To i) Probably the most controversial and protracted issues during the peace process was the question of **changes in the constitution**, specifically of paragraphs §39 and §40 on private property and expropriation.[56] Since the constitutional amendments implemented in the aftermath of the 1954-coup, debates had re-appeared on whether or not to change these paragraphs. For example during the constitutional amendments following the putsch by Coronel Enrique Peralta Azurdia in 1963 or during the constitutional changes in 1984, paragraphs §39 and §40 were at stake. With the peace process, the topic re-entered the political stage.

The URNG and many popular organizations demanded the stipulation of the **"social function of property"** in §39 as part of a larger policy plan to tackle poverty in the country. They cherished the hope that the "social function of property" could form the basis for the redefinition of land ownership and a more equal distribution of wealth. But precisely because of this, the amendment was unacceptable for the entrepreneurs. They, in contrast, wanted to stick to the more liberal formulation, speaking of the function of private property for "the individual progress and the national development for the benefit of all Guatemalans". In the view of the business sector, an amendment would have paved the way for a land reform and a loss of protection for private property. However, whereas most observers considered the constitutional amendment as a key issue in the negotiations, stipulating the difference between a liberal economic orientation and a more social one, others regarded it as a rather symbolic, politicized debate and as a remnant from the Cold-War-Area. The two formulations would only differ marginally from each other and not imply the basis for real changes.

---

56   A number of other agreements that were signed prior and after the socioeconomic accord, e.g. the indigenous agreement or the agreement on the role of the army provided for changes in the constitution (see for example chapter 7.3.4 and 8.4). Many of those amendments were of fundamental importance for Guatemalan society, in particular for the indigenous population. But for the private business sector, probably none of those amendments were so sensitive and important as potential changes in the paragraphs 39 and 40.

To ii) Closely related to the issue of constitutional amendments, was the issue of a **land reform**, including its various sub-themes. The topic was historically anathema for the Guatemalan business sector. Any attempt, by the government, the church or international organizations to realize a more equal distribution of land, had failed due to the business sector's resistance. The *finqueros* feared to loose their property and entrepreneurs from other economic branches – even if not linked to the agricultural sector – conjectured that a land reform would be the beginning of declining protection of private property. CERIGUA for example cited an entrepreneur as follows: "'We oppose any attempt at land reform' said Preti, adding that if the government was to respond to irresponsible calls for land distribution, it would soon be giving away the country's factories, industries and business." (CERIGUA 19 July 1995).

The socio-economic accord did not pose a threat to the entrepreneurs in this respect, since it only provided for a redistribution of land "through the market" and did not impose a land-reform. Less in accordance with private sector's initial ideas, however, were the related themes of a new land register and the protection of communal lands. The socio economic agreement stipulated for both, the realization of a new land survey and the implementation of measures in protection of communal land.

The entrepreneurs overall rejected the compilation of a **new land register**, even though the existing land register was generally considered incomplete and unreliable. Many, especially indigenous people, did not possess official land titles and a considerable number of documents had been destroyed during the civil war. A new land register would not only generate juridical certainty, but would also mitigate land problems by providing land for landless people (Palma Murga 1997). Although directly after the signing of the socioeconomic accord the entrepreneurs officially favoured a new land survey, some entrepreneurs argued that a wave of land disputes would scare away potential investors (for example Crónica 1996) and that a new land register would simply be too expensive[57]. Many observers, however, assumed that the actual reason for the resistance was down to the fact that entrepreneurs had profited from the irregular distribution or illegal occupations of land during the civil war.

Linked to this issue is the question of the **protection of communal land**. Since the expropriation of indigenous communal land (*ejidos*) in the 18th and 19th centuries for the purpose of expanding private property for the cultivation of coffee, this had been a sensitive issue (see chapter 4). In CACIF's document "*Guatemala: Reflexiones del Pasado, Consideraciones del Presente y Recomendaciones para el Futuro*", for example, the business organizations had argued that "collective systems of ownership have never in practice been as successful as it was claimed they were".

---

57 CACIF calculated costs of more than USD 100 million (Siglo XXI 1996c).

To iii) The third most important "bone of contention" during the peace negotiations was the issue of **tax reform**. It was mentioned earlier that attempts by the government to modify the national tax system had often resulted in vehement rejection by the business community (see chapters 6.2.1, 6.3.1.3 but also 8.5.2.1 in post-conflict for more detailed debate). As a consequence, Guatemala had one of the lowest tax rates in Latin America and the Guatemalan state was notoriously short of resources. The socio economic accord attempted to tackle this issue by stipulating among others a raise of the ratio of taxes to GDP, by providing for a land tax on underused and idle land etc.

The taxation issue as a whole, but the **taxation of fallow land**, in particular, had caused much heated debate previous to the signing of the socio-economic agreement but also immediately afterwards. The business sector, namely agriculturalists such as Humberto Preti from the CAG, or Edgar Alvarado from the Cotton Association claimed that there would be barley any ideal land in Guatemala, arguing that the land was only unused because the civil war and invasions on *fincas* made investments impossible. The farmers, and more importantly, the loan giving banks tended to avoid the risk. Shortly after the signing of the socioeconomic treaty, the AGA publicly requested the elimination of the tax on idle land from the socio-economic agreement, claiming that it would hamper new, necessary investments in the agricultural sector.

Seemingly less contentious in the immediate phase after the signing of the socio-economic accord, were the stipulations demanding an increase in the **ratio of tax**. Although potentially a costly agreement for the business community, there were few reactions to it. Probably one reason for this was the fact that the treaty did not entail detailed provisions that mandated, which sector in society had to pay for the increase in national tax-income. Only a few years later, this subject turned out to be controversial.

None of these three contentious issues was decided (fully) against the interest of the private sector. **Peace related costs**, in other words, were minimal for the entrepreneurs. Neither a fully-fledged land- or tax-reform, nor changes in paragraphs §39 and §40 were stipulated. The risk of land reform was averted by providing a market-assisted land redistribution. The paradigm of private property remained secure by not mandating the "social function of property". The only setbacks the private sector had to accept were an increase of the tax ratio, a progressive tax system, taxes on ideal land and protection of communal lands. It will be shown in chapter 8 that the private sector attempted to thwart in the post-conflict phase exactly those provisions that went against their interests.

For many observers, the watery results were a direct consequence of massive **corporate influence on the negotiations** (Alvarez 2002a)[58]. How much direct

---

58 Yet, it is also important to consider the influence of the international finance institutions on the contents of the accord, which were significant. Gustavo Palma Murga (Palma Murga 1997) for example wrote: "The second agenda [additionally to the 'peace agenda'] was the overriding concern of the government to 'do the right

influence the private business sector and namely CACIF, however, had de facto in the negotiations, remains subject to debate. The private business sector itself has not been consistent on this subject and opinions range from "big influence" to "no influence at all"[59]. Also Gustavo Porras denied that COPAZ had granted CACIF a special role in the negotiations since he himself met only twice or three times with representatives of the business sector[60]. Yet, it seems likely that the entrepreneurs' leverage was considerable. At least two factors commend this assumption:

i. The Arzú administration was closely linked to the private sector. Or as Porras had put it: "[...] The PAN is a political party of the entrepreneurship, consequently they are neoliberals, their plan is neoliberal; consequently, when the Peace Accords appear in the Program [refers to the general political program of the PAN], the Peace Accords are neoliberal [...]" (cited in Aguilera Peralta et al. 1996: 340).

ii. The composition of COPAZ with Richard Aitkenhead as contact for the private business sector institutionalized the corporate exertion of influence on the peace process. Aitkenhead – conditional to his function – met various times with different corporate interest groups and representatives, including CEPAZ, CACIF's individual member associations and business associations not affiliated to CACIF.

Despite the uncertainty if the lobbying of the private sector is a major reason for the weak outcomes in the area of social development and poverty alleviation, just the possibility draws into question the desirability and **advantages of business involvement in peace negotiations**. It was suggested in chapter 2.2 that economic elites tend to have a structural advantage in realizing their interests. In the case of Guatemala, the business elite potentially used their influence in a way that is perceived by many as detrimental to the common good. If, for example, a land reform, would in deed have significantly improved the living conditions of the impoverished population or not, cannot be discussed here appropriately. It seems however important to give allowance to the thought that the involvement of (parts of the) business sector in peace talks may lead to an outcome, undesirable for the overall peace process.

---

thing' in the face of pressure from the international financial institutions, particularly the International Monetary Fund. Now clearly paramount in government thinking, this agenda comprises two main priorities: the implementation of mechanisms to 'manage' macroeconomic imbalances (particularly fiscal), and 'modernisation' of the state".

59 Some representatives of CACIF such as Humberto Preti in an interview with the daily newspaper (El Gráfico 1996a) criticised the secrecy during the negotiations. Others stated that the private business "had to say this" in order to pretend that they had no influence.

60 For example one meeting Jorge Briz, than president of CACIF, on the promotion of investments in the post-conflict period.

7.4.2 The last six months of the peace negotiations

In the following months, until the end of October 1996, the **peace negotiations progressed** without any serious impediments. The URNG and the government passed the last substantive accord in the midst of September 1996 – the "Accord on Strengthening of Civilian Power and the Role of the Army in a Democratic Society"[61] – and entered into negotiations on operational issues. CEPAZ continued to give direct statements and proposals on the different issues, but the intensity of its involvement decreased significantly with the conclusion of the socioeconomic accord, since the topics at stake were all in all of less relevance for the corporate sector.

At the end of October, however, a case of **kidnapping** nearly thwarted the entire peace process. ORPA commander "Isaías" (Rafael Valdizón Nuñez) was held responsible for the kidnapping of 86-year-old Olga Alvarado de Novella, member of one influential Guatemalan entrepreneur's family. Arzú's government attempted to hush up the incidents and to liberate Señora de Novella in exchange for Commander "Isaías"[62]. When information about the incident leaked out, the government suspended the peace talks for two weeks. MINGUA condemned the crime as a grave violation against human rights by the URNG. For CACIF the kidnapping was an offence against the entire business sector.

ORPA's involvement in the crime seemed to confirm the judgement of those factions in the business sector, which considered the insurgency as a group of terrorists, not interested in ending the civil war and acting outside the legal framework. In addition, ORPA was regarded the least radical of the three guerrilla groups, enjoyed most confidence amongst the government, and ORPA-commandant Gasper Ilom (Rodriguez Asturias) was considered the most promising presidential candidate for the URNG in future elections[63]. CACIF strongly supported the government's decision to suspend the peace talks. They demanded to hand over those responsible for the crime and as before, assured that it would support the peace process – but only as long as it complied with the national laws (El Gráfico 1996b; El Gráfico 1996e).

The insurgency was aware that the kidnapping may lead to a long-term interruption of the peace talks. They presented the kidnapping as an isolated and rough incidence committed by Commander Isaías' group, unauthorized and without knowledge of ORPA leadership and made concessions so that the nego-

---

61 For many, this accord was the most central agreements of all. It disbanded the PACs, limited the budget of the army, created a new civilian police, and restricted the army's responsibility to defending national borders instead of providing 'inner security'.
62 Together with Isaías the bodyguard Mincho was captured. Probably seriously hurt, he disappeared and the URNG as well as the government denied his existence. The "case Mincho" has never been fully cleared.
63 A couple of weeks earlier, the URNG declared that they would establish their own political party.

tiations could continue. The **URNG** offered an early cease-fire, a stop to propaganda activities and Gasper Ilom's withdrawal from the negotiation table. The four still pending accords – the Agreement on a Definitive Cease Fire, the Accord on Constitutional Reforms and the Electoral Regime, Basis for the Legal Integration of the URNG; and the Timetable for the Peace Accords – were settled in double quick time and paved the way for the signing of the final peace agreement.

On 29 December 1996, the URNG and the Guatemalan government signed the last peace agreement in Guatemala City. CACIF welcomed the formal ending of the civil war in a campo pagado and Carlos Vielman Montes (Chamber of Industry) promised that the private business sector would invest and generate jobs so that the peace agreements could be implemented successfully.

8 Complying with the Peace Accords: The Private Business Sector's Role during Peace Building

The battle for peace reached a new stage after the signing of the final peace treaty. The terms of peace were set in the thirteen peace accords with numerous, single commitments, but they were only the scaffold and the house had still to be built. The signing of a peace agreement did not bring an end to a conflict but transferred large parts of the original struggle from the battlefield to the political arena (e.g. Ramsbotham 2000).

The majority of the Guatemalan population, the majority of the private business sector included, had (finally) welcomed the negotiated settlement of the violent conflict. Even though many were disappointed by the outcome of the peace process, the peace accords challenged many aspects of the traditional social order in Guatemala, such as in the context of the indigenous agreement. The treaties were a historic opportunity for the country to usher into a better future. However, there was justified scepticism as to whether or not the reforms stipulated in the agreements could be brought to fruition.

The following chapter outlines the role and position of the private business sector in the post-conflict recovery phase. It was argued earlier that in particular for the post-conflict reconstruction phase expectations are high that corporate engagement can contribute to a more successful peace building process, such as through economic investments or support to the overall reconciliation process. It will be shown that the private sector did little to contribute to the implementation of the peace agreements. Business associations and individual executives attempted to avoid costs resulting from the peace, in some cases even if this went against the peace treaties (e.g. in the context of the fiscal pact); the ultra-conservative fractions of the corporate sector continued to actively obstruct the implementation of the peace accords (e.g. in the referendum); and private business activities and investments increased only very modestly.

The chapter focuses on the period between 1997 and 2002, with some excursions into later periods. The structure of the chapter is thematic and deals first with some general issues (overview of the implementation of the peace agreements, some general considerations on private business actors in post settlement phases), followed by a description and analysis of the private business sector's role in dialogue forums and its role in the referendum of May 1999, before entering into the issues of fiscal policy, labour relations and conditions, and rural development. The different themes are selected on the basis of either having special relevance for the peace process in general (e.g. national referendum) or for the private business sector in particular (e.g. the area of labour relations).

8.1 No war but no success: A brief overview of the implementation of the peace accords

The post-conflict phase was a success in the sense that the war between the Guatemalan government and the guerrillas did not rekindle. But the Guatemalan peace accords contained more than a mere truce and operational agreements. Although in the view of many observes, the peace agreements did not sufficiently tackle all seeming root causes of the violent conflict, in particular in the socio-economic sphere, the treaties contained numerous provisions of substantial nature that could have brought about a far reaching process of **sustainable conflict transformation**.

In the first phase, after the signing of the final peace accord, the institutional **infrastructure for the compliance and monitoring** of the peace accords was established. Tania Palencia Prado counted fifteen institutions, founded only between January and March 1997 in order to manoeuvre and supervise the implementation (Palencia Prado 1997). Most commissions specialized in particular thematic areas, many of them arranged as *Comisiones tripartitas* or *paritarias*, which comprised representatives of the government, popular organizations and corporate associations alike (for more details on the different commissions, see the thematic chapters below).

The highest ranking committees were the ***Secretaría de la Paz*** (Peace Secretariat of the Guatemalan Government – SEPAZ) and the ***Comisión de Acompañamiento*** (Follow-up Commission). The presidential peace secretariat served as a continuation of COPAZ, with the largely technical task of ensuring that governmental activities were in keeping with the peace agreements (Zelaya 2002)[1]. The *Comisión de Acompañamiento* was designed to monitor and support the implementation of the peace accords and to devise consensus among the actors involved in the peace process. The commission comprised representatives of the

---

1 SEPAZ was already founded in 1995 but it became more relevant after the signing of the final peace accord.

URNG, the government, a member of the National Congress, four honourable members of the Guatemalan society.

Probably one of the first, most obvious indications for the massive **delays in complying with the more substantive peace commitments** was the necessity in 1999 to reschedule the timetable for implementation. The *Comisión de Acompañamiento* had to agree on a new calendar, granting four more years to accomplish 119 still pending commitments (Comisión de Acompañamiento 2000).

The original timetable for the implementation of the peace agreements had provided three phases. According to this schedule, all agreements were to be fulfilled by 31 December 2000. The short-term agreements, such as the demobilization of ex-combatants, disarmament or the establishment of thematic follow-up commissions were scheduled for the first 90 days. Most of them had been accomplished satisfactorily (United Nations 1997c; United Nations 1999b). The medium- and long-term agreements (such as tax and land-issues), however, faced severe difficulties. Also the balance of the progress in the implementation of the agreements five years after the signing of the final peace treaty showed that the peace process made only **limited advancements**. The Agreement on Strengthening of Civilian Power and the Role of the Armed Force, the Human Rights Accord, and the Socio-economic Accord were only partly realised and the Indigenous Accord was even barely implemented (Salvesen 2002: 9-17). The United Nations Secretary General expressed in his sixth and seventh report on the verification of the peace agreements (covered the periods between July 2000 to March 2001 and April 2001 to April 2002) his grave concern about the "scant progress" (for an overview of the implementation see for example Canadian Foundation for the Americas 2000; Stanley/Holiday 2002).

Major reasons for the delays were certainly insufficient commitment by the government as well as the Guatemalan population. In contrast to the short-term agreements that were primarily of operational nature, the more substantial medium- and long-term agreements required greater impetus and compassion from all forces of Guatemalan society. But much of the momentum the peace process had experienced during 1996 was already lost in the first year of the post-conflict period. President Arzú proved to be less devoted to the peace process than one might have expected after the positive course of the negotiations in 1996. His successor in office, President Alfonso Portillo (2000-2003) and the leading FRG were even less committed to the agreements. Although the FRG paid lip-service in favour of the peace process, it was fairly clear to most observers that the party was ideologically opposed to the peace treaties. Instead of becoming a priority for the **governments**, the realization of the reforms mandated in the peace accords were often ignored or exploited for peculiar interests (indigenous groups in the referendum; private business sector in the Pacto Fiscal).

In addition and as hoped by the private business sector, the **URNG** had lost most of its political influence after the end of the peace negotiations. In the national elections in the year 2000 the URNG only won only eight percent of the votes. Internally fragmented and with declining support from their former constituency, the URNG did not become a guardian for the implementation of the peace agreements or a protagonist for further reforms.

For the **private sector** the end of the violent conflict implied that the costs resulting from the violent conflict had ceased. The corporate costs of peace, in addition, seemed to remain limited, in part because the provisions in the peace agreements did only in few cases encroach on the interests of the private sector and in part because governmental commitment to enforce the pace agreements seemed small, providing many opportunities to avoid peace related costs.

The general population witnessed little improvements in their every day living conditions and after Portillo assumed office, serious human-rights violations and threats against NGOs, journalists etc. raised doubts as to whether the peace process had really made a difference. On the contrary, **corruption and violence** (primarily less politicized violence such as car thefts and bank robberies) reached to levels higher than during the war (Moser/McIlwaine 2000; van der Borgh 2001).

The **corporate sector** was particularly affected by this trend. The number of invasions of private *fincas* increased. More than 400 cases of robberies on roads, in particular against trucks, were reported between midst 1996 and late 1999 (Vela/Solares 2001: 286). 277 cases of kidnapping were registered between 1997 and 1999, from which more than 50 percent were committed against private businessmen (see Table 14)[2].

Table 14: Kidnappings between 1997-1999

Businessmen	141
Workers	36
Students	28
Civil servants	27
Foreigners	15
NGO officials	14
Academics	11
Security Forces	5
Total	**277**

Source: Vela et al. 2001: 314

Consequently, instead of declining **costs for security services**, many businessmen found themselves spending more after the end of the armed conflict. Although the war-related costs had stopped, new security risks emerged and caused

---

[2] In 1997, other sources counted 1,739 cases of kidnapping, making Guatemala one of the countries with the highest number of kidnappings globally (Moore 2004: 147).

expenses for the private sector. In 2002, the total number of private police was estimated at 45,000 to 50,000 – the national police comprised about 25,000 men. David Keen stated: "The private police is mostly made up demobilised soldier, as well as a number of ex-PACs. They have been prominent in the armed protection of landed estates at risk from Mayan peasants who feel they got little from the long years of revolutionary war." (Keen 2003: 11).

Economically, the GDP increased slightly between 1996 and 1998, but sharp jumps in consumer prices and heavy disputes over Arzú's privatization politics left disillusion about the positive economic effects many had expected from the settlement. Hhurricane Mitch hit Guatemala in November 1998 and left almost 900,000 Guatemalans with property damages, losses and devastated infrastructure, which contributed even more to the **difficult economic conditions**. Since 1999/2000 the global crisis in the coffee sector took a heavy toll on Guatemalans and further compounded the implementation of the peace agreements. In other words, already shortly after the signing of the final peace agreements large parts of the population and the government had lost confidence in the peace process. Prospects for the future were overall gloomy.

8.2 Is there a role for the business sector in the post-settlement phase? Some general thoughts

Before the private business sector's role in the implementation of a range of specific aspects of the peace agreements is addressed, it is important to dedicate some more general thoughts on the **"functions" the Guatemalan corporate sector** could and was assumed to fulfil in the post conflict phase of the peace process.

The current invitations and demands on corporate engagement in post-conflict peace-building emphasis the role companies can play in economic reconstruction as well as reconciliation. In the case of Guatemala, which specific **roles** were non-state actors, and the private sector in particular, supposed to assume **after the peace talks**? Were the ideas for corporate engagement that had been outlined in chapter 2 in any way reflected in the case of Guatemala? As mentioned earlier, the peace process in Guatemala largely occurred before the idea of corporate engagement in conflict management became a broadly discussed concept. It is therefore not self-evident that the peace-agreements provided space for corporate post-conflict engagement.

However, it was shown earlier in the context of the **peace negotiations**, that although the Guatemalan peace agreements fell short of being a truly consensual national document, civil actors had been granted some room to influence the outcomes of the negotiations, such as through the ASC (respectively CEPAZ) (see chapter 7.3.1.1)³. The ASC channelled the voice of "the" civil society to the negotiation table, but popular organizations did not have the formal right to decide over the contents of the agreements. With the exception of FEPYME, the organized private sector had shaped the peace negotiations from outside the ASC.

Formally, the peace agreements were agreements between the **URNG and the government** of Guatemala. The state and the URNG also had the clear lead function in the implementation of the peace accords (see for example Wallensteen 2003: 143). But without civil support, the peace process was doomed to failure. Or as Woodward has put it for peace agreements in general: "Peace agreements are commitments signed by leaders, but the population must also be persuaded to make a commitment to peace" (Woodward 2002: 186).

The Agreement on the Implementation, Compliance and Verification Timetable for the Peace Agreements (signed also 29 December 1996) for example stated that: "the execution of the Implementation, Compliance and Verification Timetable for the Peace Agreements should encourage all social and political forces to join together in an effort to open a new chapter of development and democratic coexistence in the history of the country" (United Nations 29 December 1996).

The government and the URNG committed themselves in the same document "to promote the effective participation of all social sectors in meeting their needs" (iba.). With regard to the private sector, none of the peace accords laid down any duties or formal obligations for them to fulfil in the post-conflict phase. The socio-economic accord requested from the private business sector to contribute to the accomplishment of the peace process by participating in follow-up commissions or by investments, but did **not contain any specific** commitments. The perception that there has been no particular role for the private sector in the post-conflict recovery phase was reflected and confirmed in many interviews. Governmental officials did not consider the private sector a force that could support the post-conflict phase in any of the ways suggested in the current proposals for corporate engagement in conflict management. However, the private sector was not a neutral player during the civil war or the peace process. Unequal distribution of land from which a group of landowner profited, exploitative labour practices by parts of the economic sector etc. were considered part of the factors leading to the emergence of the violent conflict. The peace accords addressed some of those aspects and made the private sector thereby part of the post-conflict settlement phase.

Peace agreements of such a comprehensive nature as the Guatemalan agreements consequently **provided room for non-state actors** to support or hamper the principals endorsed in the peace accords. Specifically provisions in fields

---

3   Much has been written on the issues. While some argue that the ASC never had significant influence (Pásara 2002: 107), others considered the peace process as a truly national endeavour.

such as labour conditions, land issues, minimum wages and taxation implied that the private sector together with other civil actors was inevitably involved in fine-tuning and implementing these targets.

8.3 Difficult dialogues:
Still no climate for peaceful conflict settlement?

The establishment of the **infrastructure** to comply with the peace accords such as the formation of *Comisiones tripartitas* or the *Comisión de Acompañamiento*, was one of the first important accomplishments after the signing of the final peace agreement. They were a precondition for peacefully mediating the interests of all members of society and a tool to hold the government and the URNG accountable to the commitments made in the peace treaties. However, post-conflict societies tend to be highly fragmented and characterised by a high level of distrust. Commissions, boards, meetings, conferences, workshops etc. just provide the physical infrastructure. They only come truly alive if trust, ownership, confidence and commitment complement the formal mechanisms and if dialogue, consensus and compromise are the outcomes.

In the Guatemalan context, the socio-economic and indigenous accords in particular emphasised political participation and empowerment of the traditionally excluded sectors of society and provided for the establishment of mechanisms, which sought to facilitate dialogues among all social, political, and cultural groups. Numerous interviews, however, agreed that a major obstacle for the implementation of the peace accords has been the **continued distrust and suspicion** within society. Opinions and goals often have been "irreconcilable opposed" and a "dialogue-culture" has not been sufficiently established.

The private sector did little to change this. It kept an overall recalcitrant position and rarely compromised with other non-state actors. CACIF, for example, did not back the national truth and reconciliation efforts. When the *Comisión para el Esclarecimiento Histórico* (CEH) was installed at the beginning of 1997, the German university professor and human rights expert, Christian Tomuschat, was appointed president of the CEH. His nomination was well received by the international community and the Guatemalan population but the Guatemalan agricultural sector criticised the choice vehemently. Humberto Preti, for instance, argued that Tomuschat would hold a biased position. Tomuschat, who had already worked before as human rights expert for the UN in Guatemala (1991 to 1993), had published critical reports about the human rights conditions in the country.

One of the major objectives of the CEH was to "contribute to the formation of a culture of mutual respect" in Guatemala (CEH 1999d: 77). When in February 1999, the CEH published its report *"Memoria del Silencio"*, CACIF assessed the document as incomplete and partial. In a public statement the business organization argued: "A first reading of the historic interpretation, the consideration of facts and the treatment that was give to the different parts in the report, makes one conclude that one has to be reserved with regard to its focus, objectivity, and fundament." (Prensa Libre 1999).

CACIF and other **business associations** (e.g. ANACAFÉ) had contributed data to the CEH–report, but they did not acknowledge their role in the emergence of the violent conflict (for more details on shame and responsibility for the counter-insurgency strategies, see Keen 2003: 20-29). They continued to publicly interpret the civil war as a mechanism to defend Guatemala from communism and as a sole responsibility of the Guatemalan government, in particular the military regimes.

Similarly difficult was the cooperation in many of the forums and dialogues that were founded in the course of the peace-building phase. In the first period after the signing of the final peace accord, various attempts were made to launch **forums for dialogue**. The forums focused on different themes, such as labour conditions or land regulations and will be introduced in more detail in the thematic chapters. However, it should be mentioned already here that hardly any of these initiatives turned out to be a success.

Slightly more successful were those initiatives that had a more general focus. Three attempts will be introduced further:

The first example that should be mentioned in this context is the **"Meetings for Modernization"**. Arzú launched (together with the Canadian Center of Studies and International Cooperation) in June 1997, a National Dialogue that, though not directly linked to the peace agreements, aimed at supporting consensus building on issues of national relevance. Government officials, the private business sector (represented by CACIF), and popular organizations participated in the meetings. Yet shortly after the initial meeting on privatization and tax issues, the Dialogue was suspended: The gap between the private business sector, governmental officials and popular organizations was more difficult to bridge than expected and no consensus could be reached[4].

Two other attempts for a national dialogue followed. They differed from the "Meetings for Modernization" in that they were not launched by the government but were rooted in initiatives by non-state organizations. Both attempts have to be seen against the background of the change of government in the year 2000. Arzú's PAN had been widely regarded the party of the private business sector. The FRG, in contrast, which came to power in the same year, directly confronted the entrepreneurs. The **tensions** between Portillo's **government and the private business** reached unprecedented levels. Rumours of attempted coup d'états cir-

---

4   Before, PAN's plans to privatize more than 50 state companies (e.g. airports, maritime docks, parts of the Guatemalan electric company, or the telephone company, GUATEL) had caused waves. Various social groups, the URNG as well as MINUGUA expressed concern that the concomitant social costs of the privatization plans – although not direct subject of the peace agreements – would contradict their spirit.

culated and Portillo publicly accused private businessmen of being involved. Moreover, vice-president Juan Francisco Reyes López, himself former president of CACIF (!), was accused by Jorge Briz, longstanding president of the Chamber of Commerce, of launching a 'dirty' slanderous campaign against him (Crónicas 2001e: 8). In August 2001, out of protest against the government, the private sector staged a national work stoppage (*paro*) against new tax measures and bad governance.

MINUGUA wrote in some of their verification reports for this time that "conditions for dialogue did not exist" (United Nations 2002: 2) and that: "political polarization is further impeding the peace process: Cooperation between the Government of President Alfonso Portillo, political opposition parties, the private sector and groups in civil society became increasingly difficult as the 2003 elections approached and allegations of official corruption continued to surface." (United Nations 2003: § 8)

FRG's anti-oligarchic discourse and social populism first attracted parts of the **civil society**, which had hoped to gain more influence in the processes of political decision-making. But the emergence of powerful "parallel-forces" (arguably closely linked to the government and the military sector), increasing drug trafficking, further deteriorating public security, high levels of corruption, impunity and human rights violations, and a poorly performing economy all alienated not only the private sector but also most popular organizations and repelled them from the FAR.

Gradually **escalating tensions** between the government and the private business sector on the one hand and between the government and the popular sector on the other, formed the fruitful environment for the formation of two remarkable civil initiatives: The *Foro Guatemalteco* and the *Movimiento Cívico*.

The ***Foro Guatemala*** was founded in 2001 by two Guatemalan universities, the University San Carlos and University Rafael Landívar, in cooperation with more than ten civil organizations, including the *Fundación Myrna Mack*, UASP (Unidad de Acción Sindical y Popular – Labour and Popular Action Unity), Central General de Trabajadores, FEPYME and CACIF. The private business sector's participation was surprising for many. But the *Foro* provided a platform for the entrepreneurs to alley with popular organizations and to thereby sustain a certain level of political influence, which they had lost when the FRG assumed power (see also chapter 8.5.1).

Initial impulse for the *Foro* was the work stoppage in August 2001 (see above) that – although organized by the private business sector – was supported by most popular organizations. The *Foro* **demanded improvements** in the government's accountability, a reactivation of the peace process, more transparency, "clear rules", a strengthened rule of law, the implementation of concrete and reliable political decision with regard to labour relations, tax issues, trade etc. (Foro Guatemala 2001; Foro Guatemala 2002). However, the *Foro* had little political force. The government showed hardly any interest to enter into a meaningful debate with the *Foro* and relatively soon after its foundation, the *Foro* disappeared again.

Just a couple of month afters the *Foro* was established, another, relatively similar initiative was set up: the **Movimiento Cívico**. About 40 civil and popular organizations joined the movement, fighting for similar objectives as the *Foro*. Major differences between the *Movimiento* and the *Foro* were a clear lead function of the private business sector (in particular the Chamber of Industry) in the *Movimiento*, and a much more aggressive policy: The *Movimiento's* goal was evidently to force president Portillo into resignation. Already in one of their first press conferences, the *Movimiento* demanded Portillos's withdrawal from office (Prensa Libre 2002d) and shortly afterwards they formed a nationwide petition that aimed at resulting in Portillo's renunciation. Similar to the *Foro*, the initiative come to nothing.

There is much speculation about why the dialogue forums lost impetus and failed. Some analysts speculated that external pressure made them stop; others assume that internal differences were key. What remains, however, is that there was enough **political discontent** amongst all civil sectors to came together for a joint initiative. Businessmen reported that not in the course of the peace negotiations but in the course of the *Movimiento*, they, for the first time, met former guerrilla leaders, "just for having a beer and a *charla*." Although the initiatives failed, and although the central reason for the private business sector's participation was the government's anti-business-sector discourse, the fact that traditionally antagonistic parties coalesced to stand up for joint political ideas, was clearly a positive development (see also the chapter on the Fiscal Pact below).

8.4 The constitutional referendum of May 1999

In a referendum in May 1999, the Guatemalan population voted on a package of constitutional reforms that (partly) derived from the peace accords. A number of accords, in particular the indigenous treaty and the treaty on the role of the armed forces, included commitments for the government to promote constitutional reforms in congress. Together with the tax-reform, the constitutional amendments therefore formed the **central pillars for the consolidation of peace**. The result of the referendum decided whether or not key elements of the peace treaties, especially in the field of indigenous rights, would get the legal basis they required. In view of the importance of the referendum for the peace process, it seems essential to analyse the private sector's commitment for this element of the post-conflict phase. It will be shown that the business sector kept its overall recalcitrant position, although opinions varied within the corporate community.

The majority of the electing population **voted against the constitutional reforms**[5]. Although the rejection of the reforms did not make the peace process impossible, it established a major hindrance for its implementation (e.g. Salvesen 2002). The "No" gave fresh impetus to those who had argued all along that the peace accords were only an agreement between the government of Arzú and the URNG, without much support from the population or binding for future governments.

Already the preparations for the plebiscite consisted of time-consuming hurdling. Instead of end of 1997 as stipulated in the timetable for the implementation of the peace agreements, the referendum was held with an eighteen months delay. Political games between and within political parties, hurricane Mitch and insufficient devotion by the PAN were prime reasons for the **postponement**. By the time the proposals for the amendments had finally passed congress to be than passed on to the referendum, the number of constitutional reforms at stake had swollen from thirteen that derived directly from the peace agreements, to about 50 amendments. Different political parties as well as popular organizations (especially the *Coordinadora de Organizaciones del Pueblo Maya de Guatemala*; Coalition of Mayan Peoples Organizations- COPMAGUA) saw in the referendum an opportunity to realize some of their political demands, which had not been considered in the peace agreements. From the thirty-seven additional reforms, some were completely unrelated to the signed peace accords and were legally awkward. The mushrooming number of amendments clearly alienated parts of the population and increased the strength of those against the peace process.

Another factor that contributed to the rejection of the referendum was the mode it was realized in. In early 1999, congress bundled the fifty amendments into **four thematic packages**[6], so that voters could only mark four ballots for 50 constitutional amendments, instead of holding a vote on each of the changes. Grouping the amendments in such a way was largely criticised: thematically very different reform proposals were clustered together and no difference was made between reforms originating from the peace agreements and reforms being added in the political process afterwards.

Given the importance of the referendum for the future of Guatemala, the process was broadly discussed among the population. Since the end of 1998, the **opponents and advocates** of the amendments started to raise their voices. Cam-

---

5 The actual winner of the referendum was abstention. Less than 20 percent of Guatemala's registered voters participated in the referendum. Confusing and contradictory information about the contents and effects of the constitutional reforms and frustration about the political games previous to the referendum kept the population away from the polls.
6 The first package was on the (re)definition of the Nation and on social rights. The second package was on reforms in the executive branch; the third on reforms in the legislative branch and the forth on reforms of the judicial branch.

paigns of those supporting and of those rejecting the referendum, swamped Guatemala.

CACIF barely got officially involved in the campaigns. Only two days before the referendum was held, **CACIF** published a *campo pagado*, advocating a vote against the constitutional reforms. **FEPYME**, the only business association that had participated in the ASC, also published a statement promoting to vote "No". The text of CACIF's *campo pagado* as well as the fact that they intervened at a very late stage in the opinion-shaping process exhibited the strong disunity within the ranks of the private business sector. CACIF had originally viewed the constitutional amendments resulting from the peace process as political a necessity (Ríos de Rodríguez 1999: 45). And: the twelve reforms mandated in the peace agreements barely affected the business sector's immediate economic interests. The amendments instead largely concentrated on the role of the armed forces in the Guatemalan society and on the rights of the indigenous population. Changes in paragraph §39 and 40 of the constitutions had been averted already in the negotiations for the peace accords. However, the multiplication in the number of amendments, the opacity of the political processes leading to the increase, the contents of some of the additional reforms, as well as the massive international involvement in the "Sí" campaign that – in the view of the private business sector – "constitute an interference in political affairs that only concern the Guatemalans" shrunk the entrepreneurs' support for the reforms.

Already in 1998, when the number of constitutional modifications was about to increase, CACIF had expressed its **concern** for the first time. Later the same year, when the referendum was postponed another time due to the destructions caused by hurricane Mitch, the business organization again appealed for a reconsideration of the contents of the reforms, but without success (Ríos de Rodríguez 1999: 46). Then, in May 1999, and similar to many other organizations, CACIF publicly advocated the "No" (CACIF 1999).

Very likely, the majority of CACIF **would have supported** the constitutional changes if no further amendments had been added. Some of the businessmen were, for example, sceptical about those constitutional reforms that extended indigenous rights beyond of what had been stipulated in the peace agreements (e.g. a broad interpretation of the officialization of the 24 indigenous languages and indigenous customary law). Some entrepreneurs feared that this would lead to inefficient bureaucratic processes and a confusing legal system. Others objected to changes in paragraph §94 of the constitution that significantly broadened governmental responsibility for health care.

CACIF's late involvement in the runoff to the referendum was also due to **little consensus** within the organization on whether or not to publicly endorse the "No" campaign. First, the entrepreneurs feared the political cost of taking a public stance against the reforms. Being aware that the international community favoured the constitutional changes, CACIF was reluctant to publicly advocate the "No" campaign. Secondly, although the majority of the members of CACIF favoured a "No" vote, some influential associates vehemently supported the "Sí" campaign. Luis Reyes Mayen, for example, participated in the activities of the "Sí" campaigners. However, the corporate advocates for the amendments did not organize a unified front within CACIF and their opponents got upper hand.

More radical corporate antagonists to the constitutional changes supported the "No" vote-campaigners all along. But little is known about how much money flowed into the "No"-activities and who the sources were. It is however certain that **CONAGRO** and Anzueto Vielman backed the No-movement. They stirred up fears that the amendments would grant privileges to the Mayas, leading to an indigenous state within Guatemala that would suppress the Spanish language and Christianity, and would confiscate private property located in indigenous holy sites. Many of the resisters, CONAGRO included, collaborated closely with the University Fransico Marroquin whose students spread the No-campaigners' arguments cheaply and effectively throughout Guatemala.

The arguments utilized by the corporate opponents to the referendum clearly went beyond mere economic reasoning. Even if the some amendments would have resulted in economic costs for the private sector, the tone and the line of argumentation did hardly follow a economic rational. Much rather it appealed to **racist and anti-indigenous** feelings and fuelled a highly "polarized ideological climate" (Jonas 2000: 202). Those entrepreneurs belonged largely to those factions within the Guatemalan business community whose conservative and *caudillo*-like worldview was threatened by the constitutional reforms. The amendments did not so much imperil their immediate economic interests but put to the vote the long-established structure of Guatemalan society in which the indigenous population was discriminated against and debarred from participating in the political, economic and social life (Plant 1999).

The private business sector's position(s) during the referendum primarily revealed two things:
i. the agreements on the issues of indigenous rights achieved in the peace accords, were the **maximum of possible concessions** that could find a majority within the private business sector,
ii. the private business sector was **fragmented** over the referendum and the cleavages – similar as during the peace negotiations – ran along ideological lines, much rather than along economic branches.

In the light of the rejected referendum, the advocates of the peace process hastened to explain that the changes proposed in the referendum could still be achieved through ordinary legislation processes instead – although at a much slower pace. The FRG's victory in the general elections end of 1999, however, shifted this option further away.

8.5 Economic dimensions of peace

"The peace accords of Guatemala, in difference to peace accords in the rest of the world, cover the economic theme" (Fuentes 2002: 161). Essentially, the three areas labour relations, rural development, and fiscal policy were addressed in the peace treaties. Although these three themes were interdependent and linked with other key issues in the accords, such as the topic of indigenous rights, the following will concentrate on these three topics. Due to its relevance for the entire peace process, the role of the private business sector in the context of fiscal policy is outlined first.

8.5.1 The fiscal policy

Together with the constitutional reforms, changes in the national tax system were the most **important pillars** for the Guatemalan peace process. Whereas the constitutional amendments sought to provide key parts of the legal framework for the post-conflict peace process, the changes in the fiscal system were intended to endow the peace process as well as the long-term social development efforts with the necessary financial resources. In particular, the targets set in the socioeconomic accord to address the socioeconomic inequality were doomed to failure without the necessary financial resources (Stanley/Holiday 2002). The fiscal commitments made in the peace agreements (see chapter 7.4.1) should firstly, mobilize internal resources and establish a sustainable tax base and secondly, generate donor money from those countries, for which the fulfilment of the fiscal agreements were prerequisite for the disbursement of funds pledged to the Guatemalan peace process[7].

Guatemala is after Panama the country with the lowest rate of national tax-income to GDP in Latin-America. The Guatemalan state has historically been **short of fiscal income**. The compliance with paying tax was dramatically low. In the last 40 years, the average tax burden did not augment eight percent of GDP and the presumed rate of tax evasion is more than 40 percent of the potential tax revenue (United Nations 2000a: 193). Constant signs of corruption, inefficient and opaque use of tax money further diminished tax payers' willingness to fulfil their fiscal duty.

---

7   Already in the first Donors Meeting after the signing of the final peace accord in Brussels in January 1997, some donors decided to wait with making contributions in order to see which measures the Guatemalan government takes to increase tax collection. The consultative group had approved a USD 1.9 billion aid package to be distributed equally for the next four years. This was more than the government had expected. In a meeting with the IMF, the organisation clearly stated that the USD 1.9 million loans and donations for the peace process would only be paid if the government raises tax.

As was shown in earlier chapters, most attempts to structurally alter the tax system failed. Between 1980 and 1994, five tax reforms were brought down, in most cases due to pressure from the private business sector[8]. MINUGUA wrote for example in its first verification report: "In the past, attempts to increase the tax burden were repeatedly frustrated by powerful economic interests" (United Nations 1997c: § 29). However, when the socio economic accord was signed, the private business sector endorsed the agreement – including the paragraphs on the tax reforms. CACIF's appraisal of the socio-economic agreement had therewith raised expectations that an increase of the ratio of internal taxes to GDP from eight percent to twelve percent by the **year** 2000 and the establishment of a progressive tax system would be possible.

In 1998, however, the government of Arzú solicited from the *Comisión de Acompañamiento* a rescheduling of the target of a 50 percent increase in the national tax revenue for two years to 2002. But also by 2002 this goal was not attained. Why the compliance with this agreement failed and what the role the private business sector was, is the focus of this chapter.

8.5.1.1 Prior to the Fiscal Pact: Fiscal conditions and first reform initiatives

The reform of the tax had a weak start during Arzú's term in office. Already shortly after the signing of the final peace agreement, it became fairly clear that **Arzú's tax policy** was rather half-hearted. One of Arzú's reform attempts was the Single Property Tax Act (*Impuesto Único Sobre Inmuebles* – IUSI), passed by Congress at the end of 1997. In keeping with the principals stipulated in the peace agreements, the IUSI sought to affect large landowners more than small and medium property-owners. The government, however, failed to involve civil society in the process leading to the passing of the IUSI and did not sufficiently explain the new tax to people. As a result, a broad coalition, including FRG and Rigoberta Menchu ("used" by the FRG) finally turned down the reform proposal. **CACIF** criticised the implementation of the tax measure as:
i. inappropriate given the difficult economic conditions the country was going through, and;
ii. unrealistic since a reliable land register was a necessary precondition to its implementation.

It argued that the government should instead focus on improved measures to collect taxes and more effective modes of expenditure, instead of implementing new taxes. Interestingly, however, CACIF remained relatively uninvolved in the pub-

---

8 For a historic retrospective of the private business sector's resistance to tax payments, see Montenegro 1998; Valdez/Prado 1998.

lic discussion regarding Arzú's proposal, presumably being aware that the chorus rejecting the IUSI was already loud enough.

Following the repeal of the IUSI, the *Comisión de Acompañamiento* formulated a reform proposal, based on a consensus of URNG and different civil representatives. Arzú's government, however, did nothing to push the proposal through congress. Instead, a couple of months later the government passed a short-term **"minimum programme"**, including the indefinite extension of the already existing commercial and agricultural enterprise tax (IEMA) and the formation of a new *Superintendancy of Tax Administration* (Superintendencia de Administración Tributaria – SAT) in order to improve tax collection. The business tax IEMA aimed to make the tax system more progressive, but CACIF's vehement rejection frustrated the attempt and its indefinite extension was restricted to five years. And beyond: when the SAT was about to be established, CACIF suggested the granting of "fiscal amnesty" to corporate tax evaders (Valdez/Prado 1998: 380-383; Gamboa M./Trentavizi 2001: 3-33). Although CACIF's request was rejected, it left little doubt about their resistance vis-à-vis the reforms.

In September 1998, when it was apparent that Arzú's tax measures would be insufficient to reach the twelve percent target, the *Comisión de Acompañamiento* recommended the creation of a national **Pacto Fiscal**. The *Pacto Fiscal* was thought to be a platform in which CACIF and popular organizations (later united in the *Colectivo de Organizaciones Sociales;* Collective of Social Organizations, COS) would seek consensus on medium and long-term fiscal policies that could than be the basis for government fiscal policy measures. It had become clear that without the full support of these actors, reform attempts were doomed to failure. The establishment of the *Pacto Fiscal* aimed to address this.

8.5.1.2 The Fiscal Pact

The *Pacto Fiscal*[9] in the end defeated its purposes, but it was without doubt the key event in the course of post-conflict fiscal policy discussion. Numerous earlier attempts to launch a national dialogue on fiscal issues had failed. With the Fiscal Pact, fiscal policy became an issue of truly broad national debate for the first time in Guatemala's history. It therefore broke with a tradition, in which the formulation of tax policies was a de facto reserved right of the political and economic elites. With the Fiscal Pact, traditionally antagonistic sectors of society come together and reached a consensus on an issue that is not only complex and difficult in itself, but also extremely controversial.

The first step leading to the *Pacto Fiscal* was the inauguration of the *Comisión Preparatoria del Pacto Fiscal* (**CPPF, Preparatory Commission of the Fiscal Pact**) in March 1999. The CPPF was composed of four citizens, all inti-

---

9 This chapter is based on the following publications: Valdez/Prado 1998; Gamboa M./Trentavizi 2001; MINUGUA 2001; Noriega et al. 2001; UNDP 2001.

mately familiar with fiscal issues and all with high credibility within Guatemalan society. Amongst others, Richard Aitkenhead participated. After ten months of preparation, the CPPF published the document *"Hacia un Pacto Fiscal en Guatemala"* (Towards a Fiscal Pact in Guatemala) that served as a fundament for the Fiscal Pact.

In February 2000, the *Comisión de Acompañamiento* invited numerous civil organizations, representing different areas in society to comment on the CPPF document. A technical team systemized the 48 submitted proposals according to similarities and differences. From the 48 statements, eight came from private business organizations. In addition to CACIF, the Chamber of Agriculture, the Chamber of Commerce, the Chamber of Industry, the Sugar Association, the Chamber of Finance, AGEXPRONT and FEPMYE presented their individual (although seemingly partly arranged) proposals. The strategy not to submit one concerted document for the entire private sector, but various proposals resembled CACIF's position in the context of the *Asamblea de la Sociedad Civil* in 1994. CACIF had then refused to participate in the assembly, arguing that the private business sector was "too important" to be restricted to a single voice only. However, the way the Fiscal Pact was composed forced the business associations to **search for consensus with the popular groups**. Popular organizations still formed the majority in the Fiscal Pact and in a majoritarian voting, the private sector would have been defeated.

In a following process of negotiation, 'pendulum diplomacy', dialogue, consultation and debate the participants of the Pact aimed to reach compromises on those ten issues that the technical team had identified as most controversial. The majority of the disagreements were situated between the popular and the private business sector, not between different popular organizations. Key **disparities** were:

i. the private sector's demand that the annual economic growth rate of six percent, which was laid down in the socio-economic accord had to be achieved *first*, before the twelve-percent-tax-target was to be debated;
ii. the concept of a progressive tax system that the private sector rejected;
iii. the private sector's rejection of the establishment of a tax audit unit in the SAT, which specialized in big taxpayers;
iv. tax privileges for certain economic sectors or businesses.

With the private sector's rejection of a progressive tax system and a number of other details, they de facto attempted to renegotiate subjects that had already been agreed on in the peace treaties. For all other participants in the *Pacto Fiscal* the peace accords of 1996 were the *starting point* for the debate on the fiscal policy, and not subject of renewed discussion. Moreover and seemingly as an additional sign of **CACIF's hard-line position**, the organization sent Adolfo Menédez "Chiqui" Castejón as official negotiator to the *Fiscal Pact*. Castejón had represented CACIF in numerous other negotiations with different governments. He had much experience in negotiating fiscal matters, had circumvented various tax reforms and was known for his uncompromising negotiating style.

Nevertheless, CACIF was aware that by upholding its rigid position for too long and insisting on debating issues already stipulated in the peace agreements, this would undermine its national and international credibility. After contentious debates, the parties **reached agreements** for all points. In May 2000, a final consensus document was approved that delineated the general principals and obligations of a national fiscal policy[10]. 131 organizations signed the *Pacto Fiscal para un Futuro con Paz y Desarrollo* (Fiscal Pact for a Future with Peace and Development), already a big success for the country.

In a third, even more complex step, two further commissions were established:

i. The *Comisión de Seguimiento del Pacto Fiscal* (Follow-up Commission of the Fiscal Pact) that was to support the *Comisión de Acompañamiento,*
ii. and the *Comisión Ad Hoc,* which originally served as a junction between the commissions of the Fiscal Pact and the government and congress[11]. The Ad Hoc commission – composed of representatives of CACIF, the COS and representatives of two academic think tanks – turned into a negotiation table for the formulation of concrete policy measures, leading to the compliance with the twelve-percent-target by 2002.

In about one month time, the Ad Hoc commission was supposed to develop a consensus document on specific taxes and policy measures and submit it to the National Congress. But **negotiations stalemated** over divergences on the increase of the value-added tax, IVA (*Impuesto Sobre Valor Agregado*), and tax privileges. Although various technical reports had portended that the twelve-percent target could not be reached without raising the IVA and although CACIF had offered a four percent increase in salaries as a countervailing compensation, popular sectors rejected an increase. On the issue of tax privileges and exemptions, CACIF showed less willingness to compromise. As a result, when the deadline for submitting a consensus document to the congress approached, the *Comisión de Acompañamiento* had to announce publicly that no agreement had been reached[12]. CACIF thereafter withdrew from the commission.

However, the public admission of failure surprisingly triggered new momentum. One day after the break up, the commission started a new round of negotiations between entrepreneurial and popular organizations. Within a couple of hours, consensus was reached on all those issues that had hitherto thwarted a

---

10 For instance, the pact stipulated the balance between income and expenditure of the state, the priorities for social expenditure and a simple tax system.
11 Until then there was only little formal connection between the governmental organs and the Fiscal Pact.
12 Other conflictive issues were free trade zones and maquilas, as well as the tax over distribution and/or generation of electricity.

resolution. In the document *Acuerdo Político para el Financiamiento de la Paz, el Desarrollo y la Democracia en Guatemala* (**Political Accord on the Financing of Peace, Development and Democracy in Guatemala**), the arrangements were laid down. It contained six components, including the strengthening of tax administration and fighting tax evasion, increasing the ISR, and promoting a programme for a economic reactivation.

What followed then was an incalculable move by the government and congress that ruined the achievements of the *Pacto Fiscal*. Both institutions **rejected** most elements of the Political Accord, considering them as inappropriate. A unique process in Guatemala's recent history was thereby foiled and much of the rapprochement between popular and economic organizations was nullified. In the following years, Congress approved some of the measures provided in the Fiscal Pact, including an increase in some taxes and the strengthening of the State's sanctioning capacity, but the tax burden target of twelve percent was not reached. CACIF reassumed a hard-line position and systematically opposed government efforts to raise tax revenues.

8.5.1.3 CACIF's position vis-à-vis the Fiscal Pact

As mentioned earlier, the **private business sector**'s initial embrace of the socioeconomic accord and the peace process had made many national and international players optimistically assume that the entrepreneurs would also support the implementation of the fiscal agreements. But two important events leading to the Fiscal Pact much rather suggested the opposite:

i. The idea of a Fiscal Pact originated due to Arzú's inability or unwillingness to push through substantial tax reforms against pressure from CACIF (and popular organisations). CACIF assumed a hard-line position that seemed irrevocable.
ii. In the negotiations of the Pact, the private business sectors attempted to renegotiate essential tax-agreements that had already been stipulated in the peace accords – instead of taking the peace agreement as a starting point for the negotiations.

In addition, it was obvious that resistance within the private business sector to join the Fiscal Pact was marked. The private business sector had its own ideas of how the twelve-percent-tax target had to be reached. Concessions made in the Fiscal Pact, and in particular the renunciation of tax privileges induced **much internal irritation and resistance** (UNDP 2001: 49-52) and was oil in the fire to all those who had resisted the peace process from the very beginning. The private sector showed generally little compassion for the peace process. There was little indication that it would be willing to compromise and accept costs so that the peace agreements could be implemented.

So why did the private sector participate in the Fiscal Pact negotiations, and why had they been willing to compromise? Key **motives** were certainly:
- FRG's victory in the national elections and CACIF's declining influence on national policy;
- the private business sector's final recognition that the economic crisis required a correction of fiscal policies.

FRG's populist and anti-oligarchic political discourse had made it fairly clear to all members of CACIF that the "economic elite" was excluded from political power. They were not heard in political decision processes, let alone that the FRG "granted" the entrepreneurs a de facto right to veto. Likewise to what later stimulated the *Foro Guatemala* and the *Movimiento Cívico*, CACIF looked for **allies outside the governmental arena**. In addition to this strategic-political reason, the private business sector showed some understanding to the fact that without making fiscal concessions, the economic problems of the country could not be resolved. In other words: The private sector had no alternative but to participate in the Fiscal Pact, if they wanted their interests to be considered in any way. Participating in the Pact was primarily a defence measure against an antagonistic government and not so much a sign for the corporate support to the peace process[13].

8.5.2 Labour issues

Labour issues and the relationship between workers and *patrons* played a **vital role** in the emergence and course of the Guatemala's civil war. The landed elite based and in part still bases their wealth on the availability of cheap labour (see for example McCreery 1994), and for the guerrillas – in particular the EGP – labour issues were key themes in their revolutionary rhetoric. During the civil war, trade unions were one of the sectors most seriously hit[14], and the fear of an organized workforce has long been ingrained in many Guatemalan employers. In addition, labour issue were closely interwoven with other core themes in the armed conflict, such as the issues of ethnic identity, indigenous rights and agrarian topics (e.g. Bossen 1982).

The **peace agreements** dedicated various paragraphs to the issue of labour conditions[15]. The socioeconomic accord, for instance, required that the govern-

---

13 Some analysts interpreted the private business sector's participation in the Fiscal Pact as a sign of a "new generation of entrepreneurial leadership" in CACIF (Valdez 2000: 15). My own research does not support this view.
14 For examples see publication by MINUGUA on labour movements (MINUGUA 2003).
15 In addition, Guatemala has since acknowledged all key international labour conventions and norms. Namely these are the "fundamental labour principals and rights" (ILO, 1998) that embraces freedom of assembly, the right to collective bargaining; the prohibition of forced labour, prohibition of discrimination, and the prohibition

ment promotes legislation that "severely penalizes violations, including violations to the minimum wage, non-payment, withholding and delays in wages, health and safety conditions and the work environment"; it required that the government "facilitates the procedures for the legal recognition of unions" and "elevates progressively the real income of the workers".

But labour conditions and labour relations **improved only very modestly** in the post-conflict phase. Some unionists even perceived that the overall situation actually deteriorated after the signing of the peace accords: employers did not fear attacks by the guerrillas anymore that had motivated them to treat their workers better and on many coffee *fincas* the relationship between workers and patrons was still almost feudal (Stamm et al. 2002: 19, 38). Indeed, between 1997 and 2001, the ILO received more than 17 complaints against Guatemala about discrimination against trade unions and unionists, violations against agreements on child labour etc. (Stamm et al. 2002: 16). MINUGUA also repeatedly complained of violations against labour laws, condemned the insufficient financial resources earmarked for labour issues, the delays in legislative reforms, the poor supervision of the enforcement of labour rules etc. (MINUGUA 2000c).

The state clearly had the lead role in implementing the labour related peace agreements and international treaties. Given, however, the fact that labour relations are per se the sphere in which employees and employers meet, the involvement of the business sector was inevitable. In the subsequent paragraphs, the **role of the private business sector** in the reform of the labour code, the stipulation and implementation of the minimum wage and their relation to trade unions will be examined[16].

Most of the following chapter is anecdotal, showing the private sector's overall **recalcitrant position against reforming** the labour system in the country. The organized private sector showed an obstinate attitude in negotiations for reforms and individual entrepreneurs tended to not comply with the existing labour laws. There was basically little change in attitude in comparison to the period during the war. However, it is important to emphasise that it was not only the private sector that hampered the implementation of labour related agreements but also the government and popular organizations hold some responsibility for the failure of these agreements.

---

of child labour in its worst forms, the more specific conventions 87 and 98, 29 and 105, 100 and 111, 132 and 182. These conventions concretise in more detail those norms included in the "Basic Labour Principals and Rights", such as freedom of assembly, probation of forced labour etc. Furthermore, Guatemala has approved significant conventions such as the ILO conventions on 110 and 97 on labour conditions on plantations and for migration workers (Stamm et al. 2002: 15-16).

16 It is important to keep in mind that the stipulation of the rules may fall to a certain extend into the realm of influence of the organized private business sector. Their implementation, however, concern the individual entrepreneurs!

8.5.2.1 Reforms of the labour code

The **labour code** (*código laboral*) is the central legal document in Guatemala regulating labour conditions and relations. Impelled by the peace agreements, various amendments were implemented in the code after 1996. But the negotiations for the changes were arduous, revealing that the government as well as the business sector were both loath to support the amendments.

One of the first set of reforms was implemented in spring of 1998. Congress passed **amendments** to the labour code, including reforms to ease the formation of unions and prosecute violations of labour standards by employers. But the reforms fell far behind what was mandated in the peace agreements. In summer 2000, the government presented another reform proposal, followed by a second version published in spring 2001. Subsequent, to the publication of the reform proposals in 2001, CACIF and some trade unions objected that they have not been consulted during the development of the document. They solicited the postponement of the parliamentarian debate on the amendments so that the two groups, employers and employees, could present a consensus proposal on those elements of the governmental document that they disagreed on (Crónicas 2001f: 3-8).

In highly promising, though difficult negotiations, business and labour representatives came to agreements on a number of issues, including the Freedom of Association and Protection of the Right to Organize, or on the Application of the Principles of the Right to Organize and to Bargain Collectively. No settlements were however reached on issues such as on the abrogation of the prohibition of strikes in times of harvest.

From interviews with observers of the negotiations between CACIF and the trade unions, it emerged that some business organizations had **advocated for more far reaching changes** in the labour code. Particularly VESTEX, a group within AGEXPRONT that represents the *maquila* sector, encouraged the entrepreneurs to integrate more ILO standards into national law. Since the *maquila* sector is target of many national and international criticisms on labour rights violations, the sector had a particular interest to (at least formally) comply with international labour standards[17]. The position was, however, rejected by more traditional sectors within the business organizations, namely the agricultural sector.

The national congress adopted many – though not all – of the business sectors/labour unions proposals and passed them in decree 13-2001. The reforms meant a significant improvement to the existing labour rules but **still lagged behind the peace agreements**. MINUGUA, the ILO and the United States government criticised the amendments as insufficient and the US government threatened to exclude Guatemala from preference agreements. The Guatemalan gov-

---

17 VESTEX is also the only business association in Guatemala that had developed its own Codes of Conduct.

ernment finally yielded consent and passed a second package of amendments in decree 18-2001, which finally complied with the standards (MINUGUA 2000a: 1-2; Crónicas 2001g: 1-4; Crónicas 2001d: 5-7; Fuentes 2002: 167).

8.5.2.2 Minimum wages: Stipulation and enforcement

In the labour strike on the pacific coast of Guatemala beginning of 1980, workers had fought successfully for higher incomes. However, during the civil war the private business sector generally succeeded in avoiding an increase in the **minimum recompense**. The strike in the early 1980s had forced an increase in agricultural minimum wagers from USD1,10 to USD3,20; but in the following years the minimum wages only increased modestly.

The peace agreements provided a progressive **elevation of real wages** and mandated that the government enforces the payment. During both governments after the signing of the peace accords, i.e. the government of Arzú as well as the government of Portillo, the agricultural and non-agricultural minimum wages were raised. In 2001, the daily minimum wage for agricultural activities reached USD3,91 (Q30,46) and for non-agricultural activities USD4,21 (Q32,82). Due to high rates of inflation, however, real wages declined for about thirteen percent and were therefore still below subsistence level (MINUGUA 2000c).

But the government was not the only institution in charge of stipulating the minimum wages. Guatemala's law provided that the minimum wages and the so called *bonificación salarial* (a bonus payable by the employer) are stipulated annually in **National Salary Commissions**, separated for the agricultural and the non-agricultural sector (*Comisiones Nacionales del Salario*). The committees include representatives of business associations, the government, and trade unions. The government decides over the minimum wages and the *bonificación* only if the commission fails to come to an agreement.

In recent years however, the annually convened National Salary Commissions barely reached consensus on pay rises. Instead, the government had to **decree the increase**. But in particular since president Portillo assumed office, not only the private business sector, but trade unions, the government and private sector alike, must be held responsible. Trade unions often demanded wage increases of more than ten percent, which in view of declining coffee prices and a stagnating economy, was unacceptable to the private sector. In return, the entrepreneurs were only willing to concede maximum two percent and often less, which was intolerable for workers, given high inflation rates.

In the majority of times the business sector, and in particular the agricultural sector, had not shown much compassion for this part of the peace agreements. Instead, conditions very much resembled the situation during the civil war. The peace process only seemed to have a very minor impact on **corporate willingness** to pay salaries that contributed to "social justice" as mandates in the socio-economic accord. The situation was even aggravated since the governments failed to prioritize the issue.

In fact, during Portillo's administration, wage and labour negotiations turned more and more into a playing field for the **ideological fight** between the corporate sector and the FRG-government. In December 2001, for instance, CACIF and the CGTG (*Central General de los Trabajadores de Guatemala,* Head Office of Guatemalan Workers) agreed on a two step rise in salaries: Five percent in January 2002 and one additional percent after the harvest. But the arrangement was rejected by the government, reasoning that the agreement was reached outside the commissions and that a two-step rise contradicted the existing labour laws. At the same time, most other labour organizations rejected the settlement, arguing that the CGTG was a too "modest" trade union that did not enjoy full support from workers. The Portillo government consequently cultivated its social populism and the private business sector blamed the government for disregarding a "historic agreement" (Prensa Libre 2001).

Likewise, the **"Tripartite Commission on International Affairs"** (*Comisión Tripartita de Asuntos Internacionales*) was sacrificed for the sake of political fights. The commission comprised representatives of the private business sector, labour unions and the state and was inaugurated to discuss general labour issues. In 2001, CACIF withdrew from the commission, arguing that the government had broken an earlier governmental promise by increasing the *bonificación*, earlier the same year. Although CACIF joined the commission again nine months later, the committee remained fragile and de facto immobilized.

With regard to the **implementation side of the minimum wage**, the private business sector and in particular the agricultural sector turned out to be similarly obstinate. Despite the already low statutory wage of about 30Q for agricultural activities, most, agricultural entrepreneurs did not pay the legal salary. In deed, the minimum wage was for most agricultural activities the de facto maximum wage. The coffee sector, in particular took advantage of insufficient governmental control and enforcement activities. Even though there were highly positive examples of *fincas* that paid the minimum wage, provided good housing facilities and even hygiene education for the workers[18], the majority did not comply with the law. A study by the German Foundation for Development Policy, for instance, revealed that more than 60 percent of permanently employed workers on coffee plantations were paid less than the minimum wage. For migrating workers as well as for women the results were even worse[19]. Child labour, unpaid overtime hours, poor housing and hygiene facilities for the workers completed the picture (COVERCO 2000; Stamm et al. 2002: 24-25, 32-34). Conditions were

---

18 Role model in this regard is certainly the sugar-cane sector. For a critical analysis of the cañero's strategy, see Oglesby 2002.
19 In the coffee sector the majority of the workforce (about 80 percent) are migrating workers (COVERCO 2000: 3).

slightly better in the sugar-sector and on many banana plantations[20], but income still frequently laid below subsistence level (for the sugar cane sector see Oglesby 2002).

8.5.2.3 Trade unions and labour disputes

The socio-economic accord had mandated to **support consensus-building and cooperation in labour relations** between employees and employers (§5; §6; §26g), and to support the establishment of labour unions (e.g. §5, §6; §26g, ii, §33). But the still low number of collective agreements and collective bargaining were an indicator for persistent difficulties. Lacking consensus-building and cooperation was also the consequence of insufficient organizational capacity of the labour force.

Workers have been historically **weakly organized** in Guatemala. Massive anti-union practices during the civil war undermined much of the workers' potential power and influence. Statistics indicate that only two percent of the workers in Guatemala were organized in trade unions (Fuentes 2000: 28). At the same time, more than 1.000 trade unions were registered, ranging from big unions with more than 1.000 members for wider geographic regions or economic sectors to very small unions of twenty members at the level of an individual enterprise (Morales Modenesi/Celeso de León 1995). The sheer number of trade unions and relatively low membership makes it difficult to establish influential entities. Although trade-unions in Guatemala count a number of umbrella organizations (e.g. CGTG; UGT (*Unión Guatemalteca de Trabajadores* – Guatemalan Workers Union); UNSITRAGUA (*Unión Sindical de Trabajadores de Guatemala* – Trade Union Unity of Guatemalan Workers)), most of these entities were structurally weak and fragmented.

As was shown in earlier chapters, the **private business sector** had traditionally revealed – little surprisingly – an adverse attitude towards labour organizations, and the state had shared this attitude for a long time. There is little evidence that this situation has altered significantly with the signing of peace agreements. The worker's right to organize is still largely ignored in many enterprises. In the coffee sector, the high percentage of migrating labour significantly hampered the establishment of an organized labour force. In the sugar-sector no meaningful labour organization existed; and in some parts of the banana sector, unions were relatively strong but were often exposed to severe repression. MINUGUA for example described in its fourth report the following incidence:

"[In the city of Morales] An organized group of heavily armed individuals, claiming to represent local residents, broke into the offices of the Izabal Banana Workers Union, threatened union leaders that they must give up the Union and their jobs at

---

20 In both sectors, workers are often paid more than the minimum wage.

BANDEGUA, (Guatemalan Banana Company) forced them to call off the union mobilization planned for the next day and compelled them, on pain of death, to leave the area with their families. This episode and the murder of trade union leaders during the period under review show that genuine trade union freedom does not exist in Guatemala." (United Nations 1999a: § 61).

Previous to this event, a strong labour disputed had seized the banana sector that engulfed when a banana company fired several hundred workers, all members of the banana union SITRABI (Sindicato de Trabajadores de las Bananeras de Izabal – Labour Union of Banana Workers in Izabal). The aggressors in Morales were later linked to the local branch of the Chamber of Commerce (Crónicas 2001a: 7-8).

How deeply the **fear against labour unions** has been rooted in large parts of the Guatemalan business sector shows another example. A couple of years after the signing of the peace accords, a growing number of firms founded so-called "Hygiene and Safety Committees" in their enterprises. In keeping with the socio-economic accord, the committees were responsible for improving safety and health standards in private companies. Most firms had originally resisted the establishment of these commissions, fearing that they would be the harbinger of labour unions in their enterprise. Only when some positive examples showed the advantages of the committees for the firms themselves, more and more managers became willing to accept their establishment.

Those examples given above from the different fields of labour relations showed that the private sector did **little to contribute** to those provisions in the peace agreements that aimed at improving labour conditions in Guatemala. From a corporate point of view this is little surprising. Improving labour conditions implied direct cost for the entrepreneurs. Not complying, however, or assuming rigid positions often had little consequences since the government did little to enforce the laws.

Their recalcitrant position was moreover embedded in increasingly **difficult political environment** (in particular since Portillo assumed office) and in often uncompromising positions by the worker's representatives. Both factors did not provide a conducive environment for successful implementation of the agreements in the realm of labour conditions.

8.5.3 Rural development and land issues

As mentioned several times before, the highly **unequal distribution of land, social exclusion** and **widespread poverty in rural areas** are interpreted by many as fundamental factors contributing to the emergence of the armed conflict in Guatemala. MINUGUA for example wrote:

"The magnitude of poverty and social exclusion in rural areas is the most evident manifestation of the exclusionary model that has characterized the formation of the society and economy in Guatemala. The national territory is the background of an unequal development process that has privileged regions and social groups over the great majority, generating contradictions, so sharp that they form one of the central reasons for the internal armed conflict." (MINUGUA 2002: 5)

Overcoming these patterns and structures were by many considered **key for a truly comprehensive process** of conflict transformation. Given the complexity of these problems, ideally diverse activities have to be implemented jointly in order to successfully tackle the problems. These include the provision of infrastructure plus the provision of legal security, the development of an integrated and long-term rural development policy, the establishment of incentives and support structures (technical assistance as well as financial) for sustainable development within and outside the agricultural sector etc. (MINUGUA 2002: 6). Many of theses measures revolve around a core theme, that is the (re)distribution of and access to land.

The **peace agreements** did not contain a full set of detailed policies, tackling the problems of rural development and land issues. But the socio economic and indigenous agreements comprised some paragraphs that went into this direction. The most significant included:
- the establishment of a consistent and reliable national land registry in order to warrant legal security for landholdings;
- the provision of funds to the landless in order to facilitate the purchase of land on an open market;
- the establishment of land banks and adequate credits;
- the provision of adequate infrastructure to resolve conflicts over land;
- the implementation of taxes on unused land.

The lack of a full-fledged land reform, certainly pre-empted very conflictive negotiations with land owners in the post-conflict phase, but also the agreements that were stipulated proved to already be highly **contentions**. AGA's rejection of the tax on idle land had already provided an indicator of the problems that lay ahead on these explosive issues (see chapter 7.4).

Notwithstanding, the private business sector kept a relatively low profile on these issues in the first five years of post-conflict reconstruction. The major reason for this was the low level of **implementation of rural development related agreements**. Although some advances were made regarding the compilation of a cadastre, the government did very little with respect to the issues of land distribution and land dispute resolution. MINUGUA repeatedly expressed its concern about the lack of mechanisms to deal with demands of *campesinos*, the increasing polarization in the field of land issues, the persistent legal insecurity, and the slow progress in establishing a comprehensive rural development policy. But a continued lack of financial and human resources drastically impeded the work of commissions and funds.

The Land Trust Fund (*Fondo de Tierras* – FONTIERRAS), for instance, did not hold sufficient financial resources to purchase *fincas* for displaced and indigenous populations. The *Unidad Técnico Jurídica* (UTJ) of the *Comisión Interinstitucional para el Desarrollo y Fortalecimiento de la Propiedad sobre la Tierra* (Interinstiutional Commission for development and Strengthening of Landownership – PROTIERRA), which was responsible for coordinating the land register and regulating the award of land titles, did not adequately fulfil its duties due to scarce funds and a lack of political will. Likewise, the situation in the *Comisión Nacional para la Resolución de Conflictos de Tierra* (**National Commission on the Resolution of Conflicts over Land – CONTIERRA**), an organization established to help in disputes over land[21]. Key activities, such as the formulation of a comprehensive rural development strategy or the creation of an agrarian jurisdiction were hardly addressed (United Nations 1997c; United Nations 1997b; United Nations 1998; United Nations 1999a; MINUGUA 2000b; United Nations 2000b; MINUGUA 2002; United Nations 2003)[22].

Against this scenario, the private business sector's position and role in the fields of conflict settlement over land issues as well as rural development will be explored in the following paragraphs. It is shown that very similar as in the field of labour relations, the private sector assumed a recalcitrant position in the realm of land issues and rural development, but that this position was embedded in an overall **difficult environment**. Inadequate fiscal resources and little governmental interest in theses fields significantly obstructed the implementation of the peace agreements in this area.

This chapter also sheds some light on the increasing number of corporate philanthropy projects in Guatemala. Although often not directly linked to the peace process, those initiative frequently targeted social and economic development. The reason for placing this chapter in the context of rural development and land issues is based on the fact that the initiatives introduced here primarily target this set of challenges.

8.5.3.1 Conflict settlement over land issues

Given Guatemala's long history of conflicts over land and invasions on *fincas* the **peaceful settlement of land disputes** was vital for the post conflict peace-

---

[21] These organizations were established subsequently to the signing of the peace treaties in order to implement the agreements (Durocher 2003).
[22] There is no evidence that the state did not comply with the agreements due to pressure by private business actors. A lack of political will in general, FRG's particular resistance against the peace process, and the historically deep rooted "ban" on changes to the catch-all Pandora's Box of "land and agrarian issues" may have been much more responsible for the governments' inactivity.

building phase in Guatemala. MINUGUA, however, reported that more than a quarter of the unresolved conflicts that occurred in the first three years after the signing of the final peace accord were conflicts over land (Crónicas 2001b: 4) and CONTIERRA counted more than 2,000 land-issue related conflicts in the period from 1997 to May 2003 (Camacho Nassar et al. 2003: 258).

Indeed, especially in the years 2001 and 2002 many events that occurred in rural areas were similar to those the country had experienced prior to the signing of the peace agreements. High rates of unemployment and poverty and the deficient implementation of the peace agreements prompted *campesino* organizations (e.g. *Coordinadora Nacional de Organizaciones Campesinas*) to **block roads and invade private** *fincas*. Thousands of peasants walked to the capital in demand for land, insisting on clarification of land titles and better labour conditions for migrating workers. In April 2002, more than 3,500 families occupied about 50 coffee *fincas*, rubber estates and banana plantations. The *finqueros* however refused to talk to the squatters, since the occupations "were illegal" and *Bandgeua,* a banana company threatened to withdraw its investments from Guatemala (Prensa Libre 2002b).

In the context of the peace process, attempts were made to prevent similar developments in the future through the formation of **dialogue forums, commissions** etc. The majority of them, however, proved to be insufficient. The private business sector's relatively little propensity to negotiate and landowners' little flexible position (Fuentes 2002: 167) were nearly always one, while not the only factor leading to their failure. Hardened positions at the side of the popular organizations and lack of governmental engagement clearly contributed to the breakdown of most of these initiatives[23].

In 1998, for instance, CNOC and the Chamber of Agriculture launched a **permanent dialogue forum** with the intention of overcoming land disagreements within a consultative framework. Yet, only about one year afterwards the forum broke down and the parties accused each other of causing its failure. Some well informed observers, however, claimed that the forum had, for the most part, the character of a "coffee klatch" in which few substantial decisions were taken. The agricultural chamber had speculated that as long as a formal dialogue forum existed, the *campesinos* would be reluctant to invade *fincas*. When the peasant organization demanded from the entrepreneurs to enter into a more meaningful debate with concrete results on land disagreements, the dialogue forum disrupted.

Similar initiatives had been established on the regional level, in the form of ***Mesas de Negociación de Conflictos de Tierra*** (Negotiation table for Land conflicts), such as in Alta Verapaz or in the region of Ixil. The "negotiation tables" were sought to provide space for dialogue among *campesinos, finqueros* and governmental officials alike in order to avoid or settle conflicts over land

---

23 See also Hernández Alarcón 1998: 52-53; Prensa Libre 2002e; Prensa Libre 2002c.

(Crónicas 2001c: 2, 7). In view of the massive and nationwide disputes the regional forums proved to be important, yet, insufficient (Crónicas 2002: 4).

8.5.3.2 Economic development in rural areas

Poverty alleviation was regarded an important precondition for self-sustained peace and economic development in particular in rural areas. The peace agreements had defined the need for a national effort in attaining **sustainable development in the worn-torn regions of the country**. The socioeconomic accord, in particular, prompted private entrepreneurs to increase their investments in less developed areas in order to provide income facility outside subsistence agriculture. MINUGUA stated later in its 4th verification report that "Private sector participation in the productive diversification of small farmers would facilitate the sustainability of production activities in this sector." (United Nations 1999a: § 11)[24].

Perhaps little surprising, since typical for post-conflict situations in view of overall poor economic development and persistently meagre infrastructure, the request for **enhanced private investments and development support tailed off** (see chapter 2). Private investments and economic activities remained concentrated in the area around the capital. Neither the privatization of the national telephone and electricity companies, nor the new decentralisation law or erratic public infrastructure expenditures were incentives enough to significantly increase private investments in the more remote and less industrialized areas of the country. A survey conducted by the National Statistical Office in 2002 revealed that more than 43 percent of all registered enterprises were located in the *departamento* around Guatemala City, generating nearly sixty percent of publicly registered workplaces (Prensa Libre 2002a).

Similarly unsuccessful and closely related, was the **expansion of private banks** into the countryside. The easy provision of financial resources and small-scale credits is, however, a vital precondition for investments. MINUGUA critically noted that the: "credit coverage should be expanded and the territorial and sectoral distribution of the country's financial resources should be improved since, despite the increase in the operations of the Rural Development Bank [primarily governmental Bank], official commercial credit continues to be very limited and highly concentrated in the Department of Guatemala City" (United Nations 1999a: § 39).

Private banks scarcely opened branches in rural areas, and the government did not provide incentives, such as the creation of a guarantee fund for the provi-

---

24 When Guatemala was hit by a famine in 2001/2002 and public awareness arose with regard to increasing poverty in the countryside, appeals for private investments in these areas became even more louder.

sion of land credit, to private banks that would make the establishment of branches more attractive (United Nations 2003: §59).

In other words, with the lack of private investments in formerly war-ridden regions, one central idea of corporate engagement in conflict management was not fulfilled. Neither did entrepreneurs significantly increase economic activities in general, nor in the regions most seriously affected by the violent conflict. Although the socio-economic agreement only put secondary importance to this aspect, the accord acknowledged the central role of increased economic investments for the time after the signing of the final peace treaty. Insufficient governmental support as well as incentive structure and an overall inadequate economic environment were certainly key reasons that impeded a more dynamic economic development. Realistically, private entrepreneurs can not be asked to **increase investments** in the absence of appropriate economic conditions.

8.5.3.3 Corporate social responsibility, business philanthropy and business lead development projects: Potentials for the peace process?

Notwithstanding the rather critical evaluation of private business support for poverty alleviation and rural development, a small number of corporate initiatives are worth mentioning. The projects outlined below certainly do not imply a reversal of the trend in corporate behaviour with regards to investment, but they are positive examples of corporate activities in post-war Guatemala. Some of the private business initiatives and projects are directly related to the peace agreements, while others have only a more remote linkage. They are, however, crucial in the context of this particular discussion.

Directly linked to the Guatemalan peace agreements were the projects *Inversiones para la Paz* (**Investments for Peace, IPP**) and *Industrias para la Paz* (**Industry for Peace, INDUPAZ**). Both were joint initiatives between business and development organizations. *Inversiones para la Paz* was a project undertaken by AGEXPRONT together with USAID, while *Industrias para la Paz* was a joint activity undertaken by the Guatemalan Chamber of Industry and the United Nations Development Programme (UNDP). Both projects had similar objectives and used similar approaches. They promoted, supported and developed new forms of investments, primarily in the areas most affected by the civil war[25], aiming to obtain an adequate socioeconomic development of the population and establish a better standard of living for the region. Both initiatives contained elements such as market and feasibility studies, training, support in organization, provisions of funds and credits (in cooperation with the Banco del Café and BANRURAL) etc. INDUPAZ chose the approach of "New Business Incubators"

---

25 The regions most affected by the armed conflict are sometimes referred to as "ZonaPaz", embracing the departamentos of Huehuetenango, Quiché, southern regions of Petén, Alta and Baja Verapaz.

in the industrial sector, whereas IPP contained a broader set of economic branches, with a more centralized organizational structure in AGEXPRONT (El Periódico El Periódico 2001: 14).

The differences between the two initiatives did not lay so much in their targets and approaches, but rather in their **progress**. Whereas IPP developed into a well established institution within AGEXPRONT with decent success in the countryside, INDUPAZ was still in the preparation phase five years after its start in 1998. Neither UNDP nor the Chamber of Industry seemed to place much priority on the project.

ANACAFÉ launched a comparable programme in the field of small business promotion, although with less direct reference to the peace agreements. Honoured by MINUGUA (MINUGUA 4th report, §16), ANACAFÉ provided advisory services, training and support in finding short-term loans from commercial banks to small and new producers (**Small Producers Development Project –** *Proyecto Mejoramiento del Pequeño Productores*) (see also Boot 2002).

To another category belong the activities, outlined in subsequent paragraphs. They are largely of a mere **philanthropic** nature, without direct links to the peace agreements. Most of them can be interpreted as motivated by the global CSR trend and would have been realized – in one way or another – with or without the peace agreements. Some of the initiatives established linkages to the agreements, but the relation stayed very vague.

Since the end of the 1980s and the beginning of the 1990s, more and more economic groups in Guatemala have set up **foundations** with a social development target. The *Banco del Café*[26] was in the vanguard with the establishment of a foundation in 1978, followed by the liquor, cement, sugar and coffee branches. The foundations were especially active in the fields of education, health and culture/sports and had collectively spent approximately USD10 million by the end of 1999 (United Nations 2000a: 188-191).

FUNDAZÚCAR (*Fundación del Azúcar*), the foundation of the sugar producers, and **FUNRURAL**, the foundation of ANACAFÉ (*"brazo social de la caficultura nacional"*) are probably the two foundations that have gained most public attention in recent years.

FUNRURAL executed social investment programs and projects and made strategic alliances with other public and private organizations for social responsibility projects, e.g. with the telephone company BellSouth. The project was active in nearly all *departamentos* all over the country. Although some of the projects had direct links to the coffee sector, for instance a project addressing the eradication of child labour in the coffee sector in the *departamento* San Marcos, the majority of the projects were dedicated to rural development in general.

---

26 Eduardo González, ex president of the Banco de Café, was in 2002 invited by the United Nations as the only representative from Latin America to a high-ranking working table on corporate social responsibility.

FUNDAZUCAR, by contrast, had a much clearer focus on the sugar sector. The foundation mainly realized social development projects and programmes on the south coast[27], the central region for the cultivation of sugar cane. The focus of FUNDAZUCAR's activities lays in housing, education, health, and municipality development (community self-government) with strategic alliances with the central and local government, NGOs, national and international organizations.

In 1998, FUNDAZUCAR received a prize from the World Bank and UNDP for success in supporting new development alliances between private business, local governments and NGO's. While warmly welcomed and interpreted by some as heralding a new era of corporate social responsibility in Guatemala (e.g. the World Bank), others warned vehemently of a too one-sided and optimistic **interpretation** of these "corporate social responsibility activities". Health, housing and education, three of the key areas of Guatemala's corporate social activities, are core tasks of the sate. In view of the private business sector's steady refusal to accept tax increases, which would theoretically enable the state to fulfil these duties, the corporate social activities did not only appear as acts of philanthropy but also seemed to reflect the private business sector's *"fobia al Estado"* (aversion to the state) (Fuentes 2002: 169). The corporate sector did not trust that the state was capable of effectively handling these tasks. Selective and exclusive projects supporting only one particular sector such as in the case of FUNDAZUCAR, reveal, however, the deficiency of this "policy"[28]. Moreover, there is an apparent contradiction between the sugar sector's social image that FUNDAZUCAR has tried to convey and the numerous violations against minimum labour standards in the same sector (Oglesby 2002).

---

27 That comprehends the departamentos of Escuintla, Retalhuleu, Santa Rosa, and Suchitepéquez
28 Oglesby argues that FUNDAZUCAR's strategic goals are among others, the creation of human capital that makes the sugar industry more productive and stabilizing the sugar industry in the long run (Oglesby 2002: 160). Even more, these kinds of "corporate social responsibility activities" may also be interpreted as a strategy to circumvent labour regulations, by "produce[ing] 'governable subjects'" (Oglesby 2002: 153).

9 Conclusion and Policy Implications on Business Engagement in Conflict Management

In the following, concluding chapter the main findings of the theoretical part and the case study are brought together and discussed further. The chapter is structured in three main parts. The first one recaps the background of the work, reiterates the main research questions and reviews and discusses the main results of the case-study. In the second part, the findings from the case study are compared to other, similar cases from other research. In a final third part, policy implications are deduced and summarized.

9.1 The business sector in the Guatemalan peace processes: Findings from the case study

Background and theoretical assumptions

In recent decades, the business sector has increasingly been considered a partner in activities that hitherto were in the exclusive domain of the state: development and infrastructure projects, human rights work, HIV/AIDS advocacy, environmental protection and, more recently, peace and security issues.

While partnership with the business sector is deemed by some scholars and policy makers a panacea for all kinds of challenges, others do not subscribe to this view, alluding to numerous examples where companies' behaviour has been detrimental to the common good. In the area of peace and security, the debate about the **role of business** is probably one of the most incongruous. On one hand, it is argued that private companies form part of the web of factors leading to or perpetuating violent conflict. On the other hand, companies are assumed to have the potential to contribute to the settlement of conflicts and the strengthening of peace. "Doing good by doing business", undertaking conflict impact assessments of their investments, promoting tolerance in communities or getting engaged in business diplomacy are some of the ideas that are being discussed.

Both, the argument that private companies contribute to violent conflicts as well as the one that business actors can assist in conflict management, are substantiated by examples from various countries. However, whereas numerous studies have been written about the negative effects of business activities in conflict zones, **little empirical research** has been undertaken so far on the constructive role of private companies in conflict management. The demand and invited participation of business in conflict management has hardly been implemented systematically, making it difficult to assess the corporate potential and limits for this field. Although in a number of cases, companies have participated in the prevention or settlement of violent conflict, corporate engagement has not yet been included in the "standard toolkit" for conflict management used by NGOs and governmental organizations.

The **aim of the study** was to better understand the possibilities and restrictions of business engagement in conflict management and to shed some light on the question of whether or not private companies are likely to assume this new role. The work did, however, largely abstain from discussing if the engagement of private companies is conducive to the establishment of peace. How do private companies perceive violent conflicts and peace processes? What generates costs for companies in violent conflicts? How do private companies manage war related risks? And what makes peace conducive or detrimental for business? These were the central questions leading the study.

The idea that companies should play a role in conflict management is **rooted in different lines of argumentation**. Some experts make a case that since companies contribute to violent conflicts, they also have to be integrated into conflict settlement strategies. Others appeal to corporate philanthropy. And again others allude to the corporate self-interest for peace, trying to make the business case why companies should be partners in conflict management.

To be able to make the business case for firms to support conflict settlement and peacebuilding entails a potentially strong incentive to spur companies into action. The basic reasoning that firms have **self-interest in peace** is grounded in the assumption that companies prefer peace over war. War implies the destruction and interruption of business activities with related costs, whereas peace promises a stable business environment.

However, this line of reasoning neglects some key conditions that seem to work against corporate self interest for peace.

i. The argument does not consider that **'peace' is not a neutral process**. Peace or peace processes, defined as an "action to identify and support structures, which will end to strengthen and solidify peace" (United Nations 1992), have to go beyond a mere armistice. Political exclusion, ethnic and religious cleavages, economic deprivation, rivalling ideological convictions, and other, often interwoven causes of violent conflict have to be addressed to increase the chance for a sustainable peace. Ideally, peace processes are able to transform those economic, social and/or political grievances that gave rise to the conflict in the first place. Private business actors may be affected by those structural reforms implemented in the context of a peace process. Peace, in fact, may inflict unfavourable changes on companies, resulting in opposition rather than support for the peace process. Even though companies may generally strive for an end to the actual violence, they may resist the contents of peace negotiations and related reforms since they may encroach on corporate interests.

ii. Getting involved in conflict management may bring about **organizational and political costs** for companies. Staying neutral may, under some circumstances, be a preferred option for companies. Costs resulting from taking a public stance and participating in peace related activities might put a firm in a position of comparative disadvantage relative to its competitors, undermining the willingness to contribute to conflict management.

iii. The prime concern of the private sector is with making profits. In an **unfavourable business climate**, as it is common in conflict situations, companies will have little incentive to support specific elements of conflict management, such as increased investment to generate employment, even if peace is overall considered as more beneficial.

In a generalized manner, one can assume that companies' support for peace depends on the corporate costs of war in relation to the corporate costs of peace. **Costs of war** cover costs resulting from the destruction of production facilities and infrastructure, high levels of uncertainty or long-term destruction of markets. **Cost of peace** may include political reforms or changes in the economic rules of the game that result from a peace process as well as the costs of getting engaged in conflict management. Both – expenses for war as well as peace – are determined by factors such as the intensity of the war, geographic spread, type of conflict, branch, conflict management strategies, etc. Only when the costs of war are higher than the costs of peace, will corporations then consider the possibility of engaging in conflict management. Relatedly, branches that are more effected by warfare, for instance because they are concentrated in certain geographical areas, are assumed to have a higher stake in peace than other branches or groups with less exposure to the violence.

In the study, particular attention was given to the role of **domestic companies**. Most research so far addresses the role of TNCs, largely ignoring national businesses. However, some scholars assume that domestic corporate actors have a more pronounced self-interest in a peaceful business environment than TNCs, given their relative inflexibility over the relocation of their production facilities[1]. At the same time, domestic firms are more likely to defy a peace process and re-

---

1   This is something domestic companies have in common with most TNCs in the resource extraction sector, such as mining.

lated political changes. In many developing countries, the national private sector is typically part of the national elite that tends to defend those economic, social and political structures against which other segments of the population rebel. A political system that consolidates unequal land distribution, for example, is one such possible underlying factor leading to a violent conflict. A comprehensive peace process should hence address this matter by, for example, encouraging political measures to encourage a more equal distribution of land. By being part of the economic and political elite of a country, companies may be in a position to thwart those reforms and to concentrate on protecting their interests.

The results for the case study in Guatemala

The civil war and peace process in **Guatemala** provided an interesting test case for these theoretical arguments. The vast majority of the private sector opposed the peace talks with the guerrillas, although there was little indication that companies profited in a significant way from the war. Indeed, on several occasions entrepreneurs made it clear that they favoured an end to the war, due an acute awareness of the economic costs. But at the same time, business organizations lobbied against the peace talks, boycotted civil society initiatives that were set up to bring their voice to the negotiation table and filed law suits against the peace process.

What were the reasons for this position that seemingly contradicts the argument of corporate self-interest in peace? In line with some of the findings from the theoretical part, the following main aspects were identified as the key variables leading to the private sector's recalcitrant position:
1) low war related costs;
2) risk of high peace related costs;
3) organizational capacity and unity.

1) Low war related costs

Probably one of the most important reasons underlying the private sector's relatively little enthusiasm in supporting peace are the low levels of costs the civil war imposed on the companies. For most of the 36 years of war, the conflict inflicted only a mild toll on the Guatemalan private sector. In fact, Guatemala experienced positive macroeconomic growth rates during most of the war years. The fighting remained relatively contained in rural regions with few investments by private companies, such as in the department of Xiché. In addition, the conflict was mainly waged at a relatively low intensity. The extortion of war taxes, road blockages, destruction of production facilities (in particular on *fincas*), kidnapping, etc. affected companies, some more severely than others. But the business community as a whole suffered directly from severe hardship with high levels of **political insecurity and direct war-costs** only for a relatively short period, from the late 1970s to the early 1980s, when the civil war reached its highest levels of intensity.

A major fear of the private sector during the civil war and in particular during the war peak in the late 1970s was that the guerrillas would assume political power. The business sector considered the rebels' leftist agenda an immediate threat to its corporate interests. The **risks of socio-political changes** were perceived overall as more severe than the risks of direct destruction of production facilities. But aside from the period between 1978 and 1982, companies had only little reason to believe that the insurgency would be able to take over the state. After 1984, when the guerrillas were *de facto* militarily defeated, both types of risks – direct as well as indirect war-related risks – were even more reduced, leaving hardly any threats for the private sector from the insurgency.

The **branches most seriously affected** by the armed strife were the coffee and tourism sectors. But whereas the coffee sector was affected in terms of direct war-related costs, as well as in terms of higher levels of insecurity due to potential political changes, tourism was barely a target of direct attacks. The sugar sector also experienced negative war effects but not as severely. Industry was most strongly affected by the destruction of infrastructure but apart from occasional terrorist attacks against "big industry", this sector experienced mild costs overall. Similarly, the banking sector was only mildly affected except for rare attacks against prestigious bank buildings.

War related costs were additionally mitigated by quite successful strategies to manage war risks. Corporate **conflict management strategies** changed in the course of the civil war, primarily determined by the intensity of the armed conflict. The strategies included the establishment of strong ties with the military governments, capital flight and disinvestment, as well as political campaigning.

During the civil war, the private sector primarily attempted to manage the risks associated with the armed conflict by establishing **close relationships with the army**. The provision of security services by the military to corporate facilities curbed some of the immediate threats of the civil war. And through close political links with the army, national laws were shaped in favour of the economic elite, securing economic benefits as well as physical security. But although some individual businessmen supported the national army directly by supplying private planes or giving permission to use private estates for military bases, the private sector provided little systematic assistance to the military. Even though the army requested from the entrepreneurs, on at least one occasion, an increase in their support for the military's counterinsurgency strategy, the business sector refused, minimizing thereby their costs for managing war-related risks.

Capital flight and disinvestment as a more cost-intensive way of managing war related risk only became more common in the late 1970s when the intensity of the rebellion increased significantly. At the time, the military was unable to protect the private sector from insurgency attacks and direct war costs grew. However, the entrepreneurs in Guatemala upheld most of their assets in the country, leading seemingly to significantly lower rates of capital flight than, for example, during the civil war in El Salvador.

In addition, the business sector launched **political campaigns** (e.g. the *campanga de los mille días*), complementing the other strategies in a cost-efficient way. The campaigns attempted to convince the Guatemalan population of the economic and political disadvantages of a leftist regime. Although these initiatives were primarily directed towards the following elections, the campaigners also hoped to undermine the mobilization for the insurgency. The initiative primarily showed two things:

i. That the private sector considered the political risks linked to a leftist overthrow as a major threat.
ii. That they had not relinquished the country as a business location, despite the comparatively heavy losses in previous years.

High costs from the war that may in other conflicts have provoked a positive attitude from business organizations vis-à-vis a peace process, hardly existed in Guatemala. Even during the peak of the civil war, the private sector was not threatened to the extent that it had to abandon the country. The fact that the insurgency was de facto militarily defeated before the beginning of the peace talks in the mid 1980s certainly further undermined the self-interest of companies to support peace. Beyond this, companies did not only consider the cost of war as being low, but also they perceived the potential costs of a peace process as being comparatively high.

2) Risk of high peace related costs

The civil war in Guatemala was a drag on private economic activities with financial implications for the entrepreneurs. But the violent conflict did not bring the economy to a standstill or even close to a standstill. The end of the civil war certainly promised a reduction in direct war related expenses and the private sector clearly **benefited from the end of attacks** against their properties, the end to the collection of war taxes, increased workforce stability on some *fincas*, and an end to international isolation due to human rights violations, etc.

However, the private sector did not overall expect a drastic improvement in economic conditions with the peace process. Instead, from a corporate viewpoint a peace process **imposed risks to private companies**. The business sector was concerned for nearly the entire duration of the peace talks that the negotiations with the insurgency would bring about an outcome detrimental to its interests. As the guerrillas had reiterated throughout the violent conflict the relevance of their socio-economic goals, the private sector had good reason to believe that left-leaning economic reforms would form a crucial component of the peace treaties.

Although the Guatemalan peace process in the end resulted in few costs for the entrepreneurs, the entrepreneurs feared major **changes in the socio-economic rules** of the game, including land reform and changes in the constitution about the function of private property. Since the "Liberal Reform" in 1871 and the increase in cultivation of coffee, the descendants of the colonizers had been able to expand their economic privileges. They could establish social conditions and a state structure that secured access to land as well as cheap, indigenous labour. During most years of the civil war, the close alliances between the military rulers and parts of the private sector preserved these beneficial business conditions. The *de facto* political veto that the military regimes granted the economic elite for a long period, made possible the ability of the private sector to thwart most attempts to increase national tax revenues and realize land reform. Low wages, exemption from land reforms, low workforce organisation and low tax rates manifested a good business climate.

The peace negotiations put at risk exactly those privileges that the private sector had largely managed to secure during the armed conflict and before. The entrepreneurs had expected that the *de facto* military victory of the army over the insurgency would eradicate the threat of left-leaning changes in the political-economic structure of the country. But with the URNG as a partner at the negotiation table for the peace process, this threat was upheld. The leftwing rhetoric and the development of the Guatemalan civil war in the context of the **Cold War and its ideological battle** certainly increased the potential economic risks from the corporate standpoint. It was not only negotiating with an insurgency, it was negotiating with a leftist insurgency whose socialist ideas were diametrically opposed to the market ideals of Guatemalan business organizations.

In fact, although peace agreements are commonly characterized by an absence of poverty alleviation strategies[2], the Guatemalan peace agreements are globally one the few, which considered **socio-economic aspects.** These are, however, well cushioned by liberal market principals. The socioeconomic agreement, for example, which was signed in May 1996, endorsed liberalization and macroeconomic stabilization, but also set specific targets for increased social welfare spending as well as social and economic development. Among others, the provisions committed the Guatemalan government to raise expenditure for education, health, social security and housing, to increase minimum wages, to support labour organizations and to augment the ratio of taxes to GDP.

---

2   Contemporary peace processes in general tend to have three major features in common. They are characterised by agreements on the introduction of a democratic political system; the establishment of liberal market principals, and a lack of poverty alleviation strategies. With regard to democratization, the peace process in Guatemala did not imply an introduction but rather a reinforcement of democratic rule. Formal democratic principals had already been established with the end of the military regimes in 1986. In the context of the Serranozo and the establishment of the Instancia Nacional del Consenso in which the private sector assumed a lead role, the entrepreneurs showed their commitment to democratic rules and principles. Thus, the peace process implied a reconfirmation of a political process that was already on its way and one that was considered as favourable by the business community.

But despite these provisions to implement social reforms, the most contentious and costly demands of the guerrillas such as a land reform, were not integrated into the peace agreements and **liberal market principals** were assured. These assured that the corporate costs of peace were low. The agreements fell far behind what the guerrillas had originally demanded and what many civil society organisations considered necessary for a true improvement in the social-economic conditions for the majority of the population.

The potentially high cost of a peace process is clearly key to understanding the private sector's behaviour during the peace process. Two further thoughts should be added to support this line of argumentation:

i. It is crucial to distinguish clearly between the corporate sector's position against the **peace negotiations**, which attempted initially to address some of the root causes of the violent conflict and the corporate position towards reaching peace in terms of a mere **end to the violence**. As reiterated repeatedly, the private sector was in favour of peace but largely rejected talks with the guerrillas. A simple cease-fire agreement (or a military victory) would have implied a stop to the violence, without the need for the business sector to make concessions to the rebels in socio-economic and political terms. For the private sector, it was not a question of whether or not peace was more attractive than war. Peace in the sense of an end to violence was widely considered as more beneficial to the private sector. But the potential costs of compromising with the URNG on social-economic reforms in order to reach peace were considered too high in comparison to the moderate war-related costs.

ii. In addition, it is important to differentiate between the economic functions and causes of violence. Most of the recent literature on economic factors in civil wars alludes only to the **economic function of violence**, which suggests that the use of violence can facilitate increased economic gains for certain groups. Economic factors can, however, also be a *cause* of the violence (**economic causes of violent conflicts**). Economic grievance can contribute to the outbreak of violence. In the case of **Guatemala**, there is little evidence that violence assumed a major economic function for the belligerent parties or the business sector. Although some individuals enriched themselves through war (such as some military officials in the *Zona Transversal del Norte*), this enrichment was not systematic and endemic among the militaries, the insurgency and the corporate sector. Economic factors were instead one of the *causes* of the violent conflict. While most scholars have identified distributional inequality and poverty as important sources, the roots to Guatemala's civil are certainly multidimensional, going beyond economic factors alone. However, the existence of poverty or inequality alone also cannot explain why the Guatemalan entrepreneurs defied the peace process. The reason for the private sector's recalcitrant position is placed rather in the **overlap between the causes and the functions of economic factors**. Systematic political and economic exclusion of segments of the population, economic inequality and pervasive poverty (the *causes* of the violent conflict) were also a function for those economic groups that benefited from maintaining inequality and exclusion (de facto through the use of violence). As outlined above, segments of the economic elite in Guatemala gained from the political and economic discrimination against the indigenous people and the social economic conditions that were built around it. The major costs in the peace process were in those areas where the economic functions and causes of violence overlap, such as in the areas of land reform, increased labour rights or increased indigenous rights, which could only be upheld through a coercive state.

3) Organizational capacity and unity

The Guatemalan private sector was **not affected homogenously**, neither by the violent conflict, nor by the peace process. Consequently, it was assumed that different groups within the business community would take up different positions vis-à-vis the civil war and the peace negotiations, potentially undermining the private sector's ability for a united, recalcitrant stance. The coffee and the tourism sectors, for example, as the most seriously affected branches, were expected to have a special interest in the settlement of the violent conflict. While the potential costs of peace for the coffee sector were considerably high (e.g. the risk of land reform, higher wages and improved labour rights), the economic advantages of peace for the tourism sector seemed to significantly outnumber its disadvantages.

However, the Guatemalan private sector presented a rather unified position. The differences that emerged did not simply correlate with how the violent conflict or the peace process impinged on their business activities. They were a reflection of differences in organizational capacity as well as ideological convictions rather than a result of differences in the costs from war and peace. No organized groups splintered off from CACIF to stand for a more peace-inclined position. The **variations among different groups** instead ranged from being moderately opposed to the peace process while accepting the peace talks as a given fact to hard-line opposition against any type of negotiations with the guerrillas. The high level of unity significantly strengthened the private sector's ability to shape the result of the negotiations.

The business sector's unified stance regarding the peace process was clearly favoured by a historically high level of concord among Guatemalan entrepreneurs. This unity is based in part on family ties that crosscut branches and in part on the business sector's historical experience that only with a **unified voice** are they able to realize their interests. Among the different branches, the Guatemalan private sector shared similar views on the most crucial issues linked to the peace negotiations. Changes in the constitution regarding the role of private property, for example, were rejected unanimously, since those far-reaching changes were assumed to have a negative impact on all branches and sectors. Industrialists, commercialists and agriculturalists alike also rejected a land reform. Even if the non-agricultural sector was not directly affected by land expropriation, they all feared that an agrarian reform might scare away foreign investors and develop into "common practice" for all economic branches.

Yet, it is salient that the tourism sector, as the branch with the expected highest returns from an end to the violence, was hardly engaged in the peace process. The tourism sector's passivity was then also not so much a consequence of their economic position concerning the peace process but rather a result of a lack of organizational capacity and leadership in the tourism interest group. The **tourism industry** in Guatemala has traditionally had a weak organizational structure and lobbying position. The severe economic impacts of the civil war on the branch further impaired its ability to lobby for its interests. No organizational structures similar to the agricultural or industrial interests groups were developed through which the tourism sector could effectively articulate its views.

In contrast to these conditions where organizational weaknesses impeded a more active involvement in the peace process, other derivations from CACIF's position were largely based on **ideological and generational differences**, which could not be explained by an economic cost-benefit calculation of war and peace alone. The agricultural sector (mainly coffee), for instance, largely concurred with CACIF's view on the peace process. But from this branch also splintered of the biggest group of hardliner and organized as CONAGRO.

CACIF initially attempted to integrate the **hardliner's position** into its strategy towards the peace process, but widening discrepancies led to the foundation of CONAGRO in 1994. Although CONAGRO only represented a very small group of older businessmen (approximately only 25 individuals) they were able to temporarily stall the peace process. Being strongly shaped by fervent anti-communist sentiments and the traditional attitude of *cordillos,* the hardliners rejected the peace process per se[3].

Similarly, FEPYME's position as the organization for the **small and medium companies**, cannot be explained fully by its different perceptions towards war and peace. Through FEPYME's involvement in the ASC and other civil society initiatives, its strategy formed a counterweight to CACIF's approach to the peace process. Yet, FEPYME's views and demands concerning the peace agreements coincided in many respects with those of CACIF's, such as on the issues of privatization, social security or constitutional reforms. FEPYME's seemingly more constructive approach to the peace process was largely motivated politically and not by a mere cost-benefit analysis of war and peace. In contrast to CACIF, FEPYME did not have sufficient political leverage to influence the peace process from outside structures such as the ASC. Joining these initiatives was FEPYME's only option to allow it to effectively ventilate its views and expand its political influence.

---

3   Members of CONAGRO belonged primarily to the agricultural sector, but hard-line voices also came from other branches such as the industry and service sectors.

This analysis shows that a mere cost-benefit analysis of war and peace cannot sufficiently explain the variations in position among the different business groups. The costs of war and peace are certainly key variables for the basic tendency in perception of war and peace (in the case of Guatemala a rejection of peace talks while welcoming an end to the violence) but some of the variations were based on factors such as organizational capacity or generational and ideological differences[4].

Corporate engagement in peace – The activities of the Guatemalan business sector

In the previous paragraphs the perception of the Guatemalan business sector regarding the peace process and the civil war was discussed, along with an analysis of the reasons for its recalcitrant position. This position largely manifested itself politically but also shaped other activities. What effects did its attitude towards the peace process have in terms of specific actions related to the peace process? The starting point of this study were the different ideas that governmental and non-governmental organizations developed in order to partner with the private sector in conflict management. These ideas included activities such as business diplomacy, support for economic development and wealth creation or initiatives to foster reconciliation among the war-weary population. In the following paragraphs, it will be outlined how the corporate sector's opinion on the civil war and the peace process shaped the entrepreneurs' activities, which are comparable to the current demands and ideas of **corporate engagement in peace processes**.

It should be emphasised in this context that although the Guatemalan peace process happened largely before the issue of corporate support to conflict management was debated broadly, the Guatemalan entrepreneurs had several opportunities to get engaged. During the peace negotiations and the post-conflict peacebuilding period **specific channels** were provided for non-state groups to voice their viewpoints and support reconstruction. Moreover, the business community was traditionally an influential social group with an established lobbying capacity and the ability to shape political decision making processes. The private sector did not in fact remain passive, as one might expect from companies arguing against corporate engagement for political reasons. Companies, however, did not use this space to support an establishment of peace.

Although its tactics altered, the business sector largely followed the unspoken premise not to compromise with the insurgency, largely because it feared having to make costly concessions. On a number of occasions, **concrete demands** were made to the private sector to actively support peace and peacebuilding, in forms

---

4   It should also be mentioned in this context that in the post-conflict phase, AGEXPRONT assumed positions that showed a rather peace-inclined position. However, during the actual phase of negotiations, AGEXPRONT was not yet fully established and therefore did not get involved during this period.

very much in line with current ideas for corporate engagement in peace processes. But the private sector hardly followed up on these requests. The principal demands made to the entrepreneurs were the following:

i. During the administrations of Ríos Montt and Cerezo, demands were made to support governmental efforts for **economic development** including the improvement of working conditions.
ii. Demands to **enter into dialogue** with other non-state groups and the insurgency in order to improve mutual understanding or reach consensus on peace process related matters, e.g. in the context of the Oslo-Consultations, the participation in the ASC, or in post-conflict three-party commissions.
iii. Demands to support **economic reconstruction** and development in the post-conflict period, including the provision of financial resources through taxes.

The first requests were made during the civil war and at the incipient phase of the peace process. On both occasions, during the administrations of Ríos Montt and Cerzo, the government demanded (with the National Plan of Security and Development, 1982, and the Thesis on National Stability, 1987), that entrepreneurs engage in the national strategies of poverty reduction as a tool for conflict management. The administrations had realized that high levels of poverty and inequality made the rural population more receptive to leftist guerrilla rhetoric. Comparable to current demands for corporate engagement in conflict prevention, the governments asked the business community to improve working conditions, to pay higher wages, to accept tax increases to the government in order to enable it to implement social programmes, and to augment investments. But the entrepreneurs refused, seemingly for two reasons: First, the costs of war were 'not high enough' to justify the sacrifice of **social investments** and, second, the government did not make serious attempts to enter alternatively into peace negotiations with the insurgency (which would have implied high costs of peace at this stage).

The rejection of the private sector was certainly also a consequence of the **worsening relationship** between the business community and the two administrations. But the overriding factor was clearly the lack of willingness to tackle some of the root causes of the civil war through economic means. The widespread conviction among the business community at this time was that the best way to deal with the insurgency was through military means alone. Little consideration was given to alternative solutions.

With regard to the second type of demand made to the entrepreneurs – the request to join dialogue forums – the private sector showed similarly little willingness. Its behaviour was largely characterised by **boycotting** civil society initiatives for the peace process and by attempts to undermine the peace talks, for instance through filing law suits against the guerrilla commanders. Companies largely insisted on lobbying independently from other non-state actors and on having separate meetings with the URNG. Exceptions included the meeting in

Ottawa between the URNG and CACIF in the context of the Oslo-consultations and some attempts by the business sector after 1994 to improve the relationship with civil-society groups. Overall, however, the private sector stayed outside those mechanisms that were formally established for civil society participation in the peace process. Most business organizations did not participate, for instance, in the *Assamblea de la Sociedad Civil* or in other initiatives seeking either to bring the voice of non-state actors to the negotiation table or to reach consensus among a broader set of actors. The business community could thereby maintain an independent and strong lobbying position, partly represented by CEPAZ, whereupon they did not have to compromise with other non-state actors.

The third set of demands was made during the post-conflict period. It was largely accepted that a successful implementation of the peace agreements was not possible without the support of civil society and the entrepreneurs. The World Bank stated, for example, that a "lasting peace and faster growth require not only the cessation of violence, but addressing Guatemala's poverty and social inequality" – something that was difficult to achieve without the support of the private sector (World Bank 1997: 14). This fact became particularly clear in the context of negotiations over tax increases, attempts to improve labour rights and wages, and attempts to set up a new land register. Even though the peace treaties were in principal agreements between the government and the URNG, they had also acknowledged the relevance of **private sector activities**. For example, by asking from businesses to increase investments in war-ridden regions of the country – very much in line with the central demands in the current debate on business partnerships during post-conflict reconstruction – it was attempted to integrate the business sector into the peace process.

But although the entrepreneurs welcomed the signing of the final peace agreement, including the economic aspects, they showed little enthusiasm in supporting the **implementation of these treaties**. Their enduring rejection of a tax reform, the difficult negotiations during the three-party commissions established in the aftermath of the signing of the final peace agreement on economic issues, persistently poor labour conditions and low rates of investment contradicted sharply with the contents and spirit of the peace agreements. There was little indication that the entrepreneurs made much attempt to support reconstruction and wealth creation in the country. Sharp inequalities between the impoverished majority and the affluent minority and the systematic exclusion of large parts of the population, which were key causes of Guatemala's recurring rebel violence in the past, stayed in place and not enough was done to remedy these problems.

Certainly, an aggravating factor during the immediate post-conflict phase was the **bad political, social and economic conditions** that characterized this period. Coffee prizes sunk to a low and criminal violence augmented significantly after the formal end of the civil war. Many entrepreneurs found themselves spending more money on security measures during the post-conflict period than during the armed conflict. Also political insecurity remained high and the open antagonism against the entrepreneurs during Portillo's term in office further undermined the private sector's willingness to invest.

As stated before, to explain the corporate strategies during the civil war, the peace process and the post-conflict period, a cost-benefit analysis of war and peace is certainly a useful though not completely sufficient tool. Organizational capacity but also other factors such as the ability and willingness of national and international actors to let entrepreneurs involve in conflict management have to be considered while trying to understand companies' strategies towards peace.

9.2 Comparison of the Guatemalan case with other peace process

Overall, the private sector in Guatemala showed little propensity to get engaged in conflict management as suggested by international organizations and NGOs. Guatemalan businessmen barely changed their modes of operation, and did not support reconciliation or contribute to post-conflict reconstruction efforts. Generally, low war-related corporate costs, high (potential) peace related corporate costs, and a relatively unified organized private sector, largely overlapping with the traditional elite, are identified as the key reasons for the Guatemalan private sector's position and ability not to support a comprehensive peace process.

To what extent can the findings of this case study be transferred to other cases? What are the particularities of the Guatemalan case and what is similar to other peace processes? Or: Why did the business sector in other war-torn societies seem to reveal a more favourable attitude towards peace processes than in Guatemala? This chapter cannot draw a comprehensive **comparison** between the Guatemalan and other cases. However, it can provide some thinking about the transferability of the results from the Guatemalan case and offer some policy recommendations for attempts to engage the business sector in conflict management in general.

The findings for the Guatemalan case are compared to various countries, including Columbia, El Salvador, Fiji, Nepal, Philippines (Mindanao) and South Africa. This **selection** was primarily a result of the availability of literature on the topic. Since there is relatively little information on the role of private business in peace processes, a more systematic selection of cases for comparison was not possible. The choice had to be determined by the accessibility of information. For some of these countries, more detailed case studies were available, such as for Columbia. In other cases, such as Nepal or Mindanao, information on the private sector's role was mentioned in studies addressing broader issues of the respective conflict and peace processes.

The three factors that were identified as key for the understanding of the Guatemalan corporate position and strategy vis-à-vis the peace process will be analysed and compared to other cases. The discussions also give allowance to the fact that the costs and benefits of war and peace as well as the organizational capacity of business players are not the only factors shaping their positions and strategies (for a brief overview of the results, see Table 15).

1. Corporate costs of war

The civil war in Guatemala imposed a high human toll. More than 200,000 people were killed and many displaced. However, for the business sector, the direct as well as indirect war-related costs were, overall, moderate. This factor was identified as one reason for the entrepreneurs' incompliant stance towards the peace process. In comparison to most other violent conflicts with similar or even lower numbers of causalities, such **low economic costs are rather unusual** and explain in part, why the Guatemalan business sector could afford a recalcitrant position vis-à-vis the peace process.

Indeed, in South Africa, El Salvador or Columbia, the direct and/or indirect corporate costs of war were significantly higher, prompting corporate actors in these countries to assume a significantly **more proactive role** in conflict management. In some other cases, such as Northern Ireland, however, the position of the entrepreneurs was also more constructive but it cannot be determined clearly if in fact the costs of war were higher, or just the corporate awareness of the implications of the violence on the economy.

In **South Africa**, for example, private business activities were strongly affected by labour and township unrest as well as by economic sanctions, which were imposed as a consequence of state repression of the unrest. These events impinged negatively on the business sector, spurring formerly recalcitrant economic elites into pressing the apartheid government for political reforms and negotiations with the ANC. The private sector had held originally a reluctant attitude against the ANC, largely because of their left-leaning political and economic goals. The international pressure and other costs, as well as alterations in ANC's political demands offset its earlier concerns, making the entrepreneurs to advocate for peace and for the abolishment of the apartheid system (Wood 2000). Also in **El Salvador** (a case, in many respects, very similar to Guatemala), the prolonged rebellion and related counterinsurgency measures had a direct prejudicial impact on the private sector. Many entrepreneurs left their original agricultural activities as a result of guerrilla assaults, destruction of infrastructure and the general uncertainty in the country. Capital flight increased, GDP per capita fell significantly and the relative contribution of the different economic sectors to GDP shifted. Similar to the South African case, as a consequence, hitherto intractable businessmen became more amenable to negotiations with the insurgency and accepted some compromises on socio-political issues (Wood 2000).

There is also some indication that mounting war-related costs in **Columbia** encouraged private entrepreneurs to initiate peacebuilding measures. Until the early 1990s, entrepreneurs did not consider the violent conflict a major threat to their economic interests. Economic growth rates were positive and violent confrontation was largely contained in some rural areas. Frequent destruction of infrastructure, rising numbers of kidnappings, increasing incidences of extortion of war taxes by illegal armed forces, growing governmental taxes for military and security expenditures etc., seemed to have enhanced the corporate costs of conflict (despite still healthy growth rates). Although many domestic companies were involved in financing paramilitary groups and militias, and responded to the increasing threats and expenses with capital flight, a number of entrepreneurs launched peacebuilding initiatives aimed at tackling violence by supporting wealth creation and the empowerment of workers as well as better education for communities (Rettberg 2004).

Also not fully certain, is the case in **Northern Ireland**. In Northern Ireland, business organizations began to actively push for peace in the early 1990s, when promising peace talks were already underway, leading to the peace agreement of April 1998. Despite various sticking points, with the Anglo–Irish agreement in 1985 and the first round of talks between Hume and Adams in 1988, the Northern Ireland peace process had gained significant momentum after the failure of the Sunningdale agreement in 1974. Corporate organizations argued that since the 1990s they had become more aware of the economic impact of the conflict in terms of declining tourism, low rates of investment, destruction of plants and premises, high security costs and 'brain drain' (European Platform for Conflict Prevention and Transformation 1999). But there is no certainty whether the corporate costs of violence were indeed higher than those in Guatemala.

Slightly different also seems to be the case of **Sri Lanka**. Like Guatemala, Sri Lanka experienced positive economic growth despite the ongoing armed struggle. The country recorded growth rates of 6.2 percent in 1990 and 7 percent in 1993. In addition, the civil war was contained for long periods in restricted areas of the country, with only sporadic attacks elsewhere (Arunatilake et al. 2001). However, despite the low corporate war-related costs, companies began to participate and develop peace initiatives in the late 1990s. It seems that, in particular, requests by international organisations rose awareness, encouraged them to engage and to take a public stance in support of peace (de Zoysa 2002: 55).

This brief comparison seems to support the result from the case study in Guatemala: High economic costs from war makes the private sector more receptive for peace initiatives; low corporate war costs leads to a less amenable attitude. The analysis shows additionally, however, that not only economic factors spur entrepreneurs into supporting peace processes. The example from Sri Lanka suggests that factors such as encouragement from outside and awareness-rising stimulate entrepreneurs to engage in peace related activities.

2. Corporate costs of peace

Economic factors were among the origins of the violent conflict in Guatemala. Economic grievance, inequality and economic exclusion were reasons for the insurgency to assume its fight and for others to join the movement. The peace agreements echoed some of these causes, being at the same time reason for profound concern on the part of the Guatemalan business sector.

Although economic grievances alone hardly lead to an insurgence against the state, economic deprivation and exclusion, poverty and unequal access to resources are also of relevance for rebellion in other cases. In fact, most current intrastate conflicts are taking place in third world countries, many of which are poor, overpopulated and marked by sharp contrasts between rich and poor. In Mindanao, Namibia, Peru, Bolivia, Fiji or Sri Lanka, for instance, poverty, inequality, **economic grievances** and repression are among the root causes of intra-state tensions and violence. In particular, land issues often assume a critical role, frequently associated with racism or ethnic-based exclusion.

In **Mindanao**, for example, impoverished settlers, wealthy landowners and companies fight over land rights. The struggle over land is interwoven with the conflict between Muslims and Christians and the conflict between left-wing rebel groups (National Democratic Front and New Peoples Army) and the government (Concepcion et al. 2003).

Similar to this case, in **Fiji**, the conflict lines run along the ethnic divisions between the indigenous Fijians and the Indo-Fijians, which are descendants of the Indian labourers, brought by the British colonizers to work on the sugar plantations. In the post-colonial period a divided labour market developed, with the indigenous Fijians working on traditional smallholdings and possessing most of the land of the country and the Indo-Fijians being either tenant farmers, miners, or wage-earners. The recent conflict emerged primarily as a consequence of disputes over land ownership, employment and jobs in public administration.

If **economic factors** as those outlined above contribute to the root causes of violence, it is likely that they will be brought up again – successfully or unsuccessfully – in the context of a peace process. In cases where unequal distribution of land or other private assets are thought to be tackled in peace agreements, resistance from landowners and (economic) elites is likely to occur[5]. As in Guatemala, peace agreements of this nature potentially challenge their interests, imply possible costs for entrepreneurs and thereby weaken or undermine their self-

---

5   Land issues caused conflicts also in countries such as Cambodia, Haiti or Nepal. The problem in those countries is not, however, primarily the unequal distribution of land, with a small elite possessing the majority of land resources while an impoverished majority has to live from small estates. Environmental degradation, increased pressure on land due to population growth, high rates of landlessness and insecure land titles instigated in these cases, conflicts between communities and outsiders or constituted a good basis for the mobilization of rebel movements.

interest in peace. Only if the direct and indirect costs of war are high, are private actors more likely to concede to agreements that compromise their interests.

Similar to Guatemala, for instance, in **Mindanao** the peace agreement that was signed in 1996 between the government and the Moro National Liberation Front, "omitted many key issues, including reparations, economic redistribution, affirmative action and conflicting land claims. The latter, in particular, was considered 'too explosive' to tackle" (Concepcion et al. 2003: 12).

Seemingly contradictory to the Guatemalan outcomes is the behaviour of the private sector in **El Salvador**, where entrepreneurs over time became more receptive to the peace agreements. As in Guatemala, the Salvadorian economic elite had based large proportions of its profits on large land estates and/or the exploitation of cheap labour, which was challenged by the insurgency. By contrast to Guatemala, however, the potential costs of peace declined in El Salvador as the private sector's economic activities and interested changed, making peace talks less of a risk for these actors. Over time, the economic elite in El Salvador became less dependent on these two factors, cheap labour and land, because:

i. in contrast to Guatemala, the Salvadorian government implemented the first steps of an agrarian reform with an expropriation of more than 300 private estates in 1980.
ii. guerrilla attacks against plantations were significantly higher in El Salvador than in Guatemala.

Both factors increased insecurity in the agro-sector, prompting agriculturalists to decrease their traditional activities and move to non-agricultural branches, in particular the commerce and service industries[6]. Those increasing groups of the private sector with investments in the booming non-agricultural branches held a more constructive position vis-à-vis the peace talks, fundamentally because they had less to lose and more to gain from peace than those in the agricultural sector. Since the midst of the 1980s, these newly emerging non-agricultural groups gained palpably more influence in the El Salvadorian business community and ensured the **acquiescence of the private sector to the peace process**. In Guatemala, this shift did not occured.

In addition, in contrast to the Guatemalan guerrillas, the FMLN (Farabundo Martí Front for National Liberation) in **El Salvador** made it clear at an early stage of the peace talks that **economic issues** would not take precedence in the negotiations. Priority was given instead to electoral, judicial, political and military issues. The economic agreements focused on questions such as the reintegration of ex-combatants and the extension of credit for small and medium enterprises, but did not include economic reforms that would fundamentally reshape the rules of the game (Wood 2000). In Guatemala, instead, the URNG in-

---

6   For additional factors that made agro-export less profitable in El Salvador, see Wood 2000: 55-58.

sisted for a long time on incorporating economic topics and sensitive issues such as changes in the constitution on the function of private property. Only when Alvaro Arzú assumed power, could the business community be relatively assured that the negotiations over socio-economic reforms would only impose mild costs on the entrepreneurs. The Guatemalan insurgency held this strong position despite its military weakness. In El Salvador, the insurgency was in a much stronger position, having fought governmental forces to a stalemate, but backed off early from many conflictive economic demands. The interplay of these factors – an early restraint from sensitive economic demands by the guerrillas, higher war-related costs, a stronger bargaining position of the insurgency and a shift in the composition of the economic sector – made the Salvadorian economic elite amenable towards a negotiated settlement.

The **leftist demands** and ideas of the insurgency were diametrically opposed to the interests of the business sector. Although the peace process evolved in a post-cold war environment, with rebel groups that desisted from their original communist objectives, their demands were still founded in their left-leaning position that they had held in previous years, making the entrepreneurs anticipate high costs. In addition, the corporate hardliners in particular maintained an uncompromising and relentless position that originated in the cold war period. While large parts of the business sector moved away from fervent anticommunism and assumed more moderate positions, CONAGRO based its ideology on the cold-war experiences, feeling deeply imperiled by the negotiations with the guerrillas.

Although genuine social-revolutionary movements hardly exist today, leftist ideas have certainly not vanished. One leftist rebel movements, for instance, is the **Maoist guerrilla force in Nepal**. The civil war in Nepal has developed characteristics and implications for the business sector similar to the Guatemalan civil war that emerged in the cold-war period. Founded as the Communist Party of Nepal-Maoist (CPN-M), the group took up arms in 1996. Within six years, they managed to establish a presence in almost all of Nepal, including the capital and it is unlikely that the movement can be eliminated in the near future. The CPN-M's goal is to bring down the state and to establish a planned economy, abolish the Nepali monarchy, realize a radical land reform and foster a national industrialisation. The Maoists do not, however, plan to introduce full socialism. Instead, they aim to develop a balance between state ownership of big industries and private ownership of small and medium companies (Bray et al. 2003).

The national economy as well as private **companies have been hard** hit by the violent conflict. GDP growth rates have dropped by 0.61 percent in 2001-2002, in comparison to average annual growth rates of 4.8 percent in the preceding three years. Private corporations have faced numerous direct attacks, including banks as well as industrial plants, in particular, those of companies in foreign ownership. The extortion of war taxes by the guerrillas from businesspeople totals probably hundreds of millions of rupees. The destruction of infrastructure including airports hampered normal business life severely. Moreover, there has been a massive drop in the number of tourists, one of Nepal's major sources of income, which has affected many businesses.

The high **corporate costs** prompted the business sector to seek contact with the insurgency. "There has been some dialogue between business leaders and Maoist representatives, both on issues affecting individual companies, such as extortion demands, and on wider sectoral issues [...] (Bray et al. 2003: 125). However, "there is little sign of an emerging 'business for peace' lobby" (Bray et al. 2003: 125). A combination of factors may explain the business sector's aversion to expanding its peace efforts. First, similar to Guatemala, the Maoist demands are (despite the allowance of small and medium companies) irreconcilable with the private sector's exigency for market principals. The current, perceived disinterest of the Maoist in peace talks, makes it unlikely that peace can be established without far-reaching concessions to the rebels. It is doubtful that the business community would give its consent to this. In addition, factions of the private sector are entangled in feudal practices, which the insurgency seeks to eradicate. This would constitute additional potential losses for businesspeople, should these practices be addressed in any future peace talks.

This brief comparison seems to largely confirm the relevance of corporate costs of peace to explain companies' position vis-à-vis peace processes. In the case of Nepal as well as Guatemala, peace negotiations with the insurgency was not a promising option. Even though the Cold War environment in which the Guatemalan civil war emerged impacted the private sector's position and strategies, the fundamental arguments seem to sustain. Cases such as El Salvador or the favourable support of Northern Irish business organizations for the peace process were possible, also because peace did not negatively impact on the private sector.

Table 15: Case studies, supporting and contradicting the results from Guatemala

Category	Country	Similar results as in Guatemala	Diverging results from Guatemala
Corporate costs of war	South Africa	High costs of war resulted in support for peace process	
	El Salvador	High costs of war resulted in support for peace process	
	Columbia	Increasing costs of war seems to increase the willingness to support peace	
	Northern Ireland		Seemingly relatively low costs of war, but support for peace process.
	Sri Lanka		Seemingly low costs of war but support for peace process.
Corporate costs of peace	Philippines (Mindanao)	Exclusion of economic issues from peace agreements but little information on position of business sector.	
	El Salvador	Lower costs of peace, since guerrillas stepped back from some of the leftist economic demands and because businessmen shifted investments to less conflict vulnerable branches.	
	Nepal	High potential costs from peace process due to Maoist orientation of insurgency. Little support from entrepreneurs for peace process.	
Organizational capacity and unity	El Salvador	Seemingly well-organized private sector and strong involvement in peace process.	
	Northern Ireland	Seemingly well-organized private sector and strong involvement in peace process.	
	Sri Lanka	Seemingly well-organized private sector and strong involvement in peace process.	
	Liberia	Weakly organized sector and little involvement in peace-related activities.	

3. Organizational Capacity and unity of the private sector

Much harder to compare because of a lack of information is the third point, the organizational capacity of the private sector. Information on the internal dynamics of the business sectors and organizations regarding the peace processes necessary for a more in depth comparison with the Guatemalan case is not available. The following analysis has to stay therefore even more on the surface than the two preceding discussions.

It was argued that business organizations in Guatemala, especially CACIF, could assert much influence on the outcome of the peace process, among others because of their high level of organizational capacity and unity. Northern Ireland, Sri Lanka, and El Salvador seem similar with respect to organizational capacity, since all three countries had **well-established private business communities** that allowed them to articulate their opinion on the respective peace processes. The institutional structures were in place, and were relatively well-functioning, as well as a certain level of influence on political decision-makers.

However, for some countries it is known that despite the organizational capacity, it was difficult to agree on a common corporate position, which hampered an engagement in the peace process. In Sri Lanka, for instance, the private sector preferred for a long time to have a neutral stance concerning the conflict because sharp political divisions deterred companies from engaging in peacebuilding. Only when the private sector managed to overcome these cleavages, were they able and willing to engage (de Zoysa 2002: 55). Similarly, in El Salvador, deep discrepancies that emerged between the agricultural and the non-agricultural sectors, prevented the easy formation of a common position towards the peace process. The **strong unity** of the Guatemalan sector that gave them a relatively joint position towards the peace process may be exceptional for most developing countries.

The Guatemalan case has shown as well that a violent conflict can (further) undermine the political strength of a business sector. Countries, in particular conflict-ridden ones, may lack an organized private sector or capacity may have been depleted, similar as in the case of the tourism association in Guatemala. Liberia, for instance, only had a small domestic business sector that was weakly organized. When the violent conflict erupted, most companies fled the country, leaving a vacuum for corporate lobbying (Montclos 1999). It is very likely that the situation was similar in many other high-intensity conflicts. The economic sector flees, leaving little possibility for corporate involvement in conflict management, or only on the level of individual entrepreneurs.

9.3 Policy implications

From the case study on the role of the private business sector in violent conflict, the conflict settlement and post-conflict peacebuilding phases, including the comparison with a number of other violent conflicts, the following policy implications are derived (see Box 3) (Crónica 1988a).

Box 3: Policy Implications

1.	The private business sector may support peace in terms of an end to organized violence but it may resist a **comprehensive peace process**. A mere cease-fire tackles the corporate risks and costs that go along with violent conflict, such as attacks against production facilities, destruction of infrastructure or labour insecurity. A comprehensive peace process may, however encroach upon the interests of private business actors. In particular if i. the domestic business elites is or has been entangled in the process resulting in the conditions that gave rise to the violence in the first place and, ii. if the corporate costs of war are rather minor private business actors may be apt to resist and defy rather than support comprehensive conflict management.
2.	The corporate **self-interest argument is not sufficient** to spur companies in supporting conflict management. Corporate engagement in conflict management seems, however, desirable for the following reasons: i. Since companies may be part of the problem leading to the emergence of a violent conflict, a sustainable solution of a conflict is not feasible without their integration. Private companies have the capacity to obstruct conflict settlement and peacebuilding and should therefore be integrated into conflict management strategies; ii. Private investments in the pre as well as post-conflict phases, political pressure from companies to end a conflict, changes in the modes of production etc. can be significant and efficient corporate measures to foster the settlement of conflict and peacebuilding. They should not be ignored in conflict management strategies of governmental organizations.

3.	The business sector is **not necessarily a neutral actor**, even if it does not directly profit from warfare, such as through making business with rebel groups. Private actors in particular in third world countries, may benefit from the structures that gave rise to the violence (e.g. inequality and exclusion). Business actors consequently would lose if rebels can realize their demands either through a military victory or through negotiated compromises and may therefore not support a peace process.
4.	In situations in which the private sector may lose significantly through a comprehensive peace process, its political involvement in peace negotiations may be **detrimental to the common good**.
5.	The private sector is not likely to **initiate business-lead peace building measures** by itself. Companies, not involved in the violent conflict, may i. prefer an impartial position in a volatile conflict environment, and ii. may be apt to stay passive and internalise conflict related costs as additional operational costs. In particular small and medium companies may lack the capacity to calculate the real corporate expenses related to violent conflicts. Companies have to be educated about the direct and especially the indirect corporate costs of violent strife in order to encourage them to participate and initiate conflict management activities.
6.	The private sector may in many cases not be aware of the options to engage constructively in conflict management. Corporations should be educated about potential areas of **how to participate** in establishing a more peaceful society.
7.	The private sector is not a homogenous block with equal war related costs and experiences. In order to establish a sound **peace constituency**, those groups with the highest war-related costs have to be identified and strengthened. The variations within the business community may or may not. They may also run along geographic, social (historic economic elite versus upcoming, younger businessmen) or other lines.
8.	Each conflict is different, has different effects on companies and requires **different solutions**. Not every conflict is automatically detrimental to the business sector.

Appendices

Appendix 1: Maps

Map 1: Main geographic zones of Guatemala

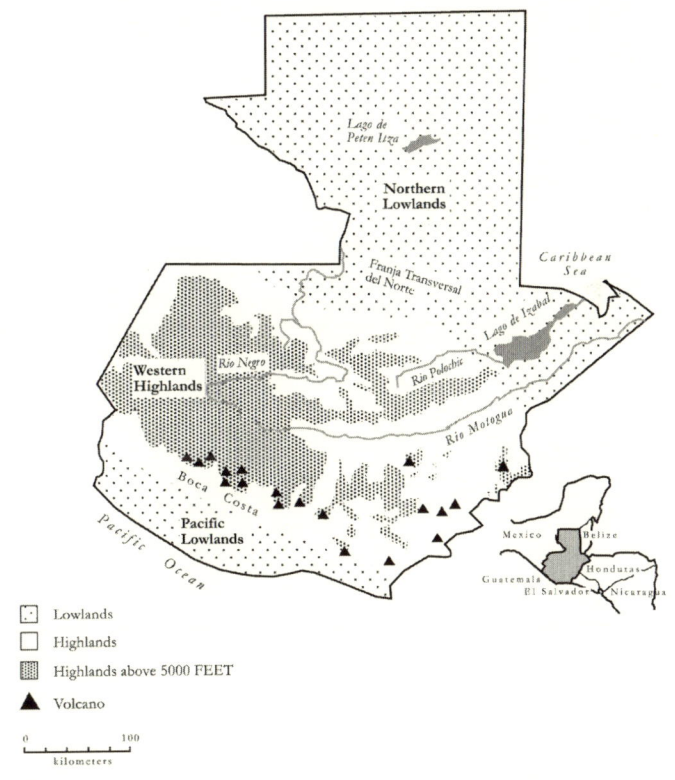

Map 2: Areas of main human rights violations during the civil war and major coffee zones in Guatemala

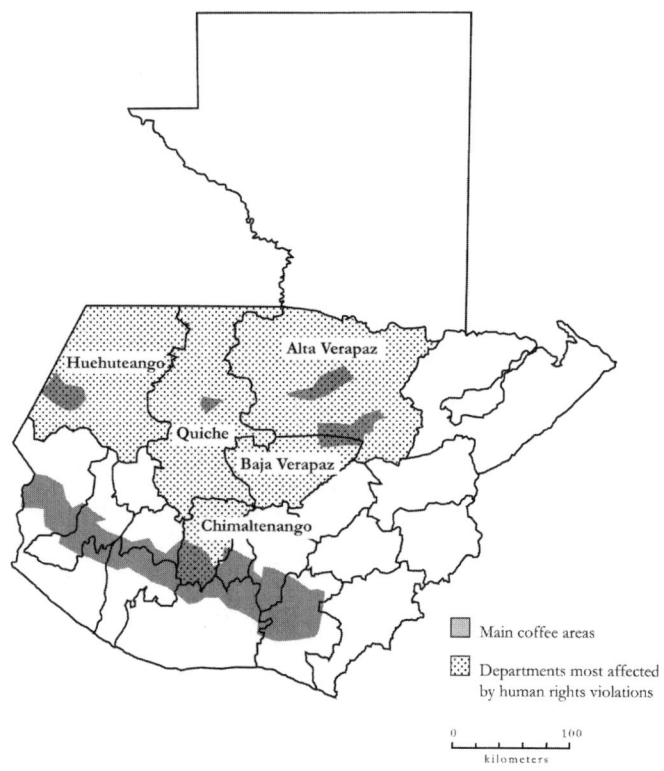

APPENDICES | 273

Map 3: Major fighting zones during the first and second phase of the civil war

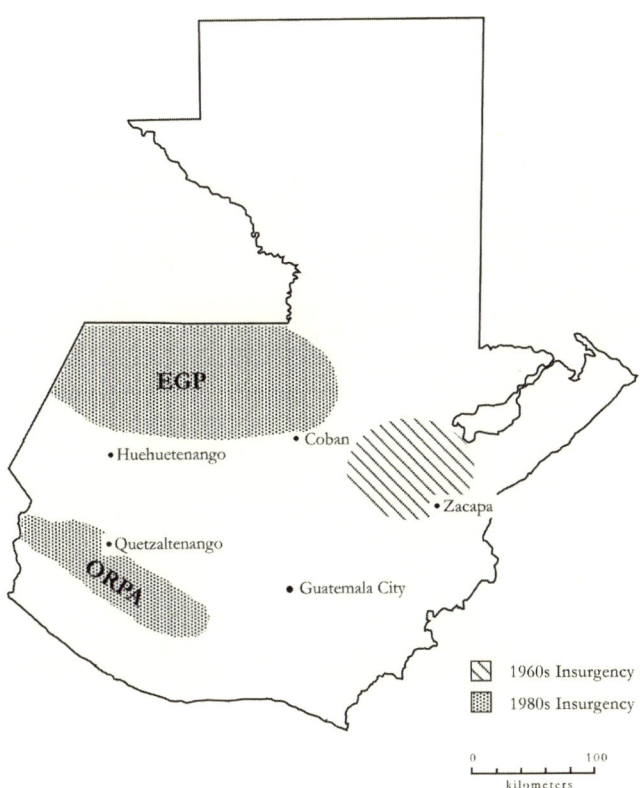

Appendix 2: Destruction and damage of fincas (1978-1994)

	Year	Department	Type of damage	Affected type of crop	Reported loss in *quetzales*
1.	1978	Mazatenango	1,500 cuerdas of cane	Cane	45,000
2.	1979		Equipment	Coffee	1,000,000
3.	1979		Equipment	Cane	
4.	1979	Retalhuleu	Equipment		
5.	1979	Retalhuleu	Equipment	Cane	
6.	1979	Mazatenango	Equipment, vehicles, plane		
7.	1979	Escuintla	Equipment	Cane	270,000
8.	1980	Costa Sur	Equipment, vehicles		3,000,000
9.	1980	Escuintla	Machines, cotton	Cotton	
10.	1980	Quetzaltenango	Equipment	Coffee	1,000,000
11.	1980	Retalhuleu	Equipment, coffee	Coffee	1,000,000
12.	1981	Santa Rosa	Equipment		5,000,000
13.	1981	Matzatenango	Tractors, vehicles		
14.	1981	Escuintla	Equipment		
15.	1981	Quetzaltenango	Equipment	Cardamom	
16.	1981	Suchitepéquez	Coffee, equipment	Coffee, cardamom	2,400,000
17.	1981	San Marcos	Roads, radio communication		2,000,000
18.	1981	Quetzaltenango	Equipment, corn, warehouse		3,000,000
19.	1981	Alta Verapaz	Roads, drying machines for coffee, tractor	Coffee	
20.	1982	Guatemala	Equipment	Coffee	
21.	1982	San Marcos	Machines, house of the patron	Coffee	800,000
22.	1982	Escuintla	Trailers with cotton and sugar	Cotton, sugar	
23.	1982	Santa Lucía	Tractors, cabezales		
24.	1982	Mazatenango	Machines		
25.	1982	Escuintla	Trailer cargados de algodón	Cotton	
26.	1982	Santa Rosa	Equipment		30,000
27.	1982	Quetzaltenango	Equipment, vehicles		
28.	1982	Alta Verapaz	Equipment		
29.	1982	San Marcos	Equipment, Coffee	Coffee	
30.	1982	Sacatepéquez		Coffee	1,500,000
31.	1982	Retalhuleu	Road	Cotton	3,500,000
32.	1982	Baja Verapaz	Machines, house of the patron		
33.	1982	Retalhuleu	Equipment		2,520,000
34.	1982	Alta Verapaz			1,500,000
35.	1982	Petén	Machines, house of the patron, warehouse		
36.	1982	San Marcos	Equipment	Coffee	
37.	1982	La Reforma	House of the patron, office, warehouse		
38.	1983	Esquintla	Equipment	Cane	900,000
39.	1983	Santa LuciaCotzumalguapa	Pacas de cotton	Cotton	

40.	1984	San Marcos	Equipment			
41.	1984	San Marcos	*Finca* completely destroyed			
42.	1985	Retalhuleu		Cane	12,500	
43.	1989	Suchitepéquez	Equipment	Coffee		
44.	1989	San Marcos	Equipment			
45.	1989	Escuintla	Equipment			
46.	1990	Retalhuleu	Vehicles, equipment, motors		125,000	
47.	1991	Alta Verapaz	Burned down *finca*			
48.	1991	Alta Verapaz	Equipment, warehouse		100,000	
49.	1991	Sacatepéquez				
50.	1993	Retaluleu	Equipment			
51.	1994	Chimaltenango	Equipment		2,000,000	
52.	1994	San Marcos	Equipment	Coffee		
53.	1994	San Marcos	Equipment	Coffee		
54.	1994	Quetzaltenango		Coffee		
55.	1994	Suchitepéquez	Equipment	Coffee	300,000	
56.	1994	Suchitepéquez	Equipment			
57.	1994	San Marcos	Equipment	Coffee		
58.	1994	Suchitepéquez	Tractors, vehicle	Coffee		

Source: based on CEH, tomo IV: 269-271

Appendix 3: Destroyed infrastructure (1981-1995)

	Year	Type of destroyed object	Department
1.	1981	Bridge	Quiché
2.	1981	Power plant	Quiché
3.	1981	Private buildings	Guatemala
4.	1981	Governmental buildings	Alta Verapaz
5.	1981	Finance centre	Guatemala
6.	1981	Postal office	Quiché
7.	1981	Governmental buildings	Huehuetenango
8.	1981	Electric Installations	Escuintla
9.	1982	Bridges	Quiché
10.	1982	Factories	Guatemala
11.	1982	Governmental buildings	Alta Verapaz
12.	1982	Installations for cattle	Alta Verapaz
13.	1982	Road	Quiché
14.	1982	Destruction on water pipes	Huehetenango
15.	1982	Transport system	Sololá
16.	1982	Destruction of electricity	Guatemala
17.	1982	Transport system	Quiché
18.	1982	Power station	Guatemala
19.	1982	Telephone system	Guatemala
20.	1982	Road	Interamericana
21.	1982	Destruction of electricity	San Marcos
22.	1982	Road	San Marcos-Quetzaltenago
23.	1982	Governmental buildings	San Marcos
24.	1982	Electricity pylon	Huehuetenango
25.	1982	Road	Huehuetenango
26.	1982	Bridge	Huehuetenango
27.	1982	Petrol station	Sacatepéquez
28.	1982	Governmental buildings	Baja Verapaz
29.	1982	Power Plant	Totonicapán
30.	1982	Road	Huehuetenango
31.	1991	Electricity pylon	Petén
32.	1991	Pipeline	Alta Verapaz
33.	1991	Bridge	Quiché
34.	1991	Electricity pylon	Guatemala
35.	1992	Electricity pylon	Guatemala
36.	1993	Electricity pylon	Sololá
37.	1993	Electricity pylon	Santa Rosa
38.	1993	Destruction of electricity facilities	Sololá
39.	1993	Electricity pylon	Guatemala
40.	1993	Bridge	Suchitepéquez
41.	1993	Bridge	Escuintla
42.	1994	Electricity pylon	Chimaltenango
43.	1994	Electricity pylon	Guatemala
44.	1994	Electricity pylon	Sololá and Qiché
45.	1994	Bridge	Road to the Atlantic

46.	1994	Lanterns	Quiché
47.	1994	Electricity pylon	Santa Rosa
48.	1994	Electricity pylon	Guatemala
49.	1994	Generators	Alta Verapaz
50.	1994	Electricity pylon	Sacatepéquez
51.	1994	Electricity pylon	Huehuetenango
52.	1994	Electricity pylon	Chimaltenango
53.	1994	Lanterns	Quiché
54.	1994	Electricity pylon	Escuintla
55.	1994	Electricity pylon	Huehuetenango
56.	1994	Electricity pylon	Sololá
57.	1994	Lanterns	Huehuetanango
58.	1994	Bridge	Escuintla
59.	1995	Electricity pylon	Chimaltenango

Source: based on CEH, tomo IV: 272-274

Bibliography

Adams, Richard Newbold (1970). *Crucifixion by Power. Essays on Guatemalan National Social Structure, 1944-1966*. Austin, University of Texas Press.
AGA (1992). *Campo Pagado*. La Hora. 18 May 1992: 15.
AGA (1994). *Campo Pagado*. Prensa Libre. 19 May 1994: 13.
AGA (1996). *Campo Pagado*. Siglo XXI. 05 March 1996: 17.
Aguilera Peralta, Gabriel (1979). "The Massacre at Panzos and Capitalist Development in Guatemala." *Monthly Review*: 13 - 23.
Aguilera Peralta, Gabriel (1996). *El Proceso de Paz en Guatemala 1987-1996*. Presented at Primera Conferencia Iberoamericana de Paz y Tratamiento de Conflictos. Bogotá, Colombia.
Aguilera Peralta, Gabriel/Bran, Rosalinda/Ogaldes, Claudinne (1996). *Buscando la Paz. El Bienio 1994 - 1995*. Guatemala, FLACSO.
Aguilera Peralta, Gabriel/Ponciano, Karen (1994). *El Espejo sin Reflejo*. Guatemala, FLACSO.
ai (1998). *Human Rights Principles for Companies*.
Alvarez, Enrique (2002a). "The Civil Society Assembly: Shaping Agreement." *Accord – An International Review of Peace Initiatives* 13.
Alvarez, Enrique (2002b). "The Grand National Dialogue and the Oslo Consultations: Creating a Peace Agenda." *Accord – An International Review of Peace Initiatives* 13.
Anderson, Ken/Simon, Jean-Marie (1987). "Permanent Counterinsurgency in Guatemala." *Telos* 73: 9-46.
Anderson, Mary B. (1999). *Do No Harm. How Aid Can Support Peace – or War*. Boulder, Lyne Rienner.
Anderson, Mary B. (2002). *Developing Best Practice for Corporate Engagement in Conflict Zones: Lessons Learned from Experience*. Public Bads – Eco-

nomic Dimension of Conflict, Bonn/Petersberg, Federal Ministry for Economic Cooperation and Development; inwent.

Anderson, Sarah/Cavanagh, John (2000). Top 2000: The Rise of Global Corporate Power

Anderton, Charles (2003). "Economic Theorizing of Conflict: Historical Contributions, Future Possibilities." *Defence and Peace Economics* 4(3): 209-222.

Anonymous (1990). *Carta abierta de un agricultor de la Costa Sur a la Guerrilla guatemalteca*. Prensa Libre. 06 June 1990: 14.

Arias, Arturo (1990). "Changing Indian Identity: Guatemala's Violent Transition to Modernity." In: *Guatemalan Inians and the State, 1540 to 1988*. Carol A. Smith, Ed. Austin, University of Texas Press: 230-257.

Arnold, Wayne (2001). ExxonMobil Curtails Gas Operations in Indonesia. March 26, 2001: 13.

Arunatilake, Nisha/Jayasuriya, Sisira/Kelegama, Saman (2001). "The Economic Cost of the War in Sri Lanka." *World Development* 29(9): 1483-1500.

ASIES (1993). *El Proceso de Paz. La percepción del Guatemalteco sobre el Proceso de Paz. Encuesta realizada a nivel nacional Mayo/Abril 1993.* Guatemala, ASIES.

Asociación de Caficultores Tumbador (1994). *Campo Pagado. Printed in Aguilera et al. 1996, p. 202.*

Austin, James E./Ickis, John C. (1986). "Managing After the Revolutionaries Have Won." *Harvard Business Review* 64(3): 103-109.

Azpuru, Dinorah (1999). "Peace and Democratization in Guatemala: Two Parallel Processes." In: *Comparative Peace Processes in Latin America*. Cynthia Arnson, Ed. Washington, DC, Woodrow Wilson Center Press: 97-125.

Ball, Nicole (1991). "The Effect of Conflict on the Economies of Third World Countries." In: *Conflict Resolution in Africa*. Francis M. Deng and Zartman, William, Eds. Washington, D.C., The Brookings Institution: 272- 291.

Ball, Nicole (2001). "The Challenge of Rebuilding War-Torn Societies." In: *Turbulent Peace. The Challenges of Managing International Conflict*. Chester A. Crocker/Hampson, Fen Osler and Aall, Pamela, Eds. Washington, D.C., United States Institute of Peace Press: 719- 736.

Ball, Nicole (2002). "Staatsversagen und die Transformation kriegszerrütteter Gesellschaften." In: *Der zerbrechliche Frieden. Krisenregionen zwischen Staatsversagen, Gewalt und Entwicklung*. Tobias Debiel, Ed. Bonn, Dietz. 13: 66-96.

Ball, Patrick/Kobrak, Paul/Spirer, Herbert F. (1996). *State Violence in Guatemala, 1960-1996: A Quantitative Reflection*. Washington, AAAS; CiiDH.

Balleis, Siegfried M. (1985). *Die Bedeutung politischer Risiken für ausländische Direktinvestitionen unter besonderer Berücksichtigung politischer Stabilität.* Nürnberg, Pauli-Balleis-Verlag.

Ballentine, Karen/Sherman, Jake, Eds. (2003). *The Political Economy of Armed Conflict. Beyond Greed and Grievance.* Boulder, Lynne Rienner.

Banfield, Jessica/Gündüz, Canan/Killik, Nick, Eds. (2006). *Local Business, Local Peace: the Peacebuilding Potential of the Domestic Private Sector.* London, International Alert.

Barnes, Catherine (2002). "Democratizing Peacemaking Processes: Strategies and Dilemmas for Public Participation." *Accord – An International Review of Peace Initiatives*(13).

Barry, Tom (1992). *Inside Guatemala.* Albuquerque, N.M., Inter-Hemispheric Education Resource Center.

Belsie, Laurent (2000). *Rise of the Corporate Nation-State.* Christian Science Monitor. 10 April 2000.

Bendel, Petra/Krennerich, Michael (1996). "Zentralamerika: Die schwierige Institutionalisierung der Demokratie." In: *Systemwechsel 2. Die Institutionalisierung der Demokratie.* Wolfgang Merkel/Sandschneider, Eberhard and Segert, Dieter, Eds. Opladen, Leske + Budrich: 315-340.

Bennett, Juliette (2002). "Public Private Partnership: The Role of the Private Sector in Preventing Funding Conflict." *Vanderbilt Journal of Transnational Law* 35: 711-717.

Bennett, Peter D./Green, Robert T. (1972). "Political Instability as a Determinant of Direct Foreign Investment in Marketing." *Journal of Marketing Research* IX: 182-186.

Bennis, Phyllis (2001). "Mit der Wirtschaft aus der Finanzkrise? Die drohende Vereinnahmung der UNO durch private Geldgeber." In: *Die Privatisierung der Weltpolitik. Entstaatlichung und Kommerzialisierung im Globalisierungsprozess.* Brühl Tanja/Debiel, Tobias/Hamm, Brigitteet al, Eds. Bonn, Dietz. 11: 130-149.

Berdal, Mats/Malone, David M., Eds. (2000). *Greed and Grievance. Economic Agendas in Civil Wars.* Boulder, Lynne Rienner.

Berman, Jonathan (2000). "Corporations and Conflict: How Mangers Think About War." *Harvard International Review* XXII(3).

Berthoin Antal, Ariane/Dierkes, Meinolf/MacMillan, Keith, et al. (2002). *Corporate Social Reporting Revisted.* Schriftenreihe der Abteilung "Organisation und Technikgenese" des Forschungsscherpunkts Technik-Arbeit-Umwelt am Wissenschaftszentrum Berlin für Sozialforschung. Wissenschaftszentrum Berlin für Sozialforschung gGmbH.

Birle, Peter (1999). "Die südamerikanischen Gewerkschaften und Unternehmerverbände im Systemwechsel – Eine historisch-vergleichende Betrachtung." In: *Systemwechsel 4. Die Rolle von Verbänden im Transformationsprozeß.* Wolfgang Merkel and Sandschneider, Eberhard, Eds. Opladen, Leske + Budrich: 181-219.

Birle, Peter/Imbusch, Peter/Wagner, Christoph (1992). *Unternehmer und Politik. Eine theoretische Annäherung an die politische Rolle der Unternehmer und ihrer Verbände mit Blick auf Lateinamerika.* Mainz.

Black, George (1984). *Garrison Guatemala.* New York, Monthly Review Press.

Black, George (1989). "Military Rule in Guatemala." In: *The Politics of Antipolitics.* Brian Loveman and Jr., Thomas M. Davies, Eds. Lincoln, University of Nebraska Press: 509-512.

Blomberg, S. Brock/Hess, Gregory D. (2002). "The Temporal Links between Conflict and Economic Activity." *Journal of Conflict Resolution* 46(1): 74-90.

Bolanos de Zarco, Teresa (1996). *La Culebra en la Corbata. Crónica del Proceso de Paz Guatemalteco.* Mexico, Editorial Diana.

Bomann-Larsen, Lene/Wiggen, Oddny, Eds. (2004). *Responsibility in World Business. Managing Harmful Side-effects of Corporate Activity.* Tokyo, United Nations University Press.

Boot, Willem J. (2002). *National Policies to Manage Quality and Quantity of Coffee in Central America*, Inter-American Development Bank.

Booth, John A./Walker, Thomas W. (1999). *Understanding Central America.* Boulder, Colo., Westview Press.

Bornschier, Volker (1997). "Zivilisierung der Weltgesellschaft trotz Hegemonie der Marktgesellschaft." In: *Frieden machen.* Dieter Senghaas, Ed. Frankfurt am Main, edition Suhrkamp: 421-443.

Borrell, Víctor Gálvez (1995). *La Gobernabilidad en Centroamérica: Sectores Populares y Gobernabilidad Precaria en Guatemala.* Guatemala, FLACSO.

Bos, Ellen (1996). "Die Rolle von Eliten und kollektiven Akteuren in Transitionsprozessen." In: *Systemwechsel 1. Theorien, Ansätze und Konzepte der Transitionsforschung.* Wolfgang Merkel, Ed. Opladen, Leske + Budrich: 81-109.

Bossen, L. (1982). "Plantations and Labor Force Discrimination in Guatemala." *Current Anthropology* 23(3): 263-268.

Bottomore, T.B. (1966). *Elite und Gesellschaft.* München, Verlag C.H. Beck.

Boyce, James K. (1996). "El Salvador's Adjustment Towards Peace: An Introduction." In: *Economic Policy for Building Peace: The Lessons of El Salvador.* James K. Boyce, Ed. Boulder, Lynne Rienner: 1-17.

Braun, Rainer (2001). "Konzerne als Beschützer derr Menschenrechte? Zur Bedeutung von Verhaltenskodizes." In: *Die Privatisierung der Weltpolitik. Entstaatlichung und Kommerzialisierung im Globalisierungsprozess*. Brühl Tanja/Debiel, Tobial/Hamm, Brigitteet al, Eds. Bonn, Dietz. EINE Welt – Texte der Stiftung Entwicklung und Frieden: 257-280.

Bray, John/Lunde, Leiv/Murshed, S. Mansoob (2003). "Nepal: Economic Drivers of the Maoist Insurgency." In: *The Political Economy of Armed Conflict. Beyond Greed and Grievance*. Karen Ballentine and Sherman, Jake, Eds. Boulder, Lynne Rienner: 107-132.

Brenes, Arnoldo/Casas, Kevin (1998). *Soldados como empresarios: Los negocios de los militares en Centroamérica*. San José, Fundación Arias para la Paz y el Progreso Humano.

Brewer, Thomas L. (1983). "The Instability of Governments and the Instability of Controls on Funds Transfers by Multinational Enterprises: Implications for Political Risk Analysis." *Journal of International Business Studies* 14(3): 147-158.

Brock, Lothar (1997). "Den Frieden erwirtschaften." In: *Frieden machen*. Dieter Senghaas, Ed. Frankfurt am Main, edition Suhrkamp: 397-420.

Brömmelhörster, Jörg, Ed. (2000). *Demystifying the Peace Dividend*. Baden-Baden, Nomos Verlagsgesellschaft.

Brück, Tilman (1996). *Macroeconomic Effects of the War in Mozambique*. QEH Working Paper Series QEHWPS11. Oxford.

CACIF (1986). *Guatemala: Pasado, Presente y Futuro*. Guatemala.

CACIF (1995a). *Campo Pagdo*. Prensa Libre. 25 October 1995: 27.

CACIF (1995b). *Guatemala: Reflexiones del Pasado, Consideraciones del Presente y Recomendaciones para el Futuro*. Guatemala.

CACIF (1999). *Campo Pagado*. Prensa Libre. 14 May 1999: 14.

Camacho Nassar, Carlos/Durocher, Bettina/Fernández Gamarro, Juan Antonio, et al. (2003). *Tierra, Identidad y Conflicto en Guatemala*. Guatemala, FLACSO, MINUGUA, CONTIERRA.

Cámara de Comercio (1991). *Campo Pagado: CCG apoya plan de paz total*. Prensa Libre. 09 April 1991: 4.

Cambranes, J.C. (1985). *Café y Campesinos en Guatemala, 1853-1897*. Guatemala, Universidad de San Carlos de Guatemala.

Campbell, Ashley (2002). *The Private Sector and Conflict Prevention Mainstreaming. Risk Analysis and Conflict Impact Assessment Tools for Multinational Cooperations*. cifp (Country Indicators for Foreign Policy).

Canadian Foundation for the Americas (2000). *Guatemala Under the FRG: Peace at a Crossroads*, Canadian Foundation for the Americas.

Carbonnier, Gilles (2001). *Economics of War-Torn Countries. A Political-Economic Approach Applied to Guatemala*, PhD-Thesis, Université de Neuchatel.

Cardenal, Ana Sofía (2000). *Élites Económicas y Democracia en El Salvador y Guatemala*. Ponencia presentada en el V Congreso Centroamericano de Historia, Universidad de El Salvador, San Salvador.

Cardoso, Fernando H./Faletto, Enzo (1976). *Abhängigkeit und Entwicklung in Lateinamerika*. Frankfurt am Main, Suhrkamp Verlag.

Carnegie Commission on Preventing Deadly Conflict (1997). *Preventing Deadly Conflict: Final Report*. New York, Carnegie Corporation of New York.

Casaus Arzú, Marta (1992). *Guatemala: Linaje y Racismo*. Guatemala, FLACSO.

Castellanos Cambranes, Julio (1996). *Café y Campesinos*. Madrid, Editorial Catriel S.L.

CEH, Ed. (1999a). *Guatemala. Memoria del Silencio*. Guatemala.

CEH, Ed. (1999b). *Guatemala. Memoria del Silencio*. Guatemala.

CEH, Ed. (1999c). *Guatemala. Memoria del Silencio*. Guatemala.

CEH, Ed. (1999d). *Guatemala. Memoria del Silencio*. Guatemala.

CEH (2000). *Guatemala: Causas y Orígenes del Enfrentamiento Armado Interno*. Guatemala, F & G editores.

Central American and Caribbean Program (1985). *Report on Guatemala. Findings of the Study Group on United States-Guatemala Relations*. Boulder, London, Westview Press with the Foreign Policy Institute, School of Advanced International Studies, The Johns Hopkins University.

Centro de Estudios de Guatemala (1995). *Guatemala: Entre el Dolor y la Esperanza*, Diputació Provincial de València, Cedsala; Universitat de València.

CERIGUA (2-16 September 1993).

CERIGUA (4-17 April 1993).

CERIGUA (7-13 March 1993).

CERIGUA (8 July 1993).

CERIGUA (12-18 May 1991).

CERIGUA (19 July 1995).

CERIGUA (21 October 1994).

CERIGUA (29 February 1996).

Champain, Phil (2002). "Engaging the Private Sector in Conflict Transformation – an overview of possibilities and challenges." *CCTS Newsletter* 19(3): 9-17.

Charney, Craig (1999). "Civil Society, Political Violence, and Democratic Transitions: Business and the Peace Process in South Africa, 1990 to 1994." *Comparative Studies in Society and History* 41(1): 182-206.

Collier, Paul (1998). "On the Economic Consequences of Civil War." *Oxford Economic Papers* 51: 168-183.
Collier, Paul (2000a). "Doing Well out of War: An Economic Perspective." In: *Greed and Grievance. Economic Agendas in Civil Wars.* Mats Berdal and Keen, David, Eds. Boulder, London, Lynne Rienner Publishers: 91-111.
Collier, Paul (2000b). *Economic Causes of Civil Conflict and Their Implications for Policy.*
Collier, Paul/Elliott, Lani/Hegre, Havard, et al. (2003). *Breaking the Conflict Trap. Civil War and Development Policy.* Washington, The World Bank and Oxford University Press.
Collier, Paul/Gunning, Jan Willem (1995). "War, Peace and Private Portfolios." *World Development* 23(2): 233-241.
Collier, Paul/Hoeffler, Anke (1998). "On Economic Causes of Civil War." *Oxford Economic Papers* 50: 563-573.
Collier, Paul/Hoeffler, Anke (2001). *Greed and Grievance in Civil War.*
Comisión de Acompañamiento (2000). *Cronograma de Implementación, Cumplimiento y Verificación de los Acuerdos de Paz 2000-2004.*
CONAGRO (1995a). *Campo Pagado.* Prensa Libre. 02 October 1995: 24.
CONAGRO (1995b). *Campo Pagado: De la Querella Presentada en relación a las Platicas de Paz.* Prensa Libre. 17 November 1995: 45.
CONAGRO (1995c). *Campo Pagado: Ya Basta.* Siglo XXI. 19 May 1995.
Concepcion, Sylvia/Digal, Larry/Guiam, Rufa, et al. (2003). *Breaking the Links between Economics and Conflict in Mindanao.* London, International Alert.
Consejo Latinoamericano de Iglesias/Consejo Mundial de Iglesias/Consejo Nacional de las Cristo en los EE.UU., et al. (1994). *Hacia una Nueva Sociedad. Informe de la Tercera Consulta Ecuménica por la Paz y la Democracia en Guatemala.* Oslo.
COVERCO (2000). *Coffee Workers in Guatemala: A Survey of Working and Living Conditions on Coffee Farms.*
Cranna, Michael, Ed. (1994). *The True Cost of Conflict. Seven Recent Wars and Their Effects on Society.* New York.
Croissant, Aurel/Merkel, Wolfgang/Sandschneider, Eberhard (1999). "Verbände und Verbändesysteme im Transformationsprozess: ein zusammenfassender Vergleich." In: *Systemwechsel 4. Die Rolle von Verbänden im Transformationsprozeß.* Wolfgang Merkel and Sandschneider, Eberhard, Eds. Opladen, Leske + Budrich: 329-355.
Crónica (1988a). Gramajo quiere reconciliación con empresarios. 28 July 1988: 18.
Crónica (1988b). MLN se refiere a pláticas en Madrid. 19 May 1988: 21-24.
Crónica (1996). Los Impuestos del CACIF. 29 March 1996: 24.

Crónicas (2001a). *El caso SITRABI en debate público*, MINUGUA: 7-8.
Crónicas (2001b). *Los conflictos en Guatemala: un reto para la sociedad y el Estado*, MINUGUA: 1-4.
Crónicas (2001c). *Mesa de negociación de conflictos de tierra en Alta Verapaz*, MINUGUA: 2-7.
Crónicas (2001d). *Nuevas Reformas al Código de Trabajo*, MINUGUA: 5-7.
Crónicas (2001e). *Pronunciamiento de MINUGUA en relación con la verificación de la denuncia presentada por el Sr. Jorge Briz, Presidente de la Cámara de Comerico de Guatemala*, MINUGUA: 8.
Crónicas (2001f). *Reformas al Código de Trabajo*, MINUGUA: 3-8.
Crónicas (2001g). *Reformas al Código de Trabajo, positivas pero insuficientes*, MINUGUA: 1-4.
Crónicas (2002). *La mesa de concertación sobre conflictos de tierra en la región ixil*, MINUGUA: 4.
CSIS/AUSA (2002). *Post-Conflict Reconstruction: Achieving Socio-Economic Well-Being in Post-Conflict Settings*.
Dahl, R. A. (1982). *Dilemmas of Pluralist Democracy. Autonomy vs. Control*. New Haven.
Dahl, R. A./Lindblom, Ch. (1976). *Politics, Economics, and Welfare*. Chicago.
Davy, Aidan (2001). "Companies in Conflict Situations: A Role for Tri-Sector Partnerships?" *Natural Resources Cluster of Business Partners for Development*(9).
de Soto, Alvaro/Castillo, Graciana del (1994). "Obstacles to Peacebuilding." *Foreign Policy*(Spring): 69-83.
de Soysa, Indra (2000). "The Resource Curse: Are Civil Wars Driven by Rapacity or Paucity?" In: *Greed and Grievance. Economic Agendas in Civil Wars*. Mats Berdal and Malone, David M., Eds. Boulder; London, Lynne Rienner Publishers: 113-135.
de Zoysa, Tilak (2002). "The Role of the Private Sector in Conflict Resolution in Sri Lanka." In: *Public Bads – Economic Dimension of Conflict*. inwent, Ed. Bonn/Petersberg, inwent. Public Bads – Economic Dimension of Conflict. Summary Report: 54-56.
Debiel, Tobias (1996). *Kriegswirtschaft und Friedenskonsolidierung. Erfahungen und Herausforderungen in den Regionen des Südens*. Duisburg.
DiAddario, Sabrina (1997). "Estimating the Economic costs of Conflict. An Examination of the Two-gap Estimation Model for the Case of Nicaragua." *Oxford Development Studies* 25(1): 123-141.
Diamond, Louise/McDonald, John W. (1996). *Multi-Track Diplomacy: A Systems Approach to Peace*. West Hartford, Kumarian Press.

Dietrich, Wolfgang (1990). *Die Bemühungen um den Frieden in Zentralamerika 1983-1989*. Frankfurt, Campus Verlag.
Doan, David B. (1999). "The Mineral Industry of Guatemala." In: *Minerals Yearbook*. US Geological Survey, Ed., US Bureau of Mines: 15.11-15.12.
Dosal, Paul J. (1995). *Power in Transition: The Rise of Guatemala's Industrial Oligarchy, 1871-1994*. Westport, Conn., Praeger.
Duffield, Mark (2000). "Globalization, Transborder Trade, and War Economies." In: *Greed and Grievance. Economic Agendas in Civil Wars*. Mats Berdal and Malone, David M., Eds. Boulder, London, Lynne Rienner Publishers: 69-89.
Dunkerley, James (1988). *Power in the Isthmus: A Political History of Modern Central America*. London, Verso.
Dunkerley, James (1994). *The Pacification of Central America: Political Change in the Isthmus, 1987-1993*. London, Verso.
Durocher, Bettina (2002). *Los Dos Derechos de la Tierra: La Cuestión Agraria en el País Ixil*. Guatemala, FLACSO, MINUGUA; CONTIERRA.
Durocher, Bettina (2003). "El contexto de los fenómenos agrarios en Guatemala." In: *Tierra, identidad y conflicto en Guatemala*. Carlos Camacho Nassar/ Durocher, Bettina/Fernández Gamarro, Juan Antonioet al, Eds. Guatemala, FLACSO, MINUGUA, CONTIERRA: 17-70.
El Gráfico (1995). ¿Conviene que el Ejercito intervenga ante invasiones? 06 April 1995: 12.
El Gráfico (1996a). El dialogo de pacificación ha sido en ambiente muy secreto. 04 May 1996: 10.
El Gráfico (1996b). Garcia Laguardia pide a URNG aclarar el hecho. El CACIF, por su lado, respalda la suspensión de las negociaciones. 29 October 1996: 4.
El Gráfico (1996c). Preocupante cisma en la ASC. 29 June 1996: 3.
El Gráfico (1996d). Se debilita la Asamblea de la Sociedad Civil. 28 June 1996: 2.
El Gráfico (1996e). URNG propone adelantar la discusión del cese de fuego. 05 November 1996: 12.
El Periódico (2001). Del grano a la taza, una nueva forma de vender café. 22 October 2001: 14.
Elbadawi, Ibrahim A. (1999). *Civil War and Poverty: The Role of External Interventions, Political Rights and Economic Growth*. Civil Conflicts, Crime and Violence, World Bank, Washington D.C.
Eloff, Theuns (1999). "South African Business and the Transition to Peace and Democracy. From Honest Broker to Constructive Partner." In: *People Building Peace. 35 Inspiring Stories from Around the World*. European Platform for Conflict Prevention and Transformation, Ed. Brussels, European Platform for Conflict Prevention and Transformation,.

Engels, Benno (2000). "PPP – Hoffnungsträger oder trügerische Hoffnung?" *E+Z – Entwicklung und Zusammenarbeit*(2): 41-43.

Escoto, Jorge/Marroquín, Manfredo (1992). *La AID en Guatemala*. Guatemala, CRIES/AVANCSO.

ESSD/Social Development Family/Post-Conflict Unit and the World Bank Institute (WBI) (1999). *The Transition from War to Peace: An Overview*.

European Platform for Conflict Prevention and Transformation (1999). "Local Business Pushing for Peace in Northern Ireland. 'We Made it Less Easy for the Parties to Simply Walk Away'." In: *People Building Peace. 35 Inspiring Stories from Around the World*. European Platform for Conflict Prevention and Transformation, Ed. Brussels, European Platform for Conflict Prevention and Transformation.

Evangelischer Entwicklungsdienst (2002). *Coltanfieber. Wie ein seltenes Metall das Leben im kriegsgeschüttelten Osten der Demokratischen Republik Kongo verändert hat*. Bonn.

FAO (2003). *The World Banana Economy. 1985-2002*. Rome.

Feierabend, Ivo K./Feierabend, Rosalinde L. (1966). "Aggressive Behaviour in Politics,1948-1962." *Journal of Conflict Resolution* 10(Fall): 249-271.

Figueroa, Carlos (1991). *El Recurso del Miedo*. San José, Editorial Universitaria Centroamericana.

Fitzgerald, E.V.K. (1997). "Paying for the War: Macroeconomic Stabilization in Poor Countries under Conflict Conditions." *Oxford Development Studies* 25(1): 43-65.

Flora, Jan L./Torres-Riva, Edelberto, Eds. (1989). *Sociology of "Developing Societies": Central America*. Houndsmill, Basingstoke, Macmillan Education.

Foro Guatemala (2001). *Propuesta de reactivación económica. Juntos por una nueva nación*.

Foro Guatemala (2002). *Discurso de cierre. Presentación del Foro Guatemala en torno al tema corrupción y transparencia*.

Frynas, Jedrzej George (1998). "Political Instability and Business: Focus on Shell in Nigeria." *Third World Quarterly* 19(3): 457-478.

Fuentes, Homero (2000). "Breve Referencia Histórica del Movimiento Sindical, su Desarrollo y las Relaciones Laborales Guatemaltecas." In: *Derecho Colectivo del Trabajo. Seminario de Actualización*. MINUGUA, Ed. Guatemala: 19-44.

Fuentes, Juan Alberto (2002). "La dimensión económico de los Acuerdos de Paz en Guatemala." In: *A cinco años de la firma de la paz en Guatemala: Un balance crítico*. Rubén Zamora/Chamorro, Carlos F./Pásara, Luis et al, Eds. Guatemala, FLACSO. 51: 159-171.

Fundación Ideas para la Paz (1999). ¿Qué es la Fundación?

Gallardo, María Eugenia/López, José Roberto (1986). *Centroamérica. La Crisis en Cifras*. San José, FLACSO, IICA.

Galtung, John (1969). "Violence, Peace and Peace Research." *Journal of Peace Research* 6(3): 167-191.

Gamboa M., Nuria/Trentavizi, Barbara (2001). *La Guatemala Posible. La Senda del Pacto Fiscal*. Guatemala, Asociación Centroamericana Hombres de Maíz.

Garbers, Frank/Heckt, Meike (2000). "Die soziale Konstruktion der Maya. Communidad, Ethnizität und neue politische Akteure im Guatemala des 20. Jahrhunderts." *Lateinamerika. Analysen, Daten, Dokumentation. Institut für Iberoamerika-Kunde, Hamburg* 17(44): 71-81.

Gerson, Allan/Colletta, Nat J. (2002). *Privatizing Peace. From Conflict to Security*. Ardsley, Transnational Publishers.

Gladwin, Thomas N./Walter, Ingo (1980). *Multinationals under Fire: Lessons in the Management of Conflict*. New York, John Wiley & Sons.

Gleijeses, Piero (1985). "Guatemala: Crisis and Response." In: *Report on Guatemala. Findings of the Study Group on United States-Guatemala Relations*. Central American and Caribbean Program, Ed. London, Boulder, Westview Press with the Foreign Policy Institute, School of Advanced International Studies, The Johns Hopkins University. 7: 51-74.

Global Compact *Guide to the Global Compact: A Practical Understanding of the Vision and Nine Principles*. New York.

Global Witness (1998). *A Rough Trade. The Role of Companies and Governments in the Angolan Conflict*. London.

Global Witness (1999). *A Crude Awakening. The Role of the Oil and Banking Industries in Angola's Civil War and the Plunder of State Assets*. London.

Global Witness (2002). *The Logs of War. The Timber Trade and Armed Conflict*, Fafo Institute of Applied Social Science.

Gramajo Morales, Héctor Alejandro (1995). *De la Guerra... a la Guerra. La Difícil Transición Política en Guatemala*. Guatemala, Fondo de Cultura Editorial.

Gramajo Morales, Héctor Alejandro (1997). "Political Transition in Guatemala, 1980-1990: A Perspective from Inside Guatemala's Army." In: *Democratic Transitions in Central America*. Jorge I. Domínguez and Lindberg, Marc, Eds. Gainesville, University Press of Florida: 111-138.

Gutiérrez, Edgar (1995). "La Difícil Transición en Guatemala." *Verdad y Vida* (no 5, enero-marzo): 15 - 25.

Hamm, Brigitte (2002). "Der Global Compat – eine Bestandsaufnahme." In: *Public-Private Partnership und der Global Compact der Vereinten Nationen*. Brigitte Hamm, Ed. Duisburg, INEF Report. Heft 62/2002: 17-30.

Handy, Jim (1989). "Insurgency and Counter-insurgency in Guatemala." In: *Sociology of "Developing Societies": Central America*. Jan L.; Edelberto Torres-Riva Flora, Ed. Houndsmill, Basingstoke, Macmillan Education: 112-139.

Harker, John (2000). *Human Security in Sudan: The Report of a Canadian Assessment Mission. Prepared for the Minister of Foreign Affairs*. Ottawa.

Harten, Gus van (2000). "Guatemala's Peace Accords in a Free Trade Area of the Americas." *Yale Human Rightsand Development Law Journal* 3(113): 113-158.

Harvey, Michael G. (1992). "A Survey of Corporate Programs for Managing Terrorist Threats." *Journal of International Business Studies* 24(3): 465-478.

Haufler, Virginia (1997). *Dangerous Commerce: Insurance and the Management of International Risk*. Ithaca, Cornell University Press.

Haufler, Virginia (2001a). *Countering Conflict: Corporate Social Responsibility in War Torn Societies*. Annual Meeting of the American Political Science Association, San Francisco, The American Political Science Association.

Haufler, Virginia (2001b). "Is There a Role for Business in Conflict Management?" In: *Turbulent Peace. The Challenges of Managing International Conflict*. Chester A. Crocker/Hampson, Fen Osler and Aall, Pamela, Eds. Washington, D.C., United States Institute of Peace Press: 659-675.

Hernández Alarcón, Rosalinda (1998). *La Tierra en los Acuerdos de Paz: Resumen de la Respuesta Gubernamental*. Guatemala, Inforpress Centroamericana.

Holiday, David (1997). "Guatemala's Long Road to Peace." *Current History* 96(607): 68-74.

Hook, Jacob/Ganguly, Rajat (2000). "Multinational Corporations and Ethnic Conflict: Theory and Experience." *Nationalism & Ethnic Politics* 6(1): 48-71.

Howard, Lise M. (2002). "UN Peace Implementation in Namibia: The Causes of Success." *International Peacekeeping* 9(1): 99-132.

Hüfner, Klaus (2002). "Private-Public Partnership im System der Vereinten Nationen." In: *Public-Private Partnership und der Global Compact der Vereinten Nationen*. Brigitte Hamm, Ed. Duisburg, INEF Report. Heft 62/2002: 4-16.

Hummel, Hartwig (2001). "Die Privatisierung der Weltpolitik. Tendenzen , Spielräume und Alternativen." In: *Die Privatisierung der Weltpolitik. Entstaatlichung und Kommerzialisierung im Globalisierungsprozess*. Brigitte Hamm Brühl Tanja; Tobial Debiel, Hartwig Hummel, Jens Martens (ed.), Ed. Bonn, Dietz. EINE Welt – Texte der Stiftung Entwicklung und Frieden: 22-56.

Humphreys, Macartan (2003). *Economies and Violent Conflict*. Harvard College.

INCEP (1987). *El proceso de paz de Centro América*. Guatemala, INCEP.

INCORE Mediatory Roles in Marching Disputes: Selected Examples.
Inforpress Centroamérica (1987). *Guatemala 1986. El Ano de las Promesas.* Guatemala, Inforpress Centroamérica.
Inforpress Centroamérica, Ed. (1995). *Guatemala 1986-1994. Compendio del Proceso de Paz. Cronologías, análisis, documentos, acuerdos.* Guatemala, Inforpress Centroamérica.
Inforpress Centroamérica, Ed. (1996). *Guatemala 1995-1996. Compendio del Processo de Paz. Análisis, cronologías, documentos, acuerdos.* Guatemala, Inforpress Centroamérica.
International Alert (2004). *Promoting a Conflict Prevention Approach to OECD Companies and Partnering Local Business. OECD DAC Conflict, Peace and Development Co-operation Network. Briefing Paper.* London.
International Alert (2005). *Conflict-Sensitive Business Practice: Guidance for Extractive Industries.* London.
International Peace Academy (2001). *Private Sector Actors in Zones of Conflict: Research Challenges and Policy Responses,* New York.
Jean, Francois/Rufin, Jean-Chrisophe, Eds. (1999). *Ökonomie der Bürgerkriege.* Hamburg, Hamburg Ed.
Jonas, Susanne (1991). *The Battle for Guatemala : Rebels, Death Squads, and U.S. Power.* Boulder, Westview Press.
Jonas, Susanne (2000). *Of Centaurs and Doves. Guatemala's Peace Process.* Boulder, Westview Press.
Jonas, Susanne/Tobis, David, Eds. (1976). *Guatemala. Una Historia inmediata.* México, Siglo XXI Editores, S.A.
Kaldor, Mary (2000). *Neue und alte Kriege.* Frankfurt am Main, Suhrkamp Verlag.
Karl, Terry Lynn (1990). "Dilemmas of Democratization in Latin America." *Comparative Politics* 23(1): 1-21.
Kassicieh, S.K./Nassar, J. R. (1986). "Political Risk in the Gulf: The Impact of the Iran-Iraq War on Governments and Multinational Corporations." *California Management Review* 28(2): 69-86.
Kassicieh, Suleiman K./Nasser, Jamal R. (1982). "Political Risk and the Multinational Corporation: A Study of the Impact of the Iranian Revolution on Saudi Arabia, Kuwait and the United Arab Emirates." *Management International Review – Journal of International Business* 22(3): 22-32.
Keen, David (1997). "A Rational Kind of Madness." *Oxford Development Studies* 25(1): 67-75.
Keen, David (1998). *The Economic Functions of Violence in Civil Wars.* Oxford, Oxford University Press for the International Institute for Strategic Studies.

Keen, David (2003). *Demobilising Guatemala.* Annual Workshop University of the Witwatersrand, Johannesburg.

Kennedy, Charles R. (1987). *Political Risk Management: International Lending and Investing under Environmental Uncertainty.* New York, Quorum Books.

Khan, Sarah (1994). *Nigeria: The Political Economy of Oil.* Oxford, Oxford University Press.

Killick, Nick "Conflict prevention in Azerbaijan." In: *Case-studies of multistakeholder partnership.* Virginia Haufler, Ed. New York, Paper commissioned by the United Nations Global Compact Office: 13-32.

Kobrin, Stephen J. (1978). "When Does Political Instability Result in Increased Investment Risk." *The Columbia Journal of World Business* October.

Kobrin, Stephen J. (1979). "Political Risk: A Review and Reconsideration." *Journal of International Business Studies* 10(1): 67-80.

Kraus, Peter A. (1999). "Assoziationen und Interessenrepräsentation in neuen Demokratien." In: *Systemwechsel 4. Die Rolle von Verbänden im Transformationsprozeß.* Wolfgang Merkel and Sandschneider, Eberhard, Eds. Opladen, Leske + Budrich: 23-44.

Kühne, Winfried (1998). "Post-Conflict Peacebuilding: Aufgaben, Erfahrungen, Lehren und Empfehlungen für die Praxis." In: *Bürgerkriege: Folgen und Regulierungsmöglichkeiten.* Heinrich-W. Krumwiede and Waldmann, Peter, Eds. Baden-Baden, Nomos: 96-107.

Kurtenbach, Sabine (1998). *Guatemala.* München, Beck.

Kurtenbach, Sabine (2002). "Konfliktsystem Zentralamerika: Gewaltenwandel und externe Akteure." In: *Der zerbrechliche Frieden. Krisenregionen zwischen Staatsversagen, Gewalt und Entwicklung.* Tobias Debiel, Ed. Bonn, Dietz. 13: 202-225.

La República (1994a). El CACIF y la ASC. 16 June 1994: 13.

La República (1994b). Paz y propiedad. 17 August 1994: 12.

La República (1994c). Ramiro de León Carpio considera que CACIF debe integrarse a Asamblea del Sector Civil. 30 May 1994: 6.

La República (1995a). Agro acusa a MINUGUA y PDH de interferir en desalojos. 29 December 1995: 2.

La República (1995b). Conagro cuestiona las negociaciones de paz. 18 October 1995: 2.

La República (1995c). Ejército protegerá fincas amenazadas por URNG. 04 August 1995: 2.

La República (1995d). Ramiro de León calificó de absurdo la querella judicial contra Héctor Rosada. 19 October 1995: 5.

La República (1995e). Sector agrario iniciará proceso legal contra Rosada. 17 October 1995: 2.

Landau, Saul (1993). *The Guerrilla Wars of Central America. Nicaragua, El Salvador and Guatemala*. London, Weidenfeld and Nicolson.
Laurance, Edward J./Godnick, William (n.d.). *Goods for Guns in El Salvador: An Assessment of a Voluntary Weapons Collection Program.* Internet Forum on Conflict Prevention (IFCP).
Le Bot, Yvon (1992). *La guerre en terre maya: communauté, violence et modernité au Guatemala (1970-1992)*. Paris, Ed. Karthala.
Lederach, John Paul (1995). *Preparing for Peace: Conflict Transformation Across Cultures*. Syracuse, Syracuse University Press.
Lensink, Robert/Hermes, Niels/Murinde, Victor (2000). "Capital Flight and Political Risk." *Journal of International Money and Finance* 19: 73-92.
Licklider, Roy (1995). "The Consequences of Negotiated Settlements in Civil Wars, 1945-1993." *American Political Science Review* 89(3): 681-690.
Licklider, Roy (2001). "Obstacles to Peace Settlements." In: *Turbulent Peace. The Challenges of Managing International Conflict*. Chester A. Crocker/Hampson, Fen Osler and Aall, Pamela, Eds. Washington, D.C., United States Institute of Peace Press: 697-718.
Lindblom, Ch. (1977). *Politics and Markets*. New York.
Lipschutz, Ronnie D. (1998). "Beyond the Neoliberal Peace: From Conflict Resolution to Social Reconciliation." *Social Justice* 25(4): 5-19.
Lizano, Eduardo (1995). "Staat und Wirtschaft in Zentralamerika." In: *Mittelamerika. Abschied von der Revolution?* Rafael Sevilla and Torres-Rivas, E., Eds. Tübingen, Horlemann: 134-150.
Mahoney, James (2001). *The Legacies of Liberalism. Path Dependence and Political Regimes in Central America*. Baltimore, The John Hopkins University Press.
Mair, Stefan (2004). "Die Rolle von Private Military Companies in Gewaltkonflikten." In: *Kriege als (Über)Lebenswelten. Schattenglobalisierung, Kriegsökonomien und Inseln der Zivilität*. Sabine Kurtenbach and Lock, Peter, Eds. Bonn, Dietz. Eine Welt. Texte der Stiftung Entwicklung und Frieden 16: 260-273.
Man, Michael (1992). "The Rise of Corporate Social Responsibility in South Africa." In: *Power and Profit. Politics, labour, and Business in South Africa*. Duncan Innes/Kentridge, Matthew and Perold, Helen, Eds. Cape Town, Oxford University Press: 250-256.
Martínez Peláez, Severo (1998). *La Patria del Criollo. Ensayo de Interpretación de la Realidad Colonial Guatemalteca*. México, Fondo de Cultura Económica.
Matovu, John Mary/Stewart, Frances (2001). "The Social and Economic Costs of Conflict: A Case Study of Uganda." In: *War and Underdevelopment: Case*

Studies in Country of Conflict. Frances Stewart and Fitzgerald, V., Eds. Oxford, Oxford University Press. 2: 240-287.
Matthies, Volker (1995). "Der Transformationsprozeß vom Krieg zum Frieden – ein vernachlässigtes Forschungsfeld." In: *Vom Krieg zum Frieden: Kriegsbeendigung und Friedenskonsolodierung*. Volker Matthies, Ed. Bremen, Edition Temmen: 8-38.
McCartney, Clem (2002). *The Business of Conflict Resolution*. Conflict Resolution – A Breakfast Theme, Galadari Hotel, Sri Lanka.
McCleary, Rachel (1999). *Dictating Democracy. Guatemala and the End of Violent Revolution*. Gainsville, University Press of Florida.
McClintock, Michael (1985). *The American Connection: State Terror and Popular Resistance in Guatemala*. London
Totowa, N.J., Zed Books.
McCreery, D. (1994). *Rural Guatemala*. Stanford, Stanford University Press.
McMahon, Robert (2000). UN: Conference to Explore Business Partnerships in Post-Conflict Zones
Meier, Ralf (1997). *Kammern und Verbände in der Dritten Welt. Funktionsfähigkeit und Entwicklungspotential für Handwerk und Kleinunternehmen*. Göttingen, Verlag Otto Schwartz & Co.
Mendelson Forman, Johanna (2002). "Achieving Socioeconomic Well-Being in Postconflict Settings." *The Washington Quarterly* 25(4): 125-138.
Mendelson Forman, Johanna/Colletta, Nat J./Praag, Nicholas Van (1998). *Conflict Prevention and Post-Conflict Reconstruction: Perspectives and Prospects*. Conflict Prevention and Post-Conflict Reconstruction: Perspectives and Prospects, Paris, The World Bank.
Mersky, Marcie (1988). *Empresarios y Transición Política en Guatemala*. Report written as part of the project "Modalidades de los Procesos de Democratización en Centro América" under the supervision of the Consejo Superior de Universidades de Centro América (CSUCA). Guatemala.
Meyer, William H. (1998). *Human Rights and International Political Economy in Third World Nations: Multinational Corporations, Foreign Aid, and Repression*. Westport, CT, Praeger.
Miall, Hugh/Ramsbotham, Oliver/Woodhouse, Tom (1999). *Contemporary Conflict Resolution: The Prevention, Management and Transformation of Deadly Conflicts*. Malden, MA, Polity Press.
Miller, Kent D. (1992). "A Framework for Integrated Risk Management in International Business." *Journal of International Business Studies* 23(2): 311-332.
Minker, Mechthild (1990). "'Guatemala 2000'": Traditionelles Entwicklungsmodell in neuem Gewand?" *Lateinamerika. Analysen, Daten, Dokumentation. Institut für Iberoamerika-Kunde, Hamburg*(14, Juli): 19-24.

Minker, Mechthild (2000). "Zentralamerikas wirtschaftliche Entwicklung. Bilanz und Herausforderung angesichts der Globalisierung." *Lateinamerika. Analysen, Daten, Dokumentation. Institut für Iberoamerika-Kunde, Hamburg* 1744: 36-61.

MINUGUA, Ed. (2000a). *Derecho Colectivo del Trabajo. Seminario de Actualización*.

MINUGUA (2000b). *Informe de Verificación. Situación de los compromisos relativos a la tierra en los acuerdos de paz*.

MINUGUA (2000c). *Informe de Verificación. Situación sobre los Compromisos Laborales de los Acuerdos de Paz*. Guatemala.

MINUGUA (2001). *El Pacto Fiscal un Año Después*. Guatemala.

MINUGUA (2002). *El debate sobre la politica de desarrollo rural en Guatemala: Avances entre octubre de 2000 y abril de 2002*.

MINUGUA (2003). *La Libertad Sindical en Guatemala. Análisis de Pronunciamientos de MINUGUA*. Guatemala.

Misereor, Ed. (1999). *Nie Wieder-Nunca Más*. Aachen, Misereor.

Molkentin, Gudrun (1993). *Guatemala: Auf dem Weg zum Frieden. Dokumente zum Friedensprozess und zum Inhalt der Friedensverhandlungen*. Bonn, Deutsche Kommission Justitia et Pax.

Molkentin, Gudrun (2002). *Kriegsursachen und Friedensbedingungen in Guatemala. Eine historische Untersuchung über das kriegsursächliche Gewaltgeschehen und die Herausforderung an den gegenwärtigen Prozess der Friedenskonsolidierung*. Frankfurt am Main, Peter Lang.

Montclos, Marc-Antoine de (1999). "Liberia oder die Ausplünderung eines Landes." In: *Ökonomie der Bürgerkriege*. Francois Jean and Rufin, Jean-Chrisophe, Eds. Hamburg, Hamburger Edition: 219-242.

Monteforte Toledo, Mario (1998). *Vinicio. Entrevista de Mario Monteforte Toledo*. Guatemala, Artemis & Edinter.

Montenegro, Arturo (1998). "El Tema Fiscal en Guatemala." *Diálogo* 2(5): 1-10.

Moore, Marianne (2004). "Die 'Entführungsindustrie': Öl ins Feuer interner Konflikte." In: *Kriege als (Über)Lebenswelten. Schattenglobalisierung, Kriegsökonomie und Inseln der Zivilität*. Sabine Kurtenbach and Lock, Peter, Eds. Bonn, Dietz: 142-154.

Morales Modenesi, Luisa Eugenia/Celeso de León, Julio (1995). *El Movimiento sindical Guatemalteco en 1995*. Guatemala, Fundación Friedrich Ebert.

Morán, Rolando (2002). *Saludos Revolucionarios. La Historia reciente de Guatemala desde la óptica de la lucha guerrillera (1984-1996)*. Guatemala, Fundación Guillermo Toriello.

Moser, Caroline/McIlwaine, Cathy (2000). *Violence in a Post-Conflict Context. Urban Poor Perceptions from Guatemala*. Washington D.C., The World Bank.

Münkler, Herfried (2002a). *Die neuen Kriege*. Hamburg, Rowohlt Verlag.

Münkler, Herfried (2002b). *Über den Krieg. Stationen der Kriegsgeschichte im Spiegel ihrer theoretischen Reflexion*. Weilerswist, Velbrück Wissenschaft.

Murdoch, James C./Sandler, Todd (2002). "Economic Growth, Civil Wars, and Spatial Spillovers." *Journal of Conflict Resolution* 46(No. 1): 91-110.

Nelson, Jane/International Alert/Council on Economic Priorities, et al. (2000). *The Business of Peace. The private sector as a partner in conflict prevention and resolution*. London.

Neumayer, Eric (2004). "The Impact of Political Violence on Tourism." *Journal of Conflict Resolution* 48(2): 259-281.

Nordstrom, Carolyn (1992). "The Backyard Front." In: *The Paths to Domination, Resistance and Terror*. Carolyn Nordstrom and Martin, J., Eds. Berkeley, University of California Press: 260-274.

Noriega, Arnoldo/Álvarez, Enrique/Chocoj, Mario (2001). *Cuando la Sociedad Guatemalteca se Encuentra: La Negociación Política del Pacto Fiscal*. Guatemala, Instituto de Estudios Políticos, Económicos y Sociales (IPES).

O'Donnell, Guillermo (1992). "Substantive or Procedural Consensus? Notes on the Latin American Bourgeoisie." In: *The Right and Democracy in Latin America*. Douglas A. Chalmers and Campello de Souza, Maria, Eds. New York, Praeger Publishers: 43 - 47.

O'Donnell, Guillermo/Schmitter, Philippe C./Whitehead, Laurence (1993). *Transition from Authoritarian Rule. Latin America*. Baltimore and London, The Johns Hopkins University Press.

ODHAG, Ed. (1998). *Informe Proyecto interdiocesano de Recuperación de la Memoria Histórica: Guatemala Nunca Más. El Entorno Histórico*. Guatemala, ODHAG.

OECD (2000). *The OECD Guidelines for Multinational Enterprises*. Paris.

OECD (2001). *The DAC Guidelines. Helping Prevent Violent Conflict*. Paris.

Offe, Claus/Wiesenthal, Helmut (1980). "Two Logics of Collective Action: Theoretical Notes on Social Class and Organizational Form." *Political Power and Social Theory* 1: 67-115.

Oglesby, Elizabeth Ann (2002). *Politics at Work: Elites, Labor and Agrarian Modernization in Guatemala 1980-2000*. University of California, Berkeley, PhD-Thesis.

Ohlson, Thomas (1991). "Strategic Confrontation versus Economic Survival in Southern Africa." In: *Conflict Resolution in Africa*. Francis M. Deng and

Zartman, William I., Eds. Washington D.C., The Brookings Institution: 219-271.

Ohlson, Thomas/Söderberg, Mimmi (2003). "From Intra-State War to Democratic Peace in Africa." In: *Africa: A Future Beyond the Crises and Conflicts.* Ebrima Sall and Hendricks, Fred, Eds. Uppsala, Nordic Africa Institute.

Paige, Jeffery M. (1983). "Social Theory and Peasant Revolution in Vietnam and Guatemala." *Theory and Society* 12(no. 3): 699-737.

Paige, Jeffery M. (1997). *Coffee and Power. Revolution and the Rise of Democracy in Central America.* Cambridge, Massachusetts, Harvard University Press.

Painter, James (1987). *Guatemala: False Hope, False Freedom: The Rich, the Poor, and the Christian Democrats.* London, Catholic Institute for International Relations: Latin America Bureau.

Palencia Prado, Tania (1996). *Construyendo la Paz.* London, Instituto Católico de Relaciones Internacionales.

Palencia Prado, Tania (1997). "Advocates and Guarantors: Establishing Participative Democracy in Post-war Guatemala." *Accord – An International Review of Peace Initiatives.*

Palma Murga, Gustavo (1997). "Promised the Earth. Agrarian Reform in the Socio-Economic Agreement." *Accord – An International Review of Peace Initiatives.*

Paris, Roland (1997). "Peacebuilding and the Limits of Liberal Internationalism." *International Security* 22(2): 54-89.

Paris, Roland (2004). *At War's End. Building Peace After Civil Conflict.* Cambridge, Cambridge University Press.

Pásara, Luis (2002). "Las peculiaridades del proceso de paz en Guatemala." In: *A cinco años de la firma de la paz en Guatemala: Un balance crítico.* Rubén Zamora/Chamorro, Carlos F./Pásara, Luiset al, Eds. Guatemala, FLACSO. 51: 101-125.

Pastor, Manuel, Jr.; Michael E. Conroy (1996). "Distributional Implication of Macroeconomic Policy: Theory and Applications to El Salvador." In: *Economic Policy for Building Peace. The Lessons of El Salvador.* James K. Boyce, Ed. Boulder, Lynne Rienner: 155-176.

Paul, James A. (2001). "Der Weg zum Global Compact. Zur Annäherung von UNO und multinational Unternehmen." In: *Die Privatisierung der Weltpolitik. Entstaatlichung und Kommerzialisierung im Globalisierungsprozess.* Brigitte Hamm Brühl Tanja; Tobial Debiel, Hartwig Hummel, Jens Martens (ed.), Ed. Bonn, Dietz. EINE Welt – Texte der Stiftung Entwicklung und Frieden: 104-129.

Payne, Leigh A./Bartell, Ernest (1995). "Bringing Business Back In: Business-State Relations and Democratic Stability in Latin America." In: *Business and Democracy in Latin America*. Ernest Bartell, C.S.C.; Leigh A. Payne, Ed. Pittsburgh and London, University of Pittsburgh Press: 257-290.

Perry, Maura B. (1996). "A Model for Efficient Foreign Aid: The Case for the Political Risk Insurance Activities of Overseas Private Investment Corporation." *Virginia Journal of International Law* 36: 511-588.

Plant, Roger (1998). *Indigenous Peoples and Poverty Reduction: A Case Study of Guatemala*, Inter-American Development Bank.

Plant, Roger (1999). "Indigenous Identity and Rights in the Guatemalan Peace Process." In: *Comparative Peace Processes in Latin America*. Cynthia Arnson, Ed. Washington, D.C.; Stanford, California, Woodrow Wilson Center Press; Stanford University Press: 319-338.

Ponciano Castellanos, Karen (1996). *El Rol de la Sociedad Civil en los Procesos de Paz de Guatemala y El Salvador. Procesos de Negociación Comparados.* Guatemala, INCEP.

Prensa Libre – Domingo (1990). Entrevista con Adolfo Boppel; Presidente del UNGARO y ex-presidente del CACIF. 29 July 1990: 13.

Prensa Libre (1986). Cambia imagen de Guatemala, dice empresario de turismo. 8 February 1986: 38.

Prensa Libre (1987a). Agencia DPA califica de realista la exposición de los altos jefes militares. 16 August 1987: 2.

Prensa Libre (1987b). Anzueto Vielman renunció del CACIF. 22 September 1987: 6.

Prensa Libre (1987c). Exhortativa hizo el Ejército. 13 August 1987: 2.

Prensa Libre (1988). Indagaron a Anzueto. Queda libre bajo caución juratoria. 25 May 1988: 2.

Prensa Libre (1989a). Abrió Diálogo Nacional. 21 February 1989: 2.

Prensa Libre (1989b). CACIF no ha decidido. 23 February 1989: 3.

Prensa Libre (1989c). Diálogo: CACIF tiene duda. 03 March 1989: 6.

Prensa Libre (1989d). Violencia afecta la economía. Cámara de Industria hace señalamiento. 25 September 1989: 13.

Prensa Libre (1989e). Violencia daña desarrollo señala sector privado. 26 September 1989: 16.

Prensa Libre (1990a). Agroindustria azucarera mejora condición laboral. 05 Feb 1990: 6.

Prensa Libre (1990b). CACIF no obstaculizará incorporación de la URNG a la vida institucional. 03 September 1990: 24.

Prensa Libre (1990c). Cordón Shwank: URNG debe bajar armas para dialogar. 4 June 1990: 2.

Prensa Libre (1990d). No escatimará esfuerzos alguno por conseguir la paz del país. 03 September 1990: 2.
Prensa Libre (1990e). Torna la clama. Campesinos depusieron la huelga. 01 February 1990: 2.
Prensa Libre (1993a). No dialogarán con guerrilla expone directivos de CACIF. 13 August 1993: 107.
Prensa Libre (1993b). Plan de paz del Gobierno atenta contra Constitución, dice CACIF. 16 July 1993: 3.
Prensa Libre (1993c). URNG fija de nuevo impuesto de guerra. 14 November 1993: 59.
Prensa Libre (1994a). CACIF analiza incorporación a ASC. 07 June 1994: 3.
Prensa Libre (1994b). CACIF exige persecución penal contra comandantes de la URNG. 20 May 1994: 8.
Prensa Libre (1994c). CACIF pide procesar a comandantes de URNG. 20 May 1994: 8.
Prensa Libre (1994d). Comision de la Verdad contribuirá a consolidar proceso de paz, dice CAMTURA. 04 July 1994: 24.
Prensa Libre (1994e). Comisión de la Verdad, panacea de una guerra de treinta años. 25 May 1994: 8.
Prensa Libre (1994f). Fiscalía y MP no enjuiciarán a comandantes de la URNG. 28 May 1994: 6.
Prensa Libre (1994g). Necesario crear los mecanismos inmediatos para incorporar desplazados al desarrollo. 21 June 1994: 8.
Prensa Libre (1994h). URNG rechaza reunion con el CACIF. 21 May 1994: 8.
Prensa Libre (1995a). CACIF adversa propuesta socioeconomía de la ONU. 10 June 1995: 50.
Prensa Libre (1995b). CACIF exige al Gobierno desenmascarar a la URNG. 28 July 1995: 6.
Prensa Libre (1995c). CACIF pedirá al Gobierno retirarse de negociaciones de paz con la URNG. 26 September 1995: 2.
Prensa Libre (1995d). CACIF pide procesar a comandantes de la URNG. 26 July 1995: 2.
Prensa Libre (1995e). CACIF presentará denuncia contra URNG ante la Organización Internacional del Trabajo. 10 Ocotober 1995: 4.
Prensa Libre (1995f). Empresarios del agro demandan a Rosada por negociar con la URNG. 18 October 1995: 3.
Prensa Libre (1995g). Finqueros deciden no contratar a campesinos por invasiones. 06 April 1995: 3.
Prensa Libre (1995h). Finqueros pedirán extradición de los comandantes de la URNG. 27 September 1995: 3.

Prensa Libre (1995i). Juicio contra comandantes de la URNG no afecta proceso de paz: Arenales Forno. 27 July 1995: 6.

Prensa Libre (1995j). Moderadores de la ONU se reúnen con dirigentes del CACIF y la ASC. 03 October 1995: 6.

Prensa Libre (1996). Catastro agrario dará certeza jurídica a propietarios de fincas, opina Preti. 06 May 1996: 3.

Prensa Libre (1999). CACIF cuestiona informe de CEH. 26 March 1999: 3.

Prensa Libre (2001). Aumentan salario mínimo. 29 December 2001: 3.

Prensa Libre (2002a). Comercio se concentra en la capital. 24 June 2002: 19.

Prensa Libre (2002b). Dejaría el país. 18 March 2002: 3.

Prensa Libre (2002c). Denuncia contra líderes campesinos. 23 July 2002: 2.

Prensa Libre (2002d). "Hay una campaña en contra mía". 16 March 2002: 5.

Prensa Libre (2002e). La crisis agraria seguirá en 2002. 11 February 2002: 2.

Preti, Alessandro (2002). "Guatemala: Violence in Peacetime – A Critical Analysis on the Armed Conflict and the Peace Process." *Disasters* 26(2): 99 - 119.

Przeworski, Adam/Wallerstein, Michael (1988). "Structural Dependence in the State on Capital." *American Political Science Review* 82(1): 11-29.

Ramsbotham, Olivier (2000). "Reflections on UN Post-Settlement Peacebuilding." *International Peacekeeping* 7(1): 169-189.

Raynard, Peter/Cohen, Jonathan (2003). "Partnerships: The Accountability Dimension." *AccountAbility Quarterly* May 2003: 4-9.

Reno, William (2000). *Foreign Firms, Natural Resources, and Violent Political Economies*.

Rettberg, Angelika (2004). *Business-led Peacebuilding in Colombia: Fad or Future of a Country in Crisis?* London, Crisis States Programme; LSE.

Rienstra, Dianna (2001). *The Approach of the Corporate World: How Conflict-Sensitive is the Private Sector*. Mainstreaming Conflict Prevention: Concept and Practice, The Hague, Stiftung Wissenschaft und Politik (Conflict Prevention Network); Netherlands Institute of International Relations, Clingendael.

Ríos de Rodríguez, Carroll (1999). "El Sector Productivo Organizado y la Consulta Popular." In: *La Consulta Popular y el Futuro del Proceso de Paz en Guatemala*, Latin American Program, Woodrow Wilson International Center for Scholars. Documento de Trabajo No 243: 43-58.

Robinson, William I. (2000). "Neoliberalism, the Global Elite, and the Guatemalan Transition: A Crtitical Macrosocial Analysis." *Journal of Interamerican Studies and World Affairs* 42(4; Special Issue, Globalization and Democratization in Guatemala): 89-109.

Robock, Stefan H. (1971). "Political Risk: Identification and Assessment." *Columbia Journal of World Business* (July-August): 6-20.

Rodríguez, Rodrigo (1995). *Cómo y en cuanto nos venderán?* Siglo XXI. 17 June 1995: 11.

Rosada-Granados, Héctor (1992). "Parties, Transition, and the Political System in Guatemala." In: *Political Parties and Democracy in Central America.* Louis W. Goodman/LeoGrande, William M. and Forman, Johanna Mendelson, Eds. Boulder, Westview Press: 89-109.

Rosada-Granados, Héctor (1998). *El Lado Oculto de las Negociaciones de Paz. Transición de la Guerra a la Paz en Guatemala.* Guatemala, Friedrich Ebert Stiftung.

Rosada-Granados, Héctor (1999). *Soldados en el Poder: Proyecto Militar en Guatemala.* San José, FUNPADEM.

Rothchild, Donald (2004). "Liberalism, Democracy and Conflict Management." In: *Facing Ethnic Conflicts: Towards a New Realism.* Andreas Wimmer/ Goldstone, Richard/Horowitz, Donaldet al, Eds. Lanham, Rowman & Littlefield: 226-244.

Roux, Gilles/Nassar, Carlos Camacho (1992). *Caraterización de la cadena del café en Guatemala.* Unpublished document.

Rupesinghe, Kumar (1995). "Transformation innerstaatlicher Konflikte. Von den 'Problemlösungs-Workshops' zu Friedensallianzen." In: *Friedliche Konfliktbearbeitung in der Staaten- und Gesellschaftswelt.* Norbert Ropers and Debiel, Tobias, Eds. Bonn, Stiftung Entwicklung und Frieden (SEF): 304- 320.

Russett, Bruce (1964). *World Hand Book of Social and Political Indicators.* New Haven, Yale University Press.

Salvesen, Hilde (2002). *Guatemala: Five Years after the Pace Accords. The Challenges of Implementing Peace.* Oslo, International Peace Research Institute (PRIO),.

Sarti, Carlos (1989). "La Nueva Derecha: Hacia una Propuesta de Investigación." *Estudios Sociales Centroamericanos* 47: 149-153.

Schäfers, Bernhard (1995). *Grundbegriffe der Soziologie.* Opladen, Leske + Budrich.

Schirmer, Jennifer (1991). "The Guatemalan Military Project: an Interview with Gen. Héctor Gramajo." *International Review* Spring 1991: 10-13.

Schirmer, Jennifer (1998). *The Guatemalan Military Project. A Violence Called Democracy.* Philadelphia, University of Pennsylvania Press.

Schlesinger, Stephen/Kinzer, Stephen (1992). *Bananenkrieg. CIA Putsch in Guatemala.* Zürich, Rotpunktverlag.

Schmitter, Philippe C. (1974). "Still the Century of Corporatism." *The Review of Politics* 36(1): 85-131.

Schnabel, Albrecht (1997). *Challenges of Operational Conflict Prevention: From Proactive to Reactive Prevention.* UNU Global Seminar.

Schubert, Gunter/Tetzlaff, Rainer/Vennewald, Werner, Eds. (1994). *Demokratisierung und politischer Wandel. Theorie und Anwendung des Konzeptes der strategischen und konfliktfähigen Gruppen.* Demokratie und Entwicklung. Münster, Hamburg, LIT Verlag.

Schwartz, Peter/Gibb, Blair (1999). *When Good Companies Do Bad Things: Responsibility and Risk in an Age of Globalization.* New York, John Wiley & Sons, Inc.

Segovia, Alexander (1996). "Domestic Resource Mobilization." In: *Economic Policy for Building Peace. The Lessons of El Salvador.* James K. Boyce, Ed. Boulder, Lynne Rienner: 107-127.

Sereseres, Cesar D. (1978). "Guatemalan Paramilitary Forces, Internal Security, and Politics." In: *Supplementary Military Forces: Reserves, Militias, Auxiliaries.* Luis A. Zurcher, Ed. Beverly Hills, Calif., Sage: 179 - 199.

Sereseres, Cesar D. (1985a). "The Guatemalan Legacy: Radical Challenges and Military Politics." In: *Report on Guatemala. Findings of the Study Group on United States-Guatemala Relations.* Central American and Caribbean Program, Ed. Boulder, London, Westview Press with the Foreign Policy Institute, School of Advanced International Studies, The Johns Hopkins University. 7: 17-50.

Sereseres, Cesar D. (1985b). "The Highland Wars in Guatemala." In: *Latin Amércian Insurgencies.* George Fauriol, Ed. Washington D.C.

Sieder, Rachel (1997). "Reframing Citizenship: Indigenous Rights, Local Power and the Peace Process in Guatemala." *Accord – An International Review of Peace Initiatives*(13).

Siglo XXI (1992). El CACIF pide que no condenen a Guatemala en Ginebra, Suiza. 29 January 1992: 3.

Siglo XXI (1994a). CACIF: Comisión de Verificación de la ONU debe ser implementada. 19 August 1994: 5.

Siglo XXI (1994b). PDH: Verificación permitirá avance de las negociaciones. 23 August 1994: 3.

Siglo XXI (1994c). Presidente pide condenar ataques guerrilleros. 24 August 1994: 4.

Siglo XXI (1994d). Sindicatos cuestionan llamado hecho por CACIF. 20 August 1994: 3.

Siglo XXI (1995a). CACIF confirma que se reunió el pasado 9 de mayo con URNG. 25 May 1995: 3.

Siglo XXI (1995b). Inhuman restos del ex presidente de CARCOR. 16 October 1995: 6.

Siglo XXI (1995c). Preti: Existe apoyo internacional en contra del impuesto de guerra. 19 October 1995: 3.

Siglo XXI (1995d). Sector Empresarial desmiente que financie campaña oficial exterior. 13 May 1995: 3.
Siglo XXI (1995e). Sector Privado y ASC se reúnen por primera vez por tema de la paz. 24 August 1995: 6.
Siglo XXI (1996a). 24 horas para iniciar discusión del 169. 04 March 1996: 5.
Siglo XXI (1996b). Monsanto: URNG estudia cese el fuego. 02 April 1996: 3.
Siglo XXI (1996c). Preti: Más de US $100 millones necesarios para hacer catastro. 01 March 1996: 6.
Siglo XXI (1996d). URNG suspenderá impuesto de guerra cuando firmen tema socioeconómico. 10 April 1996: 3.
Smillie, Ian (2002). *Dirty Diamonds. Armed Conflict and the Trade in Rough Diamonds*, Fafo Institute for Applied Social Science.
Smith, Carol A. (1990a). "Conclusion: History and Revolution in Guatemala." In: *Guatemalan Indians and the State*. Carol A. Smith, Ed. Austin, University of Texas Press: 258-285.
Smith, Carol A. (1990b). *Guatemalan Indians and the state, 1540 to 1988*. Austin, University of Texas Press.
Smith, Carol A. (1990c). "Introduction: Social Relations in Guatemala over Time and Space." In: *Guatemalan Indians and the State, 1540 to 1988*. Carol A. Smith, Ed. Austin, University of Texas Press: 1-30.
Smith, Carol A. (1990d). "The Militarization of Civil Society in Guatemala. Economic Reorganization as a Continuation of War." *Latin American Perspectives* 17(4): 8 - 41.
Stamm, Andreas/Klaus, Liebig/Eefje, Schmid (2002). *Arbeits- und Lebensbedingungen in der großbetrieblichen Kafeproduktion von Mittelamerika: Ansatzpunkte zur Sicherung sozialer Mindeststandards unter Einbeziehung der Privatwirtschaft*. Bonn, Deutsches Institut für Entwicklungspolitik.
Stanley, William/Holiday, David (2002). "Broad Participation, Diffuse Responsibility: Peace Implementation in Guatemala." In: *Ending Civil Wars. The Implementation of Peace Agreements*. Stephen John Stedman/Rothchild, Donald and Cousens, Elizabeth M., Eds. Boulder, Lynne Rienner: 421-462.
Stewart, Frances (2004). "Horizontale Ungleichheit als Ursache von Bürgerkriegen." In: *Kriege als (Über)Lebenswelten. Schattenglobalisierung, Kriegsökonomien und Inseln der Zivilität*. Sabine Kurtenbach and Lock, Peter, Eds. Bonn, Dietz. 16: 122-141.
Stewart, Frances/Fitzgerald, Valpy (2001). *War and Underdevelopment. Country Experiences. Volume II*. Oxford, Oxford University Press.
Stewart, Frances/Huang, Cindy/Wang, Michael (2001). "Internal Wars: An Empirical Overview of the Economic and Social Consequences." In: *War and Underdevelopment. Volume I: The economic and Social Consequences of*

Conflict. Frances Stewart and Valpy FitzGerald, Eds. Oxford, Oxford University Press: 67-103.

Stewart, Frances/Humphreys, Frank P./Lea, Nick (1997). "Civil Conflict in Developing Countries Over the Last Quarter of a Century: An Empirical Overview of Economic and Social Consequences." *Oxford Development Studies* 25(1): 11-41.

Stoll, David (1993). *Between Two Armies. In the Ixil Towns of Guatemala*. New York, Columbia University Press.

Strange, Susan (1996). *The Retreat of the State. The Diffusion of Power in the World Economy*. Cambridge, Cambridge University Press.

Swanson, Philip (2002). *Fuelling Conflict. The Oil Industry and Armed Conflict.*, Fafo Institute for Applied Social Science.

Taylor, Mark (2002). *Emerging Conclusions. Economies of Conflict: Private Sector Activity in Armed Conflict*. Oslo, Programme for International Cooperation and Conflict Resolution (Fafo); fafo Institute for Applied Social Science.

Thunell, Lars (1977). *Political Risks in International Business. Investment Behavior of Multinational Corporations*. New York, Praeger Publishers.

Torres-Riva, Edelberto (1995). "Die Transition in Mittelamerika." In: *Mittelamerika. Abschied von der Revolution?* Rafael Sevilla and Torres-Riva, Edelberto, Eds. Unkel/Rhein, Horlemann: 16-28.

Torres-Rivas, Edelberto (1989). *Repression and Resistance: The Struggle for Democracy in Central America*. Boulder, Westview Press.

Trudeau, Robert H. (2000). "Guatemala: Democratic Rebirth?" In: *Latin American Politics and Development*. Howard J. Wiarda and Kline, Harvey F., Eds. Boulder, CO, Westview Press: 493-511.

UN High Commissioner for Human Rights (1993). *Situation of Human Rights in Guatemala. Sub-Commission on Human Rights resolution 1993/16*.

UN Security Council Press Release (2004). *Security Council Discusses Role of Business in Conflict Prevention, Peacekeeping, Post-Conflict Peace-Building*. New York City, Security Council.

UN Wire (5 June 2000). Partnerships: Holbrooke Lauds Business Links with UN. 5 June 2000:

UNAGRO (1988). "Campo Pagado regarding the Carta Pastoral 'El Clamor por la Tierra'." *printed in Prensa Libre, 5 April 1988, p. 12.*

UNDP (2001). *Guatemala: El Financiamiento del Desarrollo Humano. Informe de Desarrollo Humano 2001*. Guatemala, United Nations.

UNDP (2004). *Democracy in Latin America. Towards a Citizens' Democracy*. New York.

United Nations (29 December 1996). *Acuerdo sobre cronograma para la implementación, cumplimiento y verificación de los acuerdos de paz.*
United Nations (1992). *An Agenda for Peace. Preventive Diplomacy, Peacemaking and Peace-keeping.*
United Nations (1997a). *Report of the Secretary-General on the Work of the Organization. Strengthening of the United Nations System Capacity for Conflict Prevention.*
United Nations (1997b). *Segundo Informe del Secretario General sobre la Verificación de los Acuerdos de Paz en Guatemala.*
United Nations (1997c). *United Nations Verification Mission in Guatemala. Report of the Secretary General. First Report.*
United Nations (1998). *Third report on the verification of compliance with the agreements signed by the Government of Guatemala and the URNG.*
United Nations (1999a). *Fourth Report on the Verification of Compliance with the Peace Agreements.*
United Nations (1999b). *Suplemento sobre la verificación de los acuerdos de paz de Guatemala.*
United Nations (2000a). *Guatemala: La fuerza incluyente del desarrollo humano. Informe de Desarrollo Humano.* Guatemala.
United Nations (2000b). *United Nations Verification Mission in Guatemala. Report of the Secretary General. Fifth Report.*
United Nations (2002). *United Nations Verification Mission in Guatemala. Report of the Secretary-General. Seventh Report.*
United Nations (2003). *United Nations Verification Mission in Guatemala. Report of the Secretary General. Eighth Report.*
URNG (1992). *Campo Pagado.* Printed in Molkentin, 1993.
URNG (1994a). *Campo Pagado: Ante la Maniobra y la Confusión, la Claridad y la Verdad. Declaración Política de URNG.* Prensa Libre. 10 May 1994: 25.
URNG (1994b). *Derecho de respuesta de URNG a la Carta abierta de la AGA.* Prensa Libre. 11 May 1994: 48.
Valdez, José Fernando (2000). *La Viabbilidad de un Pacto Fiscal en Guatemala: para los Empresarios y la Sociedad Civil.* Guatemala, FLACSO.
Valdez, José Fernando/Prado, Mayra Palencia (1998). *Los Dominós del poder: La Encrucijada Tributaria.* Guatemala, FLACSO.
van der Borgh, Chris (2001). "Political Violence, Intrastate Conflict and Peace Processes in Latin America." *European Review of Latin American and Caribbean Studies* 70(April 2001): 115-127.
Vela, Manolo/Solares, Hugo Antonio (2001). "La Transfiguración de la Violencia." In: *El Lado Oscuro de la Eterna Primavera. Violencia, criminalidad y*

delincuencia en la postguerra. Manolo Vela/Sequén-Mónchez, Alexander and Solares, Hugo Antonio, Eds. Guatemala, FLACSO: 217-380.

Vines, Alex (1998). "The Business of Peace. 'Tiny' Rowland, Financial Incentives and the Mozambican Settlement." *Accord – An International Review of Peace Initiatives*(3): 66-74.

von Alemann, Ulrich (1989). "Organisierte Interessen. Von der 'Herrschaft der Verbände' zum 'Neokorporatismus'?" In: *Regierungssysteme und Regieungslehre*. S. von Bandemer and Wewer, G., Eds. Opladen, Leske + Budrich: 219-234.

Wagner, Christoph (1997). *Uruguay: Unternehmer zwischen Diktatur und Demokratie: eine Studie zu Politik, Wirtschaft und der politischen Rolle der Unternehmerverbände*. Frankfurt am Main, Vervuert Verlag.

Wallensteen, Peter (2003). *Understanding Conflict Resolution. War, Peace and Global System*. London, Sage Publications.

Washington Office on Latin America (1988). *Who Pays the Price? The Cost of War in the Guatemalan Highlands*. Washington, Washington Office on Latin America.

Waterman, Harvey (1993). "Political Order and the 'Settlement' of Civil Wars." In: *Stopping the Killing. How Civil Wars End*. Roy Licklider, Ed. New York, New York University Press: 292-302.

Weaver, Frederick Stirton (1994). *Inside the Volcano. The Histroy and Politcal Economy of Central America*. Boulder, Westview Press.

Weaver, Jerry L. (1970). "Political Style of the Guatemalan Military Elite." *Studies in Comparative International Development*(5): 63-81.

Wenger, Andreas/Möckli, Daniel (2002). *Conflict Prevention. The Untapped Potential of the Business Sector*. Boulder, Lynne Rienner.

Wiarda, Howard J. (2001). *The Soul of Latin America. The Cultural and Political Tradition*. New Haven, Yale University Press.

Wiarda, Howard J./Kline, Harvey F. (2001). *An Introduction to Latin American Politics and Development*. Boulder, Westview Press.

Wickham-Crowley, Timothy P. (1990). "Terror and Guerrilla Warfare in Latin America, 1956-1970." *Comparative Studies in Society and History* 32: 201-237.

Wickham-Crowley, Timothy P. (1991). *Guerrillas and Revolution in Latin America: A Comparative Study of Insurgents and Regimes Since 1956*. Princeton, N.J., Princeton University Press.

Williams, Robert G. (1994). *States and Social Evolution. Coffee and the Rise of National Governments in Central America*. Chapel Hill, The University of North Carolina Press.

Wood, Elisabeth Jean (2000). *Forging Democracy from Below. Insurgent Transitions in South Africa and El Salvador.* Cambridge, Cambridge University Press.

Woodward, Susan L. (2002). "Economic Priorities for Successful Peace Implementation." In: *Ending Civil Wars. The Implementation of Peace Agreements.* Stephen John Stedman/Rothchild, Donald and Couses, Elizabeth M., Eds. Boulder, Lynne Rienner: 183-213.

World Bank (1997). *Guatemala – Investing for Peace: A Public Investment Review.* Washington D.C.

World Bank (2003a). *Inequality in Latin America and the Caribbean: Breaking with History? Advance Conference Edition.* Washington, DC, World Bank.

World Bank (2003b). *Poverty in Guatemala.* Washington, D.C.

Zadek, Simon (2004). "Civil Governance and Partnerships." *Partnership Matters. Current Issues on Cross-Sector Collaboration*(2): 11-19.

Zammit, Ann (2003). *Development at Risk. Rethinking UN-Business Partnerships.* Geneva, South Centre, UNRISD.

Zandvliet, Luc (2004). "Redefining Corporate Social Risk Mitigation Strategies." *Social Development Notes* The World Bank(16).

Zelaya, Raquel (2002). "La institucionalidad de la paz." In: *A cinco años de la firma de la paz en Guatemala: Un balance crítico.* Rubén Zamora/Chamorro, Carlos F./Pásara, Luis et al, Eds. Guatemala, FLACSO. 51: 175-185.